# A FOUNDATION IN THE PRINCIPLES OF MANAGEMENT

*First Edition*

By Daniel Kipley, Ronald Jewe, Roxanne Helm-Stevens
*Azusa Pacific University*

cognella®
academic publishing

Bassim Hamadeh, CEO and Publisher
Michael Simpson, Vice President of Acquisitions
Jamie Giganti, Managing Editor
Jess Busch, Senior Graphic Designer
Marissa Applegate, Acquisitions Editor
Gem Rabanera, Project Editor
Alexa Lucido, Licensing Coordinator
Mandy Licata, Interior Designer

First published in the United States of America in 2015 by Cognella, Inc.

Trademark Notice: Product or corporate names may be trademarks or registered trademarks, and are used only for identification and explanation without intent to infringe.

Cover image credit: Copyright © 2011 Depositphotos Inc./Olivier26.

Printed in the United States of America

ISBN: 978-1-62661-968-5 (pbk)/ 978-1-62661-969-2 (br)

www.cognella.com          800-200-3908

# CONTENTS

# PART 4: LEADING

# PART 5: CONTROLLING

## Acknowledgements

We would like to express our greatest appreciation and indebtedness to our graduate assistant Jordyn Ferraro. This project would not have been possible without her support in gathering the necessary data and information required for the compilation of this text. Jordyn was consistently a source of positive encouragement as well as valuable advice and was instrumental in the successful completion of this project.

# PART 1  Introduction

# CHAPTER 1

## An Introduction to Management

*"Your work is going to fill a large part of your life, and the only way to be truly satisfied is to do what you believe is great work. And the only way to do great work is to love what you do. If you haven't found it yet, keep looking. Don't settle. As with all matters of the heart, you'll know when you find it."*

–Steve Jobs

### Chapter Learning Objectives:

After reading this chapter you should have a good understanding of:

- The importance of management to organizations, society, and individuals.
- The basic role and the four functions of management.
- The different kinds of managers and what companies look for in managers.
- The definitions of managerial effectiveness and managerial efficiency.
- The basic skills of management and their relative importance to managers.

What is a manager? What do managers do? What is management? Why is learning about management so important? Answering these questions is what makes the study of *Management Principles* so interesting. Consider for a moment the broad scope that manager's play in all phases of modern industries. For example, consider the I-phone or Galaxy phone that you are using. That phone required design, development, manufacturing and sales, those different stages required different managers with specific skills. To build the phone an R&D manager was required for the design and development, a manufacturing manager was required for the production, and a sales manger required for the marketing and sales of the phone. In addition to those managers, human resource managers were required to hire and train the right people in the right jobs to complete the process. Finally, finance and accounting managers were required to account for the costs and to determine firm performance.

As you can see, not all managerial jobs are the same and the demands and requirements will be different in various industries. Managing people is a very rewarding experience but it is not easy. However, like any other skill, management is something that you can improve with study and practice.

 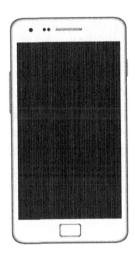

Apple and Samsung Dominate the smartphone industry with over 44% of the worldwide market selling a total of 83.1 million phones Q3, 2012.

The next 8 manufacturers combine equal the remaining 56%.

## What is a Manager?

A *manager* is one who is responsible for planning and directing the work of a group of individuals. Managers supervise their work, take corrective action when necessary and provide guidance and motivation for task completion. Managers may instruct workers directly or they may instruct other supervisors who instruct the workers.

The manager must be knowledgeable about the work that all the groups he/she supervises, but does not need to be an expert in any or all of the areas. It is more important for managers to know how to manage the workers than to know how to do their work well.

Managers influence all phases of modern organizations, they have the power to hire, fire, promote, or change the work assignments of their employees. Managers run manufacturing operations that produce the clothes we wear, the food we eat, and the cars we drive. Managers are the catalysts for new and exciting products and services that keep our economy and standard of living advancing.

There are many management functions in business and, therefore, many manager titles that reflect what job he/she is responsible, for example; an *accounting manager* supervises the accounting function;

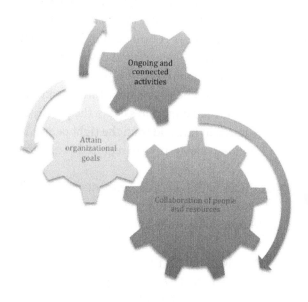

Figure 1.1: The 3 Management Characteristics

an *operations manager* is responsible for the operations of the company, the *research and development manager* supervises engineers and support staff engaged in design of a product or service, and a *marketing manager* identifies new markets, oversees new product introduction, and develops pricing strategies.

Regardless of title, the manager is responsible for planning, directing, monitoring and controlling the people and their work.

## What is a Management?

The term **management** can be used in different ways. As an example, management can refer to those processes that are followed in order to achieve the organizational goals. Management can also be referred to as the accumulation of knowledge that provides insight on how to manage. Finally, management can also refer to the individuals who guide and direct organizations or a career devoted to the task of guiding and directing organization.

In this text, the definition commonly used for management is; *the process of reaching organizational goals by working with and through people and other organizational resources.* There are three interrelated characteristics of management that are commonly accepted by contemporary management thinkers (Figure 1.1).

1. It is a process or a series of ongoing and connected activities.
2. It involves and focuses on attaining the organizational goals.
3. It reaches these goals by collaborating with and through people and other organizational resources.

Management principles are universal; they apply to all types of organizations (e.g. businesses, churches, sororities, athletic teams, hospital, etc.) and organizational levels. Managers jobs vary somewhat from one organization to another however, the job similarities are found across organizations because of the basic management functions; planning, organizing, leading, and controlling are common to all organizations.

## Management Functions

One of the most influential contributors to the modern concept of management is Henri Fayol (1841–1925). Fayol has often been credited with the development of the management theory and it is Fayol's tools that have a significant influence on how managers lead and manage in today's modern business environment. When he was 19, he began working as an engineer at a large mining company in France.

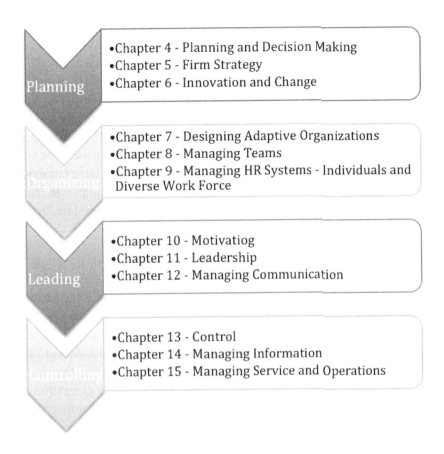

•Chapter 4 - Planning and Decision Making
•Chapter 5 - Firm Strategy
•Chapter 6 - Innovation and Change

•Chapter 7 - Designing Adaptive Organizations
•Chapter 8 - Managing Teams
•Chapter 9 - Managing HR Systems - Individuals and Diverse Work Force

•Chapter 10 - Motivatiog
•Chapter 11 - Leadership
•Chapter 12 - Managing Communication

•Chapter 13 - Control
•Chapter 14 - Managing Information
•Chapter 15 - Managing Service and Operations

Figure 1.2: The Functions of Management

He eventually became the director, at a time when the mining company employed more than 1,000 people. Through the years, Fayol began to develop what he considered to be the 14 most important principles of management. Essentially, these explained how managers should organize and interact with staff. In 1916, Fayol published one of the earliest theories of management, his "14 Principles of Management" in the book "Administration Industrielle et Generale."

Fayol also created a list of the five primary managerial functions to be successful; planning, organizing, coordinating, commanding, and controlling. Fayol's list has been revised from five functions to four by dropping the coordinating function and referring to the commanding function as 'leading'.

It is Fayol's four functions of management that is used as the organizational layout of this textbook (Figure 1.2). Chapter 1 provides an overview of management, Chapter 2 covers the history of management, and Chapter 3 focuses on the organizational environment and culture.

As we have seen managers are required in every industry. However, no matter what type of industry a manager may work, all managers share the same four functions of management each function is important and one cannot work without the others. The four functions are described in the following sections.

**Planning**: The first component in management is planning. *Planning* involves choosing tasks that must be performed to attain organizational goals, outlining how the tasks must be performed, and indicating when they should be performed. Planning actively focuses on attaining goals and is one of the best ways to improve performance. Planning encourages people to work harder for extended periods of time with behaviors that are directly related to goal achievement. Planning is concerned with the success of the organization in the near term (profit making) as well as in the long term (strategic development). Research has proven that companies that plan have larger profits and faster growth than companies that do not. Examples of types of plans for a new restaurant would most likely include a marketing plan, hiring plan, operational plan, and a sales plan.

**Organizing**: The second function of management is getting prepared and getting organized. Managers are responsible for the organization of the company and this includes organizing the people as well as the resources. *Organizing* can be thought of as assigning the tasks developed in the planning stages to various individuals or groups within the organization. Organizing is to create a mechanism to put plans into action. People within the organization are given work assignments that contribute to the company's goals. Tasks are organized so that the output of each individual contributes to the success of departments, which, in turn, contributes to the success of divisions, which ultimately contributes to the success of the organization. An organization that is not organized is one indicator that management as critically unprepared to conduct successful business activities.

**Leading**: The third component of the management functions is leading. Leading is also referred to as motivating, influencing, directing, or actuating and is concerned primarily with people within the organization. Work under this function helps the management control and supervise the actions of the staff. It also enables them to provide assistance to the employees by guiding them in the right direction to achieve the organizations goals. *Leading* can be defined as guiding the activities of organization members in the direction that helps the organization move towards the fulfillment of the goals. The purpose of leading is to increase productivity. Human-oriented work situations usually generate higher levels of production over the long term than do task oriented work situations because people find the latter type distasteful.

**Controlling**: Controlling is the last of the four management functions, it includes establishing performance standards that are aligned to the organizational objectives. Controlling also involves evaluation and reporting of job performance. The *Controlling* function is an ongoing process that provides a means to check to validate if the tasks being assigned are performed on time and according to the standards set by management. Managers play the following roles in controlling:

- Gather information that measures performance
- Compare present performance to pre-established performance norms.
- Determine the next action plan and modifications for meeting the desired performance parameters.

In order to achieve the organizational goals managers are involved in daily activities that plan, organize, lead, and control the company Resources.

Unfortunately, managers commonly make mistakes when planning, organizing, leading, and controlling. Figure 1.3 provides a list of such mistakes managers make related to each function. It is important for new managers to learn from the mistakes of others and avoid repeating them.

**Planning**
- Not establishing objectives for all important organizational areas.
- Making plans that are too risky
- Not vetting viable alternatives for reaching objectives

**Organizing**
- Not establishing departments appropriately
- Not emphasizing coordination of organizational members
- Establishing inappropriate spans of management

**Leading**
- Not taking the time to communicate properly with organizational members
- Establishing improper communication networks
- Being a manager, but not a leader

**Controlling**
- Not monitoring progress in carrying out plans
- Not establishing appropriate performance standards
- Not measuring performance to see where improvements might be made

Figure 1.3: Classic Management Mistakes

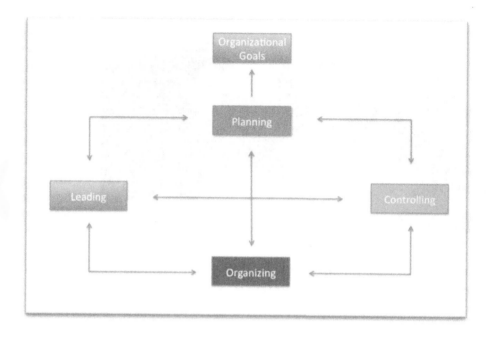

Figure 1.4: Management Function Relationship

## Management Function Relationship

As mentioned in the previous section the performance of one function depends on the performance of the others. Hence, the four functions of management are integrally related and therefore cannot be separated in practice. To be effective, a manager must understand how the four functions are practiced. The inter-relationship nature of the four functions is illustrated in Figure 1.4 as well as how managers use each of the functions to achieve the organizational goals. As an example, organizing is founded on well thought out plans developed during the planning process, and leading must be adapted to reflect both these plans and organizational structure used to implement them. Controlling is necessary for possible modifications to the existing plans, organization structure, or the motivation used to develop a more successful effort.

## Management Levels and Types

Although all managers share the same four functions of management, not all managerial jobs are the same. For an example, the demands and requirements placed on Larry Page the CEO of Google is significantly different than those placed on a manager of the local Subway restaurant. There are five kinds of managers each with different jobs and responsibilities: top-level managers, middle-level managers, frontline managers, functional managers, and general managers.

**TOP-LEVEL MANAGERS** *Top-level managers* include boards of directors, presidents, vice-presidents, CEOs, general managers, and senior managers. All of the important decisions are made at this level.

Top-level managers are responsible for controlling and overseeing the entire organization. They do not direct the day-to-day activities of the firm but develop goals, strategic plans, company policies, and make decisions on the direction of the business, they are responsible for creating a context for change. Additionally, top-level managers play a significant role in the mobilization of outside resources and are accountable to the shareholders and general public. They are also responsible for framing policies for the business, creating a positive organizational culture through company values, strategies, and lessons, and are responsible for closely monitoring their customers needs, competitors moves, and long-term business, economic, and social trends.

**MID-LEVEL MANAGERS** are the intermediate management of a hierarchical organization, being subordinate to the top-level management but above the lowest levels of operational staff. *Mid-level managers* consist of general managers, branch managers and department managers. They are accountable to the top-level management for their department's function. They dedicate more time to organizational and directional functions. Mid-level managerial roles include:

- Executing organizational plans in conformance with the company's policies and the objectives of the top management.
- Defining and discussing information and policies from top management to lower management.
- Inspiring and providing guidance to lower level managers towards better performance to achieve business objectives.

Mid-level managers may also communicate upward, by offering suggestions and feedback to top-level managers. Because mid-level managers are more involved in the day-to-day workings of a company, they may provide valuable information to top-level managers to help improve the organization's performance. Because mid-level managers work with both top-level managers and first-level managers, mid-level managers are expected to have excellent interpersonal skills to communicate, motivate, and mentor. Leadership skills are also important in delegating tasks to first-level managers.

**FRONTLINE MANAGERS** Most organizations have three management levels: top-level, mid-level, and first-line or frontline managers. *Frontline managers* hold positions like office manager, shift supervisor, section leads, foreman, or department manager. These managers are classified in a hierarchy (Figure 1.5) of authority and perform different tasks.

Frontline managers are managers who are responsible for a work group to a higher level of management. They are normally in the lower layers of the management hierarchy and the employees who report to them do not themselves have any managerial or supervisory responsibility. Frontline management is the level of management that oversees a company's primary production activities and must generate efficient productivity and control cost as such they must have high technical skill. Furthermore, frontline managers are critical to a company's success and are also required to have high interpersonal skills, as they must encourage, motivate, monitor, and reward those employees who perform those essential production duties.

**TEAM LEADERS** are a relatively new role in management as a result of companies shifting to more self-managed teams. A *team leader* is one who may not have any legitimate power over other members and as such has no authority to hire or fire workers. Typically, a team leader is appointed on either a permanent or rotating basis to represent the team to the next higher reporting level. Job duties of a team

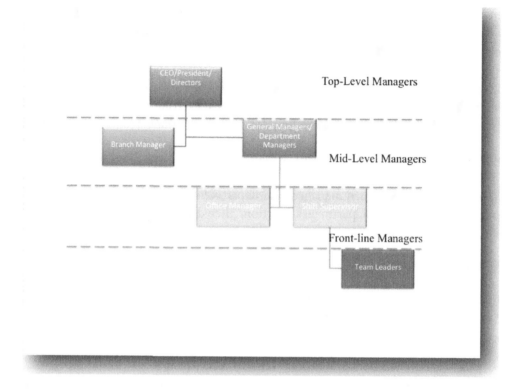

Figure 1.5: Hierarchy of Management

leader include making decisions in the absence of a consensus, resolve conflict between team members, facilitating team activities toward accomplishing organizational goals and providing intellectual, emotional, and spiritual resources to the team.

Team leaders also assist their team members plan and schedule work, learn to solve problems, and work effectively with each other.

**FUNCTIONAL MANAGERS** a *functional manager* is a person who has management authority over an organizational unit such as a department, within a business, company, or other organization. Most companies are grouped into areas of specialties, within which different functions of the organization occur (e.g., finance, marketing, R&D, engineering) hence functional management is the most common type of organizational management.

The company top management team typically consists of several functional heads such as the chief financial officer (CFO), the chief operating officer (COO), and the chief strategy officer (CSO). Functional managers have ongoing responsibilities and are not often directly affiliated with project teams, other than ensuring that the organizational goals and objectives are aligned with the overall corporate strategy and vision.

**GENERAL MANAGERS** refers to any executive who has responsibility of the day-to-day operations of a business. *General managers* include owners and managers who head small business establishments whose overall responsibilities include managing both the revenue and cost elements of a company's income statement and overseeing the firm's marketing and sales functions. Frequently, general managers are responsible

**Mintzberg's Managerial Roles and Sub-roles**

1.  **Interpersonal:**
    a.  Figurehead
    b.  Leader
    c.  Liaison

2.  **Informational:**
    a.  Monitor
    b.  Disseminator
    c.  Spokesman

3.  **Decisional:**
    a.  Entrepreneur
    b.  Disturbance handler
    c.  Resource allocator
    d.  Negotiator

Figure 1.6: Mintzberg's Manager Roles

for effective planning, delegating, coordinating, staffing, organizing, and decision making to attain desirable profit-making results for an organization.

## Mintzbergs Manager Roles

Professor and author Henry Mintzberg shadowed five American CEO's for a week analyzing their managerial activities. From his research he concluded that although managers were engaged in planning, organizing, leading, and controlling managers also fulfilled three main roles while performing their jobs: interpersonal, informational and decisional roles. Within the three main roles there are 10 sub-roles of management activities (Figure 1.6).

**INTERPERSONAL ROLES** involve working and interacting with people, it is very people intensive. In fact, some estimates of the amount of time that managers spend interacting with people face-to-face ranges from two-thirds to four-fifths of their entire workday. As such, if you prefer to work alone or have a difficulty in dealing with people, management may not be your career. In meeting the interpersonal role of management, managers perform three sub-roles;

1.  *Figurehead:* as a figurehead of the company the manager performs a number of routine duties of a legal or social nature such as greeting company visitors, speaking at openings of new facilities, or representing the company at community functions.
2.  *Leader:* Mintzberg specifically defines the role of leader as one who is responsible for the motivation, training, and encouragement of subordinates to accomplish the organizational objectives.
3.  *Liaison:* the manager liaison role networks by connecting people inside the company as well as externally. This role is not about dissemination of information however more about identifying the challenges and goals faced by others and connecting them with resources that will enable them to overcome obstacles or advance an agenda.

**INFORMATIONAL ROLES** of managers depends on gathering and disseminating information with employees. Mintzberg's studies found that managers spend as much as forty percent of their time communicating and acquiring information from others. Therefore, one might consider managers role as an information processor, gathering information by scanning the business environment and listening to others, processing that information, and then disseminate it to others both inside and outside of the organization. Mintzberg identified three sub-roles of the informational role;

1. *Monitor:* involves actively seeking and obtaining a wide variety of information, both internal and external, to develop a thorough understanding of the organization and its environment.
2. *Disseminator:* managers share information they have received from outsiders or from other subordinates to members of the organization; some information is factual; however, some information may involve management's interpretation and integration of other pertinent information in order to make managerial decisions.
3. *Spokesman:* in this role managers share the information (plans, policies, results, etc.) within and outside of the organization and may also serves as an expert on the organization's industry.

**DECISIONAL ROLES** in order to make good sound decisions, Mintzberg found the simply obtaining and sharing of the information with people inside and outside of the organization was not sufficient. Managers must integrate perspectives of others when making sound decisions. Mintzberg identified four sub-roles of the managerial decision role;

1. *Entrepreneur:* searches both within the organization and its environment and initiates improvement projects to bring about change; supervises design and improvement of certain projects as well.
2. *Disturbance Handler:* responsible for corrective action when organization faces important, unexpected disturbances.
3. *Resource Allocator:* responsible for the allocating of the organizations resources, who will get what resources and how many resources will they get; makes or approves of all significant organizational decisions.
4. *Negotiator:* responsible for representing the organization at major negotiations including schedules, projects, goals, outcomes, resources, and employee raises.

UPS provides a good example of how managers play an entrepreneurial role in management. UPS found that nearly 30 percent of its driver candidates were failing the UPS driver-training program. Managers abandoned the traditional model of driver training and instead used high-tech training methods including video games and simulators designed to allow candidates to practice specific scenarios (Such as running on ice). Thanks to the new approach to driver training, only 10 percent now fail.

A manager's job is never static, and is always in movement. At any given time, a manager may be carrying out some combination of these roles to varying degrees, from none of their time to 100 percent of their time. Over their working life, a person may hold different management positions that call upon different roles.

### Organizational Resources And Management

*Organizational resources* include the people, raw material, capital, and money that comprise the inputs necessary for the production of a finished product. Human resources (people) are those that work for the organization, they possess the skills and knowledge of the work system to transform the resources into products. Raw materials are those ingredients used directly in the manufacture of the product. Capital resources are the machines used during the manufacturing process. Monetary resources are the amounts of money that managers use to purchase goods and services fro the organization.

Managing Organizational Resources is the ability to creatively think about allocation of organizational resources to support the transformation into finished products. It may involve taking strategic risks with organizational resources, and incorporating ingenuity to maximize results. It includes the ability to look for improvements that do not require significant resourcing while committing to fully resourcing when necessary. As Figure 1.7 shows, the organizational resources are combined, used, and transformed into finished products during the production process.

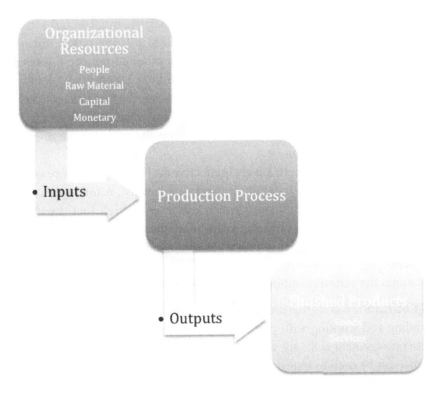

Figure 1.7: The Transformation Production Process

### Managerial Efficiency vs. Effectiveness

Effectiveness and efficiency are very common terms found in business. However, most people are unclear of their meanings and occasionally mix their usage. If you were to Google search the definitions for both terms you'll find very similar definitions, which unfortunately adds to the confusion. For this text the definition found from Dictionary.com is most appropriate: ***Effective*** (adj.): adequate to accomplish a purpose; producing the intended or expected result. ***Efficient*** (adj.) performing or functioning in the best possible manner with the least waste of time and effort.

An easier way to remember the difference in the terms is to remember this sentence: *"Being effective is about doing the right things, while being efficient is about doing the things in the right manner."*

**MANAGERIAL EFFECTIVENESS** refers to management's use of organizational resources in meeting organizational goals. If organizations are using their resources to attain their goals, the managers are considered to be effective. However, managerial effectiveness is not simply measured as effective or not effective, the closer an organization comes to achieving its goals the more effective the managers are considered. Hence, managerial effectiveness is then on a continuum ranging from ineffective to effective. The effectiveness of a workforce has an enormous impact on the quality of a company's product or service, which often dictates a company's reputation and customer satisfaction.

**MANAGERIAL EFFICIENCY** is the proportion of total organizational resources that contribute to productivity during the manufacturing process. Efficient managers complete tasks in the least amount of time possible with the least amount of resources possible by utilizing certain timesaving strategies. Inefficient managers use or waste more resources during the production time. Similar to effectiveness, management efficiency is best described as being on a continuum ranging from inefficient to efficient. For example, suppose a manager is attempting to communicate more efficiently. He can accomplish his goal by using email rather than sending letters to each employee. Efficiency and effectiveness are mutually exclusive. A manager who's efficient isn't always effective and vice versa. Efficiency increases productivity and saves both time and money.

As an example, a manager could be relatively ineffective and the consequence is that the organization is making little progress toward goal attainment. In contrast, a manager could be somewhat effective despite being inefficient if demand for the product is so high that the manager can get an extremely high price per unit and therefore absorb the inefficiency costs. Hence, a manager can be effective without being efficient. In order to maximize organizational success, managers must be both effective and efficient.

Figure 1.8 illustrates the various combinations of managerial effectiveness and managerial efficiency.

**MANAGEMENT SKILLS** are skills that are necessary to make business decisions to reach the organizations goals by leading and working with people and utilizing other organizational resources within a company. Because management skills are so critical to the success of the organization, companies often focus on tactics that can be used to improve the skills of their managers. There are two widely accepted views on management skills; the classic view and the contemporary view. The following section will discus both.

Figure 1.8: The Combinations of Managerial Effectiveness and Efficiency

**CLASSIC VIEW OF MANAGEMENT SKILLS** In his famous article, "Skills of an effective administrator", Robert Katz, a famous writer, manager, and consultant defines three skills which are essential for administrative work. These are technical, human and conceptual skills:

1. *Human skills*—the ability to interact and motivate well with others. They involve working with people and groups building cooperation and communication. Human skills are working with 'people'.
2. *Technical skills*—the knowledge and proficiency in the trade required to get the job done. Requires the able to apply specialized knowledge and expertise to work related techniques and procedures. Technical skills are working with 'things'.
3. *Conceptual skills*—the ability to see the organization holistically, understand how the different parts of the company affect each other, the skill to develop ideas, concepts, and implement strategies. Conceptual skills are working with 'ideas'.

As a manger moves from a lower level of management to top management the required skills mix change. At the lower level (supervisor or operations manager) there is a high need for technical skills and human skills with little need for conceptual skills. As managers progress to middle management, technical skills are less necessary, human skills are important, and now conceptual skills also become necessary. Finally, as top managers, both human skills and conceptual skills are critical. The relationship of the three management skills with management levels is illustrated in Figure 1.9.

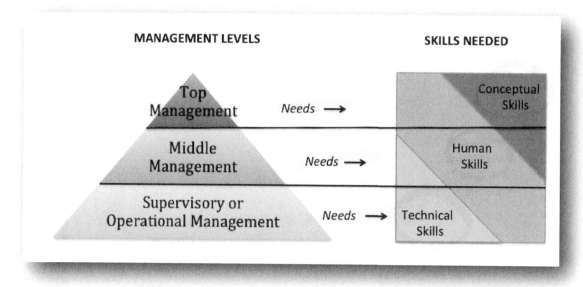

Figure 1.9: Managerial Levels and Required Skills

**CONTEMPORARY VIEW OF MANAGEMENT SKILLS** is a more current thought regarding management skills. The contemporary view is an expansion of the classic view with two unique differences; 1) the contemporary view defines the major activities that managers typically perform, and 2) the contemporary view lists the skills required to carry out those activities successfully.

The three basic types of major activities that modern managers typically perform are;

1. *Task related activities* are defined as the critical management related activities such as short-term planning, clarifying objectives of jobs in organizations, and monitoring operations and performance.
2. *People-related activities* are focused on managing people within the organization. Activities include providing support and encouragement to employees, providing recognition for achievements and contributions, developing skill and confidence of workers, consulting when making decisions, and empowerment of employees to solve problems.
3. *Change-related activities* are aimed at modifying organizational components such as; proposing new strategies and vision, encouraging innovation, risk taking to promote needed change.

The preceding sections discussed both the classic and contemporary views of management skills in modern management. A number of critical management skills were presented and related to top, middle, and lower-level management positions.

Because management skills are a prerequisite for management success, managers should spend time defining the most formidable task they face and sharpen those skills that will help them become successful. The following list provides 7 important competencies that will increase the probability of managers becoming successfully in carrying out management activities.

To increase the probability of being successful, managers should be competent in;

1). Clarifying roles: assigning tasks and explaining job responsibilities, task objectives, and performance objectives.
2). Monitoring operations: checking on the progress and quality of the work, and evaluating individual and unit performance.
3). Short-term planning: how to use resources and personnel to accomplish a task efficiently, and to determine how to schedule and coordinate unit activities efficiently.
4). Consulting: checking with people before making decisions that affect them, encouraging participation in decision-making, using ideas and suggestions of others.
5). Supporting: showing consideration for others, acting with empathy and support, providing encouragement when there is a difficult task.
6). Recognizing: provide recognition and acknowledgement of accomplishments, special contributions, and effective performance.
7). Developing: help employees learn how to improve their skills, provide coaching, advice and opportunities for skills development.

### The Value of People—A Competitive Advantage

Well-managed companies are more competitive because their workforce is smarter, better trained, more motivated, more committed, and provide better service to their customers. Furthermore, companies that practice good management consistently out performed companies in revenue, profits, and stock market performance than companies that do not. Stanford University professor Jeffrey Pfeffer wrote in his books; *Competitive Advantage through People* and *The Human Equation: Building Profits by Putting People First*, that companies cannot succeed without valuing their workforce, what separates top-performing companies from their competition is the way that management treats their people. According to Pfeffer, companies that invest in their people will create long-lasting competitive advantages that are difficult for other companies to duplicate

A ***competitive advantage*** is the favorable position an organization seeks in order to be more profitable than its competitors. The idea is to create customer value in an efficient and sustainable way.

John Stumpf, Chairman and CEO of Wells Fargo and Company believe fully in the value of his people and the creation of a competitive advantage. He states, '*our most important value is this: we believe in people as a competitive advantage. We strive to find the best people from a diversity of backgrounds and cultures, give them the knowledge and training they need, allow them to be responsible and accountable for their businesses, and recognize them for outstanding performance. Products and technology do not fulfill the promise behind a brand—people do, people who are more talented, more motivated, more energized than their competitors. We believe our people will out execute our competitors every time because they care more than our competitors do. While we do this, we expect to have fun, too.*

Management Practices for a Competitive Advantage

1. Employee security – eliminating the fear of job loss provides the security necessary for employees to be innovative and productive.
2. Hire selectively – managers must hire the most talented employees available. This means having an aggressive recruitment policy and selectively screen for the most qualified applicants.
3. Self-managed teams and decentralization – Self-managed teams can produce enormous increases in productivity through increased employee commitment and creativity. Decentralization increases employee satisfaction and commitment by allowing those employees who are closest to the problems and customers to make the decisions.
4. High wages based on organizational performance – In order to attract and retain the most qualified employees, managers must pay higher than average wages. Additionally, providing for employees a share in the rewards in the organizational performance creates a feeling of ownership and that they have a financial stake in the long-run performance of the business.
5. Training and Skills development – Companies whose competitive advantage is based on its people must continue to invest in their training and skills development.
6. Reduce status differences – Managers must treat everyone the same. This means no reserved parking, providing similar benefits, and everyone eating in the same cafeteria.
7. Information Sharing – Providing employees information about costs, finances, productivity, development, and strategies enable them to make more informed decisions which will better for the long-run of the organization.

Figure 1.10: Competitive Advantage through People

Research has shown that companies that invest in their employees were able to improve their average return on investment. They did this by adopting management techniques as simple as setting performance expectations, coaching, reviewing, and rewarding employee performance. A full list of management practices to help gain a competitive advantage are provided in Figure 1.10, these practices help organizations develop workforces that are better trained, smarter, better motivated, and are more committed in achieving the organizational goals.

## Managerial Life Cycle and Performance

Similar to a product and an industry, managers go through a series of performance stages. These evolving stages; exploration, establishment, maintenance, and decline are illustrated in Figure 1.11 which highlights the performance levels and age range most commonly associated with each stage.

1. **Exploration Stage** is the first stage of the career evolution. Individuals at this stage are generally between 15 and 25 years of age and are involved in some form of formal training such as college or vocational school. Due to the time commitment required from formal training, often individuals at this stage are involved in part-time work which may also provides a greater understanding of what a career in a particular organization may involve.

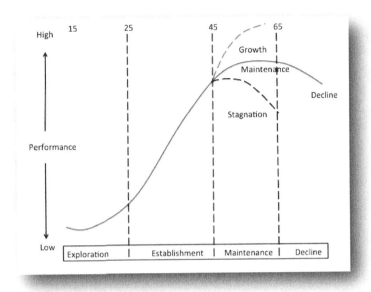

Figure 1.11: Managerial Life Cycle and Performance

2. **Establishment Stage** is the second stage in the evolution of a career wherein the participants age ranges from 25 to 45. Individuals at this stage become more productive and high performers. Employment sought during this stage is guided by what was learned during the exploration stage. Employment is often full-time and movement between jobs either within or outside of the company or industry is common.

3. **Maintenance Stage** the third stage in the career evolution. In this stage the age of the participants range from 45–65 years old. Three performance paths may occur at this stage; participants may experience increased performance (career growth), stabilized performance (career maintenance), or decreased performance (career stagnation). For obvious reasons, companies try to eliminate career plateauing and encourage continued career growth.

4. **Decline Stage** is the last stage in the career evolution. This stage involves those who are over 65 years old and whose productivity has declined. At 65 workers are close to retirement, semi-retired, or fully retired. Individuals at this stage may find it difficult to maintain prior performance levels due to loss of interest or inability to maintain skills training.

## Summary of Chapter

1. This chapter has focused on outlining the importance of management to society and has presented a definition of management and the management process.

2. We explored the three characteristics of management and Henry Fayol's part in determining the four functions; planning, organizing, leading, and controlling of managers.

3. This chapter looked at the five kinds of managers each with different jobs and responsibilities: top-level managers, middle-level managers, frontline managers, functional managers, and general managers.

4. We read that during Henry Mintzberg's research on managers, he defined three distinct roles of managers while performing their jobs: interpersonal, informational and decisional roles and within those three main roles there are 10 sub-roles of management activities.
5. We looked at the differences between managerial efficiency and managerial effectiveness as they relate to organizational performance.
6. This chapter discussed the importance of management skills to the success of the organization and what tactics can be used to improve the skills of their managers.
7. We discovered that there are two widely accepted views on management skills, the classic view and the contemporary view and that there are 7 important competencies that will increase the probability of managers becoming successfully in carrying out management activities.
8. We learned that a company's workforce can create a competitive advantage if management invests in their employees.

## Discussion Questions

1. Explain the four functions of management. ← "POLC"
2. Describe what management is. *process of working w/ people/resources in an organization's goals*
3. Briefly describe the different types of managers.
4. Discuss the key roles manager's play in organizational performance. Why is it important to recognize the interdependence nature of these roles?
5. Explain what companies look for in managers. *leaders,*
6. List the top mistakes that managers make in their jobs. *unorganized*
7. Explain how and why companies can create a competitive advantage through people.
8. How can 'controlling' help a manager become more efficient?

## References

Demos, T., 'Motivate without Spending Millions', *Fortune,* April 12, 2010, 37–38.

Fayol, H. (1949) *General and Industrial Management.* London; Pittman & Sons.

Hale, C.P., 'What Do Managers Do? A Critical Review of the Evidence', *Journal of Management Studies* (1986) (1): 88–115.

Huy, Q., 'In Praise of Middle Managers', *Harvard Business Review* (September 2001): 72–79.

Hill, L. A. (1992) *Becoming a Manager: Mastery of a New Identity.* Boston: Harvard Business School Press.

'How Investing in Intangibles—Like Employee Satisfaction Translates into Financial Returns', Knowledge@ Wharton, Janauary 9, 2008, accessed April 17, 2014, from http://knowledge.wharton.upenn.edu/article .cfm?articleid+1873.

Hunsaker, P. L., (2005) *Management: A Skills Approach.* Upper Saddle River, NJ: Pearson Prentice Hall. 24–25.

Huselid, M. A., (1995) 'The Impact of Human Resource Management Practices on Turnover, Productivity, and Corporate Financial Performance', Academy of Management Journal (38), 635–672.

Katz, R. L., (1974) 'Skills of an Effective Administrator,' *Harvard Business Review* (May–June): 132–142.

Levitz, J. 'UPS Thinks Out of the Box on Driver Training,' *Wall Street Journal,* April 6, 2010, accessed April 17, 2014, from http://online.wsj.com/article/SB10001424052702300391210457516457382418844.html?mod=WSJ_hp_editorsPicks.

McCall Jr. M. W. & Lombardo, M. M. (1983). 'What Makes a Top Executive?' *Psychology Today*, February 26–31.

McDonald, D., & Smith, A. (1995) ' A Proven Connection: Performance Management and Business Results,' *Compensation and Benefits Review* (27)(6) :59.

Mintzberg, H. (1973). *The Nature of Managerial Work.* New York: Harper & Row.

Pfeffer, J. (996) '*The Human Equation: Building Profits by Putting People First*' Boston: Harvard Business School Press.

Schmidt, F. L., & Hunter, J. E., (1992) 'Development of a Causal Model of Process Determining Job Performance,' *Current Directions in Psychological Science,* (1): 89–92.

Steckler, N., Fondas, N., 'Building Team Leader Effectiveness: A Diagnostic Tool,' *Organizational Dynamics* (Winter 1995): 20–34.

Stagner, R., 'Corporate Decision Making', *Journal of Applied Psychology* (1969) (53), 1–13.

Tully, S., 'What Team Leaders Need to Know', *Fortune*, February 20, 1995, 93.

'What Makes Teams Work?' *Fast Company*, November 1, 2000, 109.

Wren, D. A., Bedeian, A. G., & Breeze, J. D., 'The Foundations of Henri Fayol's Administrative Theory', *Management Decisions* (2002) (40), 906–918.

# CHAPTER 2

## The History of Management

---

*"The kind of people I look for to fill top management spots are the eager beavers, the mavericks. These are the guys who try to do more than they're expected to do-they always reach."*

– Lee Iacocca CEO, Chairman of Chrysler Corporation

---

### Chapter Learning Objectives:

After reading this chapter you should have a good understanding of:

- Frederick Taylor's contribution to management and job efficiency.
- Weber's view on bureaucracy and performance.
- Fayol's administrative principles and his description of managerial duties and practices.
- Mary Follett position on organizations as communities of cooperative activities.
- The Hawthorne study and is focus on the human side of the organization.
- Maslow's hierarchy of human needs with self-actualization as the top need.

- The self-fulfilling prophecies of managerial assumptions by McGregor.
- Argyris position that when management treat workers as responsible adults, those workers will become more productive.
- The concept of open and closed systems and how they interact with their environment.
- The concepts of Senge's Learning organization and how employee involvement in problem solution is important.

# The Classical Approach to Management

The classical management theory was one of the first schools of management thought and was developed during the Industrial Revolution as a way to solve the new problems management faced related to the factory system. During the Industrial Revolution Henry Ford and other were making mass production a mainstay of the emerging economy but these advancements were not made without experiencing difficulties such as how to train employees (many of which were non-English speaking immigrants) and dealing with increased labor dissatisfaction. As a result, the classical management theory was developed in an effort to 'find the best way' to perform and manage tasks. This school of thought is comprised of three branches: ***Classical Scientific, Classical Administrative***, and ***Classical Bureaucratic*** (Figure 2.1). We will cover the three branches in the following section.

The ***classical scientific branch***, or ***scientific management*** arose because of the need to increase productivity and efficiency. The emphasis was on trying to find the best way to get the most work done by examining how the work process was actually accomplished. To do this, theorists studied the basic steps and motions and determined the most efficient ways of doing them. Once the job was defined, workers could then be trained to follow it, and supervisors could be trained to best support and encourage workers to perform to the best of their abilities. Scientific management is based on four core principles:

1. Develop a 'science' for each job that includes rules on motion, standard work tools, and proper work conditions.
2. Hire workers with the right skills and abilities for the job.

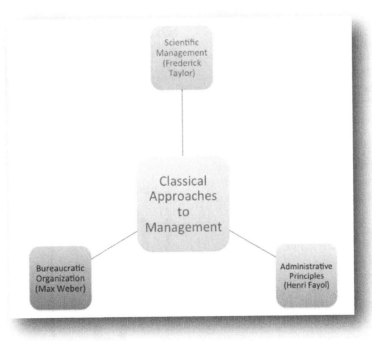

Figure 2.1: Classical Management's Three Branches

3.  Train and motivate workers to do their jobs according to the 'science'.
4.  Support workers by planning and assisting their work by the job science.

Scientific management owes its roots to several major contributors, including Frederick Taylor, Henry Gantt, and Frank and Lillian Gilbreth.

***Frederick Taylor*** is often called the "father of scientific management." Taylor believed that organizations should study tasks and then develop precise procedures to complete the tasks. This belief stemmed from his observations of how workers did their jobs, most in their own way, seemingly haphazard, and with little consistent supervision. As an example, in 1898, Taylor calculated how much iron from rail cars Bethlehem Steel plant workers could be unloading if they were using the correct movements, tools, and steps. The result was an amazing 47.5 tons per day instead of the mere 12.5 tons each worker had been averaging. In addition, by redesigning the shovels the workers used, Taylor was able to increase the length of work time and therefore decrease the number of people shoveling from 500 to 140. In 1909, Taylor published 'The Principles of Scientific Management.' Wherein he proposed that by optimizing and simplifying workers tasks, productivity would increase. Lastly, he developed an incentive system that paid workers more money for meeting the new standard. Productivity at Bethlehem Steel shot up overnight. As a result, many theorists followed Taylor's philosophy when developing their own principles of management.

Managers today continue to seek ways to improve organizational efficiency and productivity. Companies like UPS track their own time and generate reports showing how many times work activities are performed, the time spent, and recommendations for improving worker productivity based on the results.

A few years ago, UPS was facing pressures to cut costs. UPS also had an environmental stewardship policy. In thinking about how to solve their budget challenge, UPS put two seemingly unconnected ideas together.

After analyzing driving routes and realizing left turns resulted in wasting gas waiting in traffic, UPS rearranged their routes so that drivers turned right 90% of the time. Some drivers were skeptical but were willing to give the right turn policy a try.

The results of this policy were impressive. In 2007 alone, this helped UPS:

* Reduce nearly 30 million miles off already streamlined delivery routes.
* Save 3 million gallons of gas, and
* Reduce $CO_2$ emissions by 32,000 metric tons, the equivalent of removing 5,300 passenger cars from the road for an entire year.

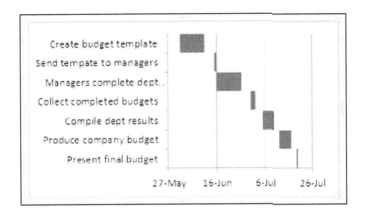

Figure 2.2: Sample Gantt chart for creating a Budget

*Henry Gantt* was an American engineer and famous management consultant who was best known for his planning methodology, the Gantt chart (Figure 2.2) a bar graph that measures planned and completed work along each stage of production. This methodology helped him realize major infrastructure projects including the construction of the Hoover Dam. Gantt also developed the task and bonus system of wage payment and measurement instruments to provide an insight to worker efficiency and productivity.

*Frank and Lillian Gilbreth* was a pioneering team in work and motion studies. In Frank's early career as an apprentice bricklayer, he was interested in standardization and method study. He watched bricklayers and saw that some workers were slow and inefficient, while others were very productive. He discovered that each bricklayer used a different set of motions to lay bricks. From his observations, Frank isolated the basic movements necessary to do the job and eliminated unnecessary motions. Workers using these movements raised their output from 1,000 to 2,700 bricks per day. This was the first *motion study* designed to isolate the best possible method of performing a given job.

Doctors to this day owe a debt to the Gilbreth's since it was Frank who first came up with the idea that surgeons should use a nurse to hand them their instruments as and when they were needed. Previously, surgeons had to search for their own instruments while operating.

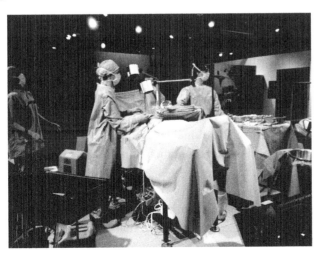

A surgical nurse is the backbone of a surgical team. Surgical nurses work in a dynamic and challenging environment, taking a key role in life-saving surgical procedures and the surrounding care.

The *classical administrative* approach is unlike from the scientific management approach as it focuses on the total organization and the importance of the development of managerial principles versus the productivity and study of work methods of individuals.

Contributors to this school of thought include Henri Fayol, and Chester I. Barnard. These theorists studied the flow of information within an organization and emphasized the importance of understanding how an organization operated.

**Henri Fayol** is generally regarded as the pioneer of the classical administrative theory. Fayol was a French mining engineer who developed 14 principles of management based on his management experiences. These principles; planning, organizing, commanding, coordinating, and control are still considered the elements under which we study, analyze and affect the management process today. The general principles provide today's managers with the guidelines on how to supervise and manage.

1. *Division of work*—Division of work and specialization produces more and better work with the same effort.
2. *Authority and responsibility*—Authority is the right to give orders and the power to exact obedience. A manager has official authority because of her position, as well as personal authority based on individual personality, intelligence, and experience. Authority creates responsibility.
3. *Discipline*—Obedience and respect within an organization are absolutely essential. Good discipline requires managers to apply sanctions whenever violations become apparent.
4. *Unity of command*—An employee should receive orders from only one superior.
5. *Unity of direction*—Organizational activities must have one central authority and one plan of action.
6. *Subordination of individual interest to general interest*—The interests of one employee or group of employees are subordinate to the interests and goals of the organization.
7. *Remuneration of personnel*—Salaries—the price of services rendered by employees—should be fair and provide satisfaction both to the employee and employer.
8. *Centralization*—The objective of centralization is the best utilization of personnel. The degree of centralization varies according to the dynamics of each organization.
9. *Scalar chain*—A chain of authority exists from the highest organizational authority to the lowest ranks.
10. *Order*—Organizational order for materials and personnel is essential. The right materials and the right employees are necessary for each organizational function and activity.
11. *Equity*—In organizations, equity is a combination of kindliness and justice. Both equity and equality of treatment should be considered when dealing with employees.
12. *Stability of tenure of personnel*—To attain the maximum productivity of personnel, a stable work force is needed.
13. *Initiative*—Thinking out a plan and ensuring its success is an extremely strong motivator. Zeal, energy, and initiative are desired at all levels of the organizational ladder.
14. *Esprit de corps*—Teamwork is fundamentally important to an organization. Work teams and extensive face-to-face verbal communication encourages teamwork.

Fayol's 14 principles cover a broad range of topics, but three common themes resonate throughout: organizational efficiency, how to manage people, and the use of appropriate managerial action.

*Chester Barnard*, who was president of New Jersey Bell Telephone Company, introduced the idea of the *informal organization*, defined as exclusive groups of people that naturally form within a company. Barnard felt that these informal organizations provided a necessary and vital communication functions for the overall organization and that they could assist the organization accomplish its goals.

Barnard felt that it was particularly important for managers to develop a sense of common purpose where a willingness to cooperate is strongly encouraged.

Barnard is credited with developing the *acceptance theory of management*. According to Barnard, directives, rules, regulations, and orders from the organization must be considered legitimate or they will not be effective. Hence, in order for employees to accept that managers have legitimate authority to act four factors that affect the willingness of employees to accept authority must be first met:

1. The employees must understand the communication.
2. The employees accept the communication as being consistent with the organization's purposes.
3. The employees feel that their actions will be consistent with the needs and desires of the other employees.
4. The employees feel that they are mentally and physically able to carry out the order.

Barnard also discusses the role of an executive. The primary function of the executive is to maintain the organization in a state of internal and external equilibrium (balance). Here, we are talking about a balance between the internal and external factors effecting the organizations such as resources, labor, market conditions, and investments.

Executives serve three basic functions in maintaining the cooperative system:

1. They must maintain and develop a system of communication.
2. They must induce individuals to join the organization and contribute to its mission.
3. Finally, and perhaps most importantly, they must define the purpose and objectives of the organization (Strategic Planning).

Using the fundamental principles that Barnard outlines, an application of these principles is made to the area of strategic management. The analysis focuses specifically on two main areas: the movement from static to a dynamic model and the role that the environment plays in affecting firm performance.

*Classical Bureaucratic Management* has two essential elements. First, it entails structuring an organization into a *hierarchy*. Secondly, the organization and its members are governed by clearly defined rational-legal decision-making rules. Each element helps an organization to achieve its goals.

An *organizational hierarchy* is the arrangement of the organization by level of authority in reference to the levels above and below it. For example, a vice-president of sales is below the company's president/ CEO but at the same level as the vice president of Operations, and above the supervisor of the company's social media department. Each level answers to the level above it with the ultimate leader of the organization at the top (Figure 2.3).

*Max Weber* is considered to be the father of *Bureaucratic management*, Weber believed that organizations should be managed impersonally and that it should follow a formal organizational structure where specific rules were followed. This non-personal, objective form of organization was called a *bureaucracy*.

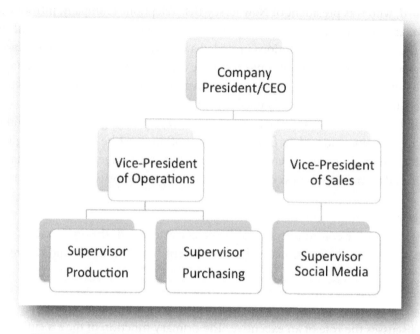

Figure 2.3: Organizational Hierarchy

Weber believed that all bureaucracies have the following characteristics:

- *A well-defined hierarchy*—all positions within a bureaucracy are structured in a way that permits the higher positions to supervise and control the lower positions. This clear chain of command facilitates control and order throughout the organization.
- *Division of labor and specialization*—All responsibilities in an organization are specialized so that each employee has the necessary expertise to do a particular task.
- *Rules and regulations*—Standard operating procedures govern all organizational activities to provide certainty and facilitate coordination.
- *Impersonal relationships between managers and employees*—Managers should maintain an impersonal relationship with employees so that favoritism and personal prejudice do not influence decisions.
- *Competence*—Competence should be the basis for all decisions made in hiring, job assignments, and promotions in order to foster ability and merit as the primary characteristics of a bureaucratic organization.
- *Records*—A bureaucracy needs to maintain complete files regarding all its activities.

## Delimitations of the Classical Approach to Management

The classical view of management focused primarily on the efficiency and productivity of workers rather any human needs that workers may have and is limited and more complex for use in larger organizations. Scientific management theory involved metrics and tools for improving efficiency that may not be appropriate in all workplace settings. Using metrics to examine specific employee behavior may be feasible in a smaller organization but becomes more difficult when trying to accomplish this at an organization that has hundreds of employees. In short, the classical approach ignored the human variables of motivation and behavior.

Due to the criticisms of the classical management theory, doors were opened for theorists that emphasized more of the human and behavioral aspects of management such as George Elton Mayo and Abraham Maslow who will be covered in the following section.

# The Behavioral Approach to Management

The *behavioral management theory* is often called the human relations movement because it addresses the human dimension of work and studies the behavior of people in groups in terms of their psychology and fit with companies rather than viewing workers as interchangeable parts with little value.

Behavioral theorists believed that having an understanding of the human behavior at work and what factors create motivation, cause conflict, builds expectations, and form group dynamics, can improve productivity.

The theorists who contributed to this school viewed employees as individuals, resources, and assets to be developed and worked with—not as machines, as in the past. Several individuals and experiments contributed to this theory.

*Elton Mayo* is known as the founder of the Human relations movement. Mayo studied people's work performance and concluded that the level of performance is dependent on both social issues and job content. In short, workers had higher levels of cooperation and higher output because of a feeling of importance whereas physical conditions or financial incentives had little motivational value.

*Mary Parker Follett* stressed the interactions of management with workers and the importance of an organization establishing common goals for its employees. She stressed the importance and value of allowing employees to participate in the decision-making process—a concept quite ahead of its time. Follett looked at management and leadership holistically, foreshadowing today's modern systems approaches. Follett defined a leader as "someone who sees the whole rather than the particular" and was one of the first to integrate the idea of organizational conflict into management theory. Due to her pioneering work on organizational conflict she is considered to be the "mother of conflict resolution.

Much of what managers do today is based on the fundamentals that Follett established more than 80 years ago.

# The Hawthorne Studies

*Hawthorne studies*, a series of experiments that rigorously applied classical management theory only to reveal its shortcomings. The Hawthorne experiments consisted of two studies conducted at the Hawthorne Works of the Western Electric Company in Chicago from 1924 to 1932. The first study was conducted by a group of engineers seeking to determine the relationship of lighting levels to worker productivity.

What he found, however, was that work satisfaction depended to a large extent on the informal social pattern of the work group. Where norms of cooperation and higher output were established because of a feeling of importance, physical conditions or financial incentives had little motivational value. Mayo concluded that people naturally form work groups that can be used by management to benefit the organization. In short, he concluded that people's work performance is dependent on both social issues and job content.

*The Bank Wiring Observation Room Experiment*, Mayo and F. J. Roethlisberger conducted a second study wherein they supervised a group of five women in a bank wiring room. They gave the women special privileges, such as the right to leave their workstations without permission, take rest periods, enjoy free lunches, and have variations in pay levels and workdays. This experiment also resulted in significantly increased rates of productivity.

Mayo and Roethlisberger concluded that human relations and the social needs of workers are crucial aspects of business management. This principle of human motivation helped revolutionize theories and practices of management.

## The Human Relations Movement

*The Human Relations Movement* refers to the researchers of organizational development who studied the interactions of people in organizations. The ultimate objective of the approach is to enhance organizational success by building appropriate relationships with people. When management is able to stimulate high productivity and worker commitment to the organization and its goals, human relations are said to be effective. The ability of a manager to work with people in a way that enhances organizational success is called *human relations skills*.

**Abraham Maslow**, a practicing psychologist, developed one of the most widely recognized **need theories**. A need is defined as a physiological or psychological deficiency that a person wants to satisfy. His theory of human needs had three assumptions:

1. Human needs are never completely satisfied.
2. Human behavior is purposeful and is motivated by the need for satisfaction.
3. Needs can be classified according to a hierarchical structure of importance, from the lowest to highest.

Maslow broke down the needs hierarchy into five specific areas from lowest to highest in order:

1. **Physiological needs**. Most basic of all human needs are in this category: such as food, water and physical well-being. After the need is satisfied, however, it is no longer is a motivator.
2. **Safety needs**. These needs include the need for basic security, stability, protection, and freedom from fear. A normal state exists for an individual to have all these needs generally satisfied. Otherwise, they become primary motivators.
3. **Social needs**. After the physical and safety needs are satisfied and are no longer motivators, the need for belonging, affections, and love emerges as a primary motivator.

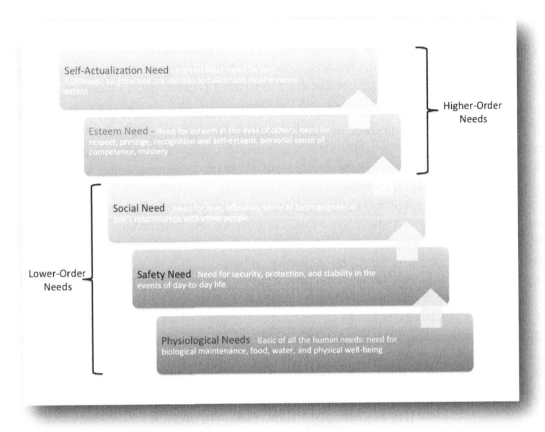

Figure 2.4: Maslow's Hierarchy of Human Needs

4.  **Esteem needs**. Is the first of the higher order needs. When an individual has the need for esteem in the eyes of others, need for respect, prestige, recognition and self-esteem, and a personal sense of competence and mastery.
5.  **Self-actualization needs**. Highest level of needs. Need for self-fulfillment, to grow and use abilities to their fullest and most creative extent.

Maslow's hierarchy of needs theory helped managers better understand people's needs and help find ways to satisfy them through their work. Maslow's Hierarchy of Human Needs is illustrated in Figure 2.4.

Another prominent management theorist is **Douglas McGregor**. He was heavily influenced by both the Hawthorne studies and Maslow and believed that two basic kinds of managers exist. One type, the **Theory X manager**, has a negative view of employees and assumes that they generally dislike work, lack ambition, act irresponsibly, resist change, are untrustworthy, and incapable of assuming responsibility. Type two are the **Theory Y managers**, this group of managers assumes that employees are not only trustworthy and capable of assuming responsibility, but also have high levels of motivation, creativity, and are willing to work.

An important aspect of McGregor's idea was his belief that managers who hold either set of assumptions can create **self-fulfilling prophecies**, that through their behavior, these managers create situations where subordinates act in ways that confirm the manager's original expectations.

As a group, these theorists discovered that people worked for inner satisfaction and not materialistic rewards, shifting the focus to the role of individuals in an organization's performance.

The research of both Maslow and McGregor revealed that people worked for inner satisfaction and not materialistic reward thus helping modern managers better understand the human component in organizations and how to appropriately work with it to enhance organizational success.

**Chris Argyris**, of Harvard University, noticed that large majorities of the people in the workplace today are still treated as immature human beings. In attempting to analyze this situation Argyris compared **bureaucratic/pyramidal value** organizational structures to organizations with a more humanistic/democratic value system. Argyris results revealed that following bureaucratic structure leads to poor, shallow, and mistrustful relationships.

These relationships do not permit the natural and free expression of feelings, resulting in decreased interpersonal competence. "Without interpersonal competence or a 'psychologically safe' environment, the organization is a breeding ground for mistrust, intergroup conflict, rigidity, and so on, which in turn lead to a decrease in organizational success in problem solving."

Argyris claims that if **humanistic or democratic values** are adhered to in an organization, a trusting, authentic relationships will develop among people and will result in increased interpersonal competence, intergroup cooperation, flexibility, resulting in increases in organizational effectiveness.

In this kind of environment people are treated as human beings, both organizational members and the organization itself are given an opportunity to develop to the fullest potential, and there is an attempt to make work exciting and challenging.

# The Management Science Approach

The **management science approach**, or operations research approach, was first developed during World War II to find solutions to warfare issues such as which gun sight would best stop German attacks on the British mainland. The management science approach was also known at the quantitative approach because it used mathematical models to solve problems by analyzing a mix of variables, constraints, and costs to enable management in making the optimal decisions. The management science approach combines rational thought with intuitive insight to resolve management concerns such as cost, production and service levels.

Management science is primarily concerned with exploring how a business can manage itself with the aim to maximize productivity. Through adopting a system that allows integration of scientific thought, the managers and owners solve or prevent the range of problems and issues arising from managerial weaknesses, which can be primary reasons small firms are viewed as marginal or unprofitable businesses. The core function of the management science approach is to compare possible outcomes and dictates that scientists:

1. Systematically observe the system whose behavior must be explained to solve the problem.
2. Use these specific observations to construct a generalized model that is consistent with the specific observations and from which consequences of changing the system can be predicted.
3. Use the model to determine how the system will behave under conditions that have not been observed but could be observed if the changes were made.
4. Test the model by performing an experiment on the actual system to see whether the effects of changes predicted using the model actually occur when the changes are made.

In short, a problem is encountered, it is systematically analyzed, an appropriate mathematical model and computations are applied, and an optimal solution is identified. Consider the following two examples of the management science approach.

- An oil exploration company is concerned about future oil reserves in various parts of the world. *Quantitative solution:* Mathematical forecasting helps make future projections for reserve sizes and depletion rates that are useful in the planning process.
- A manufacturer wants to maximize profits for producing four different products on four different machines, each of which can be used for different periods of times and at different costs. *Quantitative solution:* Linear programming is used to determine how best to allocate production among different machines to maximize profits.

## Application of Management Science Today

Today, small-business owners and mangers can use the management science approach to design specific measures that identify and evaluate the effectiveness of certain processes or decisions. For example, they can develop basic computer applications that can help predict and analyze optimal inventory levels considering both the demand and costs. Managers use the techniques and tools of this quantitative approach to management to plan, organize, lead and control operations within the workplace. For the company, the approach can result in increased production, industrial peace and benefits of specialization.

## Contingency Approach to Management

The **contingency approach** to management can be summarized as an "it all depends" approach. In other words, the appropriate management action and approach depends on, or is 'contingent' upon, a given set of circumstances. This approach emphasizes the "if-then' scenarios. 'If' this occurs, 'then' a manager would probably take this course of action. Managers with a contingency view use a flexible approach, draw on a variety of theories and experiences, and evaluate many options as they solve problems.

Contingency management recognizes that there is no one best way to manage. In the contingency perspective, managers are faced with the task of determining which managerial approach is likely to be most effective in a given situation. For example, the approach used to manage a group of new student employees working in the university cafeteria would be very different from the approach used to manage a medical research team trying to find a cure for a disease. The main challenges in using the contingency approach are the following:

1. Perceiving organizational situations, as they actually exist.
2. Choosing the management tactics best suited to those situations.
3. Competently implementing those tactics.

Contingency thinking avoids the classical "one best way" arguments and recognizes the need to understand situational differences and respond appropriately to them. It does not apply certain management principles to any situation. Contingency theory is recognition of the extreme importance of individual manager performance in any given situation; they must consider the realities of the specific situation before taking the appropriate action.

# The Systems Approach to Management

The **systems approach** to management is based on the general systems theory proposed in the 1940's by biologist Ludwig von Bertalanffy. The main premise of the theory is that to fully understand the operations of an entity, the entity must be viewed as a system. A **system** is a number of interdependent parts functioning as a whole for some purpose. Each system executes its functions as a largely independent unit. For example, according to Bertalanffy, in order to fully understand the operations of the human body, one must understand the workings of it interdependent parts (eyes, ears, heart, and brain).

In management, understanding how each functional area of the firm operates allows managers to steer the company into the directions it wishes to go. Each system must determine how best to reach those strategic goals to fulfill the mission of the leadership. A systems approach makes the assumption that each unit of the company operates at peak efficiency.

According to von Bertalanffy, there are two basic types of systems; open systems and closed systems. An **open system** is continuously interacting with its environment. Von Bertalanffy uses a plant as an example of an open system as the plant continuously interacts with its environment influencing the plant's state of existence and determining whether the plant will have a future.

The open-system approach serves as a model of business activity; that is, business is a process of transforming inputs to outputs while realizing that inputs are taken from the external environment and outputs are placed into this same environment (Figure 2.5). The open system concept helps to explain why today's firms strive so hard to continually meet the needs of their customers.

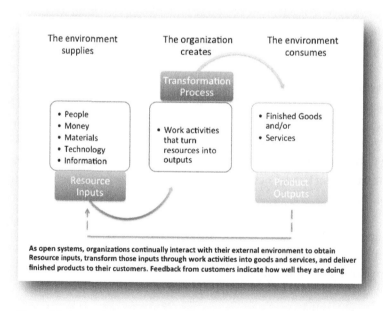

Figure 2.5: Open System and External Environment

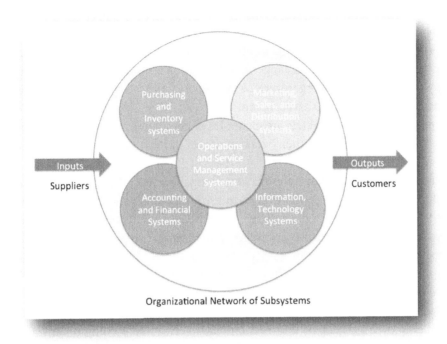

Figure 2.6: Organizational Subsystems

A *closed system* is not influenced by, and does not interact with its environment. It is mostly mechanical and has predetermined motions or activities that must be performed regardless of the environment. A watch is an example of a closed system. Regardless of its environment, a watch's wheels, gears, and other parts must function in a predetermined way if the watch as a whole is to exist and serve its purpose. A production line is an example of a closed system within an organization. The daily work that takes place on production or assembly lines can be insulated from outside factors such as day-to-day meetings between upper-level executives, or information from other similar, competing production lines. Instead, workers on an assembly line are generally only responsible for completing their tasks on the line, depending on what type of line it is.

Companies use inputs such as labor, funds, technology, and materials to produce goods or to provide services and they design their *subsystems* to attain these goals. Subsystems, either individually or collectively supports the work of the larger system. Figure 2.6 illustrates the importance of cooperation among organizational subsystems. For example, the operations and service management systems serve as a central point. They provide the integration among other subsystems such as purchasing, accounting, sales, and information, all of which are essential to the work and success of the organization.

## A New Approach to Management: The Learning Organization

Changes in the external environment, like an increasingly global marketplace, rapid technological advances, and growing pressure to do more with less, require managers to implement needed change as they build their organization.

A new approach to management is found in the ***learning organization approach***, wherein all employees systematically participate in identifying and solving organizational problems that will enable continuous change and improvement, increasing the organizations capacity to grow, learn, and achieve its purpose.

A learning organization promotes exchanges of information among employees, which creates a more knowledgeable workforce. Learning organizations exhibit flexibility because employees accept and adapt to new ideas and changes through a shared vision.

Honda, Corning, and General Electric are examples of company's that are able to quickly shape and motivate their workers, transforming their work practices to keep pace with the constantly changing environment.

Leadership in learning organizations requires something more than the traditional approach of setting goals, making decisions, and directing the troops. In learning organizations, managers learn to think in terms of "control with" rather than "control over" employees. They "control with" employees by building relationships based on shared visions and shaping the cultures of their organizations so that all can help achieve the same visions. A leader in this learning environment can help facilitate teamwork, initiate change, and expand the capacity of employees to shape their organization's future. Leaders who understand how the learning organization operates can help other leaders adapt to this organizational style.

Visionary leadership, a team-based structure, participative strategy, a strong, adaptive internal culture, empowered employees, and open information characterize the learning organization. Consultant **Peter Senge**, author of the popular book, ***The Fifth Discipline***, identifies the following ingredients of learning organizations:

- **Challenging of mental models**—members routinely challenge the way business is done, setting aside of old ways of thinking.
- **Personal mastery**—members are committed to gaining deeper self-awareness and ability to remain open to others.
- **Systems thinking**—every organizational member understands his or her own job and how the jobs fit together to provide final products to the customer.
- **Shared vision**—members have a common purpose of the organization and a sincere commitment to accomplish the purpose.
- **Team learning**—member's work together, develop new solutions to new problems together, and apply solutions together to accomplish the plan of action.

The concept of the learning organization places high value on developing the ability to learn and then make that learning continuously available to all organizational members.

## Summary of Chapter

1. This chapter has focused on the advanced quantitative techniques in decision sciences and operations management that help managers solve complex problems.
2. We read that the systems view depicts organizations as complex networks of subsystems that must interact and cooperate with one another if the organization as a whole is to accomplish its goals.

3. We learned the importance of Maslow's Needs theory and how it relates to the Human Relations movement in management thinking.
4. This chapter looked at the Contingency thinking and how it avoids the 'one best solution' argument, recognizing instead that managers need to understand situational differences and respond appropriately to them.
5. We discovered that in a Learning organization the leadership and internal environment encourages continuous learning from experience to improve work methods and processes.
6. We learned that evidence-based management uses finding from rigorous scientific research to identify management practices for high performance.

# Discussion Questions

1. Discuss the primary limitations of the classical approach to management. Would this approach be more significant to managers today than managers in the more distant past? Explain.
2. What is the 'systems approach' to management? How do the concepts of closed and open systems relate to this approach?
3. Explain how the Contingency thinking might influence a manager's choice in designing the organizational structure.
4. How does Henry Fayol's contribution to management differ from the contributions of Frank and Lillian Gilbreth?
5. Is a learning organization something that comes about because of the actions of manages, workers, or both?
6. Can you use the concepts of open system and subsystem to describe the operations of an organization in your city?
7. In addition to the choice of organization structures, in what other areas of management decision-making to you think contingency thinking plays a role?
8. Provide an example of how the principles of scientific management can be applied in organizations today.
9. How do the deficit and progression principles operate in Maslow's hierarchy?
10. Compare the Hawthorne effect with McGregor's notion of self-fulfilling prophecies.

# References

Anderson, D. R. (2012). *An Introduction to Management Science: Quantitative Approaches to Decision Making.* Mason, OH: South-Western/Cengage Learning.

Argyris, C. (1957). *Personality and Organization.* New York: Harper & Row.

Barnard, C. I. (1952). *Organization and Management.* Cambridge, MA: Harvard University Press.

Brodie, M. B. (1949). *Fayol on Administration. London: Pitman.*

Drucker, P. F. 'Looking Ahead: Implications of the Present' *Harvard Business Review.* (1997) 18–32.

Emshoff, J. R. (1971). *Analysis of Behavioral Systems.* New York: Macmillan.

Fayol, H. (1949). *General and Industrial Management*. London: Sir Isaac Pitman and Sons.

Follett, M. P. (1949). *Freedom and Coordination*. London: Management Publications Trust.

Gantt, H. L. (1916). *Industrial Leadership*. New Haven CT: Yale University Press.

Graham. P. (1995). *Mary Parker Follett-Prophet of Management: A Celebration of Writings from the 1920's*. Boston: Harvard Business School Press.

Hays, D. W. Quality Improvement and its Origin in Scientific Management, *Quality Progress* (1994) 89–90.

Heil, G., Stevens, D. F., & Bennis, W. G. (2000). *Douglas McGregor on Management: Revisiting the Human Side of Enterprise*. New York: Wiley.

Henderson, A. M., & Parsons, T. (1947). *Max Weber: the Theory of Social Economic Organizations*. New York: Free Press.

Hopkins, M. S. 'Putting the Science in Management Science,' *MIT Sloan Management Review*, (2010).

Jones, S. 'Worker Interdependence and Output: The Hawthorne Studies Reevaluated,' *American Sociological Review*. (1990) 176–190.

Karwatka, D. 'Frank Gilbreth and Production Efficiency,' *Tech Directions* (2006) 65–6.

Lock, E. A., 'The Ideas of Frederick W Taylor: An Evaluation,' *Academy of Management Review*, (1982) (7) 14.

Maslow, A. H. (1965). *Eupsychian Management*. Homewood, IL: Richard D. Irwin.

Maslow, A. H. (1970). *Motivation and Personality*. New York: Harper & Row.

Metcalfe, H. C., & Urwick, L. (1940). *Dynamic Administration: The Collected Papers of Mary Parker Follett*. New York: Harper & Brothers.

McGregor, D. (1960). *The Human Side of Enterprise*. New York: McGraw-Hill.

Michaels, E. A. 'Work Measurements', *Small Business Reports*. (1989) 55–63.

Mousa, F. T. & Lemak, D. J. 'The Gilbreths' Quality System Stands the Test of Time,' *Journal of Management History*. (2009) (15–2) 198–215.

Shane, S. & Ulrich, K. 'Technological Innovation, Product Development. And Entrepreneurship in Management Science,' *Management Science* (2004) (2) 133–145.

Taylor, F. R. (1947). *The Principles of Scientific Management*. New York: Harper & Bros.

Urwick. L. (1943). *The Elements of Administration*. New York: Harper & Brothers.

Von Bertalanffy, L. 'The History and Status of General Systems Theory,' *Academy of Management Journal*, (1972) (15) 407–426.

Wren, D. A. (1993). *The Evolution of Management Thought*. 4th Edition. New York: Wiley.

# CHAPTER 3

## Ethics and Social Responsibility

*"It's not hard to make decisions when you know what your values are."*

– Roy Disney, American Film Writer, Producer,
Nephew of Walt Disney

*"Management is doing things right; leadership is doing the right things."*

– Peter Drucker

---

### Chapter Learning Objectives:

After reading this chapter you should be able to:

- Explain the importance of ethical decision making in the practice of management
- Identify different ethical perspectives and ethical decision-making models.
- Understand the importance of corporate social responsibility
- Identify different perspectives of corporate social responsibility.

We begin this chapter with a simple question, 'Is everything that is legal, ethical?' It would be tempting to say that yes, any behavior that is legal can also be considered ethical. However, if we consider some of the laws of the past we can easily see that they were not ethical. Consider the Virginia Slave Codes of 1705 that permitted slavery, laws prohibited women from voting, and laws allowing child labor to name but a few. Therefore, defining what is ethical does not necessarily depend on its legal position. *Ethics* are defined as the code of moral principles that sets standards of good or bad, right or wrong, in our conduct. *Personal ethics* are guides for our behavior helping us make moral choices among alternative courses of action. *Ethical behavior* is the term often used to describe what we accept as 'right' or 'wrong' or 'good' or 'bad'.

What do we mean by *ethical decision-making*? Are there decisions that are not ethical in that there is not still some element of ethical components to one's choice? Many definitions exist, but most depend on using some standard of ethical behavior from which to judge the individual's behavior. For this text we will define ethical decision-making as a decision that is both legally and morally acceptable to the larger community utilizing all ethical perspectives and models to inform and influence the decision-making to produce the best possible outcomes for all stakeholders.

*Business Ethics* is a form of applied ethics or professional ethics that examines ethical principles and moral or ethical problems that arise in a business environment. It applies to all aspects of business conduct and is relevant to the conduct of individuals and entire organizations. Business ethics are often guided by law, while other times provide a basic framework that businesses may choose to follow in order to gain public acceptance.

# Ethical Behavior and values

As we just discovered, not everything that is legal is ethical and many ethical problems arise at work when people are asked to do something that violates their personal beliefs even though the act is legal. So how do we go about making the decision when it extends beyond legality and moves into your individual beliefs and judgments of what is right and wrong, your personal *values?* Values are the underlying beliefs and judgments regarding what is right or desirable and that influence individual attitudes and behaviors.

Psychologist Milton Rokeach delineates two types of values: *terminal,* and *instrumental*. **Terminal values** are the goals that we work towards and view as most desirable. These values are desirable states of existence and are the goals that we would like to achieve during our lifetime such as family security, true friendship, a comfortable life, self-respect, a sense of accomplishment, and happiness to name a few. *Instrumental values* concern the *means* for accomplishing these ends. Instrumental values are core values and as such are permanent in nature comprising personal characteristics and character traits. Instrumental Values refer to preferable modes of behavior and include values like honesty, sincerity, ambition, independence, obedience, imaginativeness, courageousness, competitiveness, and also some negative traits too. Organizations also have instrumental values (which can be ascertained from the organizational culture) and these are permanent in nature and difficult to change.

Southwest Airlines is one example of an organization with clearly defined instrumental values that significantly contribute to its overwhelming success. Some of Southwest's instrumental values are: low cost, hard work, family, fun, individuality, ownership, and profitability. The low cost concept enables people who generally cannot afford an airline flight the opportunity to fly short flights in a short amount of time. The Southwest employees do a great job servicing its customers by working very hard. The employees understand the importance of working hard and fast to ensure every flight meets their scheduled flight time. They are not just working hard to meet the mission; they work hard because they are part owners of the company.

# Ethical Perspectives

**Ethical Perspectives** provide a philosophical basis for evaluating behavior and decision-making. A variety of influences inform our decision-making, many of which are rooted in classical thought concerning morality and what constitutes right and good in a world of competing interests. The following section examines four of the major ethical philosophical views: *utilitarian, individualism, justice,* and the *moral rights view* (Figure 3.1).

### Utilitarian View

19th century philosopher John Stuart Mill argued that resolution of ethical dilemmas requires a balancing effort in which we *minimize the harms* that result from a decision while *maximizing the benefits*. Accordingly, the **utilitarian view** considers that ethical decisions should be resolved by delivering the greatest good to the greatest number of people as long as the majority of those involved are helped and a minimum number are harmed. For example, a manager who decides to cut the workforce by 30 percent in order to keep the company profitable and save the remaining jobs rather than lose them all to a business failure. Utilitarianism challenges us to look at the impact of proposed solutions to ethical dilemmas from the viewpoint of all stakeholders and attempt to provide the greatest amount of good for the greatest number of people.

### Individualism View

The **individualism view** of ethical behavior would focus on the long-term advancement of self-interests. The cornerstone to this view is that people become 'self-regulating' over time as they strive for individual

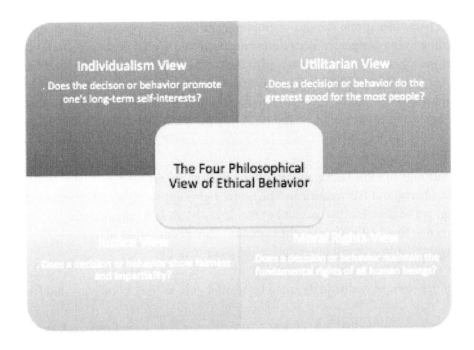

Figure 3.1: The Four Views of Ethical Behavior

advantage; ethics are maintained in the process. For example, suppose that you might think about cheating on the next exam. However, you realize that this short-term gain might lead to a long-term loss if you get caught and fail the course. For this reasoning, you reject the idea.

### Justice View

The *justice view* of moral reasoning considers the behavior ethical when people are treated impartially and fairly according to legal rules and standards. This view judges the ethical aspects of any decision on the basis of how equitable it is for everyone affected arguing that we should always choose the fairest and most just or equitable resolution of any ethical dilemma. Recently, researchers have identified three aspects of justice in the workplace: *procedural justice, distributive justice, and interactional justice.*

*Procedural justice* refers to the idea of fairness and transparency in the processes that resolve disputes and allocate resources. It reflects the extent in which an individual perceives that outcome decisions have been fairly made. The use of fair procedures helps to communicate to the employees that they are valued members of the organization. Procedural justice can be examined by focusing on the formal procedures used to make decisions and then to communicate to the employees that the process involves fair procedures. *Distributive justice* involves the perceived fairness of the allocation of outcome without respect for individual characteristics such as ethnicity, race, age, or gender. For example, when workers of the same job are paid different salaries, group members may feel that distributive justice has not occurred. To determine whether distributive justice has occurred, individuals often seek the distributive 'norm' of their group. A *distributive norm* is the standard of behavior that is required, desired, or designated as normal within a particular group (length of employment with the company). If rewards and costs are allocated according to the designated distributive norms of the group, distributive justice has occurred. Example follow-up, some workers have been with the company for a longer period of time, hence their salary is expected to be higher. **Interactional justice** focuses on the interpersonal treatment of others with dignity and respect received when procedures are implemented. For example, does a bank loan officer take the time to fully explain to an applicant why he or she was denied a loan.

### Moral Rights View

Based on the teachings of John Locke and Thomas Jefferson the **moral rights view** considers the rights of people to life, liberty, and fair treatment. The moral rights approach asserts that human beings have fundamental rights and liberties that cannot be taken away by an individual's decision. Thus, an ethically direct decision is one that best maintains the rights of those people affected by it.

Six moral rights should be considered during decision-making:

1. *The right of free consent:* Individuals are to be treated only as they knowingly and freely consent to be treated.
2. *The right to privacy:* Individuals can choose to do as they please away from work and have control of information about their private life.
3. *The right of freedom of conscience:* Individuals may refrain from carrying out any order that violates their moral norms and religious norms.
4. *The right of free speech:* Individuals may criticize truthful ethics or legality actions of others.
5. *The right to due process:* Individuals have a right to an impartial hearing and fair treatment.
6. *The right to life and safety:* Individuals have a right to live without endangerment or violation of their health and safety

To make ethical decisions managers need to avoid interfering with the fundamental rights of others. For example, a decision to eavesdrop on employees violates the right to privacy. Sexual harassment is unethical because it violates the right to freedom of conscious. The right of free speech would support whistle blowers who call attention to illegal or inappropriate actions within a company.

## Ethical Views across Cultures

How we view ethics in the United States is often at odds we how other view ethics in other parts of the world. Consider the following scenario: A 12-year old girl is working in a garment factory in Vietnam. She is the only source of income for her family. She often works 12-hour days and was once badly burned by a hot iron at work. One day her supervisor tells her that she cannot work and is fired. Her employer was given an ultimatum by his firm's major U.S customer stating 'no child workers if you want to keep our contracts.' The young girl says: 'I don't understand, I did my job very well and I need the money to support my family.'

What would you do if you were put in this position? Would you allow the child to work? The previous scenario is but one of the many examples of ethical challenges facing international business. The former

CEO of Levi's Robert Haas once said that an ethical problem 'becomes even more difficult when you overlay the complexities of different cultures and values systems that exist throughout the world.'

If your one who feels that the behavior in a foreign setting should be guided by the classic rule of 'when in Rome, do as the Romans do,' your ethical position is one of cultural relativism.

*Cultural relativism* is the view that no culture is superior to any other culture when comparing systems of morality, law, politics, etc. This view considers that all cultural beliefs are equally valid and that truth itself is relative, depending on the cultural environment. Those who hold to cultural relativism hold that all religious, ethical, aesthetic, and political beliefs are completely relative to the individual within a cultural identity.

Contrasting cultural relativism is the ethical position known as **universalism**. This ethical position suggests that if a behavior or practice is not acceptable in one's home country, it is not acceptable anywhere else. In other words, ethical standards are 'universal' and should apply absolutely across cultures and national borders. For example, in our opening scenario the American executive would not do business in a setting where child labor was practiced since it is unacceptable in the United States. Critics of the universalism approach claim that it is a form of *ethical imperialism*, in attempting to externally impose one's ethical beliefs and standards on others. The concepts of cultural relativism and universalism are illustrated in the following Figure 3.2.

## A Test of Personal Ethics and Values-Ethical Dilemmas

It is easy and safe to discuss ethical theory and behavior and how one would react under hypothetical situations. We enjoy the comfort and sense of self-satisfaction having a reasonable assurance that your decision will be of the utmost ethical standard. However, at some point in your life a real personal test will occur that will challenge your ethical beliefs and standards. As an example, upon your graduation you have interviewed for several jobs and you accept one only to receive a significantly better offer from another employer two weeks later. Should you come up with an excuse to back out of the first job so that you can accept the second?

An *ethical dilemma* occurs when a person has the ability to make two choices, but can only perform one or the other. In the prior example, the person has a legitimate moral imperative for each choice: keep the first job because of commitments made or accept the second because it provides better benefits. Thus, the person ultimately "fails" in the dilemma because he ought to complete both actions, but the actions are mutually exclusive.

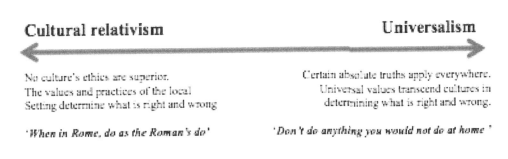

Figure 3.2: The Continuum of Cultural Relativism and Universalism

## Common Situations for Unethical Behavior at Work

- *Discrimination* – Denying people a promotion or job because of their race, religion, gender, age, or another reason that is not job-relevant.
- *Sexual Harassment* – Making a coworker feel uncomfortable because of inappropriate comments or actions regarding sexuality, or by requesting sexual favors in return for favorable job treatment.
- *Conflicts of Interest* – Taking bribes, kickbacks, or extraordinary gifts in return for making decisions favorable to another person.
- *Customer Confidence* – Giving someone privileged information regarding the activities of a customer.
- *Organizational Resources* – Using official stationary or a business e-mail account to communicate personal opinions or to make requests from community organizations.

Figure 3.3: Common Situations for Unethical Behavior at Work

William Styron provides an example of an ethical dilemma in the movie "Sophie's Choice". A Nazi concentration camp guard tells Sophie he will kill one of her two children, but she must choose which one shall die. In this scenario, Sophie has the same obligation and desire for each child. Philosophers call this a *symmetrical moral dilemma*.

In a survey of *Harvard Business Review* subscribers, managers reported that many of their ethical dilemmas arise out of conflict with superiors, customers, and subordinates. Advertising and communication with top management, clients, and governmental agencies rank as the two most frequent issues involving dishonesty followed by entertainment expenses, kickbacks, and special gifts. Figure 3.3 lists the most common situations for unethical behavior at work.

## Rationalizing Unethical Behavior

Generally, we view ourselves as being 'good'. When we do something that is or might be considered 'wrong' we are left feeling uncomfortable, anxious, and uneasy. Our natural human response is to rationalize the behavior to make it seem more acceptable in our minds. There are four common rationalizations that are used to justify ethical misconduct: *It's not really illegal; everyone does it; No one will ever know about it;* and *it's for a good cause.*

1. *It's not really illegal*—Former D.C. Mayor (and current unethical D.C. Councilman for Ward 8) Marion Barry earned himself a place in the Ethics Distortion Hall of Fame with his defense of his giving his blatantly unqualified girlfriend a high-paying job with the DC government. Barry declared

that since there was no law against using the public payroll as his own private gift service, there was nothing unethical about it. Once the law was passed (because of him), he then agreed that what he did would be wrong the next time he did it.

Ethics is far broader than law, which is a system of behavior enforced by the state with penalties for violations. Ethics is good conduct as determined by the values and customs of society. Professions promulgate codes of ethics precisely because the law cannot proscribe all inappropriate or harmful behavior. Much that is unethical is not illegal. Lying. Betrayal. Nepotism. Many other kinds of behavior as well, but that is just the factual error in this rationalization.

The greater problem with it is that it omits the concept of ethics at all. Ethical conduct is self-motivated, based on the individual's values and the internalized desire to do the right thing. Barry's construct assumes that people only behave ethically if there is a tangible, state-enforced penalty for not doing so, and that not incurring a penalty (that is, not breaking the law) is, by definition, ethical.

2. *Everyone does it*-This rationalization has been used to excuse ethical misconduct since the beginning of civilization. It is based on the flawed assumption that the ethical nature of an act is somehow improved by the number of people who do it, and if "everybody does it," then it is implicitly all right for you to do it as well: cheat on tests, commit adultery, lie under oath, use illegal drugs, cheat on taxes. Of course, people who use this "reasoning" usually don't believe that what they are doing is right because "everybody does it." They usually are arguing that they shouldn't be singled out for condemnation if "everybody else" isn't.

Since most people will admit that principles of right and wrong are not determined by polls, those who try to use this fallacy are really admitting misconduct. The simple answer to them is that even assuming they are correct when more people engage in an action that is admittedly unethical, more harm results. An individual is still responsible for his or her part of the harm.

3. *No one will ever know about it*—The habitually unethical as well as the rarely unethical who don't want to admit they have strayed are vulnerable to this classic, which posits that as long as the lie, swindle, cheat, or crime is never discovered, it hardly happened at all...in fact, one might as well say it *didn't* happen, so you can't really say anything really was wrong...right? Wrong. First of all, a remarkable percentage of time, the wrongful act *is* discovered. Even if it is not, however, the unethical nature of the act is intrinsic, and exists independently of how many people know about it. Just as a tree that falls in the forest with nobody around both makes noise and causes damage, so undetected, well-disguised or covered-up wrongs are exactly as wrong as those that end up on the front pages. They also cause the same amount of harm much of the time.

4. *It's for a good cause*—This rationalization has probably caused more death and human suffering than any other. The words "it's for a good cause" have been used to justify all sorts of lies, scams and mayhem. It is the downfall of the zealot, the true believer, and the passionate advocate that almost any action that supports "the Cause," whether it be liberty, religion, charity, or curing a plague, is seen as being justified by the inherent rightness of the ultimate goal at any price. Thus, Catholic Bishops protected child-molesting priests to protect the Church, and the American Red Cross used deceptive promotions to swell its blood supplies after the September 11, 2001 attacks.

# Ethical Intensity of the Decision

Managers don't treat all ethical decisions the same. A manager whose decision is to layoff 10 employees is going to treat that decision differently than if an employee was caught taking paper home for personal use. **Ethical intensity** is the degree of moral importance given to an issue. It is influenced by six factors:

1.  The first factor is **magnitude of consequences**. Magnitude of consequence is the harm or benefits accruing to individuals affected by a decision or behavior. An action that causes 1,000 people to suffer a particular injury has greater consequences than an action that causes 20 people to suffer the same injury.

2.  The second factor is **probability of effect**—the likelihood that if a decision is implemented it will lead to the harm or benefit predicted. The production of an automobile that would be dangerous to occupants during normal driving has greater probability of harm than the production of a NASCAR racecar that endangers the driver when curves are taken at high speed.

3.  The third factor is **social consensus** is the amount of public agreement that a proposed decision is bad or good. Actively discriminating against minority job candidates is worse than not actively seeking out minority job candidates.

4.  The fourth factor is **temporal immediacy**—the length of time that elapses between making a decision and when the consequences of that decision are known. A shorter length of time implies greater immediacy. An example of this is if Pfizer releases a drug that causes one percent of the people who take it to have acute nervous reactions within one week. This has greater temporal immediacy than releasing a drug that will cause 1 percent of those who take it to develop nervous disorders after 25 years of use.

5.  The fifth factor is **proximity of effect** is the sense of closeness (social, cultural, psychological, or physical) that the decision maker has for victims or beneficiaries of the decision. Recently, Citigroup cut 53,000 jobs. This reduced its labor force to 300,000 employees with more layoffs anticipated. This action had a greater impact on the remaining employees than the personal impact the news reporters feel when announcing this layoff.

6.  The sixth factor is **concentration of effect** -the inverse function of the number of people affected by a decision. A change in an insurance policy denying coverage to 40 people with claims of $50,000 each has a more concentrated effect than a change denying coverage to 4,000 people with claims of $500 each.

# Moral Development

Your friend Mitch has just given you the latest version of Microsoft Office. He forwarded you the download link he received when he bought it and told you to download it yourself before it expires in a few days. You're tempted. The software costs about $100, which is more than you have. Besides, all of your friends have the same version of Microsoft Office and they didn't pay for it either. You know that downloading the software to your computer without paying for it is illegal and violates copyright laws. But who would find out? Even if someone does, Microsoft isn't looking for the little guy they only go after the big fish, the companies that illegally copy and distribute software to their workers and pirates that illegally sell cheap, unauthorized copies. Ok, your computer has booted up, your email is open, and your cursor is pointing to the link in Mitch's message. What are you going to do?

Your decision, according to psychologist Lawrence Kohlberg, will be based on your level of **moral development**. Kohlberg identifies three phases of moral development with two stages in each phase (Figure 3.4).

***Phase One—The preconventional level of moral development***—people make decisions based on selfish reasons. For example, in *Stage 1* of the preconventional phase, the *punishment and obedience stage*, your primary concern will be to avoid trouble for yourself, so you won't copy the software because you are afraid of being caught and punished. However, in *Stage 2* of the preconventional phase, the *instrumental exchange* stage, your less worried about the punishment and more concerned about advancing your own wants and needs. Hence, you copy the software.

***Phase Two—The conventional level of moral development***—people at this phase of moral development make decisions that conform to societal expectations looking outside of themselves to others for moral guidance on ethical issues. *Stage 3* is influenced by what the *'good boys'* and *'nice girls'* are doing. If everyone else is copying the software illegally, you will too. But if they aren't, you won't either. *Stage 4* is the *law and order stage*, again you look externally for guidance and do whatever the law permits; since it is illegal, and you won't copy the software.

***Phase Three—The postconventional level of moral development***—at this phase of moral development people use internalized ethical principles to solve ethical dilemmas. *Stage 5* is the *Social contract stage*, wherein your decision is based on the overall rights of other, society as a whole is better off when individual rights are protected, in this case the rights of the software authors and manufacturers. Hence, you do not copy the software. At *Stage 6*, the *Universal principle stage*, you may or might not copy the software depending on your principles of right and wrong. In fact, you will stick to your principles

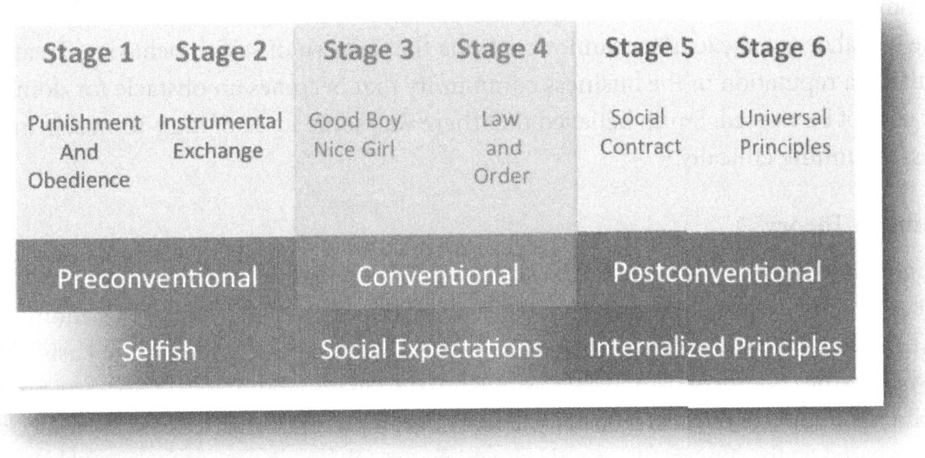

| Stage 1 | Stage 2 | Stage 3 | Stage 4 | Stage 5 | Stage 6 |
|---------|---------|---------|---------|---------|---------|
| Punishment And Obedience | Instrumental Exchange | Good Boy Nice Girl | Law and Order | Social Contract | Universal Principles |
| Preconventional | | Conventional | | Postconventional | |
| Selfish | | Social Expectations | | Internalized Principles | |

Figure 3.4: Kohlberg's Stages of Moral Development

even if your decision conflicts with the law (Stage 4) or what others believe is best for society (Stage 5). Hence, if Mitch and his friends were in a socialist or communist society they would probably copy the software believing that goods and services should be owned by society rather than by individuals and corporations.

### Problems with Kohlberg's Theory

Kohlberg's theory was based on an all-male sample and the stages reflect a male definition, or perspective, of morality (androcentric). Men's morality is based on abstract principles of law and justice, while women's is based on principles of compassion and care. Kohlberg's theory is also heavily dependent on an individual's response to an artificial dilemma bringing to question the validity of the results obtained through this research. People tend to respond very differently to real life situations that they find themselves in than they do to an artificial dilemma presented to them in the comfort of a research environment.

### Ethical Egoism Theory

*Ethical egoism* holds that we all act in our own self-interest and that all of us should limit our judgment to our own ethical egos and not interferes with the exercise of ethical egoism by others. This view holds that everything is determined by self-interest. We act as we do and decide to behave as we do because we have determined that it is in our own self-interest. One example of ethical egoism is when a person opens a bakery in a town where there is none. The individual seizes on an opportunity to make profit by selling bread in a town with no competition. In effect he has captured the market and is able to gain profit simply by *pursuing his own self-interest*. However, the town also benefits from the resource of bread.

### Moral Sentiments Theory

Adam Smith, a philosopher and an economist, wrote, in The *Theory of the Moral Sentiments*, that humans are rational and understand that fraud is in no one's self-interest, not even that of the perpetrator, who might benefit temporarily until, federal and state officials prosecute them. While many believe that they can lie in business transactions and get ahead, Adam Smith argues that although many can and do lie to close a deal or get ahead, they cannot continue that pattern of selfish behavior. Treating others this way results in a reputation in the business community that becomes an obstacle for doing business because they cannot be trusted. Smith believed that there was some force of long-term self-interest that keeps businesses running ethically.

### Divine Command Theory

The *Divine Command Theory* is an approach that incorporates religious perspectives in resolving ethical dilemmas. Decisions are evaluated according to tenets of a faith, such as the Ten Commandments for the Jewish and Christian faiths. Ultimately, decisions in ethical dilemmas are made on the basis of guidance from a divine being. The concept of natural law is similar to the Divine Command Theory and proposes that there are certain rights and conduct controlled by God. For example, in the United States, the Declaration of Independence is based on the concept of natural law, which states that we have rights granted by our Creator.

| Virtue | Definition |
|---|---|
| Ability | Being dependable and competent |
| Acceptance | Making the best of a bad situation |
| Amiability | Fostering agreeable social contexts |
| Articulateness | Ability to make and defend one's case |
| Attentiveness | Listening and understanding |
| Autonomy | Having a personal identity |
| Caring | Worrying about the well-being of others despite power |
| Charisma | Inspiring others |
| Compassion | Sympathetic |
| Coolheadedness | Retaining control and reasonableness in heated situations |
| Courage | Doing the right thing despite the cost |
| Determination | Seeing a task through to completion |
| Fairness | Giving others their due; creating harmony |
| Generosity | Sharing; enhancing others' well-being |
| Graciousness | Establishing a congenial environment |
| Gratitude | Giving proper credit |
| Heroism | Doing the right thing despite the consequences |
| Honesty | Telling the truth; not lying |
| Humility | Giving proper credit |
| Humor | Bringing relief; making the world better |
| Independence | Getting things done despite bureaucracy |
| Integrity | Being a model of trustworthiness |
| Justice | Treating others fairly |
| Loyalty | Working for the well-being of an organization |
| Pride | Being admired by others |
| Prudence | Minimizing company and personal losses |
| Responsibility | Doing what it takes to do the right thing |
| Saintliness | Approaching the ideal in behavior |
| Shame (capable of) | Regaining acceptance after wrong behavior |
| Spirit | Appreciating a larger picture in situations |
| Toughness | Maintaining one 's position |
| Trust | Dependable |
| Trustworthiness | Fulfilling one's responsibilities |
| Wittiness | Lightening the conversation when warranted |
| Zeal | Getting the job done right; enthusiasm |

Figure 3.5: List of Business Virtues

**Virtue Ethics Theory**

Aristotle and Plato taught that in order to solve ethical dilemmas there must be some element of personal development. Individuals are in a position to solve ethical dilemmas once they develop a set of virtues. Aristotle cultivated virtues in his students and taught them to resolve ethical dilemmas by using those virtues. Developing a set of virtues can provide a guide to making personal and business decisions. The following list was developed by Robert Solomon for use in business.

From A Better Way to Think About Business by Robert Solomon, copyright © 1999 by Robert Solomon.

# Training for Ethical Decision Making

Preparing employees for facing ethical dilemmas is one of the main benefits of work *ethics training*. It provides employees with a framework for decision-making and an understanding of the company's expectations from them. As we learned, ethical dilemmas can vary from accepting bribes to sacrificing customer safety to meet productivity goals. The first objective in ethics training is guiding employees into making more ethical decisions. Even when not faced with a large ethical dilemma, decisions requiring a solid foundation in ethics are made on a daily basis. For instance, the employee may regularly take home some office supplies without thinking of how it is costing the company. If an employee witnesses someone going against the company's ethical guidelines, he or she will know what to do and how to report the incident.

## A Basic Model of Ethical Decision Making

1. **Identify the problem** – What makes an ethical problem? Think in terms of rights, obligations, fairness, relationships, and integrity. How would you define the problem if you stood on other side of the fence?
2. **Identify the constituents** – Who has been hurt? Who could be hurt? Who could be helped? Are they willing players, or are they victims? Can you negotiate with them?
3. **Diagnose the situation** – How did it happen in the first place? What could have prevented it? Is it going to get worse or better? Can the damage now be undone?
4. **Analyze your options** – Imagine the range of possibilities. Limit yourself to the two or three most manageable. What are the likely outcomes of each? What are the likely costs? Look to the company mission statement or code of ethics for guidance.
5. **Make your choice** – What is your intention in making this decision? How does it compare with the probable results? Can you discuss the problem with the affected parties before you act? Could you disclose without qualm your decision to your boss, the CEO, the board of directors, your family, or society as a whole?
6. **Act** – Do what you have to do. Don't be afraid to admit errors. Be as bold in confronting a problem as you were in causing it.

Figure 3.6: Basic Model of Ethical Decision Making

The second objective for ethics training is to achieve credibility with employees. Employees often complain that outside instructors and consultants are teaching theory that has nothing to do with their jobs and the practical dilemmas they are facing. Training becomes reinforces and more credible when top-management teach the initial classes to their subordinates, who then in turn teach the classes to their subordinates. The final objective of ethics training is to teach employees a practical model of ethical decision-making. Providing employees with a basic model should help them think through how to make the different choices. Figure 3.6 provides a basic model of ethical decision making for the employees.

## Hiring Ethical Employees

An organization's ethical culture must be instilled in every employee. For many companies, ethics is a key component of the employee screening and hiring process. Ethics is not just a set of policies. Instead, it is part of the organizational culture and must be instilled from the beginning of an employee's career which usually starts with the hiring process yet it can be extraordinarily difficult to judge a candidate's ethical standards during the this process.

Hiring managers must know how to interview to find candidates with attitudes and characteristics that align with the company's mission, vision and values. Interviews that focus on more general ethical standards as well as industry issues and social norms for the local cultures in which the company operates will often yield more interesting and informative results. **Overt integrity tests** estimate job applicants' honesty by asking them directly what they think or feel about theft or about punishment or unethical behavior. For example, an applicant may be asked 'would you ever consider buying something from someone if you knew that it had been stolen?' Or, a general question such as; 'don't you feel that most people steal from their companies?' Surprisingly, unethical people believe that the world is basically dishonest and that dishonest behavior is the norm and will answer 'yes' to the question.

The second option in testing applicants' integrity is the **personality-based integrity test**. These tests indirectly estimate the honesty of the applicants' by measuring psychological traits such as dependability and conscientiousness. Result from tests like these can help companies be more selective when hiring and promoting people. A sample integrity test is provided at the end of this chapter.

## Code of Ethics

Today, almost every large corporation has an ethics code in place. A **code of ethics**, also called a code of conduct or ethical code sets out the company's values, ethics, objective and responsibilities. A well-written code of ethics should also give guidance to employees on how to deal with certain ethical situations. Every code of ethics is different and should reflect the company's ethos, values and business style. Some codes are short, setting out only general guidelines, and others are large manuals, encompassing a huge variety of situations. For example, visitors to the *Nike* website can download a 32 page comprehensive document, detailing specific ethical standards on topics ranging from bribes and kickbacks to expense vouchers and insider trading.

# Ethical Climate encourages Ethical Conduct

*An **ethical climate*** is not a thing, but a process. It is both the setting in which all the multiple large and small transactions of the groups and individuals involved in the firm take place and the net effect of all those transactions. The explicit rules and implicit understandings that govern all those transactions are built on precedent, constantly evolving, fluid, flexible, living, repetitious, and organic. So, an ethical climate is developing or deteriorating, enriching itself or impoverishing itself. It needs constant care and attention.

In 2009, a National Business Ethics Survey reported the only 39 percent of the employees who worked at companies with a strong ethical culture observed other engaging in unethical behavior. Whereas, 76 percent of those who work in organizations with weak ethical cultures have observed other engage in unethical behavior. The report also noted that employees in strong cultures are also more likely to report ethical violations through the company's reporting system, confident that management would want them reported without fear of retaliation.

***Whistleblowing*** is the act of an employee reporting suspected misconduct or corruption believed to exist within an organization. A ***whistleblower*** is anyone who has and reports insider knowledge of illegal activities occurring in an organization. Whistleblowers can be employees, suppliers, contractors, clients or any individual who somehow becomes aware of illegal activities taking place in a business either through witnessing the behavior or being told about it. Today, many federal and state laws protect the rights of whistleblowers; in fact, managers who punish whistleblowers can be imprisoned for up to 10 years.

In 2002, *Time* magazine named three women as 'Persons of the Year,' these picks were unusual in that most people cited by the magazine in the past have been well-known public figures. Time magazine explained their choice this way; *'These people were people who did right just by doing their jobs rightly, which means ferociously, with eyes open and with the bravery the rest of us always hope we have and may never know if we do.'*

> Cynthia Cooper exploded the bubble that was WorldCom when she informed its board that the company had covered up $3.8 billion in losses through the prestidigitations of phony bookkeeping.
> Coleen Rowley is the FBI staff attorney who caused a sensation in May with a memo to FBI Director Robert Mueller about how the bureau brushed off pleas from her Minneapolis, Minn., field office that Zacarias Moussaoui, who is now indicted as a Sept. 11 co-conspirator, was a man who must be investigated.
> Sherron Watkins is the Enron vice president who wrote a letter to chairman Kenneth Lay in the summer of 2001 warning him that the company's methods of accounting were improper.

# Ethical Decision Making Framework

An ***Ethical Decision Making Framework*** combines both ethical perspectives and ethical models to provide a systematic process to produce ethical decisions. Two particular approaches are noteworthy.

**The Ferrell Ethical Decision Making Framework** considers four factors when evaluating ethical dilemmas: *ethical issue intensity; individual factors; organizational factors and opportunity.*

1. ***Ethical Issue Intensity*** is the perceived relevance or importance of an ethical issue to the individual, work group, and/or organization. This reflects the ethical sensitivity of the individual and/or work group and triggers the ethical decision making process. Individuals can be subject to six spheres of influence: 1) Workplace, 2) Legal system, 3) Family, 4) Community, 5) Religion and 6) Profession. Outcomes will be affected by the degree of *Moral Intensity* involved, which is the person's perception of social pressure and the harm his/her decision will have on others.

2. ***Individual Factors***: People base their ethical decisions on their own values and principles of right or wrong. Values are learned through socialization. Good personal values decrease unethical behavior and increase positive work behavior, but values are subjective and may vary across cultures. While an organization may intend to do right, organizational or social forces can alter this intent. Gender, education, work experience, nationality and age can affect ethical decision-making. Within individual factors is ***locus of control***; this relates to individual differences in relation to a general belief about how one is affected by internal versus external events or reinforcements. Managers with external locus of control are passive because they believe that there is nothing else they can do, while those with an internal locus of control believe they can control events and trust in their capacity to influence their environment.

3. ***Organizational Factors***: Organizational culture has a stronger influence on employees than individual values. A corporate culture is a set of values, norms, and artifacts that the members of an organization share, while an ethical culture reflects whether the firm has an ethical conscience and is a function of many factors. Significant others within the organization are those who have influence in a work group. An organizational culture where obedience to authority is valued can explain why many employees unquestioningly follow superior's orders.

4. ***Opportunity*** is the conditions within an organization that limit or permit ethical or unethical behavior. Establishing formal codes, policies, and rules can reduce opportunities for misconduct; however, aggressive enforcement is often required to limit opportunities for unethical behavior. Also, knowledge can sometimes lead to unethical behavior. A person who has an information base, expertise, or information about competition has an opportunity to exploit knowledge.

**The Baird Decision Making Framework** examines ethical situations through 4 lenses: the rights lens, the relationship lens, the results lens and the reputation lens. This framework assumes that leaders are predisposed to a particular lens or set of lenses and will seek to evaluate ethical dilemmas from the values represented by each lens.

- **Rights Lens:** An action is ethical if I fulfill my duties and do the right thing as I claim my individual rights.

- **Relationship Lens:** An action is ethical if it supports a framework for continuous systemic ethical improvement for both the organization and the institutions supporting it.
- **Results Lens:** An action is ethical if good ends and good results come from the action.
- **Reputation Lens:** An action is ethical if it is consistent with the habitual development of sound character traits including habits of thoughtful reflection, good intentions and noble human virtues.

# Organizational Social Responsibility

*Social responsibility* entails developing businesses with a positive relationship to the society in which they operate. Unfortunately, because there are strong disagreements over to whom and for what in society organizations are responsible it can be difficult for managers to know what is or will be perceived as socially responsible corporate behavior. One question that managers often ask is 'does it pay to be socially responsible?' Early studies indicated that investing money into socially responsible activities did not benefit the firm. However, recent studies have dis-proven the earlier studies indicating that there is a small, positive relationship between being socially responsible and the economic performance of the firm. **Corporate Social Responsibility** (CSR) is the continuing commitment by business to contribute to economic development while improving the quality of life of the workforce and their families as well as of the community and society at large. In other words, what contributions and efforts should corporations make to others beyond their shareholders and how do corporations best contribute to communities and societies? A variety of voices shape the debate over the responsibility of corporations when it comes to social responsibility.

Honda is a good example of a company who believes is environmentally friendly technology. Honda introduced the first hybrid car in North America and has long been an industry leader in fuel efficiency. So when Honda decided to enter the private jet market with their new Honda Jet they followed the same approach to efficiency and environmental technology by constructing a plane out of light-weight composites and utilizing engines that are both powerful and fuel efficient. Although the aircraft seat a pilot and four passengers, its efficiency rivals that of larger regional jets carrying 40-50 passengers. Honda believes that if approach to being socially responsible is key in its design and in making the Honda Jet profitable.

There are two perspectives regarding to whom organizations are socially responsible: *the shareholder model,* and *the stakeholder model.*

- *The Shareholder model*—Asserts that the managers primary responsibility and duty is to maximize shareholder returns. Thus, the **shareholder theory** asserts that because shareholders advance capital to a company's managers, the manager's responsibility only extends to the expenditure of corporate funds in ways that have been authorized by the shareholders. The Shareholder theory was posited by Milton Friedman who said of social responsibility, *'There is one and only one social responsibility of business—to use its resources and engage in activities designed to increase its profits so long as it … engages in open and free competition, without deception or fraud.'*
- *The Stakeholder model*—Asserts that managers have a duty to both the corporation's shareholders and 'individuals and constituencies that contribute, either voluntarily or involuntarily, to a company's wealth-creating capacity and activities, and who are therefore its potential beneficiaries and/or risk bearers.' Hence, according to the **stakeholder theory**, managers are agents of *all* stakeholders and have two responsibilities: to ensure that the ethical rights of no stakeholder

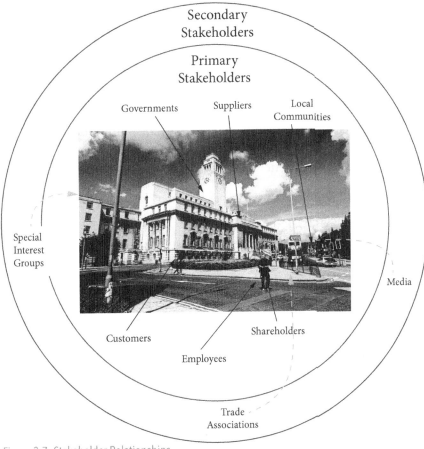

Figure 3.7: Stakeholder Relationships

**LEAST RESPONSIBLE**

**MOST RESPONSIBLE**

Figure 3.8: The Social Responsibility Continuum

are violated and to balance the legitimate interests of the stakeholders when making decisions. The objective is to balance profit maximization with the long-term ability of the corporation to remain a going concern. **Stakeholders** are persons or groups with a legitimate interest in a company. **Primary stakeholders** are groups on which the organization depends for its long-term survival; they include shareholders, employees, customers, suppliers, governments, and local communities. **Secondary stakeholders** are not engaged in regular transactions with the company and are not critical to its long-term survival. This includes groups such as the media, trade associations, and special interest groups.

Management plays a special role, for it too has a stake in the modern corporation. On the one hand, management's stake is like that of employees, with some kind of explicit or implicit employment contract. But, on the other hand, management has a duty of safeguarding the welfare of the abstract entity that is the corporation. In short, management, especially top management, must look after the health of the corporation, and this involves balancing the multiple claims of conflicting stakeholders. Owners want higher financial returns, while customers want more money spent on research and development.

Employees want higher wages and better benefits, while the local community wants better parks and day-care facilities.

**Perspectives of Corporate Social Responsibility**

The philosophical debate over the role of business in society has resulted in four schools of thought on ethical behavior based on two questions: whose interest should a corporation serve and to whom should a corporation be responsive in order to best serve that interest? The answers to these questions range from "the shareholders only" to "the larger society" and the combination of those answers defines the schools of thought noted below.

According to the **inherence school of thought**, manager's answer only to shareholders and act only with shareholders' interests in mind. This type of manager would not become involved in any political or social issues unless it was in the shareholders' best interests to do so, and provided the involvement did not backfire and cost the firm sales. Milton Friedman's philosophy, as previously expressed, is an example of inherence.

Following **Enlightened Self-Interest,** the manager is responsible to the shareholders but serves them best by being responsive to the larger society. Enlightened self-interest is based on the view that business

| |
|---|
| 1. Microsoft |
| 2. The Walt Disney Company |
| 3. Google |
| 4. BMW |
| 5. Daimler (Mercedes-Benz) |
| 6. Sony |
| 7. Intel |
| 8. Volkswagen |
| 9. Apple |
| 10. Nestlé |
| 11. LEGO Group |
| 12. Rolex |
| 13. Canon |
| 14. Kellogg Company |
| 15. Johnson & Johnson |
| 16. Colgate-Palmolive |
| 17. Danone |
| 18. IBM |
| 19. Philips Electronics |
| 20. Honda Motor |
| 21. Toyota |
| 22. Adidas Group |
| 23. Michelín |
| 24. L'Oréal |
| 25. Hewlett-Packard |

Source: Reputation Institute 2014

Table 3.1: Top 25 Best Regarded Companies for Corporate Social Responsibility

value is enhanced if it is responsive to the needs of society because it enables the business to retain a quality workforce. For example, many corporations today have instituted job sharing and child-care facilities in response to the changing structure of the American family and workforce.

The *invisible hand* school of thought is the opposite of enlightened self-interest. According to this philosophy, business ought to serve the larger society and it does this best when it serves the shareholders only. Such businesses allow government to set the standards and boundaries for appropriate behavior and simply adhere to these governmental constraints as a way of maximizing benefits to their shareholders.

The *social responsibility school* of thought, the role of business is to serve the larger society, and that is best accomplished by being responsive to the larger society. This view is simply a reflection of the idea that businesses profit by being responsive to society and its needs. These businesses believe that their sense of social responsibility contributes to their long-term success. Figure 3.11 list the top companies for social responsibility.

# Corporate Social Responsibilities

The concept of *corporate social responsibility (CSR)* means that organizations have moral, ethical, and philanthropic responsibilities in addition to their responsibilities to earn a fair return for investors and comply with the law. A traditional view of the corporation suggests that its primary, if not sole, responsibility is to its owners, or stockholders. However, CSR requires organizations to adopt a broader view of its responsibilities that includes not only stockholders, but many other constituencies as well, including employees, suppliers, customers, the local community, local, state, and federal governments, environmental groups, and other special interest groups.

Corporate social responsibility is related to, but not identical with, business ethics. While CSR encompasses the *economic, legal, ethical,* and *discretionary* responsibilities (Figure 3.12) of organizations, business ethics usually focuses on the moral judgments and behavior of individuals and groups within organizations.

- *Economic responsibilities*—Organizations basic responsibility is to make a profit by producing a product or providing a service that is valued by society. Organizations that don't meet their financial and economic expectations are under extreme pressure to take corrective actions.

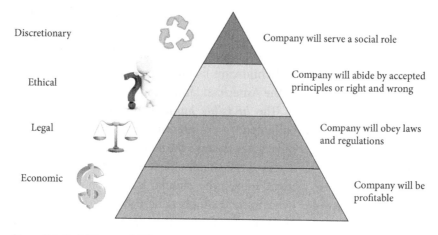

Figure 3.9: Social Responsibilities

- *Legal responsibilities*—An organization is responsible to obey society's laws and regulations as it attempts to meet it economic responsibilities.
- *Ethical responsibilities*—The firm has the responsibility not to violate accepted principles of right and wrong when conducting business. As we know, different stakeholders may disagree on what is or is not ethical. As such, meeting the ethical responsibilities may be more difficult than meeting economic or legal responsibilities.
- *Discretionary responsibilities*—Include the responsibilities that extend beyond economic, legal, and ethical such as providing relieve for flood, earthquake, and hurricanes. Companies are not considered unethical if they don't perform them.

## Summary of Chapter

As one can see from the concepts in this chapter, ethical decision-making involves understanding an ethical dilemma from a variety of ethical perspectives, ethical models and ethical decision-making frameworks. No one approach is optimal, but rather a combination of perspectives, models and frameworks are likely to yield the best outcomes when contemplating an ethical dilemma. It is important for a manager or leader to determine which ethical perspective best fits their personal values and priorities and to evaluate each situation through the ethical model or framework that seems most appropriate for them and the stakeholders they represent. Through a thoughtful process of personal evaluation and reflection, ethical dilemmas can be resolved, but rarely to everyone's satisfaction. The leader or manager should seek to do what is right, rather than what is popular.

Social responsibility is a business's obligation to benefit society. To whom are organizations responsible? According to the shareholder model the only social responsibility that an organization has is to maximize shareholder wealth by maximizing company profits.

The stakeholder model states that the organizations must satisfy the needs and interests of multiple corporate stakeholders, not simply the shareholders.

There are also a variety of viewpoints when it comes to corporate social responsibility (CSR). Some corporations feel no responsibility or obligation to the society or the community in which they operate, others feel that much of what they do centers upon "giving back" to all in the world around them. There is no one response to CSR that satisfies all stakeholders. The appropriate response for each corporation lies in the heart of their mission and the constituency they ultimately serve.

## Discussion Questions

1. Explain the difference between legal behavior and ethical behavior.
2. Differentiate terminal and instrumental values, and provide examples for each.
3. What are the four approaches to moral reasoning?
4. Explain the differences between distributive, procedural, and interactive justice in organizations.
5. What is the difference between cultural relativism and moral absolutism in international business ethics?
6. Give an example of an ethical dilemma and explain how bad management can cause ethical dilemmas.
7. List four common rationalizations for unethical behavior.

## References

Arthaud-Day, M.L. "Transnational Corporate Social Responsibility: A Tri-Dimensional Approach to International CSR Research." *Business Ethics Quarterly* 15 (2005): 1–22.

Bower, H. R. (1953). *Social Responsibilities of the Businessman.* New York: Harper & Row.

*Business Ethics: Ethical Decision Making and Cases, 9th edition,* Ferrell, O.C., John Fraedrich, and Linda Ferrell, Mason, OH: South Western Cengage Learning, 2013.

*Business Ethics, 7th Edition,* Marianne M. Jennings, Thomson, 2012.

Carroll, A.B., and A.K. Buchholtz. *Business and Society: Ethics and Stakeholder Management.* 5th ed. Australia: Thomson South-Western, 2003.

Clarkson, M.B.E. (1995). 'A Stakeholder Framework for Analyzing and Evaluating Corporate Social Performance.' *Academy of Management Review,* 20, 92–117.

*Everyday Ethics: Making Wise Choices in a Complex World, 2nd Edition,* Baird, Catherine, A., Ethics Game Press, Denver CO. 2012.

Garriga, E., and D. Mele. "Corporate Social Responsibility Theories: Mapping the Territory." *Journal of Business Ethics* 53 (2004): 51–71.

*Good Intentions Aside: A Manager's Guide to Resolving Ethical Problems,* Laura Nash, Harvard Business School Press, 1993.

Jones, T. M. (1991). 'Ethical Decision Making by Individuals in Organizations: An Issue-Contingent Model.' *Academy of Management Review.* 16, 366–395.

Marquez, A., and C.J. Fombrun. "Measuring Corporate Social Responsibility." *Corporate Reputation Review* 7 (2005): 304–308.

Morris, S., & McDonald, R., (1995). 'The Role of Moral Intensity in Moral Judgments: An Empirical Investigation,' *Journal of Business Ethic* 14, 715–726.

Novak, M. (1977), *Capitalism and the Corporation from The Fire of Invention: Civil Society and the Future of the Corporation*, p. 32.

*A Better Way to Think About Business*, Robert Solomon, copyright © 1999 by Robert Solomon.

Salopek, J. (2001). 'Do the Right Thing,' *Training & Development* 55, 38–44.

Schmidt, D. (2008). 'Ethics Can Be Taught,' accessed June 26, 2014, from www.inc.com/leadershipblog/2008/06/ethics_can_be_taught_1.html.

Schramm, J. (2004). 'Perceptions on Ethics', *HR Magazine*, 49: 176.

Schweitzer, M., Ordonez, L., & Douma, B. (2004). 'Goal Setting as a Motivator of Unethical Behavior.' *Academy of Management Journal.* 47, 422–432.

Smith, C. (2000). 'The Ethical Workplace.' *Association Management*, 52: 70–73.

Tyler, K. (2005). 'Do the Right Thing: Ethics Training Programs Help Employees Deal with Ethical Dilemma,' *HR Magazine.* February.

Wartick, S. L., & Cochran, P. L. (1985). 'The Evolution of the Corporate Social Performance Model,' *Academy of Management Review,* 10, 758–769.

*Everyday Ethics: Making Wise Choices in a Complex World, 2nd Edition*, Baird, Catherine, A., Ethics Game Press, Denver CO. 2012.

William R. Evan and R. Edward Freeman, *A Stakeholder Theory of the Modern Corporation: Kantian Capitalism*, Business Ethics Quarterly 4 (1994): Commerce Clearing House, 409–21.

*Business Ethics: Ethical Decision Making and Cases, 9th edition*, Ferrell, O.C., John Fraedrich, and Linda Ferrell, Mason, OH: South Western Cengage Learning, 2013.

R. Edward Freeman, *The Politics of Stakeholder Theory*, Business Ethics Quarterly 4 (1994): Commerce Clearing House, 409–21.

Milton Friedman, *The Social Responsibility of Business Is to Increase Its Profits*, New York Times Magazine, September 13, 1970, 32–33, pp. 122–126. Copyright © 1970 by The New York Times Company.

*Business Ethics, 7th Edition*, Marianne M. Jennings, Thomson, 2012.

Marjorie Kelly, *The Divine Right of Capital: Dethroning the Corporate Aristocracy*, (San Francisco: Berrett-Koehler, 2001).

*Good Intentions Aside: A Manager's Guide to Resolving Ethical Problems*, Laura Nash, Harvard Business School Press, 1993.

# PART 2

# Planning

# CHAPTER 4

## Planning and Decision Making

*"When planning for a year, plant corn. When planning for a decade, plant trees. When planning for life, train and educate people."*

— Chinese Proverb

---

### Chapter Learning Objectives:

After reading this chapter you should have a good understanding of:

- The definition of planning and an understanding of the purpose of planning.
- The benefits and pitfalls of planning.
- How and why managers do managers plan.
- The major steps in the planning process and their interrelatedness.
- The relationship between planning and organizational objectives.

- The various types of plan managers' use.
- Steps in Decision-making.
- Using groups for making decisions.
- What is forecasting? Why is it important? And why to managers' use forecasting in their decision-making.

# What is Planning?

Planning is a critical management activity in any organization, whether a private business, a nonprofit organization, a corporate business or a government agency and is one of the most important responsibilities of the management team. It is the process of determining how an organization's can achieve its immediate and long-term objectives, by formulating, monitoring, staffing, allocating resources, and developing specific strategies to achieve them. More specifically, *planning* is the 'systematic development of action plans focused at achieving agreed upon business objectives by the process of analyzing, evaluating, and selecting among the opportunities which are foreseen.

Planning is one of the four functions of management (Figure 4.1) setting the stage for the other three: organizing-allocating and arranging resources to accomplish a task; leading- guiding the efforts of human resources to ensure high levels of task accomplishment; and controlling- monitoring task accomplishment and taking necessary corrective actions. Managers engage in different types of organizational planning to strategically maneuver their companies towards profitable and successful futures. Planning is a critical management activity in any organization, whether a private business, a nonprofit organization, a corporate business or a government agency.

# The Purpose of Planning

The primary purpose of planning is to help the organization achieve its objectives. Every plan should be linked with some objectives and planning helps people with a coordinated sense of directions enabling a concentration of their efforts on the most important jobs rather than wasting time on the lesser important work. Planning also minimizes the cost of performance and eliminates unproductive efforts.

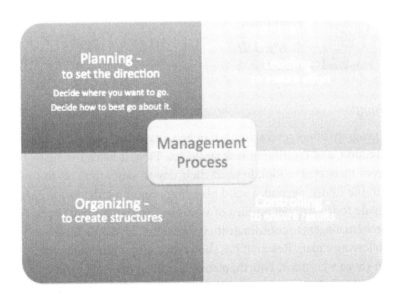

Figure 4.1: Planning in the Management Process

It helps management to adopt and adjust to the changes that take place in the environment and provides the foundation for teamwork as when the goals are properly defined assignments can be fixed and all the members can start contributing in the achievement of these objectives.

## The Advantage and Disadvantage of Planning

What type of person are you? Are you naturally organized always making a daily to-do list, writing everything down so you won't forget and never missing a deadline? Do you create a plan and stick to the plan? Do you hate 'playing things by ear' and 'seeing how you feel in the moment?' Or, do you feel energetic, flexible and adaptive when your schedule is not restrictive? Does planning 'ruin the surprises that the day holds for you? Some people are natural planners; they love its structure and can only see its benefits. Others, dislike planning and can only see its disadvantages. The fact is that *both* views have real value. Planning has advantages and disadvantages.

Are your naturally organized? Or are you one who is more adaptable to the situations and enjoys 'playing thing by Ear'?

### *Advantages of Planning*

A vigorous planning program offers several important benefits: future oriented, coordination in decisions, intensified efforts, direction, and creation of task strategies. First, it helps managers to be future oriented because planning forces managers to look beyond their day-to-day problems to predict what situations they may encounter in the future. Second, a solid planning program enhances decision coordination. No decision should be made today without an idea of what decision might have to be made tomorrow. The planning function forces managers to coordinate their decisions. Third, managers and employees put forth greater effort when following a plan. Research has shown that employees following a specific plan product at a greater level than those who don't. Fourth, plans encourage managers and employees to direct their efforts *toward* activities that help them accomplish their tasks and *away* from activities that don't. Fifth, planning encourages the development of task strategies. In other words, specific planning is the stimulus that helps managers and employees to think of better ways to accomplish their tasks. Finally, research has proven that companies with specific, formalized plans have larger profits and a higher rate of growth than companies that don't. There is no better way to improve the performance of the employees in a company than to have them develop goals and specific plans for achieving those goals.

## Disadvantages of Planning

Planning if not well executed can have some downsides. As such there are some disadvantages that managers should be aware of as they consider any planning activity, these include: 1) not involving the right people 2) spending too much time on non-essential issues 3) poor accountability and implementation.

*Not Involving the Right People*—An essential key to effective planning is including the right people or those with the information and perspectives that can best influence the process. Within the company, involvement may include supervisors or staff members in key positions. Externally, it could include advisors such as accountants, attorneys, customers, or even community leaders. Ensuring that managers have a broad range of inputs are important to avoid missing critical planning factors and can also ensure buy-in and support from key constituencies.

*Spending Too Much Time on Non-Essentials*—"Paralysis by analysis" is a problem that can hinder any planning effort. At times it can be difficult for managers to know when it's time to stop gathering and reviewing information, and when to use that information to make a decision.

*Lack of Accountability and Poor Implementation*—It has often been said in business that the biggest barrier to success is the plan's execution. 'Death in the drawer' occurs when plans are developed and then left to languish on a shelf. Instead, businesses are wise to assign specific tasks to specific individuals and to schedule regular reporting periods in order to review results.

Overall, the advantages of planning definitely outweigh the disadvantages; it is up to the managers to use the planning function properly.

# How to make a plan that works

As previously discussed, planning has both advantages and disadvantages. If done right planning increases both the organizational and individual performance; if planning is done poorly it can have the opposite effect and harm both individual and organizational performance.

In the following section we discuss the elements that are involved in making a plan that works, these include: setting goals, developing commitment to the goal, developing an effective action plan, monitoring the progress toward goal achievement, and maintaining flexibility in the planning process (Figure 4.2).

1. **Setting Goals**—The first step in planning is to set goals that will direct behavior and designed to increase effort. Hence, goals need to be specific and challenging. For example, if you were to say 'I want to pass this course' that goal won't direct and energize your efforts as much as if you were to say,' I want to achieve a score of 95 on all of my tests and homework.' Specific, challenging goals provide a target for which to aim and standard against which to measure success.

   With that in mind, there are the five SMART principles (Figure 4.3) that can help you set and achieve your personal and business goals: *Specific*—your goals must identify exactly what you want to accomplish in as much specificity as you can gather. *Measureable*—"you can't improve what you

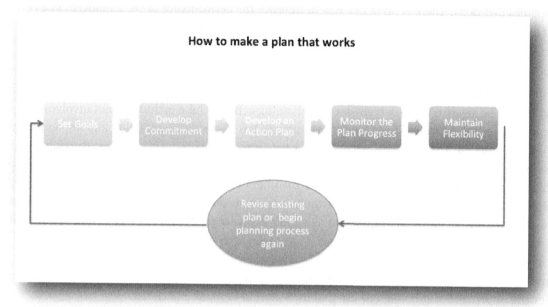

Figure 4.2: How to Make a Plan that Works

can't measure." Try to quantify the result. You want to know absolutely, positively whether or not you hit the goal. *Attainable*—is the goal that your have set one that is attainable given the resources and time. *Realistic*—A good goal should be a stretch requiring extra effort to achieve attainment. However, consider good reason when setting the goal. *Time*—Every goal needs an end date associated with it. When do you plan to deliver on that goal?

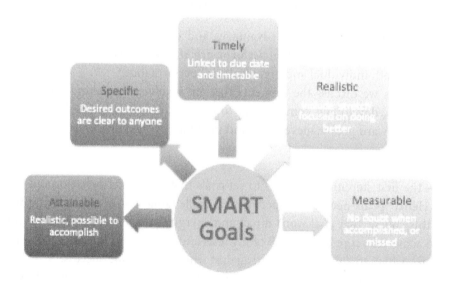

Figure 4.3: Making 'SMART' Goals

2. **Developing Commitments to Goals**—Commitment to achieve a goal does not automatically happen. Both managers and workers must consciously choose to commit themselves to a goal. The best way for managers to bring about goal commitment is to set goals with the employee rather than assigning goals. Goals that managers and employees develop together are more likely to be realistic and attainable. Another way to develop commitment to a goal is to make the goal public by announcing to others about your goal. For example, telling your parents, siblings or classmate that your will obtain a 3.75 GPA this semester. Research has shown that those who have made a verbal statement on goal achievement were more committed to achievement than those who did not and received nearly a half-grade higher than the grades of those who did not tell others of their goals.

3. **Developing and effective action plan**—An *action plan* is the 'how to' in accomplishing the goals. It lists the specific steps (how), people (who), resources (what) and time (when). One example of an action plan occurred in 2006 with Ford Motor Company and 'The Way Forward.' Ford Motors developed an action plan to return the company to profitability. In an effort to reduce its capital costs while maintaining a special focus on cars and car-based crossover vehicles, chairman Bill Ford's action plan included resizing the company to match current market realities, dropping some unprofitable an inefficient models, consolidating production lines and shuttering seven vehicle assembly plants and seven parts factories. Part of the action plan included using the new Global Product Development System (GPDS) bringing Ford's new car cycle time closer to its Japanese rivals. Other actions include sales of its subsidiaries Hertz Rent-a-Car, Jaguar, Land Rover, and Aston Martin and closure of the Mercury product line. Ford expected that these actions would result in the company returning to profitability by 2010, but they returned earlier than expected during 2009.

4. **Monitor the Plan Progress**—The fourth step in planning is to monitor or track the progress of the plan. Two acceptable methods can be used to track progress: goals and feedback. With the first method, goals can be set two ways: 1) *proximal goals*—goals that are short-term or sub-goals, which when achieved will create motivation toward the final goal, and 2) *distal goals*—which are long-term or primary goals. The second method of tracking progress is to gather and provide performance feedback. Feedback that is provided frequently allows workers and managers to track their progress toward goal achievement. Frequent feedback also allows for adjustments in efforts, directions, and strategies. Research has shown that the effectiveness of goal achievement can be doubled by the addition of frequent feedback.

5. **Maintaining Flexibility**—Sometimes action plans may be poorly conceived making the goals difficult or impossible to achieve. The last step in developing an effective plan is to maintain flexibility. One method in flexibility while planning is to adopt and *options-based approach*. This approach keeps open other options by making small, simultaneous investments in alternative plans. If or when one of these alternative plans emerge as the likely preferred option, more investment is made in these plans while discontinuing or reducing investment in the others.

The options-based plan is somewhat counter to the traditional planning method wherein a commitment is made of people and resources to a particular course of action, options-based planning leaves those commitments open by maintaining *slack resources*. Slack resources are a 'cushion' of resources such as cash, extra time, people, or production capacity, which can be used to address and adapt to unanticipated changes, problems, or opportunities.

One recent example of how slack resources were used was during the summer of 2010 when the economic recovery and the availability of credit were still uncertain. To mitigate this uncertainty and allow options, U.S companies held $1.85 trillion in cash reserves, providing those companies with the flexibility to respond to any opportunities or threats that may arise.

Another method used by managers to maintain flexibility is *learning-based planning*. This approach assumes that action plans undergo continual testing, changing, and improvement as companies 'learn' better ways of achieving goals. One example is how companies are adapting to the aging population by marketing their products focusing on the boomer preferences, such as; larger lettering on packaging, product re-design with an emphasis on healthy living.

# Types of Plans

Mangers face different planning challenges in the flow and pace of activities in organizations. In some cases the planning environment is stable and predictable. In others, it is more dynamic and uncertain. To meet those different needs, managers rely on a variety of plans.

Organizational plans are usually divided into two types: standing and single-use. A *standing plan* is one that in used over and over again because it focuses on those situations within the organization that occur repeatedly. Standing plans include: policies, procedures, and rules. A *single-use plan*, as its name implies, is only used once because it focuses on unique or rare situations within the organization.

## Standing Plans

A *policy* is a standing plan that provides broad guidelines for taking action consistent with reaching an organizational objective. Some examples of organization policies are: compensation policies, employment status policies and the international hiring policies.

*Procedures* are the 'how-to' of the policy. Procedures are also standing plans that outline a series of related actions that must be taken to accomplish a particular task. In general, procedures outline with more specificity the required actions than do policies. Organizations usually have many different sets of procedures covering the various tasks to be accomplished. The following example illustrates the relationship between policy and procedure.

A staff recruitment policy could involve the following procedures:

1. All vacant paid positions will be advertised in local and statewide newspapers.
2. The advertisements will have details of duties, salary range, closing date and contact details.
3. All interested people will be mailed job descriptions and information about the organization.

A *rule* is a standing plan that designates specific required actions of what organizational members can and cannot do and leave little room for interpretation. Rules describe the operations, definitions, and constraints that apply to the organization. Rules can apply to people, processes, behavior, and systems and are designed to help the organization achieve its goals. One example of a rule is very common in companies is that of 'no smoking'.

Although policies, procedures, and rules are standing plans, they are different from each other and have different purposes within the organization. However, in order for standing plans to be effective, policies, procedures, and rules must be consistent and mutually supportive of each other.

## Single-use Plans

There are two types of single-use plans: programs and budgets. A ***program*** is a single-use plan designed to carry out a special project within an organization. The project itself is not designed to remain in existence over the entire life of the organization; rather it exists to achieve a purpose that will contribute to the long-term success of the organization. One example of a program is the 'management development program' found in many organizations today. This program is designed to raise the skills level of the managers in one or more of the following areas: technology, conceptual, or human relations. Once managerial skills have been raised to a desired level, the program can be de-emphasized. The second type of single-use plan is the ***budget***. The budget is a financial plan designed to cover a specified period of time detailing how the funds will be spent on labor, raw material, capital goods, information systems, and marketing.

One of the most common problems in some organizations is that resource allocations get rolled over from one period to another without any real performance review. To deal with this problem, ***zero-based budgeting*** is used and views each new budget period as if it were brand new. No guarantee exists for renewing any past funding. Instead, all proposals compete for available funds at the start of each new budget cycle.

Standing plans and single-use plans and their overall relationship to the organizational plans are illustrated in Figure 4.4.

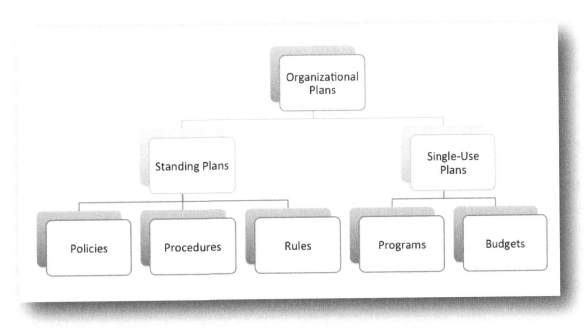

Figure 4.4: Standing Plans and Single-Use Plans

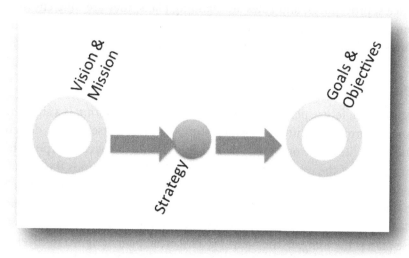

Figure 4.5: Strategy Links Vision to Objectives

## Strategic Plans

A **strategic plan** looks at all the things the organization could do and narrows it down to the things it is actually good at doing. A strategic plan is a longer-term plan that helps business leaders create the framework for where to spend time, human capital, and money for maximum long-term performance impact. Strategic planning is linked to the **vision** that clarifies the purpose of the organization and expresses what it hopes to do or be in the future. A strategic plan is what inextricably links the vision to the organizational objectives (Figure 4.5.).

**Tactics** are the means by which a strategy is carried out. Tactics can be both planned and unplanned activities meant to deal with the demands of the moment, and to move from one objective to other in pursuit of the overall goal(s). **Tactical plans**, also called **operational plans**, are highly detailed plans typically short, in respond to specific problems or opportunities; to intermediate term, such as a smaller part of the overall strategic plan, developed and deployed to implement all or parts of the strategic plan.

In business, tactical plans often take the form of functional strategies, which will be covered in the next section.

## Functional Plans

**Functional planning** refers to the process of managing the work and tasks within a given department of a larger organization such as human resources, marketing, research and development, finance, operations, and other functional areas. This work includes tasks with a specific project and general planning to improve the work environment in a department and indicate how the different components of the organization will contribute to the overall strategy. Functional planning includes identifying employees' strengths in the department, identifying the department's output and objectives and making a plan that assesses the work process. **Functional strategy** of a company is customized to a specific industry and is used to support other corporate and business strategies.

The following is an example of how the various functional areas may contribute to the organizations overall strategy.

- *Operations*—plans that deal with the methods and technology needed by people in their work and in the process of converting inputs into outputs.
- *Financial*—plans that deal with the financial resources required to support the various operations.
- *Facilities*—plans dealing with work layout and facilities requirements.
- *Marketing*—dealing with the requirements of selling, and distributing the organizations goods and services.
- *Human Resources*—dealing with the recruitment, selection, placement, and retention of qualified people necessary to complete the organizational activities.

## Contingency Plans

By definition, planning involves thinking ahead based on certain assumptions occurring. However, things often go wrong and as such no plan will be perfect. When they do this, the best managers and organizations have a back up or 'plan B'.

A ***contingency plan*** identifies a coherent alternative course of action that can be implemented to meet the needs of the changing or unplanned event. A strong contingency plan will contain 'trigger points' to indicate when to activate preselected alternatives for action if expected results fail to materialize.

## Scenario Planning

We all know that the future is going to be different. But *how* is it gong to be different?

Imagine you are sitting at your desk in September 2007. The Dow is close to 13,900; U.S. unemployment is 4.5%; and oil is $45 a barrel. You are in the middle of developing your organization's plans and budgets for 2008. How likely is it that the assumptions in your 2008 plan accurately forecast that in September 2008 the Dow will be below 9,000; U.S. unemployment will have risen to 6.5%, on its way to more than 10%; and oil prices will have risen to more than $140 a barrel before falling below $40 a few months later?

Was this simply an aberration? Unlikely, not with a European sovereign debt crisis, a massive oil spill in the Gulf of Mexico and movement toward a major health care reform in the United States.

Uncertainty, volatility and risk are here to stay. The world has been transformed from a series of loosely connected, reasonably predictable economies to a complex web of relationships where the global impact of local events is felt almost instantaneously around the world.

***Scenarios*** are possible views of the world, described in narrative forms that provide a context in which managers can make decisions. By seeing a range of possible worlds, decisions will be better informed and a strategy based on this knowledge and insight will be more likely to succeed. Scenarios do not predict the future, but they do illuminate the drivers of change, understanding them can help managers to take greater control of their situation.

***Scenario planning*** is a way of understanding the forces at work today, such as demographics, globalization, technological change and environmental sustainability that will shape the future. Scenario planning are those plans that are based on identifying several alternative future scenarios or 'what if' situations and managers plans to deal with each, should it actually occur.

Scenario planning has been used by organizations as diverse as the Australian government, Auto Nation, British Airways, Corning, Disney, General Electric, the U.S. Federal Highway Administration, JDS Uniphase, KinderCare, Mercedes, Royal Dutch Shell, UPS and the World Bank.

## Forecasting

Most planning involves the use of forecasting. **Forecasting** is a tool used that helps management in its attempts to cope with the uncertainties of the future. Typically, forecasting uses historic data and certain assumptions that are based on the management's experience, knowledge, and judgment to determine the direction of future trends to determine how to allocate their resources for an upcoming period of time.

*The Economist, Business Week, and Fortune* magazine are examples of periodicals that regularly report forecasts on industry conditions, interest rates, unemployment trends, and national economies.

These estimates are projected into the coming months or years using one or more techniques such as exponential smoothing, moving averages, weighted moving average, regression analysis, and trend projection. The following example is a forecasted demand using the moving average method.

Example—Let's say you are the HR manager and are charged with predicting the demand for personnel for the next demand period, period 8; your historical data is this:

| Month | 1 | 2 | 3 | 4 | 5 | 6 | 7 |
|---|---|---|---|---|---|---|---|
| Demand | 120 | 110 | 90 | 115 | 125 | 117 | 121 |

One method, the **simple mean forecasting method**, would be to sum the previous demand and divide by the numbers of month to obtain an average. If we follow that method the demand for period 8 would be 114. Do you notice any disadvantages using that method? What if you had hundreds of data sets, you may have a problem of storage on your computer. In addition, this method is not very sensitive to a shift in recent data if it contains a large number of data points. One solution is to use the **moving average method**, using this method you need to maintain only the N most recent periods of data point. At the end of each period, the oldest period's data is discarded and the newest period's data is added to the database. The average is then divided by N and used as a forecast for the next period. In this example we will use a three-period moving average. The following is the formula for calculating the forecasted results: $MA(3) = M_8 = [D_7 + D_6 + D_5]/3 = 121$

Any forecasting should be used with caution; a recent survey of manufacturers suggests that forecasting is an imprecise science. According to this survey, on average, sales forecasts are off by approximately 20 percent. Managers must be reminded that they are planning aids, not a substitute for planning.

## Organizational Objectives

In the previous section we noted that planning is management's focus at achieving an agreed upon business objective. However, this can only occur after there is a clear understanding of what are the organizational objectives. **Organizational objectives** serve as the foundation on which all subsequent planning efforts are built.

## Definition of Organizational Objectives

An organizational objective is a target toward which the firm is directed. Properly developed organizational objectives reflect the overall goals, purpose and mission that have been established by its management and communicated to its employees. Organizational objectives typically focus on the company's long-range intentions for operating and include its business philosophy. The **organizational purpose**, also known as the mission statement, is what the organization exists to do. Purpose statements should be enduring, inspirational, clear, and consistent with widely shared company beliefs and values. An example of a well-crafted purpose statement is that of Avon, the cosmetics company: ' to be the company that best understands and satisfies the product service and self-fulfillment needs of women globally.'

Organizations exist for various reasons and hence have differing types of objectives. The primary purpose of a business organization is to make a profit whereas the primary purpose of a hospital may include providing high-quality medical services to the community.

Deciding on the objectives for an organization is one of the most critical actions that managers can take. Objectives that are unreasonably high are frustrating for the employees and objectives that are set too low fail to drive employees to maximize their potential. The challenge for managers is to establish performance objectives that they know are within the reach of the employees, but not too easy.

## Setting Organizational Objectives

Managers should approach the development, use, and modification of organizational objectives with the greatest determination, as appropriate objectives are fundamental to the success of any organization. The necessity of predetermining appropriate organizational objectives has led to the development of a management guideline called the *principle of the objective*. This principle holds that before managers initiate any action, they should clearly determine, understand, and state organizational objectives. The following are some guidelines that managers can use to increase the quality of their objectives:

- *Include those responsible for attaining the objectives in setting the objectives*—Often the people responsible for attaining the objectives know their job better than managers and therefore can help make the objectives more realistic. Inclusion in setting objectives also encourages motivation.
- *Clearly state the objectives with specificity*—Objectives with precise statements on directions minimize confusion and ensure increased productivity from workers.
- *Relate objectives to specific actions whenever necessary*—Clear specific actions eliminate employee inferences in goal accomplishment.
- *Clearly state expected results*—Employees should know exactly how managers would determine whether an objective has been accomplished.
- *Set realistic goals*—Setting goals that require hard work but are still attainable vs. goals that are unattainable and create frustration.
- *Specify a time for expected completion*—Employees must have a time frame for accomplishing their objectives. This allows them the flexibility of work 'pacing.'
- *Set objectives only in relation to other organizational objectives*—In this way, sub-optimization can be kept to a minimum.
- *State objectives clearly and simply*—The written or spoken word should not impede communicating a goal to organization members.

We live in and work in a fast-paced world where planning horizons are becoming compressed. Businesses are continually updating and revising their plans. Long-range plans are becoming shorter and shorter due to the level of and speed of change in technology, and in industry. Given that change is occurring at such a rapid pace, organizations should set three types of objectives.

1. Short-term objectives—objectives to be achieved in one year or less.
2. Intermediate-term objectives—objectives to be achieved in one to five years.
3. Long-term objectives—objectives to be achieved in five to seven years.

# Decision Making

Imagine your boss asks you for a recommendation on sourcing raw materials for your production facilities located throughout the U.S. She has asked you to prepare a report that details the costs, supply quantity, and quality of the various suppliers both domestic and international to meet not only current demand but also future needs. She would like to have at least five different plans or options for getting the necessary raw materials to your production facilities. When your boss delegates this 'sourcing problem,' what she is actually asking from you is a rational decision. *Decision-making* is the process of choosing a solution from available alternatives. *Rational decision-making* is a systematic process in which managers define problems, evaluate alternatives, and choose the optimal solution that provides the maximum benefits to their organization.

In reality, your boss is asking you to define and analyze the sourcing alternatives, costs, quantity, and supply, and explore alternatives. In addition, your solution has to be optimal because your company will be investing a tremendous amount of time, money, and resources to support your decision. So, how will you proceed?

The following section will help you understand the process and provides six steps in the rational decision process (Figure 4.6).

1. **Define the Problem**—It is impossible to make a rational decision unless you can clearly define the problem or context in which the decision needs to be made. A problem exists when there is a gap between a desired state (what is wanted) and an existing state (the situation you currently face). Why does a decision need to be made? What will be the outcome if no decision is made? What outcome is desired? What is preventing that outcome from being realized?
2. **Identify Decision Criteria**—This step is critical because this is the process of selecting what needs to be done. Once a decision maker has defined the problem, he or she needs to identify the decision criteria that will be important in solving the problem. Typically, the more criteria a potential solution meets, the better that solution will be. In this step, the decision maker determines what is relevant in making the decision. This step frames the decision maker's interests, values and similar personal preferences into the process. Identifying the criteria that is important is critical because what one person thinks is relevant another person may not. Also keep in mind that any factors not identified in this step are considered irrelevant to the decision maker.
3. **Weight the Criteria**—The third step requires the decision maker to weight the previously identified criteria in order to give them the correct priority in the decision. Although there are numerous

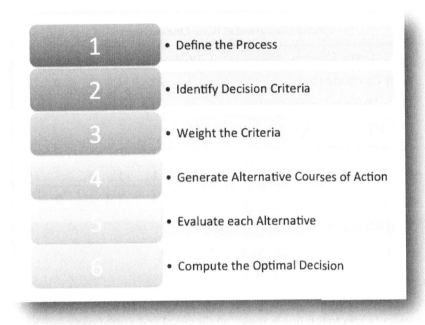

Figure 4.6: Steps in the Rational Decision-Making Process

mathematical models for weighting decision criteria, all require the decision maker to provide an initial ranking of the criteria. One method used to weight the criteria is called ***absolute comparisons***, in which each criterion is compared with a standard or ranked on its own merits. Decision makers will rank these criteria differently depending on what they value or require from each alternative. An example of absolute comparison is illustrated in Figure 4.7.

Another method used by decision makers is ***relative comparisons***, in which each of the listed criterion is compared directly with every other criterion. Figure 4.8 shows five criteria that someone might use when buying a house. As you will notice in the first column, we see that the time of the daily commute has been rated less important (−1) than the school system quality; more important (+1) than having a pool or a quiet street; and just as important as the house being brand new (0). Total weights are determined by summing

**Absolute Weighting of Decision Criteria for a Car Purchase**

Circled numbers indicate how important the particular Criterion is to a car buyer. Your ranking may be different.

| | CU | NVI | SI | I | CI |
|---|---|---|---|---|---|
| 1. Owner Satisfaction | 1 | 2 | 3 | 4 | (5) |
| 2. Reliability | 1 | 2 | 3 | (4) | 5 |
| 3. Depreciation | 1 | 2 | (3) | 4 | 5 |
| 4. Avoiding Accidents | 1 | 2 | (3) | 4 | 5 |
| 5. Fuel Economy | 1 | (2) | 3 | 4 | 5 |
| 6. Crash Protection | 1 | 2 | 3 | (4) | 5 |
| 7. Acceleration | 1 | 2 | 3 | 4 | (5) |
| 8. Ride | 1 | (2) | 3 | 4 | 5 |
| 9. Entertainment | 1 | 2 | 3 | 4 | (5) |

CU – completely unimportant, NVI – not very important, SI – somewhat important, I – important, CI – critically important

Figure 4.7: Absolute Comparison of Decision Criterion

**Relative Comparison of Home Characteristics**

| Home Characteristics | DC | SSQ | P | QS | NBH |
|---|---|---|---|---|---|
| Daily Commute (DC) | | +1 | -1 | -1 | 0 |
| School System Quality (SSQ) | -1 | | -1 | -1 | -1 |
| Pool (P) | +1 | +1 | | 0 | +1 |
| Quiet Street (QS) | +1 | +1 | 0 | | 0 |
| Newly Built House (NBH) | 0 | +1 | -1 | 0 | |
| Total Weight | +1 | +4 | -3 | -2 | 0 |

Figure 4.8: Relative Comparison of Decision Criterion

the scores in each of the columns. One can see that the daily commute and school system quality are the most important factors to this home-buyer, while a pool and a quiet street are the least important.

4. **Generate Alternative Courses of Action**—The key to this step is to not focus on the obvious alternatives or to what has worked in the past. High-quality decisions come from being open to multiple alternatives. It is often helpful to involve consultants or experts in the area in which the decision needs to be made. Once the alternatives have been generated, the decision maker must critically analyze and evaluate each one.

5. **Evaluate each Alternative**—As you evaluate each alternative, you should be looking at the likely positive and negative consequences associated with each. It is unusual to find one alternative that would completely resolve the problem and is without a doubt better than all others. As you consider positive and negative consequences, you must be careful to differentiate between what you know for a fact and what you believe might be the case. The decision maker needs to determine not just what results each alternative could yield, but how probable it is that those results will be realized. The more the evaluation is fact-based, the more confident the decision-maker can be that the expected outcome will occur.

6. **Compute the Optimal Decision**—The final step in this model requires computing the optimal decision. Evaluating each alternative using the weighted criteria and selecting the alternative with the total higher score, determines the optimal decision.

**Assumptions of the Model**: The success of the rational decision-making process just described contains a number of assumptions:

- *Problem clarity*—The problem is clear and unambiguous. The decision maker is assumed to have complete information regarding the decision situation.
- *Known options*—It is assumed the decision maker can identify all the relevant criteria and can list all the viable alternatives. Furthermore, the decision maker and can list all the viable alternatives. Furthermore, the decision maker is aware of all the possible consequences of each alternative.

- *Clear preference*—Rationality assumes that the criteria and alternatives can be raked and weighted to reflect their importance.
- *Constant preferences*—It's assumed that the specific decision criteria are constant and that the weights assigned to them stable over time.
- *No time or cost constraints*—the rational decision maker can obtain full information about criteria and alternatives because it's assumed that there are on time or cost constraints.
- *Maximum payoff*—The rational decision maker will choose the alternative that yields the highest perceived value.

**Testing the Model**—Every decision is intended to fix a problem. The final test of any decision is whether or not the problem was fixed. Did it go away? Did it change appreciably? Is it better now, or worse, or the same? What new problems did the solution create? If the problem remains or has worsened, the steps of the decision-making process need to be repeated until an acceptable resolution has been found.

## Limits to Rational Decision Making

In general, following the six step in the rational decision-making model will generate better decisions that when not using the model. It is advised that whenever possible, managers should follow the steps especially for important decisions with long-range consequences.

However, given the facts that business and managers do not exist in a perfect world with no real-world constraints, it is highly doubtful that the rational decision making method can always generate the optimal solution to provide maximum benefits to their organizations. The following six reasons are why there are limits to rational decision-making:

1. Decision makers do not have complete knowledge of all the facts surrounding the problems. They cannot foresee future events with complete accuracy. Therefore, it is not always possible to choose the optimum solution.
2. The search for decision is stopped as soon as the minimum acceptable level of rationality is reached. Most decisions involve too many complex variables all of which cannot be examined fully by a decision maker.
3. A decision-making situation may involve multiple goals all of which cannot be maximized simultaneously.
4. The environment of decision-making is often uncertain. The making and implementation of decisions are influenced by several uncontrollable factors and the consequences of various alternatives cannot be anticipated accurately.
5. A decision in one area may have an adverse effect on another area of operations. For example, a decision to produce high quality goods may result into increase in cost of production and; may not be possible to sell the product with sufficient profit margin.
6. Human factors are the main limits on rational decision-making. Personal value systems, perceptions, economic and social factors, etc., are the main human limits on rationality.

The rational decision-making method model describes the way decisions should be made. In other words, decision makers wanting to make optimal decisions *should not* have to face time and cost constraints. Certainly, very few managers actually make rational decisions the way they should. The way that managers actually make decisions is more accurately described a bounded (or limited) rationality. **Bounded rationality** states that the rationality of individuals is limited by the information they have, the cognitive limitations of their minds, and the finite amount of time they have to make decisions. Hence, in theory, fully rational decisions makers maximize decisions by choosing the optimal solutions. However, as we point out previously, limited resources along with attention, memory, and expertise, managers don't maximize—they **satisfice**, choosing the alternative that is 'good-enough'.

# Group Decision Making

Studies have shown that groups consistently outperform individuals in making decisions. **Group decision making** is a type of participatory process in which multiple individuals acting collectively, analyze problems or situations, consider and evaluate alternative courses of action, and select from among the alternatives a solution or solutions. The number of people involved in-group decision-making varies greatly, but often ranges from two to seven. The individuals in a group may be demographically similar or quite diverse. Decision-making groups may be relatively informal in nature, or formally designated and charged with a specific goal. The process used to arrive at decisions may be unstructured or structured. The nature and composition of groups, their size, demographic makeup, structure, and purpose, all affect their functioning to some degree.

## Advantages

Group decision-making has some advantages over individual decision-making as it takes advantage of the diverse strengths and expertise of its members. By tapping the unique qualities of group members, it is possible that the group can generate a greater number of alternatives that are of higher quality than the individual. If a greater number of higher quality alternatives are generated, then it is likely that the group will eventually reach a superior problem solution than the individual.

Group decision-making may also lead to a greater collective understanding of the eventual course of action chosen, since it is possible that many affected by the decision implementation actually had input into the decision. This may promote a sense of "ownership" of the decision, which is likely to contribute to a greater acceptance of the course of action selected and greater commitment on the part of the affected individuals to make the course of action successful.

## Disadvantages

There are many potential disadvantages to group decision-making. Groups are generally slower to arrive at decisions than individuals, so sometimes it is difficult to utilize them in situations where decisions must be made very quickly. One of the most often cited problems is **groupthink**. Groupthink occurs when individuals in a group feel pressure to conform to what seems to be the dominant view in the group. Opposing views of the majority opinion are suppressed and alternative courses of action are not fully explored.

Research suggests that certain characteristics of groups contribute to groupthink. In the first place, if the group does not have an agreed upon process for developing and evaluating alternatives, it is possible that an incomplete set of alternatives will be considered and that different courses of action will not be fully explored. Many of the formal decision-making processes (e.g., nominal group technique and brainstorming) are designed, in part, to reduce the potential for groupthink by ensuring that group members offer and consider a large number of decision alternatives. Secondly, if a powerful leader dominates the group, other group members may quickly conform to the dominant view. Additionally, if the group is under stress and/or time pressure, groupthink may occur. Finally, studies suggest that highly cohesive groups are more susceptible to groupthink.

*Group polarization* is another potential disadvantage of group decision-making. This is the tendency of the group to converge on more extreme solutions to a problem. The "risky shift" phenomenon is an example of polarization; it occurs when the group decision is a riskier one than any of the group members would have made individually. This may result because individuals in a group sometimes do not feel as much responsibility and accountability for the actions of the group as they would if they were making the decision alone.

# Structured Conflict

Generally, conflict is viewed as a negative and damaging event. It is believed that conflict is something bad, destructive, it is blamed for causing disagreements, arguments, divorces, violence etc., and thus it is assumed that it should be avoided at all costs. However, the right kind of conflict can lead to much better group decision-making. Conflict theorists tend to write about two types of conflict: *C-type conflict* or *cognitive conflict*, which is usually perceived as positive, and *A-type conflict* or *affective conflict*, which is considered negative.

# C-Type Conflict

In c-type conflict, group members disagree because their different experiences and expertise lead them to view the problem and its potential solutions differently. Effective groups learn to take advantage of the diversity of their members and of their capabilities. Groups can develop abilities or attributes that are essential for group effectiveness: focused activity, creativity, integration, and open communication. C-type conflict is also characterized by a willingness to examine, compare, and reconcile those differences to produce the best possible solution.

Two methods of introducing structured c-type conflict into the group decision-making process are: devil's advocacy and dialectical inquiry.

In the *devil's advocacy* method an individual or sub-group is assigned the role as critic. The following five steps establish a devil's advocacy program.

1. Generate a possible solution.
2. Assign a devil's advocate to criticize and question the solution.
3. Present the critique of the potential solution to key decision makers.
4. Gather additional relevant information.
5. Decide whether to use, change, or not use the originally proposed solution.

The second method, **dialectical inquiry**, creates c-type conflict by forcing decision makers to state the assumptions of a proposed solution and then generate a solution that is the opposite (antithesis) of the proposed solution. The following five steps are those used in the dialectical inquiry method.

1. Generate a potential solution.
2. Identify the assumptions underlying the potential solution.
3. Generate a conflicting counterproposal based on the opposite assumptions.
4. Have advocates of each position present their arguments and engage in a debate in front of key decision makers.
5. Decide whether to use, change, or not to use the originally proposed solution.

When used properly, both the devil's advocacy and the dialectical inquiry methods introduce c-type conflict into the decision-making process. Contrary to the common belief that conflict is bad, studies show that these methods lead not only to less a-type conflict but also improved decision quality and greater acceptance of decisions once they have been made.

# A-Type Conflict

In contrast, a-type conflict or affective conflict, refers to the emotional reactions that can occur when disagreements become personal rather than professional. A-type conflict often results in hostility, anger, resentment, distrust, cynicism, and apathy. Unlike c-type conflict, a-type conflict undermines team effectiveness by preventing teams from engaging in the activities characteristic of c-type conflict that are critical to team effectiveness.

**Brainstorming** is the name given to a situation when groups of people meet to generate new ideas and solutions around a specific area of interest through intensive and freewheeling group discussion. Using rules that remove inhibitions, participants are able to think more freely and move into new areas of thought and as such create numerous new ideas and solutions. The participants shout out as many ideas as possible, no matter how outlandish that they may seem. Participants then build on the ideas raised by others. All the ideas are recorded and are not criticized. Only when the brainstorming session is over are the ideas analyzed, discussed, and evaluated.

**Electronic Brainstorming** is an alternative approach to brainstorming where the group members use computers to communicate and generate alternative solutions. This approach overcomes two major disadvantage associated with face-to-face brainstorming. First, electronic brainstorming overcomes **production blocking**, which occurs when you have an idea but have to wait to share it because someone else is already presenting an idea to the group. During these times of delay, the group member may forget their idea or decide that it really wasn't worth sharing. Production blocking is avoided in electronic brainstorming as all members are at their computers and can type in their thoughts whenever they occur. The second advantage that electronic brainstorming overcomes is **evaluation apprehension**, or what everyone else may think of your idea. With electronic brainstorming, all ideas are anonymous. When you type in your idea and submit, group members only see the idea not the member from whom it was submitted. Some software randomizes the submissions adding an additional level of anonymity for the group member.

Studies have shown that in a 12-person group, electronic brainstorming produces 200% more ideas than that of traditional face-to-face brainstorming.

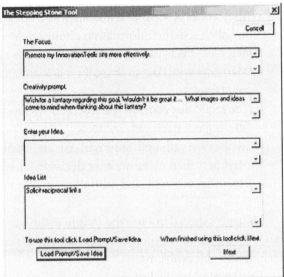

*Nominal group technique* is a more controlled version of brainstorming that encourages creative thinking. This method puts the power of voting to work while still giving individuals a chance to voice their own opinion. Each member of the group writes down his or her ideas that are then discussed and prioritized by the group. It works by allowing each voter to use tally marks to place their first, second and third choices. For decisions that must be made quickly and in a large group, this approach allows individuals to state their opinions without lengthy discussion. The nominal group technique is commonly used in market research studies or internal brainstorming sessions. The nominal group technique should be used when:

- When some group members are much more vocal than others.
- When some group members think better in silence.
- When there is concern about some members not participating.
- When the group does not easily generate quantities of ideas.
- When all or some group members are new to the team.
- When the issue is controversial or there is heated conflict.

In the *Delphi technique*, a series of questionnaires, surveys, etc. are sent to a selected panel of experts (the Delphi group) through a facilitator who oversees their responses. The group does not have to meet face-to-face affording the panel the flexibility of working from their office thus providing efficient use of the expert's time. All communication is normally in writing (letters or email). Members of the groups are selected because they are experts or they have relevant information.

The responses are collected, analyzed, and summarized to determine conflicting viewpoints on each point and then fed back to the group. The process continues in order to work towards synthesis and building consensus. The Delphi technique works as follows:

- Members are selected for the Delphi panel due to their expertise.
- They are kept separated and answer through an open-ended questionnaires, surveys, etc. in order to solicit specific information about a subject or content area. Keeping them separated avoids the negative effects of face-to-face discussions and avoids problems associated with group dynamics.
- Members are asked to share their assessment and explanation of a problem or predict a future state of affairs.
- The facilitator controls the interactions among the participants by processing the information and filtering out irrelevant content.
- Replies are gathered, summarized, and then fed back to all the group members.
- Members then make another decision based upon the new information.
- The process is repeated until the responses converge satisfactory, that is, it yields consensus.

Managers should not use the Delphi technique for common decisions because it is a time consuming, labor intensive, and expensive process. The Delphi technique is most appropriate for important long-term issues and problems.

The **Stepladder technique** is a simple and effective tool to improve group decision making by determining how and when people enter the decision-making process. The stepladder theory assumes that members contribute to the group on an individual level before being influenced by anyone else (Figure 4.9) thus ensuring that each member's contributions are independent and are considered and

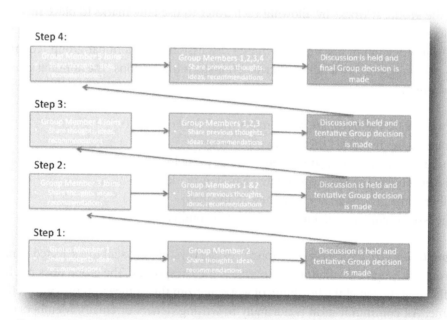

Figure 4.9: Stepladder Technique for Group Decision Making

discussed by the group. Such an approach brings a wider variety of new ideas, more flexible thinking and creative points of view.

Before a group is formed, you should present the task list or the problem list to all participants. Give everyone enough time to think over and carefully investigate what needs to be done. Each member will generate own opinion on how to accomplish the tasks or solve the problems

The following 4 basic steps illuminate how to implement the Stepladder technique:

- Step 1. Form a core group of two members. They will dispute and find the problem solution
- Step 2. Add a third member to the core group. This member will bring new ideas before hearing the first two members' conclusions and solutions. After new ideas and discussed solutions are presented, thee members start discussing new options together
- Step 3. Run this process repeatedly. A fourth member, a fifth member, and so on will be added to the core group
- Step 4: Generate the final decision only after all members have been added to the group and they've presented their new ideas.

## Summary of Chapter

1. This chapter has focused on planning; we looked at the benefits and pitfalls of planning.
2. We read that planning involves choosing a goal and developing a method to achieve that goal. Planning is one of the best ways to improve organizational and individual performance.
3. We learned that there are five steps to making a plan that works: (1) Set SMART goals, or goals that are Specific, Measureable, Attainable, Realistic, and Timely.
4. This chapter revealed that there are six steps in the rational decision making process in which managers define problems, evaluate alternatives, and compute optimal solutions.
5. The rational decision-making process describes how decisions should be made in an ideal world without limits. However, bounded rationality recognizes in a real world managers' limited resources, incomplete and imperfect information, and limited decision-making capabilities restrict their decision-making process.
6. We learned that group decisions work best when group members encourage c-type conflict. However, group decisions don't work as well when groups become hindered in a-type conflict.
7. We explored the advantages and disadvantages of group decision-making and followed group decision-making techniques such as the devil's advocate, Delphi method, Stepladder technique, and the brainstorming methods.

## Discussion Questions

1. Describe the purpose of Planning?
2. Why is planning so important as the first of four management functions?
3. What are the advantages and disadvantages of planning?
4. What is the difference between a standing plan and a single-use plan?

5. Describe the various stages involved in the planning process. Use an example to illustrate these stages.
6. What are the benefits of planning for a business or an organization familiar to you?
7. What are the benefits of planning for your personal career development?
8. What is the difference between short-range and long-range planning?
9. What is the difference between strategic and operational planning?
10. What is the importance of contingency planning?
11. What are the advantages/disadvantages when using zero-based budgeting?

# References

Aldag, R. J., & Kuzuhara, L. W. (2005). *Mastering Management Skills: A Manager's Toolkit*. Mason, OH: Thomson South-Western, 172–173.

Bavelas, J. & Lee, E. S. (1978). 'Effects of Goal Level on Performance: A Trade-Off of Quantity and Quality,' *Canadian Journal of Psychology* 32: 219–240.

Collins, J. C., & Porras, J. I. (1991). 'Organizational Vision and Visionary Organizations,' *California Management Review* (Fall) 30–52.

Dumaine, B. (1994). 'The Trouble with Teams,' *Fortune*, 86–92.

Gallupe, R. B., & Cooper, W. H. (1993). 'Brainstorming Electronically,' *Sloan Management Review* 27–36.

Janis, I. L. (1983). *Groupthink*. Boston: Houghton Mifflin.

Jenn, K., & Mannix, E. (2001). 'The Dynamic Nature of Conflict: A Longitudinal Study of Intragroup Conflict and Group Performance,' *Academy of Management Journal* (44) (2) 238–251.

Kay, G. 'Effective Meetings through Electronic Brainstorming,' *Management Quarterly* (35) 15.

Kress, G. (1995). 'The Role of Interpretation in the Decision Process,' *Industrial Management* (37) 10–14.

Locke, E. A., & Latham, G. P. (1990). *A Theory of Goal Setting and Task Performance*. Englewood Cliffs, NJ: Prentice Hall.

MacCrimmon, K. R., Taylor, R. N., & Locke, E. A. (1976). 'Decision Making and Problem Solving,' *Handbook of Industrial and Organizational Psychology*, 1397–1453.

Mason, A., Hochwarter, W. A., & Thompson, K. R. (1995). 'Conflict: An Important Dimension in Successful Management Teams,' *Organizational Dynamics* (24) 20.

Miller, C. C. (1994). 'Strategic Planning and Firm Performance: A Synthesis of More Than Two Decades of Research,' *Academy of Management Performance*, 37, 1649–1665.

Mintzberg, H. (1994). 'Rethinking Strategic Planning: Part 1: Pitfalls and Fallacies,' *Long Range Planning* (27) 12–21.

Mintzberg, H. (1993). 'Part II: New Roles for Planners,' *California Management Review* (36) 32–47.

Neck, C. P., & Manz, C. C. (1994). 'From Groupthink to Teamthink: Toward the Creation of Constructive Thought Patterns in Self-Managing Work Teams,' *Human Relations* (47), 929–952.

Pearce II, J. A. (1982). 'The Company Mission as a Strategic Goal,' *Sloan Management Review* (Spring) 15–24.

Pelled, L., Eisenhardt, K., & Xin, K. (1999). 'Exploring the Black Box: An Analysis of Work Group Diversity, conflict, and Performance,' *Administrative Science Quarterly* (44)(1).

Rodgers, R., & Hunter, J. E. (1991). 'Impact of Management by Objectives on Organizational Productivity,' *Journal of Applied Psychology (76) 322–336.*

Rogelberg, S. G., Barnes-Farrell, J. L., & Lowe, C. A. (1992). 'The Stepladder Technique: An Alternative Group Structure facilitating Effective Group Decision Making,' *Journal of Applied Psychology* (77), 730–737.

Schwenk, C. R. (1990). 'Effects of Devil's Advocacy and Dialectical Inquiry on Decision Making: A Meta-Analysis,' *Organizational Behavior & Human Decision Performance* (47) 161–176.

# CHAPTER 5

## Strategic Planning

*"It is vital to conduct Strategic Development and Profit Optimization concurrently. The goal of the strategic development process is to optimize the firm's long-term profitability."*

### Chapter Learning Objectives:

After reading this chapter you should have a good understanding of:

- The definition of strategy, strategic planning, and strategic management.
- The strategic management process and its inter-related stages.
- The impact of environmental analysis on strategy formulation.
- How to use the SWOT analysis to formulate strategy.

- Porter's Five Force model and their effect on firm pricing and profitability.
- The definitions of and differences in the vision statement and the mission statement.
- Porter's generic strategies: overall cost leadership, differentiation, and focus.
- The definition of goals and objectives and the four distinct categories of objectives.

Why do some firms outperform others? Why do high performing firms fail and struggling firms succeed? What types of strategies can a firm pursue that will provide it with a sustained advantage over time? Answering these questions is what makes the study of Strategic Management so interesting.

Consider for a moment the one time star of the 1990's, Nokia. Nokia was the industry's dominant player in the 1990's and well into the 2000's with company revenues increasing fivefold from 1996 to 2001 and in 2005, marking the sale of its billionth handset. What happened to this star of the 90's? Quite simply while Nokia was concentrating on developing markets, such as Africa, it lost focus of the smartphone revolution. Nokia's short-term view of profit maximization overshadowed the need for long-term strategic development and missed the changing consumer needs. Customers now demanded interactive application, web browsing, mail server, and GPS. All of which were provided by Apple's iPhone and RIM's Blackberry's. The result of Nokia's inability to react to the changing needs of the consumer was disastrous, In 2007, just two short years following it billionth handset sale, Nokia's market share dropped 51% and its stock price sunk 45% while Apple's shares skyrocketed 234%.

Nokia was the pioneer in the smartphone market with its Symbian phones, yet Nokia failed to respond to the iPhone and the shifting demand that came with it. As the years passed, the Symbian platform aged compared to the iOS and more and more consumers opted for pocked-sized mini-computers instead of 'feature' phones with tedious WAP

Leaders today face similar complex challenges presented by the global marketplace. This text examines the four key attributes of strategic management; In section one we look at the achievement of the overall organizational goals, satisfying the needs of the multiple stakeholders, achieving near-term profit maximization and long-term strategic development, and recognizing the tradeoff between efficiency and effectiveness.

In this section we examine the strategic management process; what constitutes a good vision and mission statement, how to construct meaningful goals and objectives, what is meant by environmental scanning, we examine the process of strategy analysis, strategy formulation, and strategy implementation.

## What is Strategy?

**Strategy** refers to the coordinated managerial action plan to pursue the organizations mission to reach its targeted goals and objectives. Simply stated, strategy is management's action plan for running the business by positioning the firm in such a way that it sells more products or services than the competition to improve the company's financial and market performance. For most firms, the preeminent goal is to maximize long-term profitability.

Basically a strategy is a set of decision-making rules for guidance of organizational behavior.

*Tactics* are the methods and actions used to accomplish the strategies. They are more specific, the 'how-to' part of the process meant to deal with the demands of the moment, and to move from one milestone to another in pursuit of the overall organizational goal(s). In an organization, the board of directors decides strategy, whereas the tactics are planned by the department heads for implementation by junior officers and the employees.

Strategy is a way of explicitly shaping the long term goals and objectives of the firm, defining the major action programs needed to achieve those objectives, and deploying the necessary resources. Strategy helps firms accomplish this goal by developing a **competitive advantage** over its competition. A competitive advantage exists when the firm is able to deliver the same benefits as competition, but at a lower cost (*Cost advantage*) or deliver benefits that exceed those of competing products (*differentiation advantage*). Cost advantage and differentiation advantage can be achieved through **Operational effectiveness**. Performing activities such as total quality, just-in-time, benchmarking, business process reengineering, outsourcing better than your rivals, are examples of operational effectiveness. A company achieves a **sustainable competitive advantage** when an attractive number of buyers have a lasting preference for the company's products or services compared to those offered by the competition. The bigger and more sustainable the competitive advantage, the better the company's prospects for winning in the marketplace and earning superior long-term profits relative to its competition. Sustainable competitive advantage cannot be achieved only through operational effectiveness; a firm must perform different activities from rivals or perform similar activities in different ways. Consider Wal-Mart, Southwest Airlines, and IKEA, each have developed unique, internally consistent, and difficult to imitate activities that have provided each with a sustained competitive advantage. A company with a good strategy is clear on its direction and avoids copying what rivals do. Imitating your rivals eventually leads to mutually destructive price competition and sub-optimal firm performance.

# Strategic Management

Before we begin to look at the *Strategic Management Process,* let's define what we mean by **Strategic Management**. Strategic Management, defined by Ansoff is;

> '*A process for managing a firm's relationship with its environment and consists of Strategic Planning, Capability Planning, and Management of Change'.*

Strategic management is focused on four managerial actions:

*Analysis*—the managerial process of evaluating of the firm's current competitive position, goal, vision, mission, and strategic objectives.

*Decisions*—involving the formulation, planning, and developing of the appropriate strategies;

*Actions*—firms must take the necessary action to implement those strategies as well as

*Evaluate*—or modify the strategies as needed in an effort to create a competitive advantage.

Hence, we define Strategic Management as, *"The systematic <u>analysis, decisions, actions and evaluations</u> an organization undertakes in order to create and sustain a competitive advantage'.*

Strategic Management combines:

- **Strategic Planning,**
- **Capabilities Planning,** and
- **Change Management**

Strategic Management includes in its decision-making those individuals, groups, and organizations that have a 'stake', hence, **Stakeholders** in the success of the organization, including the owners, employees, customers, suppliers, the community at large. Strategic Management requires management to view both **near-term profit making** and **long-term strategic development**. This view is referred to as the 'creative tension' by <u>Peter Senge</u>, as managers must maintain both a vision for the future of the organization, such as product development, as well as the focus on the firms present operating needs, current finance and resource requirements. Managers who only focus on short-term profit making will damage the future competitive position of the firm. Equally, managers who only focus on long-term strategic development will find it difficult to survive in the current competitive climate.

Strategic Management has four characteristics; as mentioned it does not focus on one specific unit of the firm, thus it is *interdisciplinary*. The second characteristic of strategic management is that it is *externally focused,* considering the affects that the external environment has on the strategic position of the firm. Strategic management utilizes *environmental scanning* to scan for those external threats and opportunities to see how they may impact—good or bad—the strategic decisions. The third characteristic of strategic management is that it is also *internally focused;* managers must have an awareness of the firm's functional and managerial capabilities as well as it resources. Knowing what it has or doesn't have will be necessary in determining the appropriate strategic aggressiveness. The final characteristic of strategic management is its *view of the future organization;* what will the future of the industry look like? How will technology play a role in the industry? Will these changes necessitate a change in our products or markets to survive?

As one can see, the strategic management process involves a critical analysis of the firm's interrelated activities as well as the causal effects of both current and future external environmental factors. From this point, we can now move to the Strategic management process.

## Management Vision

*Management vision,* alternatively called ***strategic vision*** or ***management creed***, is the image that a business must have of it s aims and goals before it sets out to reach them, it describes the shape of the firm that the influential managers of the firm propose to develop.

A **vision statement** defines what your business will do and why it will exist tomorrow, it is massively inspiring, overarching, and long-term. A Vision Statement takes into account the current status of the organization, and serves to point the direction of where the organization wishes to go.

In some firms, the charismatic leader of the firm enunciates the vision. Mr. Jack Welch of GE, who announced that he, wanted General Electric to be a company that is technologybased doing business in the growth areas of the economy.

In other firms, such as the Johnson and Johnson Corp. (which calls its vision the firm's Creed), many levels of management are involved in periodic discussions of the vision. These discussions revise the vision to reflect changing aspirations of the influential stakeholders of the firm and the changing realities of the firm's external environment.

Finally, Apple computers strategic vision is described internally as its 'purpose' statement, as such its guiding philosophy, and state; *"to make a contribution to the world by making tools for the mind that advance humankind.*

 **Vision—'a statement of the organizations future, what it is and what it is to become' ...**

A strategic vision of the firm outlines what the organization wants to be and is built upon four elements. *First,* it describes the future course of the company to its stakeholders, it is the 'where we are going' statement from management based on the organization's core values and beliefs. *Secondly,* the vision should describe a purpose for the firm. Every firm whether large or small for-profit or not-for-profit exists for a reason, a purpose. The strategic vision should explain what it is doing to achieve its purpose. The *third* element should include a brief statement on what the firm does to achieve its stated purpose. The *final* element includes a statement of broad goals for the firm; Henry Ford's vision was to 'have a car in every garage'. The strategic vision is important as it helps to focus organizational member's energies towards a common goal.

The defining characteristics of the Vision statement are what it says about the company's *future* strategic direction, where they are headed, and what the future products, markets, customers, and technology focus will be.

Although vision statements cannot accurately measure performance, they do provide a fundamental statement of an organization's values, aspirations, and goals and strive to capture both the minds and hearts of the employees.

# Mission Statement

A mission statement is an organizations vision translated into written form and designed to provide a sense of direction to guide the actions and decision making for all levels of management in the organization in its *present* business purpose.

It solidifies a leader's view of the direction and purpose of the organization. It is an enduring statement of purpose and acts as an invisible hand that defines the overall goals and serves as a vital element for motivating the people within the organization. A mission statement explains the organization's reason for being, its *'raison de etre'*, and answers the question, *"What business are we in?"*

A mission statement should:

1. • Define what the company is
2. • Define what the company aspires to be
3. • Define the limitations (what it is not)
4. • Broad enough to allow for creative growth
5. • Define what distinguishes the company from others
6. • Define framework to evaluate current activities
7. • Defined clearly for all to understand, in a limited amount of statements

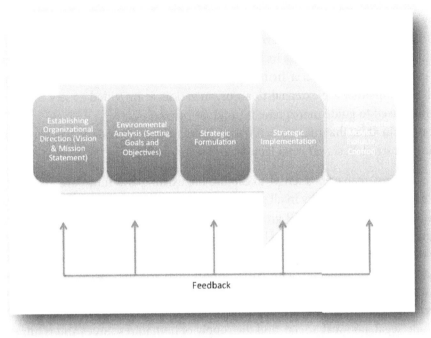

Figure 5.1: The Strategic Management Process

The difference between the Vision statement and the Mission Statement is quite straightforward. The Vision statement describes the company's 'future' business, *"where we are going"* while the Mission Statement, describes the company's present business and purpose, *"who we are, what we do, and why we are here."*

## The Strategic Management Process

The strategic management process consists of five interrelated stages; development of a strategic vision and crafting of the mission statement, setting strategic goals & objectives and conducting meaningful environmental scanning, strategic formulation, strategic implementation, and monitor, evaluate, and control. Figure 5.1.

## Creating an Organization that is Environmentally Aware

Gary Hamel and C. K. Prahalad suggest that 'every manager carries around in his or her head a set of biases, assumptions, and presuppositions about the structure of the relevant 'industry', about how one makes money in the industry, about who the competition is and isn't about who the customers are and are not ...' Environmental analysis requires managers to continually question such assumptions.

So how does a manager become environmentally aware? The follow section addresses the role of environmental scanning, monitoring, and the gathering of competitive intelligence used to develop forecasted scenarios.

**Environmental scanning** is the internal communication of external information about issues that may potentially influence an organization's decision-making process.

ES involves surveillance of a firm's external environment to predict environmental changes to come and to detect changes already under way. Its focus is on the identification of developing issues, situations, and potential events that may affect a firm's future. The information gathered, including the events, trends, and relationships that are external to an organization, is provided to key managers within the organization and is used to guide management in future plans.

There are four main areas that managers focus their attention when conducting environmental scanning: economic, industrial, basic external factors, and technology.

1. **Economic scanning**, managers attempt to capture the existing and future trends and conditions that characterize the economic activity in all geographical areas that the firm does or may want to conduct business. Such factors include: GNP growth, inflation/deflation, unemployment, disposable income, tariffs, government subsides, tax rate and historical performance as well as future projected performance.
2. **Industrial scanning** analyzes those business sectors that the firm is in or may want to enter. Trends such as market growth rate, total market share, current/future life cycle stage of the industry, past performance and future projections are all diagnosed and are requisite data for forming the firms' strategic plan.
3. **Basic external factors** consist of those factors, which are largely uncontrollable by the firm. These factors include: legal, political, social, and the supply of human resources and is imperative to define their past as well as future attractiveness when considering potential industry sector.
4. **Technology scanning** is a series of ongoing studies and assessments that tracks trends, technologies, and innovations that could influence, or be leveraged as part of, next-generation intelligent systems within a five to seven year time horizon. Technology with all its industry contributions and advancements has often been referred to as 'industry killer'.

**Environmental monitoring** records the evolution of the environmental trends, sequences of events, frequency of the events, and predictability of the events. Monitoring allows managers to evaluate what level of changeability is occurring and helps managers determine what strategic direction and resource allocation is required.

**Competitive Intelligence**, as Sun Tzu alludes, 'if you know your enemy and you know yourself, you need not fear a hundred battles' CI helps a firm define and understand their industry, identify competitors strengths and weaknesses, capitalize on opportunities, and mitigate threats. If competitive intelligence is done properly, a company can avoid surprises and reduce its response time by anticipating the competitor's next move.

## SWOT Analysis

One of the most basic tools for analyzing the firm and its industry conditions is the **SWOT Analysis**. The acronym SWOT stands for Strengths and Weaknesses, which are an assessment of the internal functional areas of the firm including management and culture of the organization. Opportunities and Threats are an assessment of the external environment. These could be factors either in the macro or competitive environment. The macro environment include factors such as; demographic, sociocultural, political/legal, technological, economic, and global. Strengths and weaknesses are assessed relative to the competition; opportunities and threats are those factors that are largely beyond the control of the firm.

The purpose of a *SWOT* analysis is to identify the strategies that will create a firm specific business model that will best align an organization's resources and capabilities to the requirements of the environment in which the firm operates. It is the foundation for evaluating the internal potential and limitations and the probable/likely opportunities and threats from the external environment. It views all positive and negative factors inside and outside the firm that affect the firm's success.

What makes SWOT powerful is that it can help you uncover opportunities that you are well placed to exploit. And by understanding the weaknesses of your business, you can manage and eliminate threats that would otherwise catch you unawares. By analyzing your firm and your competitors using the SWOT framework, you can start to craft a strategy that helps you distinguish yourself from your competitors, so that you can compete successfully in your market.

The **macro environment** includes those factors that can have a dramatic effect on a firm's strategy. Events and trends are difficult to predict in the macro environment and even more difficult if not impossible to control. Consider future political events in the Middle East or the effects of innovation in technology. Consider for a moment what your cell phone will look like and do in five or ten years. One can see the value in conducting an analysis of what the future events will become and best position its strategy to either benefit from the opportunities or mitigate the threats.

The macro environment is divided into six sections: demographic, sociocultural, political/legal, technological, economic, and global. We will briefly assess each section and provide example of the key trends and events.

## 1. Demographic

The most easily understood section of the macro environment. Demographic include population, affluence of the society, ethnicity and its changing composition, geographic distribution, density of the population, education, sex, and differences in income levels.

## 2. Sociocultural

Sociocultural include those factors that influence the lifestyle of a society and include the percentage of women in the workforce, rising dual-income families, increase in the number of temporary workers, concern for healthy diets and physical fitness, a heightened awareness of the environment, and the trend to delay starting a family. Sociocultural forces can enhance sales and service for some firms but depress sales in others.

Consider the following sociocultural fact:

> Women received 44% of MBAs in 2007, the latest year for which data is available, up from 39% a decade earlier, according to the U.S. Department of Education. That translates to a whopping 75% increase in the last 10 years.
> Despite the gains, however, women remain under represented in business graduate schools. The Department of Education numbers show that women currently receive 61% of all master's degrees awarded, some 13 percentage points higher than the number of MBA grads who are female.

## 3. Political/Legal

Political forces are governments and unilateral bodies that declare certain rules, regulations, laws or restrictions with regards the way a country is run. These affect business. An example is taxation. If taxation rises for companies then so does the price of the goods. If taxation rises in general then wages have to be increased thus making production values higher and prices for goods increase further. Legal forces are the types of law and legislation that a political body introduces. A government or state-body like the EU may decide, for example, that advertising chocolate around children's television is inappropriate, and thus ban them from advertising on children's channels and during set time periods. This is a legal constraint.

Both the political processes and legal constraints with which industries must comply, influence industry competitiveness and profitability.

## 4. Technological

Technological forces can influence organizations in various ways. They can have a sudden and dramatic effect on the environment of a firm and can significantly alter the demand for an organization's or industry's products or services.

Technological change and the rate of change vary from one industry to another and can decimate existing businesses. Moreover, changes in technology can affect a firm's operations such as processing methods, raw materials, and service delivery. In international business, one country's use of new technological developments can make another country's products overpriced and noncompetitive.

Changing technology can offer major opportunities for improving the firm's goal achievements or can threaten the existence of the firm. Hence, it is imperative that managers identify *"the key concerns in the technological environment and build the organizational capability to (1) forecast and identify relevant developments—both within and beyond the industry, (2) assess the impact of these developments on existing operations, and (3) define opportunities"*.

## 5. Economic

The economy has an effect on all industries from planned to start-up to growing businesses. Economic analysis is a comprehensive study of national, regional, and global economic performance and trends and represents a highly important phase of strategy development.

Economic factors have direct impact on the potential attractiveness of various business ventures. Key economic indicators such as: shifts in nature of economy (e.g. US shifting to a service economy), availability of credit, level of disposable income, spending propensity of people, interest rates, inflation rates, government deficits, gross domestic product trends, consumption patterns, unemployment trends, foreign currency fluctuations, stock market trends, demand shifts in various products and services in different locations, import and export trade, price indexes, monetary policies, fiscal policies, and tax rates, including economic policies of other countries and the European Economic Community have a major impact on how businesses operate and make decisions.

## 6. Global

Globalization provides to firm's both opportunities, such as access to larger potential markets, skilled labor, and a broader base of production factors, as well as risks such as political, social and economic. Key elements that managers must consider when pursuing a global strategy are: currency exchange rates, increasing global trade, trade agreements among regional blocs, terrorism, and the General Agreement on Tariffs and Trade (GATT).

# Porters Five Forces Model of Industry Competition

The Five Competitive Forces model was developed by Michael E. Porter in 1980 and described in his book *'Competitive Strategy: Techniques for Analyzing Industries and Competitors'*. Since that time it has become an important tool for analyzing an organizations industry structure in strategic decision-making.

Porter's model is based on the insight that a corporate strategy should understand the industry structures and the way they change to best meet the opportunities and threats in the organizations external environment.

Porter identified five competitive forces that determine the intensity of competition and therefore the profitability and attractiveness of an industry. Based on the information derived from the **Five Forces Analysis**, management can decide how to influence or to exploit particular characteristics of their industry. The objective of corporate strategy should be to modify these competitive forces in a way that improves the position of the organization.

The Five Competitive Forces (Figure 5.2) are typically described as:

## 1. Bargaining Power of supplier

How strong is the position does the seller have over the buyer? How much power does your supplier have on controlling the price of supplies? Suppliers can exert a tremendous amount of power on the price of goods and services squeezing the profitability of firms and making it difficult to recover the cost of the raw materials. The bargaining power of the supplier is determined by assessing the level of threats that the suppliers may raise prices or reduce the quality of purchased goods and services.

## 2. Bargaining Power of Buyers

Similarly, the bargaining power of buyers is determined by how much customers can impose pressure on margins and volumes. If one customer has a large enough impact to affect a company's margins and volumes, (e.g. Walmart) then the customer hold substantial power.

## 3. Threat of New Entrants

The competition in an industry will be the higher when it is easier for other companies to enter the industry. In such a situation, new entrants can raise the level of competition, and market environment (e.g. market shares, prices, customer loyalty) thereby reducing its attractiveness.

The threat of new entrants largely depends on the barriers to entry. High entry barriers exist in some industries (e.g. aircraft mfg.) whereas other industries are very easy to enter (e.g. real estate agency, restaurants).

## 4. Threat of Substitutes

A threat from substitutes exists when there are alternative products with lower prices offering better performance for the same purpose. These substitutes could potentially attract a significant proportion of market share and therefore reduce the potential sales volume for existing players. This category also relates to complementary products.

Figure 5.2: Porters Five Forces

## 5. Industry Rivalry

This force describes the intensity of competition between existing players (companies) in an industry. High competitive pressure results in pressure on prices, margins, and hence, on profitability for every single company in the industry. These situations make the reasons for advertising wars, price wars, modifications, and ultimately costs increases as such, make it difficult to compete.

## 6. Complementors—The 6th Force

Often considered to be Porter's 6th force of his industry analysis framework. Complementors are companies or entities that sell or offer goods or services that are compatible with, or 'complementary' to and that have a potential impact on, the goods or services produced and sold in a given industry.

Complementary goods offer more value to the consumer together than apart. Consider a powerful computer, it is of little value unless there is software that runs on it.

When one product or service complements another there exists a condition called **complementarity**; a sort of commercial symbiosis.

An example of a complementary good is the hotdog and the hotdog bun. Rarely would one purchase a hotdog without also purchasing the hotdog buns, and rarely would one purchase hotdog buns without also purchasing hotdogs. Under the six forces model, these two products are complementary.

# Firm Capabilities

**Capabilities** refer to the firm's ability to effectively transform its inputs to outputs to meet its objectives and to exploit its resources. Capabilities are functionally based (marketing, operations, R&D, finance, etc.) and are expressed in terms of:

- **People:** enough people, with the necessary competencies and experience?
- **Physical resources:** the necessary machinery, equipment, and buildings?
- **Financial resources:** enough money and credit?
- **Business systems:** processes and infrastructure sufficient?
- **Information:** the necessary knowledge, data, and information systems?
- **Intellectual property:** copyrights, patents, and designs adequately protected?
- **Supplier relationships:** reliability and continuity of supply?

# Competency, Core Competencies, Distinctive Competencies

A **competency** is a cross-functional integration and coordination of firm capabilities and is the product of organizational learning and experience that represents real proficiency in performing an internal activity. A **core competency** is a collection of competencies that crosses divisional boundaries, is collaborative, and widespread within the organization, and is something that the organization can do exceedingly well. A core competence gives a company a potentially valuable competitive capability and represents a definite **competitive asset**.

When a firm's core competencies are superior to the competition, they become **distinct competencies**. Hence, distinctive competencies are those competitively significant activities that a company performs better than its competition that cannot be easily matched or imitated by its competitors.

An example of distinctive competency is found in the following story of Nordstrom's outstanding customer service and product quality;

---

**Nordstrom Tire Story**

Nordstrom is a fashion specialty retailer founded in 1901 as a shoe store in Seattle. Today, Nordstrom operates more than 150 U.S. stores across 27 states, and is steadfastly committed to the principles the business was founded on more than a century ago – exceptional service, selection, quality and value.

'A man walked into the Fairbanks, Alaska, Nordstrom department store with two snow tires. He walked up to the counter, put the tires down and asked for his money back. The clerk, who'd been working there for two weeks, saw the price on the side of the tires, reached into the cash register and handed the man $145'.

Nordstrom has become synonymous with great customer service. No other retailer has been able to achieve that level of marketing status. Whether or not the tire story is true doesn't matter. What matters is that based on Nordstrom's reputation of providing the best customer service, people actually believe the story could be true.

---

A **competitive advantage** exists when the superiority gained by the distinctive competencies are exploited, thus allowing the firm to provide the same value as its competitors but at a lower price, or allowing the firm to charge higher prices by providing greater value through differentiation. A firm achieves a **sustainable competitive advantage** when the competitive advantage is long-term, not easily duplicable or surpassable by the competition.

This chapter evaluates the importance of a company's resources, capabilities, and competencies to ascertain whether they are internal strategic factors that will help to determine the future of the company.

## Porters Generic Strategies

For an organization to obtain a sustainable competitive advantage Michael Porter suggested that they should follow either one of three generic strategies (Figure 5.3). The following three generic strategies are defined along two dimensions: 1). *Strategic scope* is a demand-side dimension and looks at the size and composition of the market in which you intend to compete. *Strategic strength* views the supply-side and looks at the core competencies of the firm. The first, *overall cost leadership*, is based on creating a low-cost position. Here a firm must manage the relationships and lower its costs throughout the value-chain. Porter's second strategy, *differentiation*, requires a firm to create products and/or services that are unique and valued. The primary focus is now on the 'non-price' attributes for which the consumer will pay a premium. Porter's last generic strategy is *focus* based, directing the 'focus' toward a narrow product line, buyer segment, or targeted geographic market.

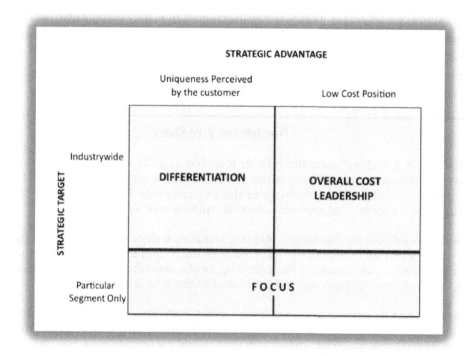

Figure 5.3: Porters Generic Strategies

## Overall Cost Leadership strategies

This strategy focuses on being the lowest cost producer within the industry. The firm's goal is to drive cost down through all the elements of the production of the product from sourcing of raw materials, to labor costs. A great deal of managerial attention to cost control is required for a firm to become successful using this strategy. The market position for this strategy is usually aimed at the broad market so sufficient sales can cover costs.

One key strategy to obtaining overall cost leadership is achieved when a business learns to lower its costs. The **experience curve** is gained when a firm has 'learned through experience' how to improve and subsequently lower, its costs. With experience, unit costs decrease as output increases.

Examples of low cost leadership include; Ryan Air, Walmart, Motel 6. One advantage to the overall cost leadership position is that it provides the firm an above average return in its industry despite the presence of strong competition.

To be successful, this strategy usually requires a high relative market share or other advantage such as preferential access to raw materials, components, labor, or some other important input.

## Differentiation strategies

Porter's second strategy calls for differentiating the product or service offered by the firm. To be different or unique *industry-wide* is what firm's strive for. Having a competitive advantage that allows the company and its products to stand out in the sea of competitors is crucial for their success. Achieving the differentiation strategy enables above-average returns in an industry because it creates a defensible position for coping with the five competitive forces.

With a differentiation strategy the organization aims to focus its effort on particular segments and charge for the added differentiated value.

## Focus or Niche strategies

The final strategy Porter presents focuses on a particular buyer group, segment of the product line, or geographic market and becomes well known for providing products/services within the segment. The strategy rests on the premise that the firm creates a competitive advantage for this niche market and either succeeds by being a low cost producer or differentiator within that particular segment.

With both of these strategies the organization can also focus by offering particular segments a differentiated product/service by better meeting the needs of the particular market or a low cost product/service, or both. The key is that the product or service is focused on a particular segment.

The firm achieving focus strategy may also potentially earn above-average returns than the industry average (differentiation focus). Examples of a focused or niche strategy are found with Ferrari and Rolls Royce in the automobile industry. Both companies have a niche of premium products available at a premium price yet have a very small percentage of the total worldwide market, a trait characteristic of the niche strategy.

Challenges with the focus strategy are that the niche market typically is small and may not be significant or large enough to generate the economies of scale to justify a company's attention.

In order for a firm to achieve above average performance in either low cost or differentiation strategies, a firm must first achieve **competitive parity**. Parity is similarity to competitors or being 'on par' with respects to low costs or product differentiation.

# Industry Life Cycle (ILC)

History has shown that both business and products experience periods of growth interrupted by periodic recessions, and subsequent recoveries restored to pre-recession growth rates. History has also shown that some industries the growth continued to occur and for others, the growth slowed down and even declined. Furthermore, these stages of movement can be extended from an entire industry to that of a single product or service.

This life cycle was based on what economist for many years called the **Gompert growth curve**. This curve has been renamed as the **Demand Product or Industry Life cycle** (Figure 5.4) which describes a typical evolution of need demand and can be subdivided into several distinctive parts:

1. **Emergence (E)**—a turbulent period during which an industry is born, and a number of aspiring competitors seek to capture leadership.
2. **Accelerating Growth ($G^1$)**—the period during which the surviving competitors enjoy the fruits of their victory. During $G^1$ the demand growth typically outpaces the growth of supply.

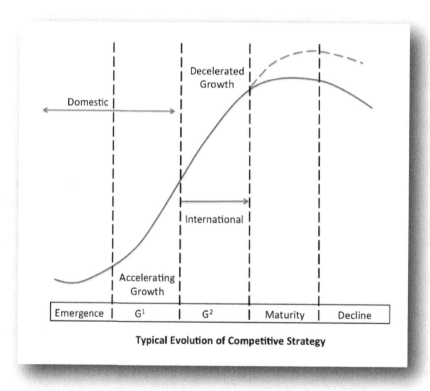

Figure 5.4: Stages of the Industry Life Cycle

3. *Decelerating Growth (G²)*—when the early signs of saturation appear, and supply begins to exceed demand.
4. *Maturity (M)*—when saturation is reached and there is a substantial overcapacity.
5. *Decline (D)*—to a lower volume of demand (or no demand). This cause may by economic factors, demographic factors, rate of product obsolescence, or product consumption.

# Portfolio Analysis

There are several different **portfolio analysis** tools that help managers assess how best to identify opportunities and to allocate resources across a set of products or businesses. The portfolio analysis framework is valuable to assess business units on the basis of market share and growth rate of the industry or sector in which they compete to identify individual business units' growth cycle stages.

A portfolio analysis is also used to identify business units or products in the context of overall growth in their respective industries with a view to optimize resources and maximize overall portfolio performance.

Portfolio analysis also seeks to evaluate the strength of a company's competitive strength within an industry or sector, using inputs such as its rate of change of market share, cost base, and product factors such as cost per unit and the strength of its new product pipeline. Using these inputs, portfolio analysis can help to promote success by highlighting areas with the potential to deliver the most attractive future profits, while highlighting other areas with limited prospects, thus helping management to guide resources toward areas where they can best be invested.

Two of the most popular portfolio analysis techniques are the **BCG Growth-Share Matrix** and the **GE McKinsey Business Screen**.

## BCG Growth Share Matrix

The **BCG**, Figure 5.5 is a simple, well-known management portfolio tool based on the ***Product life cycle (PLC)*** theory. This portfolio-planning model classifies products (and implicitly the company's business units) into four categories based on the combination of *market growth* and *market share* relative to the largest competitor.

A business unit's relative competitive position is defined as its market share in the industry divided by that of the largest other competitor. By this calculation, a relative market share of 1.0 belongs to the market leader. The business growth rate is the percentage of market growth, that is, the percentage by which sales of a particular business unit classification of products have increased.

The basic premise of the BCG matrix is that a company should have a balance portfolio of products including ***high-growth*** products as well as ***low- growth*** products.

A high-growth product is one that requires resources and effort to market but expects to generate substantial return on investment. A low-growth product is a well-established product whose customers are familiar with what they are buying that generates continual cash flow for the company. The product has a limited budget for marketing with stable product characteristics and a price that changes very little over time.

The BCG matrix helps managers decide which products (and by default SBU/SBAs) are selling and to assign priorities for allocation of resources.

*Stars*—(high growth/high market share) have high market share in a growing market that still requires considerable resource support. Maintaining market share, Stars can grow into Cash Cows.

*Question Marks*—(high growth, low market share) typically these are new products in a growing market where buyers have not yet discovered them. Question marks have high demand and low return due to low market share and without significant investment, can quickly turn into dogs.

*Cash Cows*—(low growth, high market share) typically companies strive for these products. Ones that have high market share in a mature market and if a competitive advantage exists, generate substantial cash flow. Because of low growth, marketing and placement investments are also low.

*Dogs*—(low growth, low market share) are to be avoided and divested as soon as possible. Typically, turnarounds are expensive and unsuccessful.

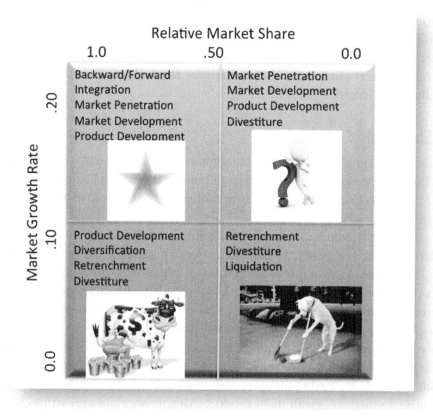

Figure 5.5: BCG Growth Share Matrix

The BCG Growth-Share Matrix has some clear advantages. It is quantifiable and easy to use. *Cash Cows*, *dogs*, *question marks*, and *star* are easy to remember identifiers for referring to a corporation's business units or products. However, as the BCG has advantages it also has disadvantages:

- It can be argued that growth rate is only one aspect of industry attractiveness.
- It can be argued that market share is only one aspect of overall competitive position.
- The use of high and low to form four categories is too simplistic.
- The relationship between market share and profitability is debatable. Low share businesses can also be quite profitable.
- Product lines or business units are considered only in relation to one competitor, the market leader. Small competitors with fast-growing market share are ignored.

## GE/McKinsey Matrix

The **GE/McKinsey** is similar to the BCG Growth-share matrix in that it maps the various SBUs on a grid to show their performance relationship to the industry.

The GE/McKinsey matrix, Figure 5.6 although similar, has three marked improvements over the BCG matrix.

1. The GE/McKinsey uses nine cells to the four cells used by the BCG, adding a further dimension of relationship.
2. The GE/McKinsey uses *'Industry Attractiveness'* vs. 'market growth' and 'Business Unit Strength' vs. 'market share' as its axes.
3. A circle on the matrix represents each SBU with market size reflected by the size of the circle. The portion of market share that the SBU has is indicated by a 'pie slice' of the circle. Finally, the direction of the circle, indicated by an arrow, reflects the future position of the SBU.

Each of the factors listed are assigned a weighting that is appropriate for the industry. The Industry Attractiveness is then determined based on the overall weighted total.

---

### Industry Attractiveness factors:

| | |
|---|---|
| Market Growth rate | Market Size |
| Demand Variability | Industry Profitability |
| Industry Rivalry | Global Opportunities |
| Political Factors | Environmental Factors |
| Social Factors | Technological |

### Business Unit Strength Factors:

| | |
|---|---|
| Access to Distribution channels | Market Share |
| Growth in Market Share | Production Capacity |
| Profit margin vs. competition | Brand equity |

---

The Business Unit Strength is then determined by assigning a weighting that is appropriate for the industry in the same manner used to determine the Industry Attractiveness.

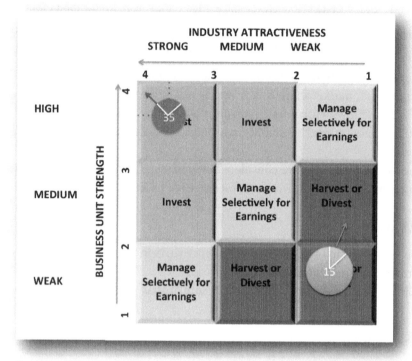

Figure 5.6: GE/McKinsey Matrix

The matrix is a useful tool for management as it visually represents the relative strength of the SBU in its industry. From this information, management can determine to allocate resources enabling SBU growth, maintain resources to hold the position, or withdraw resources and harvest the unattractive SBU.

- *Grow*—strong and average SBUs in attractive industries, and strong SBUs in average industries.
- *Hold*—average SBUs in average industries, strong
- SBUs in weak industries, and weak SBUs in attractive industries.
- *Harvest*—weak SBUs in average and unattractive industries and average SBUs in unattractive industries.

Although the GE/McKinsey is an improvement over the BCG model, it still fails to represent the interactions between the various SBUs and the core competencies that each may have.

## Advantages and limitations of Portfolio Analysis

The completion of a portfolio analysis is typically done during the strategic formulation stage because it offers certain advantages:

- It encourages decision makers to evaluate each of the firm's businesses separately and to set objectives and allocate resources for each.
- It inspires the use of externally oriented data to supplement management's judgment.
- It raises the issue of cash flow availability for use in expansion and growth.
- It provides graphic depictions that facilitate communication.

Completing a portfolio analysis does have some real limitations and as such, have caused some companies to reduce their use of this approach.

- Defining the products and/or market segments can be problematic.
- Portfolio analysis provides generic strategic advice that if followed, can cause the firm to fall short of performance optimality.
- The portfolio analysis provides an illusion of scientific rigor when in reality positions are determined using subjective inputs.
- It is difficult and sometimes unclear what makes an industry attractive or where a product is on it life cycle.
- Naively following the prescriptions of a portfolio analysis without considering the input and results of any other analyses may actually reduce the firm's performance.

# Organizational Strategies

After analyzing the organizational environment both internal and external. Decision makers now have the foundation on which to formulate an organizational strategy. It is at the corporate level that the determination on how capital, staffing, and other resources are allocated for firms. This includes decisions regarding the flow of financial and other resources to and from a company's product lines and business units. Additionally, market definition, diversification strategies, and decisions to add new products or services to the existing offerings, falls under the purview of corporate level strategy.

There are three common groups of organizational directional strategies that management can choose based on their earlier analysis of the firm.

1. **Growth strategies**—*expand* the company's activities.
2. **Stability strategies**—*maintain* the company's current activities.
3. **Retrenchment strategies**—*reduce* the company's level of activities.

**Growth Strategies** are those designed to achieve growth in sales, assets, profits, or a combination of the three. Growth Strategies are aimed at winning larger market share even at the expense of short-term earnings and are a popular strategy because larger businesses tend to survive longer than smaller companies due to greater financial resources, organizational routines, and external connections.

**Stability strategy** may be chosen by an organization over a growth strategy by simply continuing its current activities without little to any substantial change in direction. Although some would view this approach as a lack of strategy, stability strategies can be appropriate for a successful corporation operating in a reasonably predictable (stable) environment. Stability strategies are quite popular with small-to-medium sized firms (SME's) who have found a niche and are happy with their success and the managerial size of their firms.

When a company finds it in a weak competitive position in some or all of its product lines resulting in poor performance such as declining sales, profits stagnate or turn to loss; a firm may decide to follow a **retrenchment strategy** to reduce the diversity or the overall size of the operations of the company.

This strategy is often used in order to cut expenses with the goal of becoming a more financial stable business. Typically the strategy involves withdrawing from certain markets or the discontinuation of selling certain products or service in order to make a beneficial turnaround. Management may follow one of several retrenchment strategies ranging from turnaround, becoming a captive company, selling out, bankruptcy, or liquidation.

# Summary of Chapter

1. A strategy is management's action plan for running the business by positioning the firm in such a way that it sells more products or services than the competition to improve the company's financial and market performance.

2. The strategic management process consists of 5 components, they are: defining the mission and vision, determining the major goals and objectives of the firm and conduct meaningful environmental scanning, formulation of the strategy that align an organization's strengths and weaknesses with external environmental opportunities and threats, implementation of the strategy adopting controls and appropriate organizational structure to support the chosen strategy, monitor and adjust.

3. A vision statement defines what your business will do and why it will exist tomorrow, it is massively inspiring, overarching, and long-term.

4. A mission statement explains the organization's reason for being, its 'raison de etre' and answers the question, "What business are we in?"

5. *Goals* are broad, general statements of what the organization intends to accomplish whereas objective are a precise and measurable desired future state that the company attempts to realize.

6. Environmental scanning involves the process of continuous surveillance and monitoring of a firm's external environment, including competitive intelligence, to predict environmental changes to come and to detect changes already under way. Managers must analyze the external environment to mitigate or eliminate threats and exploit opportunities.

7. The competitive environment consists of industry related factors and has a more direct impact that the general environment. Porter's five-forces model of industry related factors include; the threat of new entrant, buyer power, supplier power, threat of substitutes, and industry rivalry. A sixth force called 'Complementors', are companies or entities that sell or offer goods or services that are compatible with and that have a potential impact on, the goods or services produced and sold in a given industry.

8. We also discussed the concept of the Industry life cycle and its critical importance to management when formulating a new strategy as well the ILC's five stages: introduction, growth[1], growth [2], maturity, and decline and provided suggested strategies for each stage.

# Discussion Questions

1. How is 'strategic management' defined in the text?
2. Briefly discuss the key activities in the strategic management process. Why is it important to recognize the interdependence nature of these activities?
3. How are goals different than objectives?

4.  List the five characteristics of a well-stated objective.
5.  What is the difference between the Vision statement and the Mission statement of the firm?
6.  According to Porter, what determines the level of competitive intensity in an industry?
7.  How can a decision maker identify strategic factors in a firm's external environment?
8.  What are some of the limitations in using the five-forces analysis?
9.  List four limitations to the BCG Matrix by this calculation, a relative market share of 1.0 belongs to the market leader. .... NOT above 1.0?
10. Describe each of Porter's three generic strategies: overall cost leadership, differentiation, and focus.

# References

P. Brews and D. Purohit, "Strategic Planning in Unstable Environments," *Long Range Planning* (February 2007), pp. 64–83.

Wilson, "Strategic Planning isn't Dead—It Changed," *Long Range Planning* (August 1994), p. 20.

R. Dye and O. Sibony, "How to Improve Strategic Planning," *McKinsey Quarterly* (2007, Number 3), pp.40–48.

D. Rigby and B. Bilodeau, *Management Tools and Trends 2007,* Bain & Company (2007).

R. M. Grant, "Strategic Planning in a Turbulent Environment: Evidence from the Oil Majors," *Strategic Management Journal* (June 2003), pp. 491–517.

Ansoff, H. Igor. (1972). "The Concept of Strategic Management." *The Journal of Business Policy.* (Summer). Vol. 2, No. 4.

Ansoff, H. Igor & McDonnell, E. (1992). *Implanting Strategic Management.* London: Prentice Hall International.

Drucker, Peter. (1980). *Managing In Turbulent Times.* London: Heinemann.

Mintzberg, Henry. (1973). 'Strategy making in three modes,' *California Management Review.*

Porter, M.E. (1980). *Competitive Strategy, Techniques for Analyzing Industries and Competitor.* New York, NY. The Free Press.

R. T. Lenz, "Managing the Evolution of the Strategic Planning Process," *Business Horizons* 30, Number 1 (January–February 1987):37.

R. Grant," The Resource-Based Theory of Competitive Advantage: Implications for Strategy Formulation," *California Management Review,* Spring 1991, 114.

H. Weihrich, " The TOWS Matrix: A Tool for Situational Analysis," *Long Range Planning* 15, Number 2 (April 1982): 61.

G. Dess, G.T Lumpkin, and A. Eisner, *Strategic Management: Text and Cases* (New York: McGraw-Hill/Irwin, 2006), 72.

H. Rowe, R. Mason, and K. Dickel, *Strategic Management and Business Policy: A Methodological Approach* (Reading, MA: Addison-Wesley, 1982), 155–156.

F. David, "The Strategic Planning Matrix—A Quantitative Approach," *Long Range Planning* 19, Number 5 (October 1986): 102.

R. T. Lenz, "Managing the Evolution of the Strategic Planning Process," *Business Horizons* 30, Number 1 (January–February 1987):37.

R. Grant, "The Resource-Based Theory of Competitive Advantage: Implications for Strategy Formulation," *California Management Review,* Spring 1991, 114.

H. Weihrich, "The TOWS Matrix: A Tool for Situational Analysis," *Long Range Planning* 15, Number 2 (April 1982): 61.

# CHAPTER 6

## Innovation, Change, and Conflict

*"The Secret of Change is to focus all of your energy,
Not on fighting the old, but on building the new"*

– Socrates

---

### Chapter Learning Objectives:

After reading this chapter you should have a good understanding of:

- What is innovation, and why is it important to organizations.
- The definition of organizational innovation.
- What is organizational change?
- The relative importance of change and stability to an organization.
- What kinds of changes should be made within an organization?

- Why it is important to consider the effects of change on people within the organization.
- How to evaluate change.
- How organizational change and stress is related.
- How to handle conflict as a factor of organizational change.

# The Importance of Innovation

We begin this chapter with a definition of innovation to set the foundation for organizational innovation. **Innovation** is defined as, the renewing, changing or creating more effective processes, products or ways of doing things.

Defining innovation is important, as it is a critical function for an organizations success. Innovation is one way to make your product unique from your competition. If you are unable to compete on price, you'll need to have innovative products and ideas to make your business stand out from the crowd.

In the past, many organizations have been able to survive even with very limited amounts of innovation. They focus on providing quality products and simply update them to a level that maintains their competitiveness in the market.

Today's consumers are more informed and have more options in terms of what they buy and from whom they buy; they expect innovation in the marketplace. Customers are used to products that continually improve and make their life easier and will not accept mediocrity. If your products are seen as obsolete or out of date, your customers will go elsewhere.

In addition to meeting the changing needs of the consumers, there are other forces that drive innovation in business today and are more powerful than they have ever been. Forces such as globalization and outsourcing increase the push to improve efficiency and effectiveness that can drive down costs and improve productivity in organizations. The amount of innovation your competitors are doing is also a driver of innovation and being first to market with a new product can provide you with a significant advantage in terms of building a customer base.

Innovation is important to the advancement of society around the world. New and innovative products can increase the standard of living and provide people with opportunities to improve their lives. Breakthroughs in medicine and technology have significantly improved living standards around the world. Innovation has also lead to significant improvements in the way businesses operate and has closed the gaps between different markets.

# Organizational Innovation

**Organizational innovation** is the implementation of a new organizational method in the undertaking's business practices, workplace organization or external relations. **Creativity** is the production of novel and useful ideas and is a form of organizational innovation.

**Spotify** is one example of a company that spotted a gap in the market and exploited it through creative and innovative thinking. The subscription music service allows paying users to stream unlimited music on their computers and phones. Launched at a time when piracy was at a high level, and people were reluctant to pay above the odds to download music, the service addressed a clear new market, and offered individuals an affordable and revolutionary way to enjoy high quantities of music, without having to resort to illegal downloads.

Of one thing we can be certain, innovations will continue to change our lives. For a moment, consider the devices that you use on a daily basis and what they will look like in 20 years. Today's iPhones, Android, and Windows phones; what will they look like and how will they function? What about solar power or wind power; will it become cheap enough to power your home as a stand-alone power source and off the main electrical grid? Finally, how about the ubiquitous HDTV; it already has 3D capabilities, will it have 3D imaging holograms?

# Technology Cycles

*Technology* is the purposeful application of knowledge, tools, and techniques in the design, production, and utilization to transform inputs (raw materials and information) into outputs (products and services). Technology is generally divided into five categories:

1. *Tangible*: Prototypes, models, blueprints, and operating manuals.
2. *Intangible*: Problem-solving, training methods, and consultancy.
3. *High-tech:* Consisting entirely or almost entirely of automated or intelligent technology that manipulates ever-finer matter and ever-powerful forces of mechanics.
4. *Intermediate-tech*: Consisting of semi-automated, or partially intelligent technology that manipulates refined matter and medium level forces of mechanics.
5. *Low-tech*: Consisting of labor-intensive technology that manipulates only raw materials and weaker forces of mechanics.

A *technology-cycle* describes the business cycle approach of how a technology affects a products life, and how the stages of technology impacts the business processes from the research and development stage, to the growth, maturity, and decline stages of the technology.

Technology life cycle is different from a product life cycle in that a product life cycle deals with the performance of the product in the market place, whereas the technology life cycle describes the stages of technology in the stage of development of a product and utilization of the technology in the business. The following are the prominent stages of a technology life cycle:

1. *Research and development*—stage where the costs are greater than the returns from the technology that is installed in the business.
2. *Growth stage*—where the incremental utilization of the technology is very high.
3. *Maturity*—where the growth of the utilization of the technology is reduced.
4. *Decline*—the decay stage in which the utility of the technology is reduced.

Nearly all technology cycles follow the typical **S-curve pattern of innovation** (Figure 6.1). Early in the technology cycle there is much to learn so progress is slow, as depicted by point A on the S-curve. Point B indicates that researchers have figured out how to improve the performance for the innovation only to by followed by point C, the flat slope indicating maturity of innovation and that increased effort (in time, money, and R&D) brings only a modest improvement in technological performance and eventual limit to the technology. After technology has reached it limits at the top of the S-curve, significant improvements in performance usually come from radical new designs or new performance enhancing materials.

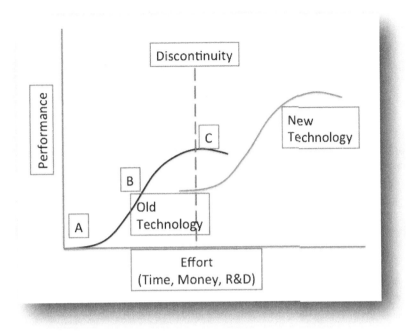

Figure 6.1: S-Curves Pattern of Innovation

This is represented in the second S-curve, the changeover or discontinuity between the old and new technologies is represented by the dotted line. Typically, both old and new technologies co-exist until the new technology becomes the dominant in the marketplace at which time the old technology cycle will be complete and the new technology cycle will begin.

## Innovation Streams

As mentioned previously, innovation is important to the survival of the organization. Companies that innovate are able to create competitive advantages; companies that can create streams of innovation are positioned to sustain competitive advantages. A company's competitive advantage becomes sustainable if other companies cannot duplicate the benefits obtained from that distinctive competence. However, technological innovation can enable competitors to duplicate the benefits obtained from a company's distinctive advantage. Hence, managers must be keenly aware that although they may possess a competitive advantage, technology is a great equalizer and their competitive advantage may become a competitive parity, or worse, a disadvantage.

In order to sustain a competitive advantage, companies must protect themselves from the strategic threat of innovation. The best way for a company to accomplish this is to create *innovation streams*, patterns of continuous innovation that over time can create sustainable competitive advantages. Figure 6.2 shows three such technological cycles. The cycle begins with a *technological discontinuity*, in which a unique combination of prevailing technologies or a scientific advance creates a substantial breakthrough in performance or function. Technological discontinuities are followed by a *discontinuous change*,

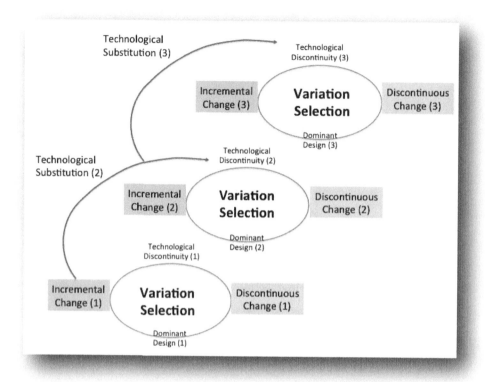

Figure 6.2: Innovation Streams

the phase of the cycle characterized by technological substitution and design competition. ***Technological substitution*** occurs when consumers purchase new technologies to replace older technologies.

One example of technological substitution is the change in consumer preferences in video rentals from the brick-and-mortar stores like Blockbuster and Hollywood video to on-demand, streaming services available through Netflix and Amazon. Both Blockbuster and Hollywood video experienced a phenomenon known as ***technological lockout***, which is the inability of a company to competitively sell its products because it relied on old technology or a non-dominant design.

Discontinuous change is further characterized by ***design competition***, wherein the old technology and several new technologies compete to become the technological standard. The competition at the design competition stage can become intense, as consumers are reluctant to switch to the new technology for the following reasons:

- The investment in the old technology is significant, as such companies will usually improve the performance or functionality of the old technology in response to the treat of the new technology in an attempt to hold the market for a longer period of time.
- The old and new technology is often times incompatible with each other; companies and consumers making the switch to the new technology may have to deal with compatibility issues.

The cycle continues with the emergence of a ***dominant design***, which becomes the new accepted market standard for technology. Dominant design may occur in several ways, one method is through *critical mass*, meaning that a particular technology can become the dominant design through sheer numbers of users. One recent example of dominant design occurred between Toshiba's HD DVD and Sony's Blu-ray for establishing the new format for high definition home video. Sony won the design competition when Warner Bros. decided to go exclusively with the Blu-ray technology. Retailers soon joined Warner Bros. deciding only to sell the Blu-ray equipment and movies. Dominant design can also emerge through independent standards bodies. The International Telecommunication Union (ITU) is an independent organization that establishes standards for the communications industry (Internet, telephone, satellites, and radio). Standards are discussed, proposed, negotiated, and changed until an agreement is determined on the final standards that communications industries worldwide will follow.

Within the innovation stream, dominant design is a key event; the emergence of dominant design indicates that innovation is both competence enhancing and competence destroying. Dominant design also signals a shift from design experimentation and competition to *incremental change*, a phase that is identified by lowering of costs and improving the functionality and performance of the dominant design. Some examples of incremental change are Microsoft's Windows 7 to Windows 8 or Apple's I-Phone 4S to the I-Phone 5S.

# Managing Innovation

Effective management during the technology cycles and innovation streams require two very different approaches. First, during the discontinuous change, managers must anticipate change and position the firm to survive the technological shifts that can suddenly transform industry leaders into industry losers. Second, following the emergence of a new dominant design, managers must focus on incremental improvements and innovation. Companies that can't manage incremental innovation will slowly weaken as they fall farther behind the industry leaders.

Unfortunately, what works well when managing innovation during discontinuous change doesn't work well when managing innovation during periods of incremental change.

### Managing the Sources of Innovation

Managing innovation is to manage where the ideas come from. Although it is impossible for companies to command their employees to be more creative, managers can assist innovation by building a creative work environment, one where workers realize that creative thoughts and ideas are not only welcomed but valued. A strong creative work environment has six components that encourage and drive creativity: challenging work, an organization that is encouraging, supervisors that are encouraging, work groups that are encouraging, freedom, and few of organizational obstacles (Figure 6.3).

1. *Challenging work*—Challenging work requires effort, demands attention and focus, and is recognized as important to others in the organization. A central element in creating a challenging work environment is to achieve a balance between skills and task challenge. Workers become bored when they can do more than what is required of them and apprehensive when their skills aren't sufficient to complete the task. When there is a balance between tasks and skills, creativity will occur.
2. *Encouragement*—A creative work environment requires three types of encouragement: organizational, supervisorial, and work groups. *Organizational encouragement* occurs when management

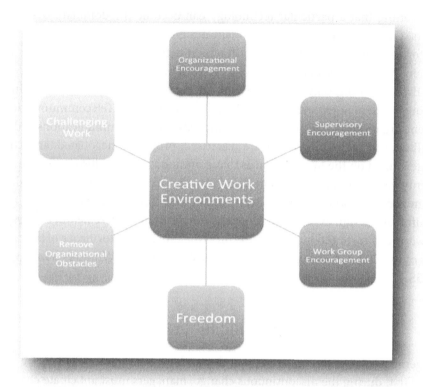

Figure 6.3: Components of a Creative Work Environment

promotes employees to be risk-takers seeking new ideas, supports and evaluate new ideas from employees equally, reward and recognizes creativity in employees, and supports and encourages the sharing of ideas throughout the entire organization. *Supervisory encouragement* supports innovation by providing clear goals, encouraging open interaction with other subordinates, and openly supporting the development team's work and ideas. *Work group encouragement* occurs when group members have experiences, education, and backgrounds that are diverse. Innovation is further supported when the group fosters a mutual openness to ideas, maintains positive and constructive challenges to ideas, and all share a deep commitment to ideas.

3. *Freedom*—Creativity thrives when management allows workers autonomy over their day-to-day work and control over their ideas.

4. *Remove organizational obstacles*—To foster creativity, companies should remove impediments to the workers environment. Obstacles to creativity such as internal conflict, power struggles, rigid management structures and a conservative bias toward a status quo position, discourage creativity.

**Managing Innovation during Discontinuous Change**

During periods of discontinuous change (characterized by technological substitution and design competition), companies that are successful have typically followed an ***experiential approach to innovation***. This approach assumes the innovation is occurring within a highly uncertain and dynamic environment and that the key to rapid product innovation is to use intuition, flexible options, and hands-on experience to mitigate uncertainty and accelerate both learning and understanding. The experiential approach has five characteristics: design iterations, testing, milestones, multi-functional teams, and powerful leaders.

*Design iteration* is a repetitive cycle wherein the company tests a prototype of a new product or service, from these tests improvements are then made to the design, after which, the improved design of the product prototype or service prototype is then tested. *Testing* is an essential step it the process as it compares the different product or service designs or design iterations systematically. Testing has several benefits: 1). Testing speeds up and improves the innovation process by testing product or service designs against each other, the new design iteration is tested against the previous iterations; strengths and weaknesses quickly become evident. 2). Testing uncovers errors in the design process making them easier and less costly to fix. 3). Testing accelerates learning and understanding by forcing engineers and product designers to examine hard data about the product performance. When there is compelling data that the prototypes are testing well, the confidence of the design team builds. Also, testing provides the performance data necessary for team members to make final decisions on product or service design.

*Milestones* are scheduled regular assessments on innovation project progress. By performing regular assessments, people know how well they are doing and whether or not corrective actions are required. Meeting or exceeding regular milestones is beneficial to the group members because it helps to build momentum by providing a sense of accomplishment. *Multi-functional teams* are teams that are composed of people from different functional departments of the organization. By involving all key departments (R&D, marketing, and manufacturing) in the development from the start, multi-functional teams are able to speed innovation, accelerate learning and understanding, and identify new ideas or problems. *Powerful leaders* are critical to the innovation process. Strong leadership provides the vision, discipline, motivation, and the essential resources that are essential in keeping the project on time and on target. On average, strong leadership can get innovation-related projects completed nine-months faster than leaders with little power or influence.

## Managing Innovation during Incremental Change

The *compression approach* is used to manage innovation in more certain and stable environments during periods of incremental change. The goals of the compression approach are to lower costs and incrementally improve products and/or services of the existing dominant design. The general strategy of the compression approach is to condense, as rapidly as possible, the time and steps needed to bring about small, consistent improvements in performance and functionality. Hence, the compression approach to innovation assumes that innovation is a predictable process and that incremental innovation can be planned using a series of steps, and that compressing the time it takes to complete those steps can speed up innovation. Similar to the experiential approach, the compression approach has five characteristics as well: planning, supplier involvement, shortening the time of individual steps, overlapping steps, and multi-functional teams.

*Planning* for incremental innovation involves a general strategy to create a series of planned steps to accomplish the compressing and reducing of the development time. A well conceived plan helps to avoid unnecessary steps and enables developers to sequence steps in the correct order to avoid wasted time and delays between process steps.

One way to shorten development time is to have ***supplier involvement***. Having a strong collaborative relationship with your suppliers reduces the amount of work that internal development teams must do. Suppliers can provide a good source of alternative ideas and expertise that can lead to better designs.

Another way to reduce development time is to ***shorten the time of individual steps*** in the innovation process. A common method used today to shorten the time is through computer-aided design (CAD). CAD allows designers and engineers to make and test changes using a computer program rather than physically testing expensive prototypes. With CAD, designers and engineers can 'see' how the new design will affect engineering, purchasing, and production. ***Overlapping steps*** reduce the development process by reducing the delays or waiting periods between the development steps.

# Defining Organizational Change

***Organizational change*** is simply the shift from its present state toward a desired state to increase performance and/or effectiveness. This can involve virtually any organizational segment, but typically affect the lines of organizational authority, the levels of responsibility held by various organizational members, and the established lines of organizational communication. The business environment is constantly dynamic and ever evolving, organizations must adapt to these changing events in order to survive.

In addition to organizational change, some degree of stability is required for an organization's long-term success. Figure 6.4 illustrates a model by Hellriegel and Slocum showing the relative importance of change and stability to organizational survival. The model stresses that organizational survival and growth are most probable when both stability and adaptation are high within the organization. The model also indicates that organizational survival is low when stability and adaptation (change) are low.

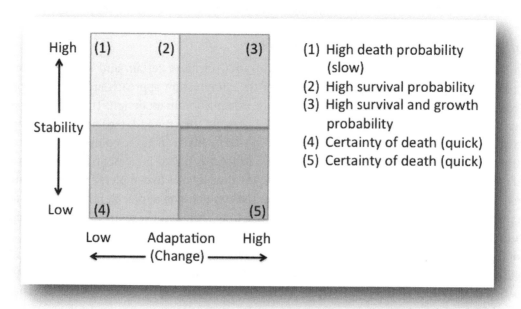

Figure 6.4: Stability/Adaptation Organizational Survival

# Drivers of Change

You may recall from Chapter 5 that many environmental forces have an effect on the firm performance. If managers are slow to respond to the effects of these forces the organizations perform will degrade and will begin to lag behind its competition.

*Competitive Forces* are a driver of change because unless the organization can match or exceed its competitors in at least one of its functional areas, it will not survive. Managers must continually work to achieve a competitive advantage over their rivals by performing their tasks in a more effective way.

Changing *Economic, Political, and Global Forces* affect organizations and compels them to adjust how and where they produce goods and provide services. No organization can afford to ignore the effects of the global economic and political forces on its interests. The effects of low-cost competitors and the development of new technologies erode a company's competitive advantage forcing companies to either take advantage of the low-cost inputs of labor and material from abroad or become uncompetitive.

Changing *Demographic and Social Forces* have motivated managers to find better ways to supervise and motivate minority and female employees. Through both equity in recruitment and an affirmative promotion process companies have had to change to accommodate the increasing diversity in the workplace. For example, companies have had to adapt to the changing needs of dual-career and single parent families by providing employees with childcare facilities and allowing flextime work hours. Many companies have helped employees stay current with the changing technology by providing advanced education and training.

*Ethical Forces* are driving companies to change their rules and SOP's to promote ethical behavior and to protect the interests and reputation of the organization and the people affected by unethical actions. Organizations are giving employees direct access to important decision makers and providing protecting for whistleblowers that expose ethical lapses in the organization. Additionally, firms must now consider how they are conducting business in a foreign country where bribery and sweatshops are common. Firms must take steps to impress on their employees that they should not engage in such kinds of behavior in order to protect the organization's interests.

# Resistance to change

Mark Twain once said, '*I'm all for progress, it's change I object to.*' In the last decade many of America's best-known companies such as Chrysler, General Motors, Kodak, Circuit City, Blockbuster, and Dell have seen their performance decline. Circuit City, Kodak, and Blockbuster have all gone bankrupt and Dell is in serious financial straits.

How did such large and well-established firms, Kodak was established in 1888, lose their ability to compete in the global marketplace? The main explanation for their decline in performance is most always the inability of an organization to change to the changing environmental conditions.

Logically we understand that in order for a firm to grow and improve the organization must adapt to changing environmental conditions. Hence, also logically, no organization can escape change. So, why do manager encounter resistance to change? Why do some level resist more than others? How should managers use their power to influence change? These are questions that have and will challenge managers for decades and decades to come.

People and organizations at all levels are prone to inertia, slow to learn, slow to adjust, and in general, do not like to change! The simple thought of change raises anxieties in people due to the fear economic loss, inconvenience, uncertainty, and a break in normal social patterns.

*Resistance to change* is caused by self-interest, misunderstanding and distrust, and general intolerance for change. The amount of resistance is proportional to the degree of discontinuity in the culture and/or the power structure introduced by the change. As well, the resistance will be inversely proportional to the time that the change is spread (Ansoff, 1979).

Researcher have identified five common reasons why people are resistance to change:

1. **Organizational inertia** is the tendency to have the status quo remain in place. Concerns that the company may be 'throwing good money after bad decisions' despite negative performance feedback. Most often resistance is due to the lack of understanding of what is happening or why changes are taking place. Employees may simply need accurate information as to the reasons for the change.

2. There may exist **systemic barriers** from the organization's structure. An organizational structure that is highly bureaucratic consisting of multiple layers, burdensome procedures, rigid rules and requirements will create a 'natural' barrier to change.

3. **Behavioral barriers** are those that are created by myopic managers and their inability to view issues or change unbiased. This barrier may be as a result of limited education, training, or work experience.

4. An outcropping of issue one is **political barriers**. Political barriers are those that arise from power conflicts such as vested interests, refusal to share information or resources, differences between departments or divisions and even personal differences.

5. Gresham's law of planning states *'that operational decisions will drive out the time necessary for strategic thinking and reflection'*. The fifth reason why people resist is **personal time constraints**, a barrier to change that stems from people not having the amount of time required for implementing strategic change.

## Reducing Resistance to Change

To ensure the success of needed change, managers must be able to reduce the effects of the resistance that typically is associated with change. The following steps can improve the likelihood of a successful change implementation:

1. *Invite employee participation in the process of change*—Participation allows everyone to give opinions, to feel a part of the change process, and to identify their own self-interests regarding the recommended change. Most importantly, those individuals who will be affected by a change should be involved in the decision to make the change and in decisions about how to implement the change

2. *Provide motivation and/or incentives to implement change*—Self-interest can be the most important motivator. Offer training and development workshops so that managers and employees can adapt to those changes

3. *Communication*—Effectively communicate the need for change. People can understand the purpose for the changes if the reasons are clearly stated and communicated.

4. *Provide a feedback loop*—Be transparent and open! Employees enjoy knowing how things are going and how much progress is being made.

5. *Avoid surprises*—Provide time for evaluation of the propose change by those who will be affected by the change before management implements it. Employees will be less resistant to change if they have been given time to absorb how the change will affect them. Whenever possible, individuals

who will be affected by a change should be informed of the kind of change being considered and the likelihood that the intended change will be adopted.

6. *Reduce fear of the change*—When fear of personal loss related to a proposed change is reduced, opposition of change is also reduced. People should be given information that will help them answer questions such as:

- Will I lose my job?
- Will I be required to learn new skills?
- Am I capable of producing effectively under the new system?
- Will my power and prestige be diminished?
- Will I have to work longer or different hours?
- Will I take on greater responsibility than I can assume?

Organizations that simply react to change will find their performance lacking. Organizations must consider change as a continuous process adapting to the shifts in their competitive environment rather than viewing change as a singular project or event. Therefore, managers must anticipate change and ideally be the creator of change.

## Lewin's Three Phases of Planned Change

Psychologist **Kurt Lewin** describes change as a function of the forces that promote change and the opposing forces that slow or resist change. These **change forces** lead to the differences in the form, quality, or condition of an organization over time. The opposite forces, known as **resistance forces** are those forces that support the status quo of the organization.

Managers seeking change in an organization can benefit from a simple but effective model developed by Lewin (Figure 6.5). The 3 phases of the Lewin model provide guidance on how to go about getting people to change: a manager will implement new processes and re-assign tasks, but change will only be effective if the people involved embrace it and help putting it into practice it.

*Phase 1—Unfreezing*—When a structure has been in place for a while, habits and routine have naturally settled in. The organization as a whole is going in the right direction, but people or processes may have strayed off course. For example, tasks that are not relevant or useful anymore are still being performed by force of habit, without anyone questioning their legitimacy. Similarly, people might have learned to do things one way, without considering other, more efficient methods. **Unfreezing** means getting people to gain perspective on their day-to-day activities, unlearn their bad habits, and open up to new ways of reaching their objectives. Basically, the current practices and processes have to be reassessed in order for the wheels of change to be set in motion.

*Phase 2—Changing*—Once the unfreezing phase has opened up the employee's minds to change, phase 2 can start. Phase 2 can be a very dynamic one and, if it is to be effective, it will probably take some time and involve a transition period. In order to gain efficiency, people will have to take on new tasks and responsibilities. This means a learning curve that will at first slow the organization down. A change process has to be viewed as an investment, both in terms of time and the allocation of resources: after the new organization and processes have been rolled out, a certain level of disorder might ensue, but that is the price to pay in order to attain enhanced effectiveness within the structure.

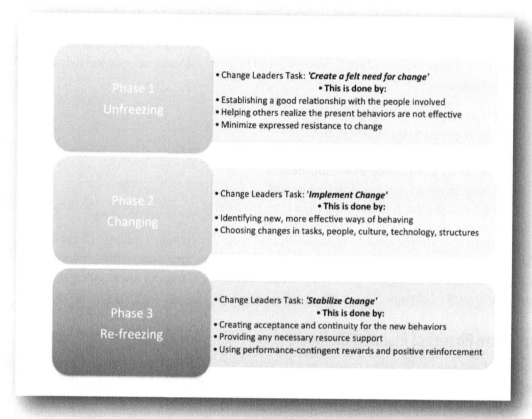

Figure 6.5: Lewin's 3- Phases of Planned Organizational Change

*Phase 3—Refreezing*—Change will only reach its full effect if it's made permanent. Once the organizational changes have been made and the structure has regained its effectiveness, every effort must be made to 'freeze' them and make sure the new organization becomes the standard. Linking change with rewards, positive reinforcement, and resource support all helps with refreezing.

## Change Strategies for Managers

When it comes to actually implementing organizational change, managers have available three common change strategies; coercive change strategy, shared power strategy, and rational persuasion strategy.

***Coercive change strategy*** involves the use of position power to create change by decree and formal authority, giving orders, and enforcing those orders to overcome resistance; this approach has the advantage of being fast, but low commitment, high costs, being extremely socially disruptive and causing high resistance plague it.

The second method of change is ***rational persuasion strategy***. Although change does not work to everyone's advantage, this approach attempts to convince individuals through rational argument,

| Change Strategy | Power Base | Managerial Behavior | Likely Results |
|---|---|---|---|
| Using position power to create change by decree and formal authority | Legitimacy Rewards Punishment | *Direct forcing* And unilateral action *Political maneuvering* And indirect action | Faster, but low Commitment and only Temporary compliance |
| Creating change through rational persuasion and empirical argument | Expertise | *Informational efforts* Using credible knowledge, demonstrated facts, and logical argument | |
| Developing support for change through personal values and commitments | Reference | *Participative efforts* To share power and involve others in planning and implementing change | Slower, but high Commitment and longer Term internalization |

Figure 6.6: 3 Change Strategies, Power Base & Behavior

information, facts, and special knowledge, that the overall benefit to change is to their personal advantage and when successful, change can be relatively easy to accomplish.

A *shared power strategy* is a collaborative approach that empowers people in a process of participation that identifies values, assumptions, and goals from which support for change will emerge. Although a shared power strategy is slow, the process is likely to yield high commitment. The change leader works together with others as a team to develop the consensus needed to support change. This requires being comfortable and confident in allowing others to influence decisions that affect the planned change and its implementation. Figure 6.6 summarizes the three common change strategies, force-coercion, rational persuasion, and shared power.

## Evaluating Change in the Organization

As with any managerial action, managers should evaluate the changes they make to not only gain insight into how the change itself might be adjusted but also to determine what steps should be taken the next time to increase the overall organizational effectiveness.

Evaluation from change often involves watching for symptoms that indicate further change is necessary. As an example, if people are reluctant to shift from past methods of task completion to the new methods or if they have greater allegiance to departmental goals than to the overall organizational goals, further change is necessary.

A word of caution is needed at this point. Although the symptom just provided generally indicate that further change is required, the decision to make additional change should not be made solely on that basis.

Decisions for further change should include other objective information such as increasing profitability, raising job satisfaction, increasing customer satisfaction, or contributing to the overall welfare of society.

## Stress and Change

Stress from change is a natural part of life. Unfortunately, without appropriate stress management it can have a negative affect any improvements that were anticipated from the change not to mention the affect on workers physical, mental, and emotional health. Therefore, understanding how change leads to stress, as well as how to manage that stress is an important part of leading a healthier, happier life.

*Stress* is the body's reaction to a change that requires a physical, mental or emotional adjustment or response. It can come from any situation or thought that makes you feel frustrated, angry, nervous, or anxious. A *stressor* is an environmental demand that causes people to feel stress. Stressors are common in situations where individuals are confronted by circumstances for which their usual behaviors are inappropriate or insufficient and where negative consequences are associated with failure to deal properly with the situation. Organizational change characterized by continual layoffs or firings is an obvious stressor, buy many other factors related to organizational policies, structure, physical conditions, and processed can act as stressors. In organizations, these 'stressor' cause the human body to unconsciously mobilize energy when confronted with the demands of work.

## Stress and Work

Job stress can wear on you nerves, cause sleepless nights, and contribute to health problems such as heart disease and depression. "Chronic job stress can put both your physical and emotional health at risk," says Paul J. Rosch, MD, the president of the American Institute of Stress. Controlling stress at work is important for several reasons:

1. Stress can have a damaging effect on employee's psychological and physiological health. It can limit employee's concentration and decision-making skills as well as decrease productivity. Stress is also associated with heart disease, increased psychiatric symptoms and adverse effects on family relationships.
2. Stress is a major factor in employee absenteeism and turnover.
3. A stressed employee can affect the safety of other workers or even the public.
4. Stress is expensive to organizations. Some estimates of the cost of stress to the U.S. economy are in excess of $150 billion per year. As such, many organizations spend a great deal of money treating stress-related employee problems through medical programs and legal fees when handling stress-related lawsuits.

Managers often find it difficult to identify the employees in the organization who are experiencing high levels of stress. Part of this difficulty stems from the fact that people respond differently to high stress and that the signs of physiological reactions, such as high blood pressure, pounding heart, and gastrointestinal disorders are difficult to observe or monitor.

Nevertheless, managers can learn to recognize several observable symptoms of undesirably high stress levels such as: constant fatigue, low energy, moodiness, increased aggression, excessive use of alcohol, temper outbursts, compulsive eating, high levels of anxiety, and chronic worrying.

Additionally, the following list provides 8 'risk of stress' employee types that managers should look for:

1. *The Overworked worker*—Employees are busy from the time they get to work until the time they leave and have little freedom while at work. Employees have say over how to do the work or the types of projects they are assigned.
2. *The Frustrated worker*—Employee that works his/her tail off to make their bosses look good, yet receives little to no credit—or compensation for their work.
3. *The Castaway worker*—Employee feels like they are all alone, and not in a good way. If they require help or guidance, the boss or supervisor won't give it to them, and when they need to vent there are no colleagues to turn to.
4. *The Doormat worker*—Employee's that constantly deal with demanding and verbally abusive customers yet are required to swallow any resentment they may feel and maintain a facade of professionalism, calm, and courtesy.
5. *The Technology-prisoner worker*—Thanks to the smartphone, laptop, and tablet your company has so generously provided, your boss can now reach you 24/7. This worker is constantly (if virtually) connected to the office, work and personal life now become indistinguishable.
6. *The Burned-out employee*—This employee is terminally exhausted, both physically and emotionally to the point where it becomes difficult to function. Employees at this stage feel as if they are on the verge of a breakdown.
7. *The abused employee*—This employee is a victim of the manager's insults often in front of their colleagues. Frequently given impossible deadlines to meet or assigned busywork just because the manager 'can'.
8. *The wronged victim worker*—For this employee work is not fair. The manager plays favorites and the decisions made by management are confusing and arbitrary. The manager treats the employees like children.

## Stress and Worker Performance

To deal with stress at work, managers must understand the relationship between the amount of stress felt by an employee and the employee's performance. Figure 6.7 illustrates the relationship between stress and performance. One will notice that both low and high stress has negative effects on performance and a certain level of stress is actually good for employee performance. In sum, an appropriate amount of stress is generally considered to be advantageous for the organization because it increases productivity. However, when employees experience too little or too much stress, productivity is negatively affected.

## Reducing Stress in the Workplace

Stress is difficult to reduce until the stressors causing it have been dealt with satisfactorily or eliminated from the environment. For example, if too much organizational change is creating conditions of high stress for workers, management may be able to reduce the level of stress by initiating a training program that is preparing workers for the demands of the new change, thus reducing worker anxiety. Management

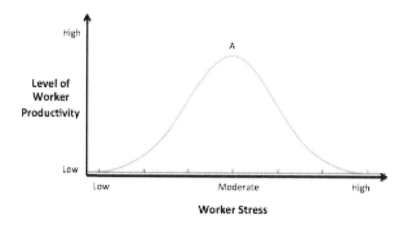

Figure 6.7: Relationship of Stress and Performance

may also curtail additional changes until the organizational culture as first 'absorbed' and adjusted to the current changes. The following four strategies are examples that management can adopt to mitigate the initial development of unwanted stressors in organizations:

1. *Create a climate of support for individuals*—Organizational climate clearly influences the success of an organization. Companies that utilize progressive human resource focus on supporting workers realized a greater impact on areas such as customer commitment, communication, empowerment, innovation, rewards and recognition, community involvement, environmental responsibility, and teamwork than organizations with less progressive practices.

2. *Initiate courses that focus on stress management*—Research has proven that employees who participated in a stress management course that focused on stress identification, coping strategies, and stress prevention, were less likely to become depressed than employees who did not participate. Clearly, the implementation of a stress management course could be beneficial for the whole workplace.

3. *Create stimulating jobs*—Jobs that are routine and mundane often do not allow employees any freedom of expression resulting in employee stress. Managers should strive to make employees jobs as interesting as possible to prevent the stressor stemming from a routine, boring job.

4. *Design and operate career-counseling programs*—Career path development can become a stressor for employees. If employees do not know what their next steps could be in their career development they may become discouraged and stressed. Designing and operating a career-counseling program that will assist employees with their next career path steps from both a realistic and achievable approach will reduce the stress levels.

## Conflict and Change

At times, organizational change will result in conflict. **Conflict** pertains to the opposing ideas and actions of different entities, thus resulting in an antagonistic state. Conflict is an inevitable part of life. Each of us possesses our own opinions, ideas and sets of beliefs. We have our own ways of looking at things and we act according to what we think is proper. Hence, we often find ourselves in conflict in different scenarios; may it involve other individuals, groups of people, or a struggle within our own selves. Consequently, conflict influences our actions and decisions in one-way or another.

However, managers are fortunate to have four useful techniques for handling conflict. These techniques are depicted in Figure 6.8 and include *compromising, avoiding, forcing,* and *resolving.* Each technique is discussed in the following sections.

One approach to resolving conflict is ***compromising***. Compromising is when the two sides agree on a solution to give up some of their demands for a solution that gives each party *part* of what they originally want. Managers who choose to compromise generally feel that a solution completely acceptable to everyone would be difficult to achieve and they would rather not force someone to accept a completely disagreeable choice. Compromise is appropriate to adopt as a conflict management technique if a planned change is relatively minor and the time to make an organizational change is somewhat limited.

The second technique that managers can adopt to manage conflict is ***avoiding***. As simple as it sounds, avoiding is a conflict management technique whereby managers choose to ignore the conflict. For example, if the R&D manager finds that the individuals in the production department are becoming a continual source of conflict because they are unwilling to provide any constructive feedback and resist proposed change, the manager can avoid dealing with the department. The manager can opt to propose and implement desirable change by dealing with others in the organization that may have power over the production department.

The avoiding strategy is logical if you assume that all conflict is bad. If you are successful in avoiding all conflict, the work environment could seem to be positive. However, managers often disagree and those with opposing viewpoints have important ideas that should be considered through conflict.

From an employee's viewpoint, manages who use the avoiding technique can be seen as irritating, puzzling, or unprofessional. It is important that managers give equal attention to the views of all employees, not just the views that are easily understood by the manager. Hence, to make sure that organizational change is designed and implemented most effectively and efficiently, a manager must ensure that employees know the manager wants to be aware of any employees' thoughts about how to improve organizational change.

The third technique available to managers is a more direct approach. ***Forcing*** is a technique for managing conflict in which managers use their authority to declare that conflict is over. In effect, this declaration ends any conflict because they have the authority to do so. As an example, a worker may complain to the manager that the recent changes are unfair because the worker has lost overtime hours. The manager can force closure on this issue by simply saying that 'I make the work assignments, and your job is to do what you are told.'

The advantage to forcing as a solution to conflict is that it is a relatively fast way to manage a conflict, and it may be the best approach in an emergency. The downside is that by forcing a conclusion to the conflict, employees may become frustrated and the frustration may build to form another later conflict.

The final technique used by managers in conflict management is ***resolving***. Resolving is the most direct and sometimes the most difficult solution in managing conflict. With this technique, the manager identifies the differences between the manager and the employees and then listens to the viewpoints of others in an honest effort to understand rather than argue. Next, both sides should identify the issues

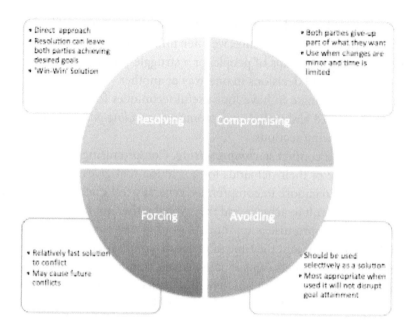

Figure 6.8: Techniques for Handling Conflict

about change on which they agree and the ways they can both benefit from implementing the change that reflects the ideas on which they agree. Both sides should be honest and diligent to reach a mutually agreed-upon, change related strategy.

Resolving is different from the other techniques as they tend to assume managers and employees are in a *win-lose conflict.* In other words, the outcome of the conflict will be that one side achieves a desired goal (wins) and the other side does not (loses). Resolving assumes that conflict can be *win-win conflicts,* wherein the conflict resolution can leave both parties achieving a desirable outcome and as such, help the organization maximize organizational success.

## Summary of Chapter

1. Technology cycles typically follow an S-curve pattern of innovation. Wherein early in the cycle, technological progress is slow and improvements ion technological performance is small. As technology matures, performance improves until the limit of technology is reached at which only incremental improvements occur.
2. The best approach to protect a competitive advantage is to create streams of innovative ideas and products.
3. Dominant design emerges because of critical mass and solve a practical problem, or because of the negotiation of independent standards bodies.
4. We discussed that technological innovation is both competence enhancing and competence destroying.

5. We learned that to successfully manage innovation streams, companies must manage the sources of innovation an learn to manage innovation during both discontinuous and incremental change.

6. This chapter covered the experiential approach to innovation, which assumes that intuition, flexible options, and hands-on experience can reduce uncertainty and accelerate learning and understanding.

7. The second approach to innovation was the compression approach. This approach works best during periods of incremental change and assumes that innovation can be planned using a series of steps and that compressing the time it takes to complete those steps can speed innovation.

8. We learned that Lewin's three phases of planned change are unfreezing, changing, and refreezing.

9. Resistance to change stems from self-interest, misunderstanding, distrust, and an intolerance for change but can be managed through education and communication, participation, negotiation, support, and coercion.

## Discussion Questions

1. What role should organizational stability play in the organizational change process?

2. Provide an example of how you might use 'unfreezing, change, and refreezing' in making specific organizational changes.

3. When is it better to pursue incremental change rather than discontinuous change?

4. Can the refreezing phase of planned change ever be completed in today's dynamic environment?

5. Should managers avoid the force-coercion change strategy altogether?

6. How do manager's responsibilities for change leadership vary among Lewin's phases of planned change?

7. What may be the differences in outcomes for managers using the force-coercion versus the shared power change strategies.

## References

Abernathy, W., & Utterback, J. (1978). 'Patterns of Industrial Innovation.' *Technology Review (2)*. 40–47.

Amabile, T. M., Conti, R., Lazenby, J. & Herron, M. (1966). 'Assessing the Work Environment for Creativity.' *Academy of Management Journal (39)* 1154–1184.

Anderson, P., & Tushman, M. L. (1991). 'Managing through Cycles of Technological Change. '*Research/Technology Management*. 26–31.

Deutschman, A. (2005). 'Making Change: Why is it so Darn Hard to Change Our Ways?' *Fast Company* (May) 52–62.

Duck, J. D. (1988). 'Managing Change: The Art of Balancing.' *Harvard Business Review on Change* (Boston: Harvard Business School Press). 55–81.

Eisenhardt, K. M. (1995). 'Accelerating Adaptive Processes: Product Innovation in the Global Computer Industry.' *Administrative Science Quarterly (40)*. 84–110.

Ettlie, J.E., & O'Keefe, R. D. (1982). 'Innovation Attitudes, Values, and Intentions in Organizations.' *Journal of Management Studies. (19)* 163–182.

'How Companies Overcome Resistance to Change.' (1972). *Management Review* 17–25.

Kahn, W. (2004). 'Facilitating and Undermining Organizational Change: A Case Study.' *Journal of applied Behavioral Science (40).* 7.

Kanter, R. M. (1989). 'The New Managerial Work.' *Harvard Business Review.* 85–92.

Kotter, J. P., & Schlesinger, L. A. (1979). 'Choosing Strategies for Change.' *Harvard Business Review.* 106–114.

Kotter, J. P. (1995). 'Leading Change: Why Transformation Efforts Fail.' *Harvard Business Review (73)* 59.

Lawless, M. W., & Anderson, P. C. (1996). 'Generational Technological Change: Effects of Innovation and Local Rivalry on Performance.' *Academy of Management Journal* (39). 1185–1217.

Lewin, K. (1951). *Field Theory in Social Science: Selected Theoretical Papers.* New York: Harper & Brothers.

Morgan, J. S. (1972). *Managing Change: The Strategies of Making Change Work for You.'* New York: McGraw-Hill.

Robertson, W. J., Roberts, D. R., & Porras, J. I. 'Dynamics of Planned Organizational Change: Assessing Empirical Support for a Theoretical Model.' *Academy of Management Journal. (36).* 619–634.

Rothwell, W. J., Sullivan, R., & McLean, G.M. (1995). '*Practicing Organizational Development: A Guide for Consultants.* San Diego: Pfeiffer & Co.

Selye, H. (1956). *The Stress of Life.* New York: McGraw-Hill.

Smereka, C. M. (1990). 'Outwitting, Controlling Stress for a Healthier Lifestyle.' *Healthcare Financial Management (44)* 70–75.

Tribus, M. (1989). 'Changing the Corporate Culture: A Roadmap for the Change Agent.' *Human Systems Management (8)* 11–22.

Van de Ven, A. H., & Poole, M. S. (1995). 'Explaining Development and Change in Organizations.' *Academy of Management Review.* (20) 510–540.

Zimmerman, J. H. (1995). 'The Principles of Managing Change.' *HR Focus.* 15–16.

# CHAPTER 7

## Managing Global Business and Trade

*"In Globalization 1.0, which began around 1492, the world went from size large to size medium. In Globalization 2.0, the era that introduced multinational companies, it went from size medium to size small. And then around 2000 came Globalization 3.0, in which the world went from being small to tiny."*

– Thomas Friedman

---

### Chapter Learning Objectives

After reading this chapter you should have a good understanding of:

- What is Global business and why is it important?
- What are Trade barriers and their impact on global business?
- What are Trade agreements and why are they important to countries?
- The importance of balancing global integration and local responsiveness

- The different ways that a company can organize to do business globally.
- The importance of identifying and adapting to cultural differences.
- The value and importance of Prof. Geert Hofstede's research on cultural differences.

# The Importance of Global Business

Everyday, we are all involved in global business. Consider the shoes you are wearing, the shirt and pants you have on, or even your cellphone. There is a high probability that all of these items were manufactured in different countries such as Vietnam, Indonesia, and Korea. The above quote is from author and columnist **Thomas Friedman** on his experiences he gained when on a business trip to India visiting the CEO of *Infosys*, a consulting and information technology company. During his trip, Friedman observed global business in action when the CEO, Nandan Nilekani showed him the company's global videoconference room equipped with multiple, wall-sized, flat screen TV's. Above each screen were clocks, one for each region in which *Infosys* conducts business (eastern U.S., western U.S., Greenwich Mean Time, India, Singapore, Hong Kong, Japan, and Australia). These clocks served as a reminder to employees that Infosys works 24/7/365. CEO Nilekani stated 'that's what globalization is all about today,' the ability to bring together those key players from the company's entire global supply chain to discuss any project, at a moment's notice.

Infosys isn't unique; there are thousands of other multinational firms that conduct business by selling products and services worldwide with managers and employees from different continents working together as seamlessly as if they were in the same building.

# Global Business and its Impact

**Business** is the activity of making, buying, or selling products or providing services in exchange for money. As an example, when you bought your cellphone, or computer it was a business transaction, work you perform and are paid for is a business transaction. **Imports** are goods and services produced in a foreign country and bought by U.S. residents. It includes all goods that are shipped into the U.S., even if produced by an American company. If the consumer is a U.S. resident, and the provider is a foreign resident, then it is an import. **Exports** are any good or services that passes through customs from the U.S. to be sold overseas. This includes merchandise shipped from a U.S. based company to its foreign affiliate or branch.

 **Global Business** consists of transactions that are developed and completed across national borders to satisfy the objectives of individuals, companies, and organizations. In short, it is the buying and selling of products or services by people from different countries.

This chapter examines global business from three perspectives. First, what is the impact that global business has on businesses in the U.S. Second, we look at the basic framework of the rules and agreements that govern global trade. Finally, we consider how to find the best global business climate and how to adapt to its cultural differences.

*Multinational Corporations (MNC)* are corporations that have facilities and other assets in at least one country other than its home country. MNC's have offices and/or factories in different countries and usually have a centralized head office where they co-ordinate global management. Very large multinationals such as 3M, Coca-Cola, Intel, and American Express have budgets that exceed those of many small countries.

Multinational corporations can be found in every country in the world. In 1990 there were about 30,000 multinational companies. Today there are more than 60,000, and while the number of multinational companies continues to grow, their average size is falling.

The level of *foreign direct investment* also impacts global business. Foreign direct investment occurs when a company builds new business (*greenfield investment*) or buys an existing business (*brownfield investment*) in a foreign country.

Foreign direct investment can be achieved ether by setting up a subsidiary or associate company in the foreign country, by acquiring shares of an overseas company, or through a merger or joint venture. The accepted threshold for a foreign direct investment relationship, as defined by the OECD, is 10%. That is, the foreign investor must own at least 10% or more of the voting stock or ordinary shares of the investee company. An example of foreign direct investment would be an American company taking a majority stake in a company in Vietnam. Another example would be a Chinese company setting up a joint venture to harvest lumber contracts in Brazil. Whether U.S companies invest abroad or foreign companies invest in the U.S, direct foreign investment is an integral and common approach in conducting global business strategy.

## Barriers to Trade

Is it important from where you buy your products? Most consumers really don't think of or care where the products they buy originate. However, national governments do! For economic reasons governments prefer that consumers buy products that are domestically made in hopes that such purchases would increase the number of domestic businesses and workers. One method that governments can use to leverage their will is to use *trade barriers*. A trade barrier is a form of restriction used to control the amount of trade that one economy conducts with another economy, either for selfish or altruistic purposes. Typically, trade barriers make it more expensive or more difficult for consumers to buy or consume imported goods. For example, the U.S. government artificially inflates sugar prices by imposing quotas that cap the amount that food manufacturer and consumers in the United States can buy from producers in other countries. If a bakery or a candy company wants to import more sugar than is allowed under the government's quota, it must pay a prohibitive tariff of 15.36 cents per pound for raw sugar. At current prices, that works out to a whopping 62 percent tariff rate. By imposing these restrictions and taxes, the U.S government is engaging in *protectionism*, which is the use of a trade barrier to protect local companies and their workers from foreign competition.

Generally, there is two kinds of trade barriers governments can use: *tariff* and *non-tariff* barriers. A tariff is a direct tax imposed on imported goods and services. There are two types of tariffs; *specific tariff* and *ad-valorem tariff*.

Each tariff is a tool used to restrict trade as they increase the price of imported goods and services, making them more expensive to consumers. Ad-valorem tariff is levied based on the item's value. As an example; if the ad-valorem tariff on a Mercedes Benz is 10 percent, this means that the U.S consumer must pay $27,500 for an imported car valued at $25,000, with $2,500 going to the U.S government. A specific tariff is levied as a fixed fee based on the type of item (e.g., $1,000 on any car).

*Non-tariff barriers* are a method of increasing the costs or reducing the volume on imported good. There are many different types of non-tariff barriers including; quotas, voluntary export restraints, government import standards, government subsidies, embargoes, sanctions, and customs valuation/classification. One of the most important non-tariff barriers is the **Quota**. A Quota is a direct quantitative restriction on the amount allowed of a commodity to be imported or exported. There are two types of quotas; absolute and tariff-rate quotas. *Absolute quotas* are quotas that limit the amount of a specific product that may enter a country. *Tariff-rate quotas* allow a quantity of a good to be imported under a lower duty rate; any amount above this is subject to a higher duty.

Similar to quotas are *voluntary export restraints* (VER's). This is a self-imposed limit placed on the export of a good to another country. Typically, VER's are a result of requests made by the importing country to provide a measure of protection for its domestic businesses that produce substitute goods. VER's are often created because the exporting country would prefer to impose their own restrictions than risk sustaining worse terms from tariffs and/or quotas.

One of the most notable VER's occurred in the 1980's when Japan imposed a VER on its auto exports into the U.S. as a result of American pressure. The VER gave the U.S. auto industry some protection against a flood of Japanese cars. One strategy companies use to avoid VER's is to build a manufacturing plant in the country to which it exports. By doing so, the company will no longer need to export and should not be bound by the country's VER's.

*Government import standards* were established to protect the health and safety of the consumers. However, such standards have been used to restrict or ban imported goods. For example; Canada controls the import of dairy, chicken, eggs, and turkey in part for consumer safety and also for control of foreign competition.

Many governments use *subsidies* to develop and protect companies in special industries. Subsidies are benefits given by the government to companies usually in the form of a cash payment or tax reduction. The purpose of the subsidy is usually to remove some type of burden (competitive disadvantage) and is often considered to be in the interest of the public. For example, the farming industry may receive government subsidies to compete in a highly competitive international industry with low prices, by providing cash subsidies to farms they can sell at the low market price and still achieve financial gain.

The previously discussed controls were mainly focused at a particular industry. An *embargo* is focused at restricting trade or commerce for the entire country. Typically an embargo is established as a result of unfavorable political or economic circumstances between nations restricting anyone from exporting to the target nation. Because many nations rely on global trade, an embargo is a powerful tool for influencing a nation. One of the longest embargos is between the U.S and Cuba. This embargo dates back over 54 years as a reaction to events of the Cuban revolution and the missile crisis.

*Sanctions* are a tool used by countries or international organizations to persuade a particular government or group of governments to change their policy by restricting trade, investment or other commercial activity. There are two types of sanctions; economic and trade. *Economic sanctions* are punitive in nature and

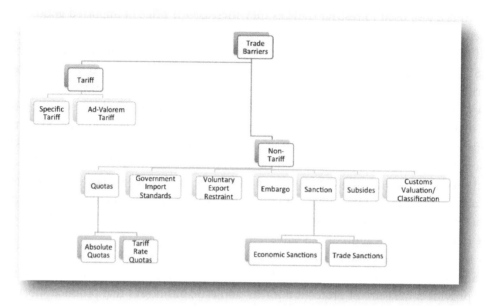

Figure 7.1: Barriers to International Trade

meant to isolate the target. Economic sanctions may include trade embargoes or boycotts, freezing of assets, bans on cash transfers, bans on technology transfer and restrictions on travel. The US Government has placed sanctions against North Korea, Cuba, and Iran among other countries. *Trade sanctions* are the most common kind and are the least onerous. They could be revocation of preferential treatment such as Most Favored Nation (MFN) status or import quotas against a country not abiding by agreed international rules of trade. Some recent examples of sanctions are; UN Security Council supported economic sanctions against North Korea for their possession of nuclear weapons. In 1980, President Carter boycotted the Moscow Olympics can be viewed as sanctions in protest against the invasion of Afghanistan by the Soviet Union.

The last type of nontariff barrier is *customs valuation/classification*. As products are imported into a country, customs agents examine them and decide into which of nearly 9,000 categories they should be assigned. Classification is important because the category assigned by the agent can affect the size of the tariff and whether the item is subject to import quotas. Figure 7.1 illustrates the various trade barriers discussed in this section.

# Trade Agreements

*Trade agreements* are when two or more nations agree on the terms of trade between them. There are many different types of trade agreements. The easiest and most numerous of trade agreements are the *Bilateral trade agreements* as they are negotiated between two countries. The more difficult trade agreement is the *multi-lateral trade agreement*, as these are between three countries or more.

So, why do trade barriers and trade agreements matter to consumers? Trade agreements increase the consumer's choices, competition, and purchasing power and as such, lower the amount that they pay for clothing, food, luxuries, and necessities. With these obvious benefits, consumers care little where their products and services come from.

In an effort to regulate trade and reduce tariffs and other trade barriers the *General Agreement on Tariffs and Trade (GATT)* was implemented to further regulate world trade to aide in the economic recovery following World War II. GATT's main objective was to reduce the barriers of international trade through the reduction of tariffs, quotas, and subsidies. GATT, which existed from 1947 to 1995 was eventually replace by the *World Trade Organization (WTO)* in 1995, the objectives remains the same as the GATT, that of encouraging international trade. The WTO is headquartered in Geneva, Switzerland and has three main objectives; it provides a forum for negotiating trade, administers trade agreements, and it helps to settle trade disputes.

- *Negotiating forum*—the WTO is a place where member governments go, to try to sort out the trade problems they face with each other. The first step is to talk. The WTO was born out of negotiations, and everything the WTO does is the result of negotiations. For example; where countries have faced trade barriers and wanted them lowered, the negotiations have helped to liberalize trade.
- *Administers Trade agreements*—WTO's overriding purpose is to help trade flow as freely as possible so long as there are no undesirable side effects. Because this is important for economic development and wellbeing it means removing obstacles to trade. It also means safeguarding that individuals, companies and governments know what the trade rules are around the world and giving them the confidence that there will be no sudden changes of policy.
- *Settle trade disputes*—Trade relations often involve conflicting interests represented in complex agreements. At times the WTO may be called upon to interpret these agreements for clarification and to settle these differences through some neutral procedure based on an agreed legal foundation.

Figure 7.2 provides a brief overview of the WTO and its functions.

Location: Geneva, Switzerland
Established: 1 January 1995
Created by: Uruguay Round
negotiations (1986-94)
Membership: 159 countries on 2
March 2013
Budget: 196 million Swiss
francs for 2011
Secretariat staff: 640
Head: Roberto Azevêdo
(Director-General)

Functions:
• Administering WTO trade agreements
• Forum for trade negotiations
• Handling trade disputes
• Monitoring national trade policies
• Technical assistance and training for developing countries
• Cooperation with other international organizations

Figure 7.2: The World Trade Organization

# Regional Trading Zones

*Regional trading zones* were developed to reduce or eliminate the tariff and nontariff trade barriers between countries within the trading zone. The largest and most important trading zones are in Europe (Maastricht Treaty), North America (the North America Free Trade Agreement, NAFTA), Central America (Central America Free Trade Agreement, CAFTA-DR), South America (Union of South American Nations, UNASUR), Asia (the Association of Southeast Asian Nations, ASEAN), and Asia-Pacific Economic Cooperation, (APEC).

The ***Maastricht Treaty*** (formally known as the Treaty on European Union), was signed on February 7, 1992, and created the European Union. The treaty consisted of three main pillars: the *European Communities*, a *common foreign and security policy*, and *enhanced cooperation in home (domestic) affairs and justice.*

On January 1, 2002, a single common currency, the euro, went into circulation and today 18 EU members circulate it (Austria, Belgium, Cyprus, Estonia, Finland, France, Germany, Greece, Ireland, Italy, Latvia, Luxembourg, Malta, the Netherlands, Portugal, Slovenia, Slovakia, and Spain).

The treaty changed the name of the European Economic Community to the European Community (EC), which became the primary component of the new ***European Union (EU)***. The EU was not always as big as it is today. When European countries started to cooperate economically in 1951, only Belgium, Germany, France, Italy, Luxembourg and the Netherlands participated. Today, the EU's current size is 28 member countries with the accession of Croatia on 1 July 2013. (Figure 7.3)

Figure 7.3: Map of EU Member Nations

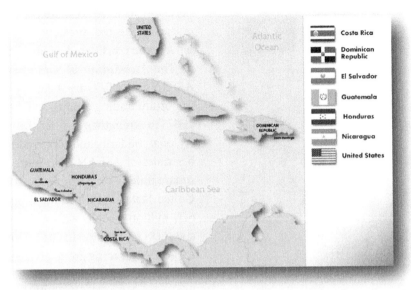

Figure 7.4: Map of CAFTA-DR Member Nations

In 1994, a comprehensive trade agreement was established between the United States, Canada, and Mexico. The **North American Free Trade Agreement (NAFTA)** created one of the world's largest free trade zones and set the foundation for a strong economic growth and rising prosperity by systematically eliminating most tariff and non-tariff barriers to free trade and investment between the three member countries. The benefits to the member nations are impressive with both Canada and Mexico exports to the U.S up over 240 percent and the U.S exports to Mexico and Canada up over 170 percent, twice the growth rate of U.S exports to any other part of the world.

The **Dominican Republic-Central America-United States Free Trade Agreement (CAFTA-DR)** was signed on August 5, 2004 with five Central American countries (Costa Rica, El Salvador, Guatemala, Honduras, and Nicaragua) and the Dominican Republic Figure 7.4). This was the first agreement facilitating trade and investment between the U.S and a group of smaller developing countries that created new economic opportunities for the member states by eliminating tariffs, opening markets, reducing barriers to services, and promoting transparency. The combined populations of the CAFTA-DR countries exceeds 48.2 million and together are the seventh largest U.S export market in the world and third largest U.S export market in Latin America, after Mexico and Brazil.

The **Union of South American Nations (UNASUR)** is an intergovernmental body modeled after the European Union. Known as UNASUR, the group acts as a forum for interaction between member-country leaders and also serves as a platform for interregional trade promotion. Its purpose is to develop a South American forum for addressing political, social, economic, environmental and infrastructure issues that will reinforce the identity of South America and will contribute to the strengthening of Latin America and the Caribbean. One aim of UNASUR is to create free movement between nations creating a common infrastructure that includes an interoceanic highway and eliminating all tariffs by 2019.

The current UNASUR members are illustrated in Figure 7.5: Argentina, Bolivia, Brazil, Chile, Colombia, Ecuador, Guyana, Suriname, Peru, Uruguay, and Venezuela. UNASUR countries suspended

Figure 7.5: Map of UNASUR Member Nations

Paraguay in June 2012 after the country's democratically elected president was impeached in what some considered a constitutional coup.

The *Association of Southeast Asian Nations, ASEAN* and *APEC* are Asia's two largest and most important trading groups. ASEAN was founded in 1967 "to strengthen further the existing bonds of regional solidarity and cooperation." The ten member states of ASEAN span more than 1.7 million square miles—over half the size of the continental United States—and include a population of over 626 million people with an economy valued at about US $2.4 trillion in 2012. Current members of the ASEAN trading group are; Brunei Darussalam, Cambodia, Indonesia, Laos, Malaysia, Myanmar, the Philippines, Singapore, Thailand, and Vietnam (Figure 7.6). An ASEAN free trade area will begin in 2015 for the six original countries (Brunei Darussalam, Indonesia, Malaysia, the Philippines, Singapore, and Thailand) and in 2018 for the newer member nations.

The *Asia-Pacific Economic Cooperation Organization (APEC)* is comprised of 21 of the world's leading economies, including the United

Figure 7.6: Map of ASEAN Member Nations

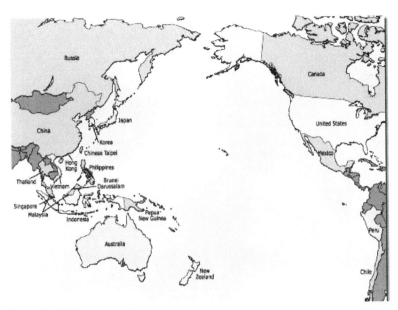

Figure 7.7: Map of APEC Member Nations

States, China, Japan, Australia, Canada, Mexico, Singapore and others who have come together to facilitate economic growth and shared strategic objectives. APEC's 21 Member Economies account for more than two-thirds of the world's population and over 50 percent of the global trade.

APEC full list of members are Australia; Brunei Darussalam; Canada; Chile; People's Republic of China; Hong Kong, China; Indonesia; Japan; Republic of Korea; Malaysia; Mexico; New Zealand; Papua New Guinea; Peru; The Republic of the Philippines; The Russian Federation; Singapore; Chinese Taipei; Thailand; United States of America; Viet Nam (Figure 7.7)

APEC's broad agenda covers topics such as social security, corporate governance, environmental issues, trade and investment; energy and climate change, food supply, security, disaster readiness, and IPR protection and transparency

### Going Global—Integration or Local Responsiveness?

Once a company has decided to go global it has the choice of four basic strategies to enter and compete in the global environment: *multi-domestic strategy*, a *global strategy*, an *international strategy*, and a *transnational strategy*.

Each of these strategies has their advantages and disadvantages depending on the firm's approach to global integration or to local responsiveness. ***Global integration*** is the coordination of the firm's value chain activities across countries to achieve worldwide efficiencies, synergies, and **cross-fertilization** (a strategy wherein firm's can improve innovation and boost revenue and profitability through collaboration with key suppliers and other companies closely tied to their operation) in order to take maximum advantage of similarities between countries. ***Local responsiveness*** requires meeting the specific needs of buyers in different countries. Figure 7.8 depicts the four basic approached to going global.

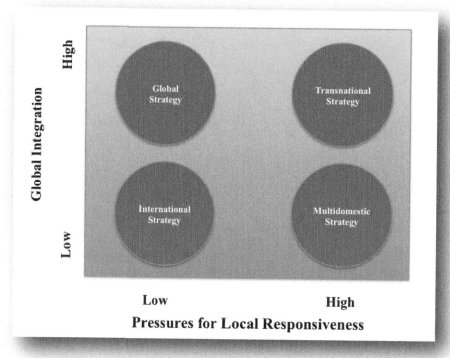

Figure 7.8: Four Basic International Strategies

## Multi-domestic Strategy

*Firms pursuing a multi*domestic strategy (sometimes called a *multi-local strategy*) focus on achieving maximum local responsiveness. One key distinguishing feature of the multi-domestic strategy is the extensive focus on product offerings, customization, and marketing strategy to match the different local markets rather than taking a more universal or global approach.

This means that companies employing a multi-domestic strategy will seek to recognize the culture of various local markets and adapt their products into those markets based on the demographic needs of that area. With this approach, a great deal of effort is made to adapt advertising and presentation to appeal to local need.

Supporting this strategy, the firm usually establishes a complete set of value creation activities including production, marketing, and R&D and distribution process in each major national market in which they conduct business as well as allowing a considerable level of autonomy to each country manager.

With the multidomestic strategy, country managers recognize and emphasize differences between each national market allowing each to vary the products and management practices specific for each country.

The multidomestic approach is usually more expensive to implement, finds difficulty leveraging its core competencies and infrequently gain benefits from the experience curve or location economies. Additionally, the multidomestic strategy takes time to research the specific needs and interests of each individual market and to design and develop a unique strategy for each country.

The multi-domestic strategy makes sense for companies competing in the food and beverage, consumer products, and clothing industries, where consumers require local responsiveness to their needs and there is little pressure for following a low-cost strategy.

*Key point of the Multi-domestic Strategy*

- Product is customized for each market.
- Decentralized control—allowing local decision-making.
- Multi-domestic strategy is most effective when there are large differences that exist between countries.
- Advantages: product differentiation, local responsiveness, minimized political risk, minimized exchange rate risk.

## Global Strategy

Firms pursuing a **Global strategy** focus on increasing profitability by achieving the cost reductions that come from the experience curve and location economies. With the Global strategy the production, marketing, and R&D functions are concentrated in a few select locations. Unlike the Multi-domestic strategy, the Global strategy tends not to customize their product offerings and marketing strategy to the local conditions as both increase costs. The global approach is to market a standardized product globally to obtain the benefits from economies of scale and the experience curve. This strategy makes sense when the firm is under cost reduction pressures and negligible demand for local responsiveness.

The Global strategy is found most often in industrial goods, such as the semiconductors, aerospace, automobiles, metals, chemicals, telecommunications, and industrial equipment, but is limited in the consumer goods industry where the demand for local responsiveness is high.

*Key points of the Global Strategy*

- The firm products are the same in all countries.
- Centralized control - negligible decision-making authority on the local level.
- Global strategy is most effective when differences between countries are limited.
- Advantages: cost, coordinated activities, faster product development.

## International Strategy

Firm's early in their internationalization strategies may pursue a natural extension of their current domestic business strategy by extending their domestic product offerings internationally to generate incremental sales. One such method is through **exporting**, one of the oldest forms of economic transfer whereby goods produced in one country are then shipped to another country for future sale or trade.

The international strategy is beneficial if a firm has valuable core competencies that native competitors' in foreign markets lack and if the firm confronts relatively weak pressures for local responsiveness and cost reductions. One challenge facing this strategic approach is that duplication of manufacturing facilities may occur creating higher operating costs making this strategy inappropriate for firms in the manufacturing industry where cost pressures are high.

Toys "R" Us, McDonald's, IBM, Kellogg, Proctor & Gamble, Wal-Mart, and Microsoft are all examples of firms that have created value by transferring differentiated product offerings developed at home to new markets overseas.

## Transnational Strategy

*Unlike the International* strategy where the flow of products in in one direction, originate in the home country and are exported to the foreign countries, the transnational strategy is a coordinated approach *to* internationalization based on capitalizing the firm's worldwide capabilities that are develop in any of the firm's worldwide operations.

A transnational organization is also known as a *global organization,* considers the entire world as its business area as such national borders are inconsequential. Transnational organizations represent the maximum level of international activity as depicted on the continuum of international involvement. Firm's following a transnational strategy will have products ship from the home country to the foreign subsidiaries and from the foreign subsidiaries to the home country, as well as from the foreign subsidiaries to other foreign subsidiaries. This process is referred to as **Global learning**. Aware of great opportunities in the global marketplace, some MNC's have transformed themselves form home-based companies with worldwide interests into worldwide companies pursuing business activities across the globe and having no claim or loyalty to any one country.

A transnational strategy makes strategic sense when a firm faces high pressures for cost reductions, high pressures for local responsiveness, and significant opportunities to leverage its distinct competencies within a multinational global network of operations.

Transnational strategy implies a flexible approach to standardize where feasible and adapt where appropriate. Managers implement transnational strategy by:

- Exploiting scale economies by sourcing from a reduced set of global suppliers.
- Concentrating the production of product offerings in few locations where a competitive advantage exists.
- Organizing production, marketing, and other value-chain activities on a global scale.
- Optimizing local responsiveness and flexibility.
- Facilitating global learning and knowledge transfer.
- Coordinating the firms competitive moves.

Firms which follow the transnational strategy are in some ways trying to simultaneously reduce costs and increase value, this type of approach is difficult to achieve as pressures for local responsiveness raise costs and internally, battling cost and differentiation, place conflicting demands on the firm.

Transnational strategy requires planning, resource allocation, and uniform policies on a global basis. Building an organization that is capable of supporting a transnational strategic posture is a complex and difficult task as firms become bogged down trying to optimize both cost and global integration.

Examples of firms competing using the transnational strategy are: IKEA, Caterpillar, Dow Chemicals, and Standard Chartered.

Global business requires a balance between integration and local responsiveness. Global integration mean coordinating the firm's value chain activities across countries to achieve worldwide efficiencies, synergies, and cross-fertilization in order to take maximum advantage of similarities between countries. Local responsiveness requires meeting the specific needs of buyers in different countries by recognizing the local culture and markets and adapting their products to those markets based on the demographic needs of that area.

# Forms of Global Business

Firms have multiple options available when deciding to expand internationally. The central primacy for managers when selecting which mode of entry is the trade-off between *risk and control*. Entry risk takes two forms: *financial* and *marketing*. Typically, **financial risk** is the major consideration at the point of market entry and is that which is minimized by low-intensity modes of market participation.

However, this reduced risk comes at the price of low control over the business strategy. As an example, exporting or licensing with a local distributor requires no investment in the country-market in the form of offices, distribution facilities, sales personnel, or marketing campaigns, low financial risk. This arrangement also affords a minimum level of control to the firm since the company will have little or no involvement in most elements of the marketing, distribution, and service standards. Hence, low intensity modes of entry minimize financial risk.

Firms that seek a high level of control and are acceptant to the increased level of risk can select a higher-intensity mode of market entry involving investments in local executives, distribution, and marketing programs. It must be clearly stated that control only comes from involvement, and involvement only comes from investment. The variety of entry modes and risk-control tradeoff can be distinguished on Figure 7.9.

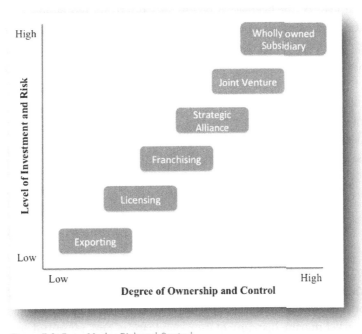

Figure 7.9: Entry Modes Risk and Control

*Exporting* is the marketing and sales of domestically produced goods from one country to another foreign market. This entry mode option is the lowest risk, requiring the least amount of investment available to a firm.

Since exporting does not require production in the foreign country, no investment in facilities is required. Most of the costs associated with exporting take the form of marketing expenses. Many countries dislike this entry approach because it provides less local employment than other entry modes.

Foreign markets typically are nationally regulated and dominated by networks of local intermediaries; as such firms should collaborate with local distributors to benefit from their expertise and knowledge in effort to create a win-win relationship.

## Cooperative Contracts

One method available to companies who wish to expand globally without making a large financial commitment is to sign a *cooperative contract* with a foreign business owner who pays the company a fee for the right to conduct that business in their country. There are two types of cooperative contracts: licensing, and franchising.

*Licensing* is an entry mode that essentially permits a company in the foreign country (licensee) to use intellectual property (IP) of the licensor in exchange of a royalty or fee. Typically, such property is an intangible such as a trademark, patent, trade secret, or other valuable item of intellectual property.

Licenses are typically non-exclusive, which means they can be sold to multiple competing companies serving the same market. In this arrangement, the licensing company may exercise control over how its IP is used but does not control the business operations of the licensee.

Licensing benefits the licensor because this mode requires little investment or risk and has the potential to provide a very large ROI. The licensee also benefits from the potential returns from manufacturing and marketing activities and gaining a competitive advantage. Examples of licensing include Microsoft's Office Suite, Disney's character Donald Duck, and Michael Jordan licensing his name to Nike.

*Franchising* is a specialized form of licensing in which the *franchisor* not only sells an independent *franchisee* the use of the intangible property (usually a trademark) but also operationally assists the business on a continuing basis through sales promotion, branding, marketing support, and training.

With this mode of entry, the franchiser maintains a considerable degree of control over the operations and processes used by the franchisee. The franchiser also ensures that branches do not cannibalize each other's revenues. Well recognized examples of franchising include: McDonalds, Subway, 7–11, and Dunkin Donuts.

## Strategic Alliances

*Strategic alliances* are partnerships in which two or more companies work together to achieve objectives that are mutually beneficial. *Garmin*, which makes satellite navigation devices, and *Volvo Penta*, which makes leisure and commercial boat engines and propulsion systems have formed a strategic alliance to jointly develop and market marine instrumentation, navigation, and communication equipment.

One major advantage of global joint ventures is that companies may share resources, information, capabilities and risks to achieve a common goal. A common reason for entering into a strategic alliance is to obtain the advantage of another company's innovations without having to invest in new research and development. While companies have used acquisition to accomplish some of these goals in the past, forming a strategic alliance is more cost-effective.

*Eli Lilly* is another example of an international firm with successful strategic alliances. Lilly has aligned with the Belgium-based company *Galapagos* to develop treatments for osteoporosis and in Japan, Lilly has partnered with *Kyowa Hakko Kogyo Co., Ltd.*, to bring a targeted cancer treatment to market. This alliance will allow Lilly the exclusive license to develop and sell the product worldwide except in Japan, and the two companies will share rights in certain Asian countries.

The most common type of strategic alliance is a ***joint venture***, which occurs when two existing companies collaborate to form a third company. The two founding companies remain intact and unchanged except that together they now own the newly created joint venture.

Joint ventures may be formed between companies that produce similar products and generate revenue in similar ways. For instance, though they are technically competitors, *Jaguar Land Rover* and Chinese automobile manufacturer *Chery Automotive* have engaged in a joint venture to develop a new manufacturing facility in Changshu, China in 2014. The joint venture, known as *Chery Jaguar Land Rover Automobile Company* is intended to blend together the heritage and experience of luxury premium vehicle manufacturer Jaguar Land Rover with the intricate knowledge and understanding of Chinese customers evident at Chery.

Managing global joint ventures can be difficult because they result in the merging of four cultures: the country and organizational culture of the first partner, and the country and organizational culture of the second partner. Because of the potential for problems to develop, companies considering global joint ventures should carefully develop detailed contracts that specify the responsibilities of each party.

## Wholly Owned Affiliates

The ***wholly owned affiliate*** is an entry mode with the highest level of risk as well as the highest level of control of all entry strategies. A wholly owned subsidiary is a company whose common stock is 100% owned by the parent company. If successful, the payoff for such a risk can be enormous. However, the losses can be equally great if the affiliate fails. One example of such a risk was with *Deutsche Telekom*, the largest telecommunications company in Europe and their acquisition of *T-Mobile USA*. T-Mobile had reported modest performance for almost a decade but more recently began to lose customers because it did not carry the i-Phone. In 2010 alone, the company lost nearly 400,000 fixed-contract customers and had twice as many customers not renew their contracts as its next nearest competitor. The poor performance of T-Mobile contributed to a 37 percent drop in profits for Deutsch Telekom and the eventual sale of T-Mobile to AT&T for $39 billion.

In many cases companies can create ***subsidiaries*** wherein the parent company has from 51 to 99 percent ownership, this is done to retain complete control of their technology. A company can become a wholly owned subsidiary through acquisition by the parent company or spin off from the parent company. **Affiliates** are those companies wherein the parent company only possesses less than 50 percent, or a minority stake in the ownership of the company in a foreign country.

# Determining the Optimal Global Market

Deciding what method to use to go global is important, equally important is deciding *where* to go global. When making this decision companies search for those countries or regions with the most promising business climate.

Two factors help companies determine the growth potential of foreign markets: purchasing power of the market and level of risk.

**Purchasing power** is measured by comparing the relative cost of a standard set of goods and services in different countries. As an example, the average price for a Big Mac sandwich in the U.S is $4.62. In India you can buy a chicken or mutton based Maharaja Mac for $1.54 and in South Africa you will pay $2.16. However, in Norway, a Big Mac cost $7.80. As such, both countries would have more purchasing power than in the consumer in Norway. Purchasing power is growing in countries like India and South Africa because basic living expenses such a food, shelter, and transportation are very inexpensive so consumers still have money to spend after paying for necessities.

As with any strategy, there are potential **risks of international expansion**. A firm must be aware of *political stability, currency stability and value, cultural values and ethics, trade restrictions and tariffs, receptiveness to foreign intervention in foreign local markets, legal barriers,* and *infrastructure* to name but a few.

To assist firms in their decisions, *Euromoney* publishes semiannually a magazine that assesses the 'Country Risk Rating' of entering foreign countries. Using a rating system to evaluate political, economic,

| Rank | Country | Total Risk Assessment | Economic Performance | Political Risk | Total Debt Indicators | Total of Credit and Access to Finance Indicators |
|---|---|---|---|---|---|---|
| 1 | Luxembourg | 99.51 | 25.00 | 24.51 | 20.00 | 30.00 |
| 2 | Switzerland | 98.84 | 23.84 | 25.00 | 20.00 | 30.00 |
| 3 | United States | 98.37 | 23.96 | 24.41 | 20.00 | 30.00 |
| 40 | China | 71.27 | 18.93 | 16.87 | 19.73 | 15.74 |
| 55 | Poland | 57.12 | 18.56 | 13.97 | 9.36 | 15.23 |
| 63 | Vietnam | 52.04 | 14.80 | 11.91 | 18.51 | 6.82 |
| 86 | Russia | 42.62 | 11.47 | 8.33 | 17.99 | 4.83 |
| 114 | Albania | 34.23 | 8.48 | 5.04 | 19.62 | 1.09 |
| 161 | Mozambique | 21.71 | 3.28 | 2.75 | 13.85 | 1.83 |
| 178 | Afghanistan | 3.92 | 0.00 | 3.04 | 0.00 | 0.88 |

Source: Adapted from worldbank.org/html/prddr/trans/so96/art7.htm.

Figure 7.10: International Country Risk Rankings

financial, credit risks and other risks that entrants potentially face. Note that a high *Total Risk Assessment* score indicates a low country risk.

Considering all of the risks previously mentioned, there are four primary risks that a firm should give priority attention: ***political risks, economic risks, currency risks***, and ***management risks***.

## Political and Economic Risks

Before entry a firm must give attention to that country's political climate. Forces such as social unrest, military turmoil, demonstrations, terrorism, and violent conflicts all may be hazardous to the health of a corporation conducting business in that environment. Such conditions increase the probability of destruction of property, disruption of operations, and the likelihood of nonpayment of goods and services. ***Policy risks*** refer to the risk associated with changes in laws and government policies that directly affect the way foreign companies conduct business.

An example of policy risk was evident with *Research In Motion (RIM)* and their Blackberry phones in Saudi Arabia. The Blackberry phone was very popular because of the secure, encrypted, electronic communication technology. However, Saudi security officials became concerned that due to the encrypted technology they were unable to monitor terrorists groups that use the Blackberry for communication. As a result, the Saudi government announced that the Blackberry phones would be prohibited. This policy change placed RIM at risk of losing over 750,000 users. After intense negotiations, RIM research agreed to install computer servers giving the Saudi government unencrypted access to monitor user communication and activities.

***Intellectual property*** and the protection of those rights can pose a significant risk for technology companies entering new countries. Apple and Microsoft are two examples of firms that have lost billions of dollars in potential revenue through piracy and counterfeit products in many countries including China, Russia and eastern European countries. Figure 7.11 lists the top 12 countries violating Intellectual Property Rights.

## Top Countries For Counterfeiting Activities

| | |
|---|---|
| 1. China | 7. Israel |
| 2. Russia | 8. Lebanon |
| 3. Argentina | 9. Thailand |
| 4. Chile | 10. Turkey |
| 5. Egypt | 11. Ukraine |
| 6. India | 12. Venezuela |

Source: International Anti-Counterfeiting Coalition (IACC)

Figure 7.11: Top 12 Counterfeiting Countries

*Currency risk* is that which arises from the fluctuation in price of one currency against another. Whenever a company has assets or business operations across national borders or in several countries they face risk of currency fluctuation. Even a small fluctuation in the exchange rate from the foreign currency into the US dollar can result in a significant difference in the cost of production or net profit. Currency risk is also referred to as the *exchange-rate risk*.

For example, consider a US company conducting business in France. If this firm had a 15 percent profit in euros at its French center of operations, this profit would be totally negated when converted into US dollars if the euro had depreciated by 15 percent against the dollar. In order to lower the risk firms use hedges and other techniques to offset any of the gains or losses from the fluctuations.

In addition to the risk of currency fluctuation, companies face risks of *currency devaluation*. Foreign governments devaluing their currency and/or not honor their foreign debts, *debt default*, as was the case with Thailand in 1997, Russia in 1998, Argentina in 2001, and Greece in 2010.

## Management Risks

The challenges and risks that face managers when entering a foreign country take on a variety of forms: customs, cultural differences, language, income level, education level, customer preferences, distribution systems, an the list goes on. Differences in culture across countries can pose a significant challenge for managers as cultural symbols take on a different set of meaning with varying cultures.

One example of management risks is the symbols found in a culture. *Symbols* are cultural representations of reality. Every culture has its own set of symbols associated with different experiences and perceptions. As an example, the color white is often associated with purity, innocence, cleanliness, in western cultures. This is why white is worn by brides and associated with marriage. In China however, white is associated with mourning and funerals. Something as simple as a hand gesture can hold many different meanings. Back in 1992 in Australia, George Bush Senior signaled the letter "V" for victory with his pointer and middle finger. Unfortunately, he didn't realize the direction the palm faced held different connotations. As he signaled the crowd with the back of his hand facing the crowd, people became offended because in Australia showing the back of your hand is an extremely derogative gesture.

# Becoming Culturally Aware

The truly global dimension of the twenty-first century's economy has redefined the playing field on which international companies compete. The ability to offer the right products and services in the right markets at the right prices is no longer the sole factor of success. Having the right people with a high level of cultural awareness and intercultural competence is now key when working across borders and cultures. *Culture* is the set of characteristics of a given group of people and their environment. The most important components of culture are norms, values, customs, beliefs, attitudes, habits, state of technology, level of education, and religion. As a company moves from a domestic corporation involving basically one culture to international involving multiple cultures, the task of managerial influence becomes more challenging. *National culture* is a set of shared values and beliefs based on specific characteristics such as language, religion, ethnic, and racial identity, and cultural history and traditions that affect the perceptions decisions, and behavior of the people from a particular country.

# Hofsteade's National Cultural Dimensions

The first step in dealing with national culture is to recognize that there are meaningful differences. One of the most widely used methods to describe the diversity of values in foreign culture was developed by Geert Hofstede. According to Hofstede, national cultural values vary on five basic dimensions: power distance, individualism, masculinity/femininity, uncertainty avoidance, and short-term versus long-term time orientation.

*Power distance (PDI)*—measures the extent to which the people in a country accept that power is distributed unequally in society and organizations. This represents inequality (more versus less), but defined from below, not from above. In countries like Sweden and Denmark where power distance is low, employees don't like their organization or their boss to have power over them or to tell them what to do. They want to have input in the decisions that affect them. However, in Japan, where power distance is high, we would expect to find high respect for age, status, and titles and as such being told by your boss what to do is more culturally accepted.

*Individualism (IDV)*—measures the degree to which societies believe that individuals should be self-sufficient. In societies with strong individualistic scores, employees put loyalty to themselves first and loyalty to their company and work groups second. The United States, can clearly been seen as individualistic (scoring a 91). The "American dream" is clearly a representation of this. This is the Americans' hope for a better quality of life and a higher standard of living than their parents'. This belief is that anyone, regardless of individual status can 'pull up their boot straps' and raise him or herself from poverty.

*Masculinity/Femininity (MAS)*—measures the degree which society values high assertiveness and materialism, versus feelings, relationship, and quality of life. Masculine traits include assertiveness, materialism/material success, self-centeredness, power, strength, and individual achievements. Whereas, according to Hofstede, feminine cultures emphasize the importance of relationship, modesty, caring for the weak, and quality of life. For example, Germany has a masculine culture with a 66 on the scale of Hofstede (Netherlands 14). The United States scored a 62 on the scale. So these two cultures share, in terms of masculinity, similar values.

*Uncertainty Avoidance (UAI)*—Uncertainty avoidance measures the degree of a society's tolerance for uncertainty and ambiguity. It indicates to what extent a culture programs its members to feel either uncomfortable or comfortable in unstructured situations. Unstructured situations are novel, unknown, surprising, and different from norm. High uncertainty avoidance cultures try to minimize the possibility of such situations by strict laws and rules, safety and security measures. As example, France scored high on the UAI and as such one would expect to find a preference for structure, order, and predictability. Conversely, Hong Kong, which scored low on the UAI, is considered a highly entrepreneurial culture and favors taking risks in business affairs.

*Long-Term Orientation (LTO)*—Long-Term Orientation is the fifth dimension of Hofstede that was added after the original four to try to distinguish the difference in thinking between the East and West. LTO addresses whether cultures are oriented to the present and seek immediate gratification or to the future and defer gratification. Americans are notoriously impatient and desire quick even instantaneous gratification. Even American companies are expected to achieve short-term results; those failing to meet quarterly financial targets often suffer immediate stock price decline. Japan, whose culture in long-term thinking, is more patient and willing to invest in long-term technology such as the hybrid even though it did not payoff in the short-term.

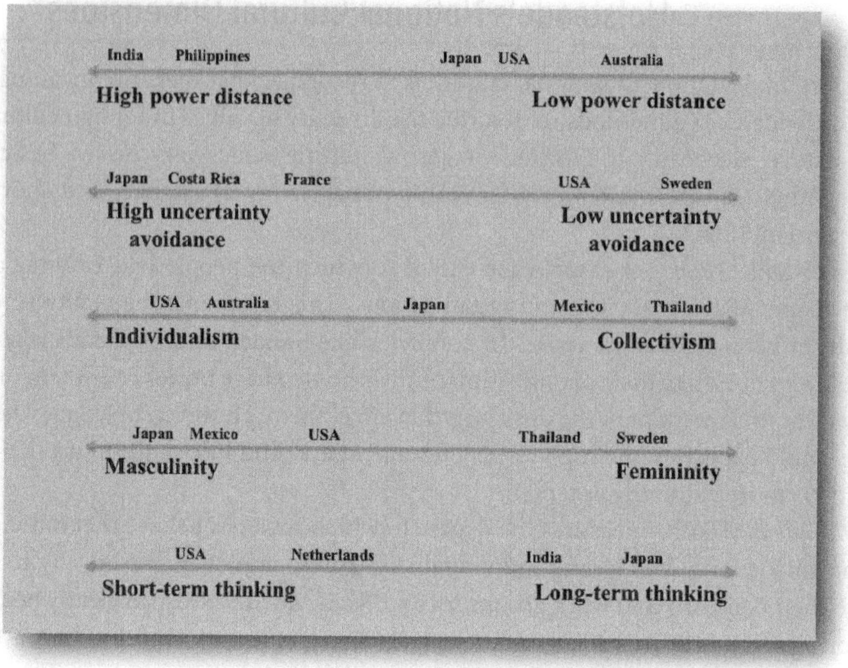

| | | | | | |
|---|---|---|---|---|---|
| India | Philippines | | Japan | USA | Australia |

**High power distance**                      **Low power distance**

Japan    Costa Rica      France             USA       Sweden

**High uncertainty avoidance**          **Low uncertainty avoidance**

USA    Australia        Japan       Mexico     Thailand

**Individualism**                       **Collectivism**

Japan   Mexico      USA         Thailand    Sweden

**Masculinity**                       **Femininity**

USA      Netherlands       India     Japan

**Short-term thinking**               **Long-term thinking**

Figure 7.12: Hofstede's Five Dimensions of National Culture

Recognizing cultural differences exist is critical to succeeding in global business. Nevertheless, Hofstede points out that descriptions of cultural differences are based on the average level of each dimension within a culture and one should not assume that all cultural statements automatically apply to an individual. Figure 7.12 uses examples of each dimension with sample countries to show how national cultures varied in Hofstede's research. Can you see how this information can be significant in business and management?

## Time, Space, Context - The 'Silent' Language of Culture

Are you able to communicate to your friends at a dinner party or social gathering through your body language or facial expressions? Is it as effective as communication with language? Most likely your answer is yes and what your are demonstrating is that people of all cultures have a 'silent language.'

Anthropologist Edward T. Hall's points out that 'silent languages' of a culture that are very significant. Hall found that how different cultures approach communication context, time, and space helps us better understand the powerful effect culture has on communication. A key factor in his theory is context. *Context* is the framework, background, and surrounding circumstances in which communication or an event takes place.

*Low-context cultures* (including North America and much of Western Europe) members emphasize communication through spoken or written words. Low-context cultures are logical, linear, individualistic, and action-oriented. People from low-context cultures value logic, facts, and directness. Solving a problem means lining up the facts and evaluating one after another. Decisions are based on fact rather than intuition. Discussions end with actions and communicators are expected to be straightforward, concise, and efficient in telling what action is expected. To be absolutely clear, they strive to use precise words and intend them to be taken literally. Explicit contracts conclude negotiations. As the saying goes: '*We say (or write) what we mean, and we mean what we say.*'

**High-context cultures** (including much of the Middle East, Asia, Africa, and South America) members rely on non-verbal and situational cues as well as spoken or written words in communication. High-context cultures are relational, collectivist, intuitive, and contemplative. This means that people in these cultures emphasize interpersonal relationships. Developing trust is an important first step to any business transaction. According to Hall, these cultures are collectivist, preferring group harmony and consensus to individual achievement. And people in these cultures are less governed by reason than by intuition or feelings. Words are not so important as context, which might include the speaker's tone of voice, facial expression, gestures, posture, and even the person's family history and status. Dinner parties and social gatherings in high-context cultures allow potential business partners to get to know one another. Only after the relationships are established and a context for communication exists is it possible to make business deals.

In his research, Hall also noticed that the way people approach and deal with time varies across cultures either in a monochronic or polychromic view. In a **monochronic culture** people like to do just one thing at a time. They value certain orderliness and sense that there is an appropriate time and place for everything. They do not value interruptions. They like to concentrate on the job at hand and take time commitments very seriously. This is typical of the United States, where most businesspeople schedule a meeting for one person or group to focus on one issue for an allotted time. If someone is late or brings an uninvited person, we tend to not like it.

Members of a **polychronic culture** are more flexible toward time, how to use it, and enjoy doing multiple things at the same time. A manager's office in a polychronic culture typically has an open door, a ringing phone and a meeting all going on at the same time. Although they can be easily distracted they also tend to manage interruptions well with a willingness to change plans often and easily. People are their main concern (particularly those closely related to them or their function) and they have a tendency to build lifetime relationships. Issues such as promptness are firmly based on the relationship rather than the task and objectives.

If you live in the United States, Canada, or Northern Europe, you live in a monochronic culture. If you live in Latin America, the Arab part of the Middle East, or sub-Sahara Africa, you live in a polychronic culture.

Interactions between the two types can be problematic. Monochronic businessmen cannot understand why the person they are meeting with is always interrupted by phone calls and people stopping by. Polychronic businessmen cannot understand why tasks are isolated from the organization as a whole and measured in time instead of part of the overall organizational goal.

Finally, Hall points out that different cultures view and value interpersonal space differently. In America, we like and value our own space. We like big offices, big homes, and big yards. In fact, we value our own 'personal space' and are uncomfortable when someone talks to us 'right in our face.' Hall describes these cultural tendencies in terms of **proxemics**, or how people use interpersonal space to communicate. However in Japan, space is very precious, respected, and carefully planned. Homes, offices, and shops are small but tidy. Gardens are tiny but immaculate and public spaces are carefully organized for the most efficient use.

In the United States, there are four types of 'distance' that people use to communicate on a face-to-face basis: intimate distance, personal distance, social distance, and public distance.

*Intimate distance (0–2ft)*—is used for very confidential communications. People in intimate distance share a unique level of comfort with each other. Those who are not comfortable with someone who approaches them in the intimate zone will experience a great deal of social discomfort or awkwardness.

*Personal distance (2–4ft)*—generally used for talking with family and close friends. Like intimate distance, if a stranger approaches someone in the personal zone, they are likely to feel uncomfortable being is such close proximity with the stranger.

*Social distance (4–12ft)*—is typically used in business transactions, meeting new people and interacting with groups of people. Social distance may be used among students, co-workers, or acquaintances. Generally, people within social distance do not engage in physical contact with one another and some people may require more physical distance than others.

*Public distance (>12ft)*—is the distance maintained between the audience and a speaker such as the professor in a lecture hall.

# Summary of Chapter

1. We learned that Global business affects the United States in two ways: through foreign direct investment in the United States by foreign companies and through U.S. companies' investment in business in other countries.

2. In this chapter we discovered that tariffs and nontariff trade barriers, such as quotas, voluntary export restraints, government import standards, subsidies, and customs classifications have made buying foreign goods much harder or more expensive than buying domestically produced goods.

3. We uncovered that worldwide trade agreements such as GATT, Maastricht Treaty of Europe, NAFTA, CAFTA-DR, UNASUR, ASEAN, and APEC have substantially reduced tariff and nontariff barriers to international trade.

4. This chapter discussed the options of integration or local-responsiveness. Integration means coordinating the firm's value chain activities across countries to achieve worldwide efficiencies, synergies, and cross-fertilization. Whereas local-responsiveness requires meeting the specific needs of buyers in different countries.

5. We discussed the different options for global business moving from exporting, licensing and franchising, strategic alliances, and wholly owed affiliates and benefits and risks with each.

6. We learned the importance of an attractive business climate for growing the company considering consumers' purchasing power, political risk, political and policy uncertainty, and foreign competition.

7. National culture is a set of shared beliefs and values that affect the perceptions, decisions, and behavior of the people from a particular country. We discovered the value to Hofstede's cultural differences such as power distance, individualism, masculinity, uncertainty avoidance, and short-term/long-term orientation.

# Discussion Questions

1. What are three similarities and three differences of international versus transnational organizations?
2. What knowledge must a manager have to successfully influence organizational members of a multinational corporation?
3. Differentiate between low-context and high-context cultures.
4. Explain the difference between monochronic and polychronic cultures? Provide an example of each.
5. List Hofstede's five dimensions of value differences among national cultures.
6. How does the American culture differ with that of other countries on each dimension?
7. Should religion be included on Hall's list of silent languages of culture?
8. Even though cultural differences are apparent around the world, is the trend today for culture to converge and become more like one another?

# References

C. A. Barlett and S. Ghoshal, *managing across Borders* (Boston: Harvard Business School Press, 1989).

CAFTA-DR (Dominican Republic-Central America FTA).' Office of the United States Trade Representative, accessed June 14, 2014, from http://www.ustr.gov/trade-agreements/free-trade-agreements/cafta-dr-dominican-republic-central-america-fta.

J. Birkinshaw, N. Hood, and S. Jonsson, "Building Firm Specific Advantages in Multinational Corporations: The Rule of Subsidiary Initiative," *Strategic Management Journal* 19 (1998), pp. 221–241.

J. Bleeke and D. Ernst, "The Way to Win in Cross Border Alliances," *Harvard Business Review,* March–April 1986, pp. 78–90.

T. S. Frost, J. M. Birkinshaw, and P. C. Ensign, "Centers of Excellence in Multinational Corporations," *Strategic Management Journal* 23 (2002) pp. 997–1018.

Friedman, T. (2005). 'It's a Flat World, After All,' *New York Times,* April 3, 33.

K. Ferdows, "Making the Most of Foreign Factories," *Harvard Business Review,* March–April 1997, pp. 73–88.

'GATT/WTO,' accessed June 12, 2014, from http://www.wto.org/english/thewto_e/whatis_e/tif_e/fact4_e.htm

P. Ghemawat, *Commitment: The Dynamic of Strategy* (New York: Free Press, 1991).

V. J. Govindarajan and A. K. Gupta, *The Quest for Global Dominance* (San Francisco: Josey Bass, 2001).

Hall, E. T. *The Silent Language* (New York: Anchor Books 1959).

Hall, E. T. *Beyond Culture* (New York: Doubleday, 1976).

Hall, E. T. *Hidden Differences* (New York: Doubleday, 1990).

Hofstede, G. *Culture's Consequences* (Beverly Hills, CA: Sage, 1984).

Hofstede, G. *Culture's Consequences: Comparing Values, Behaviors, Institutions and Organizations Across Nations* 2nd ed. (Thousand Oaks, CA: Sage, 2001).

Hofstede, G. & Bond, M. H. (1988) 'The Confucius Connection: From Cultural Roots to Economic Growth,' *Organizational Dynamics,* v.16, pp.4–21.

T. Hout, M. E. Porter, and E. Rudden, "How Global firms Win Out," *Harvard Business Review,* September–October 1982, pp. 98–108.

'Map of Euro member states,' accessed June 14, 2014, from http://www.nationsonline.org/oneworld/europe_map .htm.

X. Marin and R. Salomon, "Knowledge Transfer Theory and Its Implications for the Theory of the Multinational Corporation," *Journal of International Business Studies,* 34 (July 2003), pp. 356–360.

K. Ohmae, "The Global Logic of Strategic Alliances," *Harvard Business Review,* March–April 1989, pp. 143–154.

S. Tallman and K. Fladmoe Lindquist, "Internationalization, Globalization and 116–130.

'Selected basic ASEAN Indicators, 2012,' *Association of Southeast Nations,* February 15, 2011, accessed June 14, 2014, from www.aseansec.org/stat/Table1pdf; 'Selected Basic ASEAN Indicators, 2005.'

'The History of the European Union,' accessed June 12, 2014, from http://europa.eu/about-eu/eu-history/ index_en.htm

UNASUR, Unition of South American Nations, accessed June 14, 2014, from http://www.unasursg.org/

'Understanding the WTO,' *World Trade Organization,* accessed June 12, 2014, from www.wto.org/english/ thewto_e/whatis_e/tif_e/agrm9_e.htm.

'US Trade with CAFTA-DR Countries,' Office of the United States Trade Representative. Accessed June 14, 2014, from http://www.ustr.gov/trade-agreements/free-trade-agreements/cafta-dr-dominican-republic-central-america-fta.

# PART 3

# Organizing

# CHAPTER 8

## Organizational Structure and Design

*"Architecture does not create extraordinary organizations by collecting extraordinary people. It does so by enabling very ordinary people to perform in extraordinary ways."*

– John Kay

---

### Chapter Learning Objectives

After reading this chapter you should have a good understanding of:

- The importance of organizational structure and design.
- The five basic approaches to departmentalization.
- The definition and dimensions of organizational authority.

- The significance, functions and three common methods of job design.
- The components of the job characteristics model and its importance to managers.

This chapter begins with an explanation of the history and importance of organizational structure and design. Traditional and contemporary approaches to organizational structure and design will be covered in detail. **Organizational structure** is the division of the business as whole into departments or units. **Organizational design** encompasses the processes, roles, and formal reporting relationships of the business.

The vertical and horizontal configuration of departments, titles, and reporting relationships within an organization are generally depicted through organizational charts. Structure and reporting relationships, are generally depicted as visual representations in organizational charts. Organizational design, however, is not as clearly depicted in visual charts or graphs as it includes specifications of job design—the interior details of structuring tasks.

In the first section of the chapter, you will learn about the emergence of departmentalization and the five traditional approaches to organizational structure. The advantages and disadvantages of each approach to organizational structure will be examined.

In the second section of the chapter, you will learn about the importance of chain of command and the hierarchy of organizational authority. The degrees of centralization of authority including the benefits and shortcomings of centralization versus decentralization will be explored.

Lastly, you will learn about the traditional methods of job design and how contemporary organizations are becoming more competitive by redesigning jobs and their internal and external processes.

## The Emergence of Departmentalization

A prominent contributor to the field of organizational structure and design, **Alfred DuPont Chandler, Jr.** (1918-2007) wrote extensively on organizational structure and design. A professor of business at Harvard Business School, Massachusetts Institute of Technology, and Johns Hopkins University, Chandler crafted his Structure follows Strategy thesis based on the case studies of four American conglomerates that dominated their industries—automobile manufacturer General Motors, energy company Standard Oil of New Jersey, chemical company Du Pont, and retailer Sears Roebuck.

After studying these four large-scale enterprises, Chandler wrote extensively on their scale, management structures, and diversification strategies. His thesis argued that organizational structure and design were a derivative of strategy. Emphasizing the importance of employing a cadre of managers to organize and run complex operations, Chandler described how these organizations managed a growth and diversification strategy by creating revolutionary multi-divisional structures.

The multi-divisional or M-Form organizational structure has a corporate headquarter and a coalition of semi-independent product or geographic divisions that oversee corporate strategy and coordinate complex interdependent systems. Although the M-form was executed differently in each organization, Chandler showed that strategic shifts, such as, market changes and new technologies, fueled the need to restructure. The M-form organizational structure emerged as the design through which corporate strategy could be administered. By adopting multi-divisional structures, these businesses were able to increase profits by achieving higher productivity while lowering costs.

Chandler's works, spanning the management of small owner-operator businesses, plantations, railroads, and large conglomerates with the capacity for mass production, are credited with redefining business. In 1977, Chandler received the Pulitzer Prize for History for his work, The Invisible Hand: The Managerial Revolution in American Business.

### Five Basic Approaches to Departmentalization

Traditionally, there are five basic approaches to creating multi-divisional organizations:

1. Functional departmentalization
2. Product departmentalization
3. Geographic departmentalization
4. Customer departmentalization
5. Matrix departmentalization

In each of these approaches, organizational structures are based on some form of **departmentalization**— a method of subdividing work into separate organizational units. For example, founded in 1886, Johnson & Johnson is now a global company with headquarters in New Brunswick, New Jersey. Operating in 60 countries around the world with more than 250 companies and 125,000 employees, Johnson & Johnson is organized into three business segments—consumer healthcare, medical devices and diagnostics, and pharmaceuticals. These complex business segments are comprised of several interrelated business units and franchises.

Basically, departmentalization is a method of organizing work and workers. The approach to departmentalization and organization's design will depend on the business and industry. Businesses have unique functions and the organization of the work and workers should support the needs of the business and enable effective pursuit of organizational strategy. The five methods to departmentalization are described in the following sections.

## Functional Departmentalization

The most common organizational structure, **functional departmentalization** subdivides work and workers into separate units responsible for business functions or areas of expertise. Common business functions may include operations, sales, customer service, accounting and human resources. However, not all organizations subdivided functionally have the same business functions. The kind of business segments or units organizations adopt in functional departmentalization depend on the business.

Functional departmentalization divides and organizes work and workers into separate units responsible for certain business functions or areas of expertise.

The primary advantage of functional departmentalization is that it allows work to be done by highly qualified specialists. The research and development department will be responsible for designing a product while the operations department will assume the responsibility for manufacturing the product.

A second advantage is that is lowers costs and expenses by reducing duplication. The research and development department, responsible for designing products will not need to create the marketing plan. The third, and perhaps most beneficial advantage is communication. With shared task expertise and work experience or training in a particular department, communication and coordination are less problematic for employees and administration is less cumbersome for department managers.

Figure 8.1: Functional Departmentalization Structure

On the other hand, there are also a number of disadvantages to functional departmentalization. First, cross-department coordination can be complicated. Often, managers and employees are more interested in benefitting their department or division instead of the entire organization. Second, functional departmentalization can cause slower and less effective decision-making. Finally, this type of multi-divisional organization can produce workers and managers with narrow expertise.

## Product Departmentalization

**Product departmentalization** divides and organizes work and workers into separate units responsible for particular products or services. Both business that produce goods and offer services can be organized by product line.

Similar to an organizational structure of division by function, the primary advantage of a product departmentalization design is that it allows for specialization of skills and expertise. Employees, both managers and workers, are able to specialize; but managers and workers generally develop a broader set of experiences. So their expertise can be expanded to an entire product line. Also, product departmentalization makes it easy for managers to assess workers and work-unit performance. Finally, decision-making can be more effective and efficient. Since top managers are usually responsible for a complete product line, many of the conflicts that might arise in separate functional departments are generally avoided.

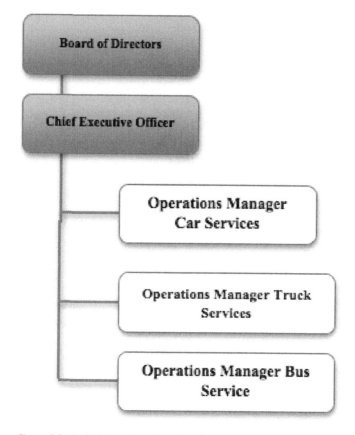

Figure 8.2: Product Departmentalization Structure

A primary disadvantage of product departmentalization is duplication, which often results in unnecessary or higher costs. Another disadvantage is that it can be difficult to coordinate and communicate across different product departments.

**Customer departmentalization** divides and organizes work and workers into separate units responsible for certain kinds of customers. Many businesses divide their organization by different types of customers, such as, business or individual customer, or online or brick and mortar customer.

The primary advantage of customer departmentalization is that it focuses on the needs of the customer. The organization's structure is designed based on customer need rather than by business function or product. By creating and adopting a customer departmentalization structure, the organization is better able to serve specific kinds of customers. This allows companies to adapt and tailor their product and service offerings to the customers' needs and wants.

Similar to product departmentalization, the primary disadvantage of customer departmentalization is duplication of resources. Additionally, it can be difficult to establish effective communication and coordination across different customer departments. Lastly, the emphasis on meeting the customers' needs and wants may lead to unbalanced decision-making. Managers and workers may make decisions with the focus on pleasing the customer but neglect to consider the needs of the business.

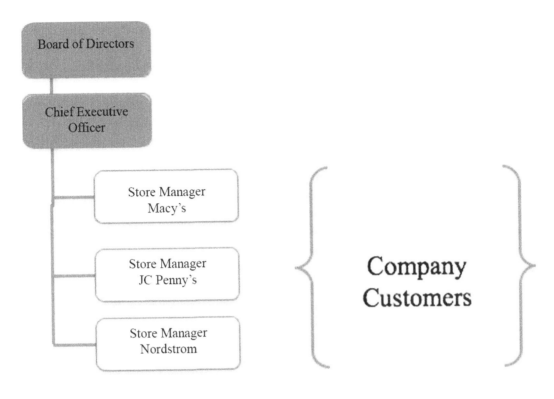

Figure 8.3: Customer Departmentalization Structure

**Geographic departmentalization** divides and organizes work and workers into separate units responsible for certain geographic areas. For example, many businesses structured by geographic departmentalization adopt a regional approach, such as, divisions in North America, Europe, and Asia.

The primary advantage of geographic departmentalization is that it allows companies to respond to the needs and demands of different markets. This approach is advantageous when the company sells it's goods and services tailored to different countries. Quite often, a company with a geographic departmentalization structure will adapt their product offering to local customs, tastes, and competitor offerings.

Similar to product and customer departmentalization, a primary disadvantage of geographic departmentalization is duplication of resources. For example, although it may be beneficial to tailor products and marketing to different geographic regions, it's unlikely that every business function requires duplication. A second disadvantage is the difficulty in establishing effective communication and coordination. Quite often managers are thousands of miles apart in organizations adopting the geographic structure and hence have limited contact with headquarters or other regions.

**Matrix departmentalization,** a hybrid structure, combines two or more forms of departmentalization. The most common types of matrix structures combine the product, customer, or geographic structural forms with the functional form of departmentalization.

Matrix departmentalization is a contemporary organizational structure created for the needs of global and multi-national firms.

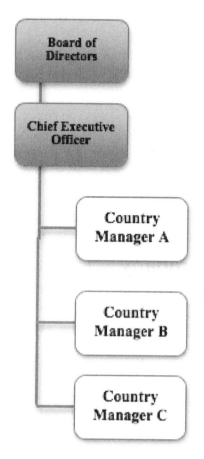

Figure 8.4: Geographical Departmentalization Structure

Three important attributes distinguish the matrix structure from the other traditional forms of departmentalization. First, and most importantly, most employees report to two bosses, one from each core part of the matrix. For example, a manager in Brazil responsible for consumer banking may report to Vice-President of Latin America and also the Vice-President of all Global Consumer Banking. Second, by virtue of heir hybrid design, matrix structures bring about more cross-functional interaction than different structural forms. Generally, employees in matrix structures are assigned to one or more project groups based on their experience or expertise. Third, significant amounts of communication and coordination are typical of matrix structures. Due to the vast amounts of cross-functional interaction, managers are commonly responsible for multiple objectives including tracking and coordinating multiple projects.

The primary advantage of matrix departmentalization is that it allows companies to gather employees from different functional areas with varying expertise and experience to manage large, complex projects and tasks. When carried out effectively the organization is able to create project teams with employees representing each necessary area of expertise or experience. Effective project teams have the ability to carry out complex tasks and avoid duplication of effort. For example, instead of having the entire consumer banking team involved in a project, managers would assign different banking team members representing specialized expertise or experience, such as credit card processing, at different stages of the project. The ability to create intricate project teams inherently creates a second advantage—the ability to execute large and complex tasks. By virtue of their design, matrix structures provide managers with access to a diverse employee pool with different expertise and skill sets.

The primary disadvantage of matrix departmentalization is the consumption of time and resources. Managing multiple projects and personnel creates a need for considerable and on-going communication and coordination. Confusion and disagreements are typical in matrix structures. The demands of the reporting structure, two or more bosses with two or more priorities, causes misunderstanding and conflict regarding schedules, resources, and timelines. This drawback leads to a second and closely related disadvantage, managers must posses finely honed management skills and the ability to work within the constructs of the matrix structure.

Because of these disadvantages, a number of matrix structures evolve from a simple matrix structure to a complex matrix structure. In a **complex matrix structure** the organization supplements the simple matrix structure by adding specialized managers and departments to the existing organizational structure. For example, managers from different parts of the matrix structure may report to one manager. All types of the complex matrix structure attempt to reduce conflicts, disagreements, and other problems.

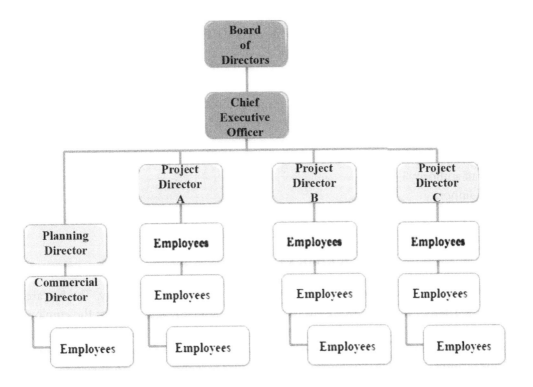

Figure 8.5: Matrix Departmentalization Structure

| Approach | Advantages | Disadvantages |
|---|---|---|
| Functional | • Work done by highly qualified specialists<br>• Reduce duplication through Lower costs and expenses | • Complicated cross-department coordination<br>• Slower and less effective decision-making<br>• Produces workers and managers with narrow expertise |
| Product | • Develops broad set of experiences and expertise for managers and workers<br>• Easier assessment for top-managers<br>• Quick decision making and fewer conflicts | • Resource duplication<br>• Difficult achieving cross- department coordination |
| Customer | • Customer-oriented organization<br>• Specialized departments serving specific needs of customers | • Resource duplication<br>• Difficult achieving cross-department coordination<br>• Emphasis on customer needs leads to decisions hurting the organization |
| Geographic | • Ability to respond to different market demands | • Resource duplication<br>• Difficulties coordinating international markets |
| Matrix | • Efficiently manage large, complex tasks<br>• Diverse set of expertise with cross-department managers | • Confusing and conflicting with multiple projects<br>• Requires more management skill |

Figure 8.6: Five Basic Approaches Advantages and Disadvantages

# Organizational Authority

A critical element of organizational structure is authority. Commonly referred to the second part of organizational structure, **organizational authority** is the responsibility for certain areas of activity including the right to make decisions, take action, and give directives and orders to achieve organizational objectives. Traditionally, organizational authority encompasses four distinct dimensions:

1. Chain of command
2. Line versus staff authority
3. Delegation of authority
4. Degree of centralization

# Chain of Command

**Chain of command,** the building block of authority, is the hierarchy of authority. The hierarchy of authority in an organization should be designed to benefit the company and support the employees in reaching organizational goals and objectives. Represented in organizational charts, chain of command is the vertical line connecting every job in the organization to a higher level of management. Simply put, it is the vertical line of authority which demonstrates who reports to whom in the organization. The chain of command for a position or personnel can be traced to the top levels of the organization.

A key assumption that underlies the chain of command authority dimension is unity of command. **Unity of command** necessitates that workers report to one boss. The principle of unity of command simply means that only one person can be in charge at one time. In practical terms, being in charge means only one person can be in charge of the organizational issue, decision, or situation at any given time. Unity of command prevents disagreements, conflicts and confusion from an employee receiving conflicting. By alleviating the situation of an employee receiving orders from different bosses, the authority to make decisions, give orders, and take action is clear.

The principle of unity of command is breached in matrix organizations. When reporting structures are unclear or when employees report to two or more bosses, then effective management is less likely to occur.

## Line Versus Staff Authority

A second dimension of authority is the difference between line authority and staff authority. **Line authority** is the organizational permission to command subordinates within the chain of command.

Figure 8.7: Delegation of Responsibility, Authority, and Accountability

While, **staff authority** is the organizational permission to advise but does not allow command of others who are not subordinates within the chain of command. For example, it is common for human resources manager to advise another manager in hiring or promotion decisions but not dictate the hiring of a particular applicant or the selection of a certain employee for promotion.

The terms line and staff also describe different organizational functions.

A **line function** is an activity or job that directly contributes to creating or selling the company's goods or service. For example, activities or jobs that take place within the manufacturing and operations or marketing and sales departments would be considered line functions. A **staff function** is an activity or job that does not contribute directly to creating or selling the company's goods or services, but is responsible to support line activities. Generally, staff functions within an organization include activities and jobs in accounting and human resource departments.

## Delegation of Authority

**Delegation of authority** is the process of assigning direct authority and responsibility to a subordinate. Simply put, delegation of authority involves transferring the decision-making authority to complete tasks to a lower-level employee.

In order for a manager to successfully delegate authority over work activities, it is essential three transfers occur. First, the manager must take full responsibility for the transfer of the work activity, task, or assignment to the subordinate. Second, the manager must transfer full authority over necessary resources. The manager should transfer the subordinate authority appropriate and necessary for the responsibility. For delegation of authority to be effective, the subordinate must be able to obtain the needed resources, access vital information, and garner the cooperation necessary to successfully complete the assignment. And, third, is the transfer of accountability. As the work activity or task is transferred from the manager to the subordinate, the employee assumes accountability for completing the assignment. In exchange for managers taking responsibility for the delegation of assignment and delegating the authority and responsibility necessary to complete the assignment, the subordinate assumes accountability for completion of the assignment.

Empowerment, closely related to delegation of authority, also involves the transfer of authority. **Empowerment** occurs when managers share authority and power with subordinates. In order for empowerment to be effective, managers must provide subordinates with the training, tools, and support necessary to accomplish the assignment. Often, the transfer of accountability impedes delegation of authority and empowerment. In many organizations, even though authority can be delegated, responsibility cannot. It is generally the manager who is ultimately responsible.

Effective delegation is advantageous to the organization, managers, and employees. There are several key benefits. A primary organizational benefit of effective delegation is increased quality of work. By transferring tasks to employees with specialized experience or expertise, improvements in the quality of work are often gained. Another key and closely related benefit is found in the employee owning the task. Subordinates are generally motivated to do a better job when they feel ownership of the assignment. Managers who practice effective delegation and empowerment free up valuable time are often found to have higher ratings with from their staff and are generally highly valued by the organization.

> ### How to be an Effective Delegator
>
> - By recognizing that others have the talent and ability to complete projects, you display trust in your staff
> - Establish standard of quality, instead of seeking perfection, with a timeline for it to be reached.
> - Make sure employees have the information necessary and job instructions to complete the job effectively and successfully.
> - Identify your true interests to ensure you can delegate the work to manager rather that completing it yourself.
> - Create checkpoints and milestones to follow up on progress.
> - Praise your staff for their efforts.
> - Delegate work routinely to avoid crisis management and delegating at the last minute.
> - Help employees complete the work assignments through asking questions, expecting answers, and assisting when able.
> - Give the same amount of resources to employees as if you were doing the work yourself.
> - In order to make the best use of organizational resources, energy, and knowledge, delegate to the lowest possible level.

Figure 8.8: Tips on How to be an Effective Manager

There are also several challenges associated with delegation of authority and empowerment. First, a manager may lack the motivation or skills needed to effectively delegate. Managers may also have a lack of trust in their employees or fear competition from their staff. Or, simply, they may delegate to the wrong employee. Additionally, improper delegation can cause organizational inefficiencies and harm both the manager and the subordinate. If the wrong tasks are delegated or a task is delegated without the necessary resources, information, or support, then the delegation or empowerment is likely to be ineffective. When this occurs, the reputation of the manager and the employee may be harmed.

## Degree of Centralization

**Centralization of authority** is defined as a concentration of authority at the upper levels of the organization. In other words, most of the authority and power resides in the higher levels of the organization. In an organization characterized by centralization, delegation of authority or empowerment is uncommon as managers make most of the decisions.

Conversely, **decentralization** is defined as the dispersing of authority throughout the organization. An organization is decentralized if there is a high degree of delegation at all organizational levels and a significant amount of authority is located in the lower levels of the organization. In other words, in decentralized organizational structures employees are equipped and authorized to make necessary decisions and solve problems.

Decentralized authority structures have many benefits, including faster decision-making, more satisfied customer and employees. Because, decentralized organizational systems are able to develop employees' capability by increasing their knowledge, skills and abilities, they also experience organizational growth and increased revenue.

Commonly, organizations adopt structural systems that utilize both centralized and decentralized processes and procedures. By embedding centralized processes and procedures where standardization is important, organizations can make the most of decentralized processes and procedures where standardization is not important or less important than a competing priority, such as, customer service. **Standardization** is the consistent application of methodology in executing organizational processes and procedures.

Generally, you can observe the centralization or decentralization of authority within an organization through a customer service call. If you call a customer service representative with a script or you are told that they cannot make a decision or an accommodation, it is likely the organization has a system of centralized authority. However, if the customer service representative is able to listen to your concerns, provide information, and offer resolution, it is likely the organization has a system of decentralized authority.

# The Origin of Scientific Management

In the previous section, we learned that organizations are deliberately structured and designed. Structure leads to greater control of the organization. This greater control, in turn, leads to greater efficiencies. **Frederick Taylor** (1856-1915), commonly credited as the founder of scientific management, aimed to explore effectiveness and efficiency. Specifically, Taylor, a mechanical engineer, was interested in determining the most effective method of completing each particular task.

As Taylor observed industrial workers, he noticed that some were more effective than others. He theorized that in order for an organization to improve its efficiency, it would need to recognize and adopt the most effective way to perform workplace tasks. Taylor's built his principles of scientific management on four key principles.

1. Work processes, techniques, and routines must be based on a scientific study of the task.
2. Employees must be scientifically selected, trained, and developed.
3. Employees must be provided detailed instruction and supervision on assigned workplace tasks.
4. Work should be divided between managers and employees with managers planning the work and employees performing the workplace tasks.

Taylor's work revolutionized the organizations of the time. His ideas are recognized as influencing the Ford Motor Company in designing the assembly line. In time, companies found that while the efficiencies of job specialization increased workers intensity, it also lowered morale and job satisfaction.

# Job Specialization

**Job specialization** occurs when a job is comprised of small, specific parts of a larger process or task. Specialized job are fast and easy to learn. Basic steps, low variety, and high repetition characterize specialized jobs. The primary advantage of specialized jobs is economic. Because a specialized job is fast and easy to learn, the organization can replace an employee with little down time or productivity loss. However, the primary disadvantage of specialized jobs is that become boring just as fast. When employees become bored, job satisfaction declines. Commonly, declines in job satisfaction lead to high absenteeism and turnover and increases in workplace injury claims.

Due of the efficiency of specialized jobs, organizations are generally slow in restructuring or eliminating specialized jobs. So, job redesign efforts have generally focused on modifying jobs. The principle intent of modifying specialized jobs is to keep benefits of specialized jobs, while reducing the disadvantages. Organizations use the job design to overcome the challenges associated with job specialization.

# Job Design

**Job design**, a critical and key component of organizational design, is defined as the number, kind, and variety of tasks performed by an individual employee. Particularly, job design examines how the characteristics of skill variety and autonomy affect the employee. Job design, also referred to as work design, is equally concerned with aligning the job specifications to organizational requirements as well as how the job affects the social and personal requirements of the worker. In principle, the goal of job design is to improve quality and employee motivation and job satisfaction and, thereby, reduce problems caused by employee moral, such as, absenteeism and turnover. Historically, there have been three major approaches of job design, each of these method attempts to overcome the disadvantages of specialized work.

1. Job rotation
2. Job enlargement
3. Job enrichment

# Job Rotation

**Job rotation**, a method of job redesign aimed at motivating employees, introduces variety into an employee's workday. The goal of job rotation is to overcome the disadvantages, such as monotony and boredom, of job specialization.

For example, a company practicing job rotation will implement processes and timetables to transfer workers through different jobs or tasks. Job rotation has several key advantages. By introducing more variety and the opportunity for employees to use different skills, the company gains a multi-skilled worker, employee attitudes and job satisfaction improves, and workplace productivity generally increases. Yet, organizations can still gain the economic benefits produced by job specialization.

# Job Enlargement

**Job enlargement**, a method of job redesign aimed at motivating employees, increases the number of different tasks assigned to an employee. Similar to job rotation, the goal of job enlargement is to overcome the disadvantages of job specialization. Unlike job rotation, the employee does not transfer to different jobs but instead takes responsibility for more tasks. The goal of job enlargement is to introduce variety into the employee's tasks. The advantage of job enlargement is that employees experience a reduction in monotony and boredom. However, the disadvantage with job enlargement is that the employee may see the variety as 'more work.' In order to execute job enlargement successfully, companies must ensure that employees have sufficient time to complete all assigned duties.

# Job Enrichment

**Job enrichment**, the third method of job redesign aimed at motivating employees through work design, increases the number of tasks *and* gives workers the authority and control to make decisions about planning and executing their work. Job enrichment allows the employee to assume more responsibility. It has the same advantages as job enlargement. However, it also has the additional advantage of giving the employee autonomy, independence, and allowing for greater participation. The disadvantage with job enrichment is that the employee may see the autonomy as decisions that should be performed by someone at a higher level.

**Frederick Herzberg** (1923—2000), a prominent contributor in the area of employee motivation, is credited with introducing the theory of job enrichment. Herzberg believed that employees could be motivated by jobs that contain a variety of tasks, challenges of varying difficulties, meaningful work, feedback, and communication and encouragement. Herzberg is also credited as having coined the terms 'horizontal job loading' and 'vertical job loading.' **Horizontal job loading** refers to the addition of inter-related tasks to the job to increase variety in the employees work. While **vertical job loading** describes the reassigning of planning and control from a higher-level employee, such as a supervisor, to the employee involved in the work allowing the employee to have more autonomy over their work.

# Job Characteristics Model

The job characteristic model, developed by **Hackman & Oldman** (1976) is a contemporary job design theory. Similar to job rotation, job enlargement, and job enrichment, the job characteristic model (JCM) attempts to overcome the deficiencies of job specialization. Building upon the traditional job design methods, the JMC model provides a comprehensive approach to job design intended to influence employee's in three psychological states—experience meaning in their work (employees must view their work as being important), understanding their contributions (employees must know who they are performing in their jobs), and feeling responsible for outcomes (employees must feel personally responsible for their work). Hackman and Oldman propose these three critical psychological states are necessary for employees to find internal motivation. Hence, the central concern of the job characteristics theory is motivation that comes from the job itself instead of motivation that comes from external or outside rewards, such as a raise. The **job characteristics model (JCM)** provides a framework for job design utilizing five core job characteristics intended to positively influence worker intrinsic motivation—skill variety, task identity, task significance, autonomy, and feedback. (Figure 8.9)

1. Skill variety. The dimension of skill variety encompasses the different skills or activities needed for the job. The more variety in an employees work, the less likely the employee is to experience boredom and the more likely the employee is to be satisfied at work.

2. Task identity. The dimension of task identity measures individual portions of tasks and the portions required to complete the entire task or assignment. The more an employee is involved in the entire activity (from start to finish), the more likely the employee is to be satisfied at work.

3. Task significance. The importance of the task significance dimension an examination of the job's influence and impact. The more an employee feels they are making a contribution and making a difference, the more likely the employee is to be satisfied at work.

4. Autonomy. The dimension of autonomy looks at the amount of individual choice and discretion allowed an employee. The more an employee is involved in the decisions surrounding their job instead of being issued commands, the more likely the employee is to be satisfied at work

5. Feedback. The feedback dimension brings about a need for continuous measurement and communication of information regarding performance and the impact of their work. The more communication and employees receives about their performance and the impact of their work on the organization, department, or customer, the more likely the employee is to interested in their work and satisfied at work.

Increasing job satisfaction and performance has become increasingly important as organizations face environmental challenges, such as globalization and the economic crisis. Managers must be alert and proactive in decreasing job dissatisfaction and increasing employee moral. By eliminating workplace

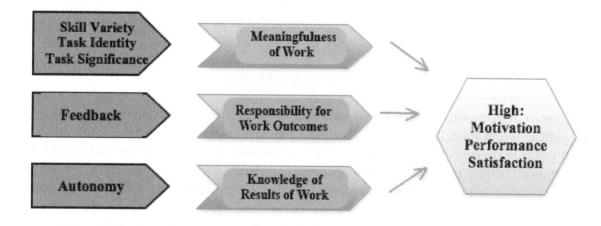

Figure 8.9: Job Characteristics Model

dissatisfaction caused by conditions like low wages and poor working environment and increasing workplace satisfaction by providing opportunities for growth and promotion and recognizing employee achievements, organizations see an increase in worker moral and productivity.

## Summary of Chapter

1. This chapter discussed the history of departmentalization and the importance of organizational structure and design.
2. We learned the five traditional approaches organizations use to create multi-divisional structures. We examined the advantages and disadvantages of each approach to departmentalization.
3. We discussed the critical element of organizational authority and the role it plays in creating organizational structure and culture. This chapter also covered chain of command and the influence hierarchical structures have on the degree of centralization.
4. We examined delegation of responsibility, authority, and accountability and discussed how managers can be effective delegators in today's workplace.
5. We learned about motivating employees through job design and the differences between job rotation, job enlargement, and job enrichment. We examined the contemporary approach to job design theory by analyzing the job characteristics model.

## Discussion Questions

1. What are five basic approaches to departmentalization available to organizations?
2. Discuss the similarities and differences between the traditional approaches to departmentalization.
3. Explain why organizational authority is significant to organizational structure and culture.
4. Differentiate between line and staff authority.
5. Explain the critical elements in delegation of authority.
6. How can managers use job design to motivate their employees?
7. What knowledge must a manager have to successfully delegate to subordinates?
8. Differentiate between job enlargement, job enrichment, and job rotation.
9. How does vertical loading differ from horizontal loading?
10. Explain the components of the job characteristics model.

## References

Burns, L.F. "Adoption and Abandonment of Matrix Management Programs: Effects of Organizational Characteristics and Interorganizational Networks," *Academy of Management Journal* 36 (1993): 106–138

Burns, T. & Stalker, G.M. *The Management of Innovation* (London: Tavistock, 1961).

Casad, Scott (2012). "Implications of job rotation literature for performance improvement practitioners". *Performance Improvement Quarterly* **25** (2): 27–41. doi:10.1002/piq.21118.

Chandler, A.D. Jr. (1962). *Strategy and Structure: Chapters in the History of the American Industrial*

Chandler, Alfred D., Jr. 1962/1998, Strategy and Structure: Chapters in the History of the American Industrial Enterprise. Cambridge, MA: MIT Press

Chandler, Alfred D., Jr. 1977, The Visible Hand, Cambridge, Mass. and London, England: The Belknap Press of Harvard University Press

Chandler, Alfred D., Jr. 1980, Managerial Hierarchies. Harvard University Press

Chandler, Alfred D., Jr. 1990, Scale and Scope. Cambridge, MA. The Belknap Press of Harvard University Press

Chandler, Alfred D., Jr. 2005, Inventing the Electronic Century. Harvard University Press

Chandler, Alfred D., Jr. 2005, Shaping the Industrial Century. Harvard University Press

Conner, G., McFadden, M., & McLean, I. (2012, January 1). Organisational Design

Designing an Effective Organization Structure. (2009, January 1).. Retrieved July 25, 2014, from http://www.bridgespan.org/getmedia/b1139597-adfe-4dd7-bbb2-ac8c67883020/effective-organizations_-structural-design.pdf.aspx

Dess, G.G., Rasheed, A.M.A., McLaughlin, K.J., & Priem, R.L. "The New Corporate Architecture," *Academy of Management Executive* 9 (1995): 7–18.

*Enterprise.* Cambridge, MA: MIT Press

Faycl, *General and Industrial Management.*

Fayol, H. *General and Industrail Management,* transl. Constance Storrs (London: Pitman Publishing, 1949).

Griffin, R.W. *Task Design* (Glenview, IL: Scott, Foresman, 1982).

Hackman, J.R. & Oldham, G.R. *Work Redesign* (Reading, MA: Addison-Wesley, 1980).

Hackman, J.Richard; Oldham, Greg R. (August 1976). "Motivation through the design of work: test of a theory". *Organizational Behavior and Human Performance* **16** (2): 250–279. doi:10.1016/0030-5073(76)90016-7.

Hall, D.J. and Saias, M.A. (1980). *Strategy Follows Structure!* Strategic Management Journal, Vol 1 No 2 (April–June 1980) 149–163

Hammer, M. & Champy, J. *Reengineering the Corporation: A Manifesto for Business Revolution* (New York: Harper & Row, 1993)

Herzberg, F. (1968). *One more time: How do you motivate employees.* Boston: Harvard Business Review. pp. 46–57.

Herzberg, F. (1968). *One more time: How do you motivate employees.* Boston: Harvard Business Review. pp. 46–57.

http://www.bridgespan.org/getmedia/b1139597-adfe-4dd7-bbb2-ac8c67883020/effective-organizations_-structural-design.pdf.aspx

http://www.cipd.co.uk/NR/rdonlyres/8C5DA6D7-99B5-41F2-859A-E2DF80539C5C/0/978184398132_sc.pdf

Lawler, Edward (1973). *Motivation in Work Organizations.* Belmont, California: Wadsworth Publishing Company INC. p. 148.

March, J.G. & Simon. H.A. *Organizations* (New York: John Wiley & Sons, 1958)

Osland, Joyce S.; [et al.] (2007). *Organizational behavior : an experiential approach* (8th ed. ed.). Upper Saddle River, N.J.: Pearson Prentice Hall. pp. 35–36. ISBN 0131441515.

Parker, Sharon K. (3 January 2014). "Beyond Motivation: Job and Work Design for Development, Health, Ambidexterity, and More". *Annual Review of Psychology* **65** (1): 661–691. doi:10.1146/annurev-psych-010213-115208.

Pink, D. "Who Has the Next Big Idea?" *Fast Company,* 1 September 2001, 108.

Rich, M. "Shut Up So We Can Do Our Jobs!-Fed Up Workers Try to Muffle Chitchat, Conference Calls and Other Open-Office Din," *The Wall Street Journal,* 29 August 2001, B1.

Rush, Harold F. M. (1971). *Job Design for Motivation.* New York: The Conference Board. p. 5.

Schultz, Duane P.; Sydney Ellen Schultz (2010). *Psychology and work today : an introduction to industrial and organizational psychology* (10th ed. ed.). Upper Saddle River, N.J.: Prentice Hall. p. 227. ISBN 0205683584.

Sheridan, "The Agile Web: A Model for the Future?"

Snow, C.C., Miles, R.E., & Coleman, Jr., H.J. "Managing 21st Century Network Organizations," *Organizational Dynamics*, Winter 1992, 5–20.

Spreitzer, G.M. "Individual Empowerment in the Workplace: Dimensions, Measurement, and Validation," *Academy of Managemetn Journal* 38 (1995): 1442–1465.

Taylor, Frederick Winslow (1903), *Shop Management*, New York, NY, USA: American Society of Mechanical Engineers, OCLC 2365572. *"Shop Management" began as an address by Taylor to a meeting of the ASME, which published it in pamphlet form. The link here takes the reader to a 1912 republication by Harper & Brothers. Also available from Project Gutenberg.*

Taylor, Frederick Winslow (1911), *The Principles of Scientific Management*, New York, NY, USA and London, UK: Harper & Brothers, LCCN 11010339, OCLC 233134. *Also available from Project Gutenberg.*

Thomas, K.W. & Velthouse, B. A. "Cognitive Elements of Empowerment," *Academy of Management Review* 15 (1990): 666–681.

Wall, T. D.; S. Parker (2001). Neil J. Smelser and Paul B. Baltes, ed. *International encyclopedia of the social & behavioral sciences* (Encyclopedia) (in English) (2nd. ed.). Amsterdam, Netherlands: Elsevier. pp. 7980–7983. ISBN 978-0-08-054805-0.

Weber, M. *The Theory of Social and Economic Organization*, transl. and ed. A. M. Henderson & T. Parsons (New York: Free Press, 1947).

# CHAPTER 9

## Managing Work Teams

*"Teamwork is the ability to work together toward a common vision. The ability to direct individual accomplishments toward organizational objectives. It is the fuel that allows common people to attain uncommon results."*

– Andrew Carnegie

---

### Chapter Learning Objectives:

After reading this chapter you should have a good understanding of:

- The difference between groups and teams.
- The importance of managing workplace teams and enhancing their effectiveness.
- The advantages and disadvantages of using teams.
- The different types of workplace teams.

- The stages of team development and effective leadership behaviors in each stage.
- The five components of designing successful teams.
- The two kinds of conflict and their definitions.

# Managing Teams

A growing number of organizations are significantly improving their effectiveness by adopting team-based environments. As organizations are forced to operate in more complex environments, it is work teams that have become the common working unit in many contemporary organizations. **Work teams** consist of a group of individuals possessing complementary skills who hold themselves mutually accountable for pursuing a common business purpose, such as, improving customer service or achieving workplace performance goals.

Recently, organizations have realized that team-based work environments have the ability to foster interaction through increased communication, generate new and innovate ideas, and introduce a sense of vitality and synergy in the workplace. And, in many industries, teams are growing in importance as they can help organizations improve interdependent work processes and respond to business challenges and specific problems.

However, work teams are not the solution for every situation or organization. When organizations create high functioning teams and the teams are utilized properly and in the right settings, work teams can dramatically improve effectiveness and efficiency and overall company performance. Additionally, when composed and managed properly work teams can achieve higher productivity and better results than other traditional management approaches. But, not all workplace groups become effective work teams. What makes some teams effective and others not?

## Work Group versus Work Team

Work groups and teams do not share definitions. A **work group** is a collection of individuals operating towards a business goal with little or no collaboration between the members of the group. For example, the work group may be responsible for work on separate parts of project or for assisting different

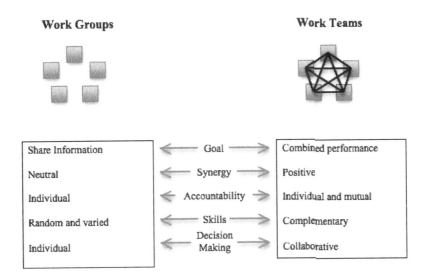

Figure 9.1: Comparing Work Groups and Work Teams

177

customers. A **work team** is a collaborative group of individuals with complementary talents and skills joined together to accomplish a common organizational objective or goal. Similar to work teams, a **high-functioning team** is generally regarded as a tight-knit team, aligned with and committed to a common goal, capable of achieving high level of collaboration and innovation. In high functioning teams, the output of the team generally exceeds the sum of the output of individual members.

## Advantages of Teams

More frequently, companies are utilizing work teams as a common part of the workplace environment. The benefits of work teams create advantages for the organization and the employee. Several of the benefits work teams bring to the organization include: shared ideas and innovation, increased speed and efficiency in product development, increased customer satisfaction, product and service quality, and employee job satisfaction. Several of the advantages work teams offer the team member include improved office relationships, development of ability or expansion of knowledge through the sharing of work, a feeling of connectedness, and job satisfaction. The advantages of teamwork are more than just organizational and business; generally, there are personal benefits for the employees.

Working in teams is a common part of today's business environment. Three primary reasons organizations adopt team based environments revolve around an increase in efficiency, the sharing of ideas fostering collaboration and innovation, and better decision-making. Increased efficiency, a key advantage of teamwork, results when team members work together to accomplish tasks. A team can work more quickly and with greater efficiency than an individual. Shared ideas, another key advantage of teamwork, results when team members contribute different perspectives and approaches. The ability to share and bounce ideas among team members produces innovation and collaboration. Decision-making in teams improves due to the sharing of ideas, perspectives and approaches. Because members posses different experiences, knowledge, skills, and abilities, the team is able to gather multiple perspectives on issues. This generally leads teams to make better decisions. Diverse viewpoints help the team to generate multiple approaches to problems and brainstorm alternative solutions. The increased knowledge generated from multiple perspectives provides the team a bed of information from which to generate more alternative solutions. Diverse viewpoints also assist the team in identifying and solving the fundamental causes of the problem rather than simply dealing with the symptoms. Additionally, team members are more committed to the solution since they were involved in the decision-making process.

## Disadvantages of Teams

Certainly, work teams can produce significant benefits for the organization and the individual. However, creating and using workplace teams does not guarantee the organization positive outcomes, as there are several inherent problems in work teams. While teamwork is generally viewed as a positive concept, work teams may experience several significant disadvantages. The two most crucial disadvantages of teamwork are social loafing and the problems associated with groupthink.

Closely connected to unequal participation, social loafing is a key disadvantage of work teams.

First documented by nineteenth-century German scientist Max Ringelman (1913), **social loafing** occurs when team members do not participate and instead deliberately exert less or entirely withhold their efforts. In other words, they do not perform their share of the work and allow others to do most of the work.

While working on rope pulling exertion, Ringelman found the larger the team, the less individual effort. Indeed, social loafing is more probable in larger groups because it can be difficult to categorize the efforts or individual team members. Social loafers are less likely to assume responsibility for a task. Social loafers count on blending into the background, where their lack of efforts isn't easily spotted. In other cases, social loafers are armed with a variety of excuses and delay tactics. In some instances this can lead to conflict, resentment, and low workplace morale.

Usually in teamwork, there can be a tendency for unequal participation as some members to contribute less and others contribute more. Unlike unequal participation, social loafing is a conscious and intentional action. Due to the importance of team-based class projects, most students already know about social loafers or "slackers."

## Reducing social loafing

Dan Rothwell (1999) claims utilizing the three Cs of motivation can reduce social loafing –collaboration, content, and choice.

1. Collaboration, a way to involve team members, is achieved by assigning special and meaningful tasks to all members of the team.
2. Content, giving meaning to involvement, is achieved by assigning worthy and meaningful tasks to team members.
3. Choice, the opportunity to have input into involvement, is achieved by providing members the opportunity to choose their tasks.

Consequently, involvement, responsibility, and motivation are deterrents to social loafing. For example, assigning group roles and tasks can cause lack of motivation, disagreements, and frustration. Whereas involving group members in the planning and discussion of assignments and the freedom to choose tasks encourages collaboration and responsibility while reduces social loafing.

Groupthink, the second key disadvantage of teamwork, can have disastrous affects. Pioneered and documented by Irving Janis (1072), groupthink is a psychological phenomenon. **Groupthink** occurs when the desire for harmony or conformity among group members results in illogical, irrational, or unscientific decision-making. In highly cohesive groups or groups constructed with unequal power distributions, group members feel tremendous pressure to agree with each other so the group can continue a particular course of action. Generally evidenced by an inadequate number of alternative solutions, a hallmark of groupthink is the lack of independent critical thinking. Additional characteristics of groupthink include restricted discussion, elimination of diverse perspectives, and poor decision-making.

Continuing his work in the field, Janis acknowledged three antecedent conditions to groupthink– high group cohesiveness, structural faults, and situational context.

1. High group cohesiveness leads to lack of individuality. The group becomes more important than the individual or their opinions and ideas.

2.  Structural faults include insulation of the group, lack of rules or norms for decision-making, lack of impartial leadership, lack of diverse experience, background and knowledge among group members.
3.  Situational context includes recent group failures, moral dilemmas, overwhelming difficulties in decision-making, and disproportionate or overpowering external threats.

Although all of these conditions underpin groupthink, it is not necessary for each of the three to be present in order for groupthink to occur. Interestingly, Janis considered high cohesiveness essential for groupthink to occur, although a high degree of cohesiveness was not guaranteed to produce groupthink.

In order to help in the identification of groupthink, Irving Janis documented eight symptoms. These symptoms, indicative of groupthink, can help managers, leaders, and groups recognize the signs of groupthink.

Type I: Overestimations of the group—its power and morality
1.  *Illusions of invulnerability* includes creating excessive optimism and encourages risk taking.
2.  *Unquestioned belief* in the group's morality. Members belief in the rightness of the cause and therefore ignore the consequences of their actions.

Type II: Closed-mindedness
1.  *Rationalizing* signs or warnings that might challenge the assumptions of the group.
2.  *Stereotyping* those who are opposed to majority opinion or the group, such as stupid or biased.

Type III: Pressures toward uniformity
1.  *Self-censorship* of opinions or ideas that deviate from the seeming group consensus are not expressed.
2.  *Illusions of unanimity* among group members. Silence is viewed as agreement and majority views and judgments are assumed to be unanimous.
3.  *Direct pressure* to conform is placed on members who question the group. Members are under pressure not to express dissenting arguments.
4.  *Mindguards*— self-appointed members who shield the group from dissenting information. Members who shield the group leader and members from information that is problematic or contradictory to existing information.

Not surprisingly, Janis also devoted a considerable amount of time investigating and documenting strategies designed to prevent groupthink. Although not every decision-making group is destined to groupthink, Janis devised eight tactics to aid in preventing groupthink:

1.  Leaders should assign each member the role of "critical evaluator". This allows each member to freely air objections and doubts.
2.  Leaders should not express an opinion, preference, or expectation when assigning tasks to the group.
3.  Leaders should remove themselves from most group meetings. This will help leaders avoid excessively influencing the outcome.
4.  The organization should set up several independent groups. These independent groups should be assigned to work on the same assignment or task.
5.  Each effective alternative should be examined.

6. Each member should discuss the group's ideas with trusted people outside of the group.
7. The group should invite one or more outside experts into meetings. Group members should be allowed to discuss with and question the outside experts, while the outside experts should challenge the members' views.
8. At least one group member should be assigned the role of Devil's advocate. This role should question assumptions and plans. This role should also be rotated –a different person should be assigned for each meeting.

Team decision-making takes a considerable amount of time. Often, team meetings can be unproductive and inefficient. At times, a minority of group members dominates team discussions and restricts critical debates. When this occurs, problems are not fully defined and few alternative solutions are generated. These types of situations can cause team members to not feel accountable for team decisions. However, in order for teams to make better decisions, time and careful consideration to the topics at hand are required.

**Create chart**

| Team Advantages | Team Disadvantages |
|---|---|
| • Team members have the opportunity to learn from each other. | • Some individuals are not compatible with team work. |
| • Potential exists for greater work force flexibility with cross-training. | • Workers must be selected to fit the team as well as requisite job skills. |
| • Opportunity provided for synergistic combinations of ideas and abilities. | • Some members may experience less motivating jobs as part of a team. |
| • New approaches to tasks may be discovered. | • Organization may resist change. |
| • Teams membership can provide social facilitation and support for difficult tasks and situations. | • Conflict may develop between team members or other teams. |
| • Communication and information exchange may be facilitated and increased. | • Teams may be time-consuming due to need for coordination and consensus. |
| • Teams can foster greater cooperation among team members. | • Teams can stymie creativity and inhibit good decision-making if "group think" becomes prevalent. |
| • Interdependent work flow can be enhanced. | • Evaluation and rewards may be perceived as less powerful; |
| • Potential exists for greater acceptance and understanding of team-made decisions. | • "Free-riding" within the team may occur. |
| • Greater autonomy, variety, identity, significance, and feedback for workers can occur. | • Less flexibility may be experienced in personnel replacement or transfer. |
| • Team commitment may stimulate performance and attendance. | |

\* *adapted from Medsker, G.J., Campion, M.A., "Job and Team Design," in Salvendy, G., Handbook of Human Factors and Ergonomics, pp. 450–489, Interscience, 18 Apr 1997.*

Figure 9.2: Advantages and Disadvantages of Teams

**Team Advantages & Disadvantages**

The advantages and disadvantages of teams also need to be considered before deciding to transition to teams. The following table of team advantages and disadvantages is an adaptation of work by Medsker and Campion (1992).* This list can also be used by existing teams to self-evaluate their efficacy.

## Types of Work Teams

In today's workplace, team-based environments are growing in popularity. Teams are important because they help businesses respond to both specific and complex problems and challenges. Organizations use different types of teams for different purposes. Generally, the type of team an organization utilizes varies depending on need and also from business to business.

Teams should be utilized for a clear purpose. Prior to creating a team, managers need to think through the purpose, scope, design and the level of autonomy of the team. **Autonomy** is the degree to which workers have the independence and authority to utilize resources, access information, and decided how and when to accomplish their tasks. Defined and discussed below are the four most common types of workplace teams.

1. Problem-solving teams
2. Self-managed teams
3. Cross-functional teams
4. Virtual teams

**Problem-solving teams**, designed for specific issues, help to solve organizational problems by offering suggestions and advice to management. Problem-solving teams share ideas and offer suggestions on how processes and methods can be improved in areas such as manufacturing safety, product quality, and customer satisfaction. Typically, teams look at improving quality, effectiveness, and efficiency. However, problem-solving teams are rarely given the authority to implement their ideas or suggestions.

**Self-managed teams**, have the greatest degree of autonomy, as they generally take on supervisory responsibilities. Self-managed teams are generally granted responsibility over their schedules, meeting times, task assignments, and processes. Typical responsibilities include managing and controlling resources, making the product or providing the service, and ensuring timely delivery. In some instances, fully self-managed team may select their own members and evaluate and provide feedback on each other's performance.

**Cross-functional teams** are intentionally composed of employees at about the same hierarchical level but from different functional areas of the organization. Generally, cross-functional teams are created to coordinate complex projects or accomplish a specific task that requires one or more areas of expertise. Because members have different functional backgrounds and specialties, cross-functional teams are effective at exchanging information and perspectives. Early communication and coordination between different functional areas of expertise, helps organizations to build better designs and improve quality.

**Virtual teams** are composed of geographically and/or organizationally dispersed employees who use technology to meet and accomplish assigned tasks. Virtual team members collaborate online and rarely meet face-to-face. Because the team members don't meet in a traditional setting, the ability to overcome time and space constraints is an advantage. Similar to more traditional teams, at times, virtual teams may include other key stakeholders, such as suppliers and customers. But, employees and other stakeholders can meet from the comfort of their own office or home. Virtual teams allow team members greater flexibility but demand less of a time commitment due to the lack of travel and are less costly for organizations to support.

# Designing Work Teams

As more organizations adopt team-based environments and create different types of teams, it is imperative for managers to understand how to construct and lead effective work teams. Arguably, team member composition, selecting the right people for the team, is an essential factor for creating well-functioning and high performing teams. Given the trend of team-based work environments, managers who understand the foundational elements of composing effective teams will be better prepared to lead in the organizations of today. Currently, there is much discussion about the team member composition. Yet, despite the different characteristics used to describe team composition, a set of common set of components are recognized as critical in designing effective work teams.

1. Team Norms
2. Team Cohesiveness
3. Team Roles
4. Team Size
5. Group diversity

## Team Norms

Over time, teams develop **norms** -implicit agreed-on standards that regulate team behavior. Although team norms are informal, they are understood codes that govern the behaviors of team members. Valuable because they let team members know what is expected of them, norms regulate team behavior and allow teams to function effectively. Team norms are often linked to positive organizational outcomes. Generally, team norms can influence stronger organizational commitment, improved job and organizational satisfaction, and a deeper trust in management. For example, effective work teams develop positive and constructive norms about individual behavior, such as, timeliness, accountability, quality, job performance, absenteeism, safety, professionalism, and transparency. Research demonstrates that norms are one of the most powerful influences on an individual's work behavior.

However, norms can also negatively influence a teams' behavior. Destructive or negative team norms are developed similarly to positive team norms. Destructive team norms can harm the organization, other employees, and team members. For example, deliberately bending or breaking the rules, developing passive-aggressive behaviors, or intentionally ignoring the chain of command are all negative team norms that can harm the organization and it's employees. Because research demonstrates that team norms are developed in the early stages of group development, it is critical that teams establish positive norms as early as possible.

## Team Cohesiveness

**Cohesiveness,** a critical characteristic of successful work teams, is the extent to which team members are attracted to a team and motivated to stay part of the team. Team cohesiveness, important for numerous reasons, promotes cooperative behavior. Primarily, research has demonstrated that high cohesiveness improves team member satisfaction, loyalty, and participation, which leads to increased team performance. Typically, morale is higher due to better communication among group members, which in turn gives individuals a feeling of being in on things. Additionally, highly cohesive teams are committed to team decisions and, hence, experience a higher shared accountability. Because cohesive groups are able to retain their members they experience lower turnover.

Research has established that cohesive teams are able to attain high levels of performance quickly as compared with team with low cohesiveness. Additionally, cohesive teams consistently perform better than teams with low cohesiveness. Conversely, teams low in cohesion may experience disagreements, conflicts, lack of participation, and low communication and coordination. Typically, teams with low cohesion are often lagging in organization and commitment to team. Additionally, teams with low team member cohesiveness may have members not fully committed to team decisions, strategies, schedules, and goals. As a result, teams low in cohesion take much longer to reach the same levels of performance.

## Team Roles

Differentiation of roles within a team leads to better team cohesiveness and productivity. Although there are many different kinds of contributions by individuals in a team, there are several key roles. Team roles can be broadly categorized as functional or non-functional. **Functional roles** assist the team to successfully and productively attain their goal. **Non-functional roles** detract from the team and hinder performance.

Functional roles include both task and socio-emotional roles. **Task roles** include individual actions that help the project stay on task and move forward. Individuals who fulfill task roles think about what it takes to do the job. They are generally organized and proficient at sequencing. Task roles directly contribute to the productivity of the team. **Socio-emotional roles** include individual actions that help communication, participation, and preserve team relationships. Individuals who fulfill socio-emotional roles work at strengthening and maintaining relationships. They are generally inclusive and encouraging. Socio-emotional roles directly contribute to the cohesiveness of the team. Although many individuals will have a dominant strength in their functional role, other individuals may operate as more of a dual role—equally comfortable in either the task or the socio-emotional role. If a group is to become a high-functioning team, then both roles must be present as either the task or socio-emotional role may be required by the team at any given time. If a team lacks balance, then it will have difficulty attaining their goal in an effective and efficient manner. A lack of socio-emotional role contribution is likely to cause quarrels and disagreements to fester and become destructive conflict. On the other hand, a lack of task role contribution is likely to cause a lack of focus and productivity.

Non-functional roles include non-participative and hindering roles. **Non-participative roles** refer to the actions of individuals that are absent either physically or mentally. Individuals who are non-participative are generally, absent, inattentive or unengaged. **Hindering roles** include individual actions

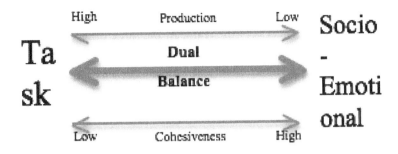

Figure 9.3: Team Cohesiveness and Roles

that impede the team's progress. Individuals who fulfill hindering roles often delay or obstruct the team's progress. Hindering actions may include such behaviors as being uncooperative, degrading others, or employing passive-aggressive behaviors.

Although As team size increases, the need to differentiate between the roles of individuals increases. With time, the roles that team members occupy may change. Different situations may cause individual roles to emerge. Regardless of the level and type of contribution, all team members should be responsible for behaving in a way that furthers the objectives of the team and advances the organization.

## Team Size

Research has established a preliminary link between team size and team performance. Recently, Chidambaram and Tung (2005) established that group size had a significant effect on group performance. In smaller groups, members have a tendency to participate. Wile, in larger groups members are more likely to appear busy. For most traditional types of teams, generally, the optimal number of team member is between 5–9 since it is conducive to high team cohesiveness. As it easy for members to contribute in positive ways and get to know other team members, team member can participate without getting lost in a large team. So, it is easier to instill a sense of responsibility and accountability in the team. Additionally, having 5–9 team members enables the team to take advantage of the diversity in team members' experience, skills, and knowledge. Obviously, very small teams or very large team have significant concerns.

Often, very large or very small team will not perform as well as moderately sized teams. If a team is too small (three or less members) there may be a lack of differences in ability, experience, skills, and knowledge. Lack of diversity may impact the team in the areas of generating alternatives, decision-making, and innovation. On the other hand, if a team is too large (10 or more members) then the team is not likely to be cohesive. When teams become too large then it is difficult to get know other team members. If this occurs, then teams may fragment into smaller sub-groups. The creation of sub-groups may create minority domination-where a few of the team members control and dominate.

There appears to be a curvilinear relationship between team size and performance. In other words, very small or very large teams may not perform as well as moderately sized teams. For most teams, the right size is somewhere between six and nine members. This size is conductive to high team cohesion, which has a positive effect on team performance, as discussed above. A team of this size is small enough for the team members to get to know each other and for each member to have an opportunity to contribute in a meaningful way to the success of the team. At the same time, the team is also large enough to take advantage of team members' diverse skills, knowledge, and perspectives. It is also easier to instill a sense of responsibility and mutual accountability in teams if this size.

## Team Member Diversity

Most importantly, diversity in teamwork is not limited to racial or ethnic diversity. **Team member diversity** refers to individualism, such as, variances in level of ability, experience, personality, education, and background. In other words, team member diversity is the significant uniqueness of the

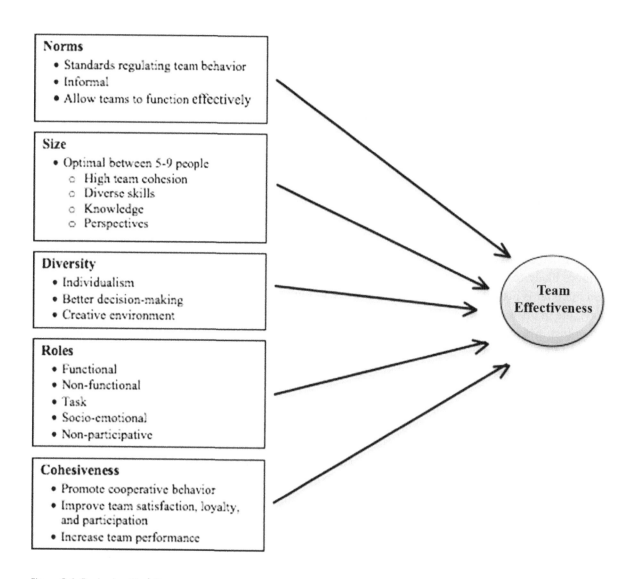

Figure 9.4: Designing Work Teams

personalities on the team. Certainly, by definition, diverse representation from the team members provides an increased likelihood that a broad range of views and perspectives will be presented. The existence and presentation of diverse views is essential to better decision-making. From fully understanding the problem to identifying to exploring a greater number of alternative solutions, diversity fosters a creative environment and allows for exploration of a task, assignment, or problem from various angles. Research has demonstrated the roll of diversity in improving and increasing team performance.

While constructing diverse teams, organizations must make sure that individuals selected posses a focus on teamwork (individualism-collectivism). Hofstede's Cultural Dimensions theory (Greet Hofstede, 1984) defines **individualism-collectivism** as "the degree to which individuals are integrated into groups." defined as the degree of difference between believing one should be self-sufficient and that loyalty to one's self is more important than loyalty to one's team or company. **Individualists**, who put their welfare and interest and those of their immediate family first, generally prefer independent tasks. They may prefer to work alone. In contrast, **collectivists**, who put group, team, or company interests ahead of self-interests, generally prefer interdependent tasks. They may prefer to work with others. However the degree of individualism-collectivism should not preempt the need for team member diversity, as individualist may be appropriate to garner wide variances.

## Stages of Team Development

In 1965, **Bruce Tuckman**, a prominent scholar in group dynamics theory and research, published his model of group development called Tuckman's stages. Understanding that teams mature experientially and in stages, Tuckman explained that teams must traverse these phases in order to mature into well-functioning teams. Tuckman's team development model suggests that as teams mature, they pass through five separate and distinct stages of development. These stages are necessary for the growth of teams as they learn to overcome obstacles, develop solutions, and deliver results. Moreover, individual relationships and leadership style change throughout the different phases of a team—from the beginning (formation) of the team through the end (adjourning). Originally, Tuckman's stages of team development offered four stages—forming, storming, norming, and performing. However, in 1977, Tuckman and colleague Mary Jensen added a fifth stage - adjourning. Widely accepted, Tuckman's model of group development has become the foundation for later models.

1. Forming
2. Storming
3. Norming
4. Performing
5. Adjourning

**Forming**, the initial stage of team development is characterized as the 'meet and greet' stage. When team members first meet each other, they are polite and try to avoid controversy and conflict. They do, however, form initial impressions, gather information, and try to assess how they fit into the group. A few of fist team norms will be established during this stage, as team members begin discussing expectations and discovering acceptable behaviors.

In the forming stage, team leaders should facilitate the 'meet and greet' ensuring that all group members get to know each other and participate and engage in conversations regarding preliminary roles, rules, and structure. During this stage, team leaders should allow time for team members to get to know each other. If possible, team leaders should help the team set early ground rules, and begin preliminary discussion on the methods of selecting and deciding upon team structure.

**Storming**, the second stage of team development is often distinguished by disagreements and conflicts. As team members become acquainted with each other, the level of comfort in expression increases. Generally, team members become more assertive at this stage and are more willing to state opinions. Team members begin voicing opinions and disagreements and arguments may erupt. Different personalities, agendas, and work styles clash and cause conflict. During this stage team members also announce their intentions and politic for positions. In addition to attempting to establish favorable roles for themselves, team members are likely to have disagreements about goals, objectives, and processes.

During the disagreements and conflicts of the storming stage, it is important for team leaders to ensure that differences are channeled in a productive manner. It is also critical that team leaders do not attempt to squash or bury the difference, but instead foster an environment of respecting different opinions and remaining professional in conversations and actions. Additionally, team leaders must keep driving the focus towards team goals and team performance. If a team remains in the storming stage or continues to the next stage without resolving the issues present, then the team is likely to be ineffective.

The establishment and acceptance of team roles and structure characterize **norming**, the third stage of team development. During this stage, team members having resolved differences can begin the process of learning to work together productively. Team members begin settling into their roles as team members and the group makes big decisions about goals and objectives. Additionally, the team should be working together to develop agreement and expectations on processes, methods, and working styles in preparation for the work that needs to be done. Team leaders should ensure that participation and engagement among team members is high and that team norms are positive and performance oriented. While monitoring for groupthink, team leaders should ensure that members are beginning to operate as a unit. If commitment and unity are strong, then team members may participate in social activities. If so, the team leaders should help the group to avoid cliques and factions.

In the fourth stage of team development, **performing**, is distinguished by performance. The team has become a well-oiled machine—an effective and efficient fully functioning team. Because team roles and structure were settled in the previous stage, brainstorming and ideas are now debated instead of personal agendas. The team improves because it can now focus on creative and innovative problem solving. During the performing stage, it is common for cohesiveness to be high as team members are committed to the team, feel responsible to other group members and accountable for the success or failure of the team. Team leaders should assure that productivity remains high by making certain the team has access to all required resources, such as, information and materials.

The last stage of team development, adjourning does not necessarily contribute to the main task of managing a team. However, it is important and relevant to individual development and critical for team development and organizational improvement. **Adjourning**, which occurs after the completion of the project or task, involves a closing of the project and a review of the successes and failures. During this stage, team leaders should conduct any outstanding evaluations and help the team celebrate successes, identify strengths to retain, and explore possible improvements for future team projects. Team leaders should also recognize the personal involvement and investment of the members and help the team transition from thinking of themselves as 'members of the team' and prepare for the next project or a return to a previous assignment.

Arguably, not all teams passes through each of these stages. However, teams that do progress through each stage tend to be become better performing teams. Conversely, ineffective teams may begin a process of decline and pass through the stages of de-norming, de-storming, and de-forming. If team cohesiveness destructs, the team becomes complacent, or ineffective leadership transpires, then the team is likely to become ineffective and inefficient. As performance declines, the group decays and the team may experience one or more stage of de-norming, de-storming, and de-forming.

**De-norming**, a reversal of the norming stage is characterized by the deterioration of team performance. A natural erosion of group guidelines and norms may occur as the interests and expectations change and group members go in different directions. De-norming can also be caused by significant

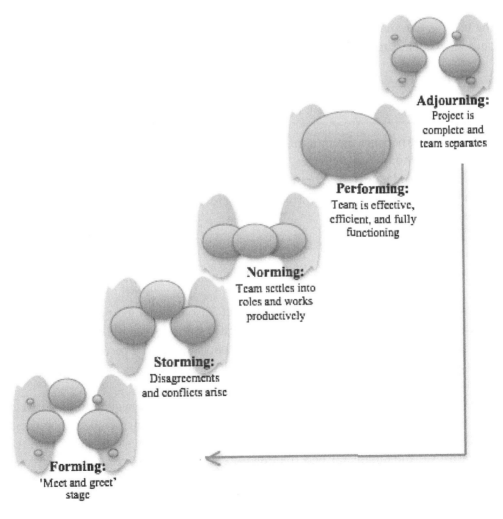

Figure 9.5: Tuckman's Stages of Team Development

shifts to the team, such as changes to the size, scope, or goals of the team. When new members are introduced, they may question, challenge, or reject group norms or previously established roles, structures, methods or work styles.

**De-storming**, a reversal of the storming phase is distinguished by a decrease in group cohesiveness. Instead of the rapid and openness of disagreements found in the storming phase, a slow undercurrent of discontent resides among group members. The team's comfort level is disturbed as team unity weakens and group members increasingly resist conforming to team norms.

**De-forming,** a reversal of the forming stage is characterized by team member isolation. As the team begins to fall apart, members battle to gain control of pieces of the project or team. As team members struggle to position themselves they begin to avoid other members and isolate themselves from the leaders. Team performance declines and those tasks or pieces of the project that are unclaimed go abandoned as the team quits caring.

Even if teams are proactively managed, decline is not inescapable. So, team leaders must not become complacent with a performing team. Additionally, recognizing the destruction of the deconstructive stages managers must be aware and informed of current team performance and group dynamics. When needed, the team leader and the manager should take the necessary steps to reinforce group norms, bolster cohesiveness, reiterate team and organizational goals, and negotiate disruptive conflict.

# Team Conflict

When groups work together, miscommunications, arguments and disagreements are to be expected. It is inevitable that people who work together are going to disagree. These conflicts may arise from a variety of issues, such as, what and how things should get done. For example, team members may disagree over resources, schedules, team goals, and priorities. There are two primary types of conflict that exist in inter-group relations:

1. Cognitive conflict
2. Affective conflict

**Cognitive conflict** is defined as task-oriented conflict. Also referred to as c-type conflict, cognitive conflict includes arguments or disagreements concentrated on task or problem-related differences in judgments or perspectives. C-type conflict is generally associated with a certain issues, such as, timelines, schedules, resources, and the work itself. For example, team members may disagree over timelines and task, such as, how or when to get the work done.

Generally, this type of conflict leads to exploration of different ideas, negotiation, creative decision-making, and improved team decision-making and performance. Team members may disagree, but c-type conflict is distinguished by a willingness to investigate and resolve differences with the goal of identifying alternatives and finding the best solution

**Affective conflict** is defined as emotional conflict. Affective conflict includes arguments or disagreements concentrated on personal differences and disputes. Also referred to as a-type conflict, affective conflict is generally associated with and drawn from emotion as disagreements become more personal than professional. Whereas cognitive conflict is about issues, affective conflict is about people.

Unlike cognitive conflict, affective conflict generally decreases team member satisfaction and commitment and team performance. In worse case scenarios, team members can hold grudges, withhold information, sabotage other members, and be uncooperative. When team members disagree, the outcome may be team members who are uncomfortable, unhappy, or apathetic due to expressions of anger and distrust. Teams can, and often do, experience both types of conflict. At times, conflict can begin as c-type and deteriorate into a-type conflict. Irving Janis proposed that constructive conflict is beneficial to groups as it aids in reducing the risk of groupthink. Conflict can lead to a better understanding of issues among group members. Additionally, conflict can also lead to creative and innovative ways to solve problems or take advantage of opportunities.

Although conflict causes frustration, constructive resolution of the conflict often generates positive results. **Constructive conflict** is defined as conflict in which the benefits outweigh the costs. However, in constructive conflict the process is as important as the result. Utilizing cognitive conflict, team members come together for the greater good. **Destructive conflict** is defined as conflict in which the damages outweigh the benefits. Often in destructive conflict the parties succumb to personal attacks and hostility and operate under the assumption that the opposing party must suffer defeat.

Done properly, cognitive and constructive conflict benefits all individuals involved and the organization. In teamwork, constructive conflict involves open communication, discussion, and provides the platform for better understanding and collaboration, which in turn produces high-quality ideas. Teams that feel comfortable with a cognitive level of disagreement and acknowledge difference of opinions develop better relationships, produce better results, and are able to increase their productivity.

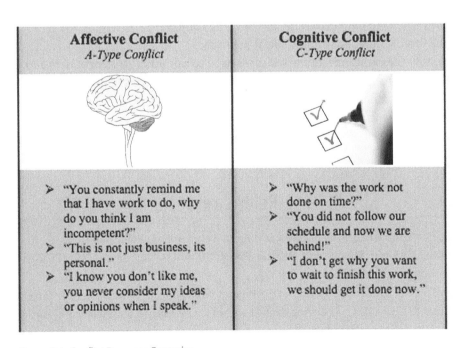

Figure 9.6: Conflict Response Examples

# Summary of Chapter

1. This chapter focused on team management; we examined the advantages and disadvantages of teams.
2. We explored strategies to minimize the disadvantages of workplace teams. We learned how the three Cs can reduce social loafing and the eight preventative measures to employ in order to minimize the threat of groupthink.
3. The four common types of workplace teams and the typical characteristics of each were discussed.
4. We revealed the five core components of designing effective workplace teams. Norms are implicit agreed-upon standards that regulate team behavior. Cohesiveness is the extent to which team members are attracted to a team and motivated to stay part of the team. Differentiation of roles within a team leads to better team cohesiveness and productivity. Team size and team member diversity are essential components for designing high quality teams.
5. We explored Tuckman's stages of team development. Understanding that teams mature experientially and in stages, we read about the team role and leader role in each stage. Conversely, ineffective teams may begin a process of decline and pass through deconstruction stages.
6. We learned about team conflict and the different types of conflicts. We revisited affective and cognitive conflict and introduced constructive and destructive conflict.

# Discussion Questions

1. What are the differences between work groups and work teams?
2. Can you compare and contrast the four common types of workplace teams?
3. Why are teams becoming popular in today's workplace?
4. What are the advantages and disadvantages of using teams?
5. What are the three Cs that can reduce social loafing?
6. Can you identify the eight preventive measures used to minimize the threat of groupthink?
7. Describe the five core components of designing effective workplace teams?
8. How do norms and cohesiveness contribute to developing high quality teams?
9. How does team size and member diversity help produce a high functioning team?
10. Describe the differences between the functional team roles and how the contribute the success of the team?

# References

Tony Alessandra, Phil Hunsaker (1993), *Communicating at Work*, Fireside Publishers, p. 92

Guffey, Mary Ellen, Kathleen Rhodes and Patricia Rogin. "Business Communication: Process and Product." Toronto: Thomson South-Western, 2010. Print.

Alessandra, Tony Ph.D. & Hunsaker, Phil Ph.D. (1993) Communicating at Work. New York: Fireside Publishers.

Cappozzoli, Thomas K. (1995, Dec). Resolving conflict within teams. Journal for Quality and Participation. v18n7, p. 28–30.

"Resolve Hot Topics with Cooler Heads." Negotiation (May 2007): 12–12.

Tuckman, Bruce (1965). "Developmental sequence in small groups". *Psychological Bulletin* **63** (6): 384–99. doi:10.1037/h0022100. PMID 14314073. Retrieved 2008-11-10. "Reprinted with permission in Group Facilitation, Spring 2001"

White, Alasdair A. K. "From Comfort Zone to Performance Management" 2009 White & MacLean Publishing ISBN 978-2-930583-01-3 [1]

Blanchard, Ken and Parisi-Carew, Eunice, *The One Minute Manager Builds High Performing Teams*, William Morrow, 2009.

Fischer, Michael D (28 September 2012). "Organizational Turbulence, Trouble and Trauma: Theorizing the Collapse of a Mental Health Setting". *Organization Studies* **33** (9): 1153–1173. doi:10.1177/0170840612448155.

Fischer, Michael Daniel; Ferlie, Ewan (1 January 2013). "Resisting hybridisation between modes of clinical risk management: Contradiction, contest, and the production of intractable conflict". *Accounting, Organizations and Society* **38** (1): 30–49. doi:10.1016/j.aos.2012.11.002.

Sophia Jowett (2007). *Social Psychology in Sport*. Human Kinetics. p. 34. ISBN 978-0-7360-5780-6. Retrieved 11 October 2012.

Janis, I. L. (November 1971). "Groupthink". *Psychology Today* **5** (6): 43–46, 74–76.

Jehn, K. A.; Mannix, E. A. (1 April 2001). "The dynamic nature of conflict: A longitudinal study.". *Academy of Management Journal* **44** (2): 238–251. doi:10.2307/3069453.

Amason, A. C.; Sapienza, H. J. (1 August 1997). "The Effects of Top Management Team Size and interaction Norms on Cognitive and Affective Conflict". *Journal of Management* **23** (4): 495–516. doi:10.1177/014920639702300401.

Eidelson, Roy, J; Eidelson, Judy I (2003). "Dangerous ideas: Five beliefs that propel groups toward conflict". *American Psychologist* **58** (3): 182–192. doi:10.1037/0003-066X.58.3.182.

Sue, Derald Wing; Bingham, Rosie P.; Porché-Burke, Lisa; Vasquez, Melba (1999). "The diversification of psychology: A multicultural revolution". *American Psychologist* **54** (12): 1061–1069. doi:10.1037/0003-066X.54.12.1061.

Michael Nicholson (27 March 1992). *Rationality and the Analysis of International Conflict*. Cambridge University Press. p. 13. ISBN 978-0-521-39810-7. Retrieved 11 October 2012.

Karau, Steven J.; Williams, Kipling D. (1993). "Social loafing: A meta-analytic review and theoretical integration". *Journal of Personality and Social Psychology* **65** (4): 681–706. doi:10.1037/0022-3514.65.4.681. ISSN 0022-3514. "the reduction in motivation and effort when individuals work collectively compared with when they work individually or coactively"

Gilovich, Thomas; Keltner, Dacher; Nisbett, Richard E. (2006). *Social psychology*. W.W. Norton. p. 60. ISBN 978-0-393-97875-9. "The tendency to exert less effort when working on a group task in which individual contributions cannot be measured"

Piezon, Sherry L., and Ferree, William D. "Perceptions of Social Loafing in Online Learning Groups: A study of Public University and U.S. Naval War College students." June 2008. *The International Review of Research in Open and Distance Learning*. **9** (2)

Krumm, Diane J. (December 2000). *Psychology at work: an introduction to industrial/organizational psychology*. Macmillan. p. 178. ISBN 978-1-57259-659-7. Retrieved 1 May 2011.

Ringelmann, M. (1913) "Recherches sur les moteurs animés: Travail de l'homme" [Research on animate sources of power: The work of man], *Annales de l'Institut National Agronomique*, 2nd series, vol. 12, pages 1–40.

Kravitz, David A.; Martin, Barbara (1986). "Ringelmann rediscovered: The original article". *Journal of Personality and Social Psychology* **50** (5): 936–941. doi:10.1037/0022-3514.50.5.936. ISSN 1939-1315.

Ingham, Alan G.; Levinger, George; Graves, James; Peckham, Vaughn (1974). "The Ringelmann effect: Studies of group size and group performance". *Journal of Experimental Social Psychology* **10** (4): 371–384. doi:10.1016/0022-1031(74)90033-X. ISSN 0022-1031.

Latané, Bibb; Williams, Kipling; Harkins, Stephen (1979). "Many hands make light the work: The causes and consequences of social loafing". *Journal of Personality and Social Psychology* **37** (6): 822–832. doi:10.1037/0022-3514.37.6.822. ISSN 0022-3514.

PsyBlog "Social Loafing: when groups are bad for productivity," 29 May 2009 (citing, inter alia, Latane).

Chidambaram, Laku; Tung, Lai Lai (2005). "Is Out of Sight, Out of Mind? An Empirical Study of Social Loafing in Technology-Supported Groups". *Information Systems Research* **16** (2): 149–168. doi:10.1287/isre.1050.0051. ISSN 1047-7047.

Christopher Earley, P. (1989). "Social Loafing and Collectivism: A Comparison of the United States and the People's Republic of China". *Administrative Science Quarterly* **34** (4): 565–581. doi:10.2307/2393567. edit

Forsyth, D. R. (2009). Group dynamics: New York: Wadsworth. [Chapter 10]

Edwards, Wattenberg, Lineberry (2005). *Government in America: People, Politics, and Policy*, 12/E (Chapter 6 summary).

Thompson, L. L. (2003). *Making the team: A guide for managers.* Saddle River, NJ: Pearson/Prentice Hall. (pp. 31–32).

Jackson, J. M. & Harkins, S. G. (1985). Equity in effort: An explanation of the social loafing effect. *Journal of Personality and Social Psychology, 49,* 1199–1206.

Snook, Scott A. (2000). *Friendly Fire: The Accidental Shootdown of U.S. Black Hawks over Northern Iraq.* Princeton, NJ: Princeton University Press. p. 135. ISBN 978-0-691-09518-9

Hoon, Hwee; Tan, Tan Min Li (2008). "Organizational Citizenship Behavior and Social Loafing: The Role of Personality, Motives, and Contextual Factors". *The Journal of Psychology* **142** (1): 89–108. doi:10.3200/JRLP.142.1.89-112. ISSN 0022-3980.

Shiue, Yih-Chearng; Chiu, Chao-Min; Chang, Chen-Chi (2010). "Exploring and mitigating social loafing in online communities". *Computers and Human Behavior* **26** (4): 768–777. doi:10.1016/j.chb.2010.01.014. Retrieved 6 February 2012.

Chung, Jae Eun; Park, Namkee; Wang, Hua; Fulk, Janet; McLaughlin, Maraget (2010). "Age differences in perceptions of online community participation among non-users: An extension of the Technology Acceptance Model". *Computers in Human Behavior* **26** (6): 1674–1684. doi:10.1016/j.chb.2010.06.016. Retrieved 6 February 2012.

Rothwell, J. Dan (27 December 1999). *In the Company of Others: An Introduction to Communication.* McGraw-Hill. ISBN 978-1-55934-738-9. Retrieved 1 May 2011.

"Pattern: Collaboration in Small Groups" by CSCW, The Computing Company, October 31, 2005, retrieved October 31, 2005

Thompson, L. L. (2003). *Making the team: A guide for managers.* Saddle River, NJ: Pearson/Prentice Hall. (pp. 29–36).

Forsythe, 2010.

Kassin, Saul; Fein, Steven; Markus, Hazel Rose. *Social psychology* (8th ed. ed.). Belmont, CA: Cengage Wadsworth. p. 312. ISBN 978-0495812401.

Latham, Gary, P.; Baldes (1975). "James, J.". *Journal of Applied Psychology* **60** (1). doi:10.1037/h0076354.

Weldon, E.; Jehn (1991). "K.". *Journal of Personality and Social Psychology* **61** (4). doi:10.1037/0022-3514.61.4.555.

Piezon, S. L. & Donaldson, R. L. "Online groups and social loafing: Understanding student-group interactions." 2005. *Online Journal of Distance Learning Administration*, 8(4).

Kraut, R. E., & Resnick, P. Encouraging online contributions. The science of social design: Mining the social sciences to build successful online communities. Cambridge, MA: MIT Press. p. 39.

Hofstede, Geert, Gert Jan Hofstede and Michael Minkov.*Cultures and Organizations: Software of the Mind, 3rd ed.* New York: McGraw-Hill. 2010.

Whatsonmymind, September 2010, Geert Hofstede

Geert Hofstede's academic website

Hofstede, Geert (1984). *Culture's Consequences: International Differences in Work-Related Values* (2nd ed.). Beverly Hills CA: SAGE Publications. ISBN 0-8039-1444-X.

http://smallbusiness.chron.com/differences-between-destructive-constructive-conflict-1202.html

http://www.isixsigma.com/implementation/teams/high-performance-teams-understanding-team-cohesiveness/

http://www.stanford.edu/group/resed/resed/staffresources/RM/training/grouproles.html#task

B. Dumaine, "The Trouble with Teams," *Fortune*, 5 September 1994, 86–92.

J. R. Katzenback & D. K. Smith, *The Wisdpm of Teams* (Boston: Harvard Business School Press, 1993).

S. G. Cohen & D. E. Bailey, "What Males Teams Work: Group Effectiveness Research from the Shop Floor to the Executive Suite," *Journal of Management 23*, no. 3 (1997): 239–290.

S. E Gross, *Compensation for Teams* (New York: American Management Association, 1995); B. L. Kirkman & B. Rosen, "Beyond Self-Management: Antecedents and Consequences of Team Empowerment," *Academy of business Management 42* (1999): 58–74; G. Stalk & T. M. Hout, *Competing against Time: How Time-Based Competition Is Reshaping Global Markets* (New York: Free Press, 1990); S. C. Wheelwright & K. B. Clark, *Revolutionizing New Product Development* (New York: Free Press, 1992).

R. D. Banker, J. M. Field, R. G. Schroeder, & K. K. Sinha, "Impact of Work Teams on Manufacturing Performance: A Longitudinal Field Study," *Academy of Management Journal 39* (1996): 867–890.

"Beating the Joneses (Learning What the Competition Is Doing)," *Industry Week 1* (7 December 1998): 27.

Stalk & Hout, *Competing Against Time.*

H. K. Bowen, K. B. Clark, C. A. Holloway, & S. C. Wheelwright, *The Perpetual Enterprise Machine* (New York: Oxford Press, 1994).

J. L. Cordery, W. S. Mueller, & L. M. Smith, "Attitudinal and Behavioral Effects of Autonomous Group Working: A Longitudinal Field Study," *Academy of Management Journal 34* (1991): 464–476; T. D. Wall, N. J. Kemp, P. R. Jackson, & C. W. Clegg, "Outcomes of Autonomous Workgroups: A Long-Term Field Experiment," *Academy of Management Journal 29* (1986): 280–304.

J. George, " Extrinsic and Intrinsic Origins of Perceived Social Loafing in Organizations," *Academy of Management Jornal 35* (1992): 191–202.

Hoerr, "The Payoff from Teamwork: The Gains in Quality Are Substantial-So Why Isnt I Spreading Faster?"

Kirkman & Rosen, "Beyond Self-Management: Antecedents and Conswquences of Team Empowerment."

S. Eaton & G. Porter, "Selecting the Right Team Structure to Work in Your Organization," in *Handbook of Best Practices for Teams,* Vol. 1, ed. G. M. Parker (Amherst, MA: Irwin, 1996).

R. J. Recardo, D. Wade, C. A. Mention, & J. Jolly, *Teams* (Houston: Gulf Publishing Co., 1996).

D. R. Denison, S. L. Hart, & J. A. Kahn, "From Chimneys to Cross-Functional Teams: Developing and Validation a Diagnostic Model," *Academy of Management Journal 39*, no. 4 (1996): 1005–1023.

A. M. Townsend, S. M. DeMarie, & A. R. Hendrickson, "Virtual Teams: Technology and the Workplace of the Future," *Academy of Management Executive 13*, no. 3 (1998): 17–29.

A. M. Townsend, S. M. DeMarie, & A. R. Hendrickson, "Are You Ready for Virtual Teams?" *HRMagazine* 41, no. 9 (1996): 122–126.

Wellins. Byham & Dixon, *Inside Teams.*

A. M. Townsend, S. M. DeMarie, & A. R. Hendrickson, "Virtual Teams: Technology and the Workplace of the Future."

W. F. Cascio, "Managing a Virtual Workplace," *Academy of Management Executive* 14 (2000): 81–90.

R. Katz, "The Effects of Group Longevity on Project Communication and Performance," *Administrative Science Quarterly* 27 (1982): 245–282.

D. Mankin, S. G. Cohen, & T. K. Bikson, *Teams and Technology: Fulfiling the Promise of the New Organization* (Boston: Harvard Business School Press, 1996).

K. Lovelace, S. G. Cohen, & L. Weingart. "Maximizing Cross-Functional New Product Teams' Innovativeness and Constraint Adherence: A Conflict Communications Perspective," *Academy of Management Journal* 44 (2001): 779–793.

S. Asche, "Opinions and Social Pressure," *Scientific America* 193 (!995): 31–35.

S. G. Cohen, G. E. Ledford, & G. M. Spreitzer, "A Predictive Model of Self-Managing Work Team Effectiveness," *Human Relations* 49, no. 5 (1996): 643–676.

M. E. Shar, *Group Dynamics* (New York: McGraw Hill, 1981).

S. E. Jackson, "The Consequences of Diversity in Multidisciplinary Work Teams," in *Handbook of Work Group Pyschology*, ed. M. A. West (Chichester, UL: Wiley, 1996).

A. M. Isend & R. A. Baron, "Positive Affect as a Factor in Organizational Behavior," in *Research in Organizational Behavior* 13, ed. L. L. Cummings & B. M. Staw (Greenwich, CT: JAI Press, 1991), 1–53.

C. R. Evans & K. L. Dion, "Group Cohesion and Performance: A Meta Analysis," *Small Group Research* 22, no. 2 (1991): 175–186.

S. M. Gully, D. S. Devine, and D. J. Whitney, " A Meta-Analysis of Cohesion and Performance: Effects on Level of Analysis and Task Interdependence," *Small Group Research* 26, no. 4 (1995): 497–520.

R. Stankiewicsz, "The Effectiveness of Research Groups in Six Countries," in *Scientific Productivity*, ed. F. M. Andrews (Cambridge: Cambridge University Press, 1979), 191–221.

F. Rees, *Teamwork from Start to Finish* (San Francisco: Jossey-Bass, 1997).

Gully, Devins, & Whitney, " A Meta-Analysis of Cohesion and Performance."

F. Tschan & M. V. Cranach, "Group Task Structure, Processes and Outcomes," in *Handbook of Work Group Pyschology*, ed. M. A. West (Chichester, UK: Wiley 1996).

D. E. Yeatts & C. Hyten *High Performance Self Managed Teams* (Thousand Oaks, CA: Sage Publications, 1998).

Ibid; J. Colquitt, R. Noe, & C. Jackson, "Justice in Teams: Antecedents and Consequences of Procedural Justice Climate," *Personnel Psychology*, 1 April 2002, 83.

D. S. Kezsbom, "Re-Opening Pandora's Box: Sources of Project Team Conflict in the '90's," *Industrial Engineering* 24, no. 5 (1992): 54–59.

A. C. Amason, W. A. Hochwarter, K. R. Thompson, "Conflict: An Important Dimension in Successful Management Teams," *Organizational Dynamics* 24 (1995): 20.

A. C. Amason, "Distinguishing the Effects of Functional and Dysfunctional conflict on Strategic Decision Making: Resolving a Paradox for Top Management Teams," *Academy of Management Journal* 39, no. 1 (1996): 123–148.

C. Nemeth & P. Owens, "Making Work Groups More Effective: The Value of Minority Dissent," in *Handbook of Work Group Psychology*, ed. M. A. West (Chichester, UK: Wiley, 1996).

J. M. Levin & R. L. Moreland, "Progress in Small Groups Research," *Annual Review of Psychology* 9 (1990):72–78; S. E. Jackson, "Team Composition in Organizational Settings: Issues in Managing a Diverse Work Force," in *Group Processes and Productivity*, ed. S. Worchel, W. Wood, & j. Simpson (Beverly Hills, CA: Sage, 1992).

Gross. *Compensation for Teams.*

J. F. McGrew, J. G. Bilotta, & J. M. Deeney, "Software Team Formation and Decay: Extending the Standard Model for Small Groups," *Small Group Research* 30, no. 2 (1999): 209–234.

J. R. Hackman. "The Psychology of Self-Management in Organizations" in *Psychology and Work: Productivity, Change, and Employment*, ed. M. S. Pallak & R. Perloff (Washington DC: American Psychological Association, 1986), 85–136.

A. O'Leary-Kelly, J. J. Martocchio, & D. D. Frink, "A Review of the Influence of Group Goals on Group Performance," *Academy of Management Journal* 37, no. 5 (1994): 1285–1301.

A. Zander, "The Originss and Consequences of Group Goals," in *Retrospections on Social Psychology*, ed. L. Festinger (New York:Oxford University Press, 1980), 205–235.

M. Erez & A. Somech, "Is Group Productivity Loss the Rule or The Expectation" Effects of Culture and Group-Based Motivation." *Academy of Management Journal* 39, no. 6 (1996): 1513–1537.

S. Sherman, "Stretch Goals: The Dark Side of Asking For Miracles." *Fortune*, 13 November 1995, 231.

K. R. Thompson, W. A. Hochwarter, & N. J. Mathys, "Stretch Targets: What Makes Them Effective?" *Academy of Management Executive* 11, no. 3 (1997): 48–60.

G. A. Neuman, S. H. Waner, & N. D. Christiansen, "The Relationship between Work –Team Personality Composition and the Job Performance of Teams," *Group & Organization Management* 24, no. 1 (1999): 28–45.

M. A Campion, G. J. Medsker, & A. C. Higgs, "Relations between Work Group Characteristics and Effectiveness: Implications for Designing Effective WorkGrops," *Personal Psychology* 46, no. 4 (1993): 823–850.

B. L. Kirkman & D. L. Shapiro, "The Impact of Cultural Values on Employee Resistance to Teams: Toward a Model of Globalized Self-Managing Work Team Effectiveness," *Academy of Management Review* 22, no. 3 (1997): 730–757.

J. Buncerson & K. Sutcliffe, "Comparing Alternative Conceptualizations of Functional Diversity in Management Teams: Process and Performance Effects," *Academy of Management Journal* 45 (2002): 875–893.

S. Caudron, "Tie Individual Pay to Team Success," *Personnel Journal* 73, no. 10 (October 1994): 40.

Gross, *Compensation for Teams.*

Cohen & Bailey, "What Males Teams Work."

R. Allen & R. Kilmann, "Aligning Reward Practices in Support of Total Quality Management," *Business Horizons* 44 (May 2001): 77–85.

J. H. Sheridan, "Yes to Team Incentives," *Industry Week.* 4 March 1996, 63

# CHAPTER 10

## Managing Human Resources

*"...while extraordinary products and unique services still afford a competitive advantage, the one advantage that stands the test of time ... is people."*
– Mark Salsbury, Human Capital Management: Leveraging Your Workforce for a Competitive Advantage

---

### Chapter Learning Objectives:

After reading this chapter you should have a good understanding of:

- The major federal laws that regulate employee-employer relationship and workplace activities.
- The role of the Equal Employment Opportunity Commission in enforcing federal labor laws.
- The different kinds of recruiting philosophies and the advantages and disadvantages of internal and external recruiting.
- How companies use interviewing methods and techniques to determine whether candidates are qualified for a job.
- Contemporary organizational compensation philosophies and the role equity plays in determining wages.

- The four kinds of employee separations and the differences between functional and dysfunctional employee turnover.
- How downsizing, outsourcing, and re-shoring decisions are affected by organizational goals and objectives.
- The basic benefits available in organizations today and value-added employment benefits of high-performing organizations.

Human resource management (HRM), the process of recruiting, developing, and retaining the right people to form a qualified work force, remains one of the most difficult and important of all management tasks. Accordingly, this chapter begins by reviewing major human resource legislation.

Understanding federal employment legislation and how it affects the workplace is a key component of human resource management. Federal employment law, often referred to as United States labor law, is the body of law that governs the rights and duties of employees, employers, and labor unions in the United States of America. Because there are employment laws that govern each stage of the human resource process—from how employees are recruited and selected to why employees are terminated—this chapter begins with an introduction to the essential federal laws governing workplace activities.

Next, we explore two distinct recruiting philosophies and how organizations use recruiting strategies and interviewing techniques to find and hire qualified employees. This section of the chapter also reviews how managers utilize performance appraisals to assess employee's contributions and develop the knowledge, skills, and abilities of their subordinates.

Lastly, this chapter concludes with a review of compensation and employee separation, that is, how companies can keep their best workers through effective compensation practices that promote employee contribution and improve workplace moral. And how organizations manage the separation process when employees leave the organization.

# Human Resource Legislation

The management of human resources occurs in a complex environment, many organizations have entire departments and personnel dedicated to the practice of human resource management. From employing dedicated and certified human resource professionals to training supervisors and managers, businesses spend countless resources to ensure compliance with federal and state laws. Certainly, most businesses require that all supervisors and managers have a basic understanding of the major federal laws that regulate employee-employer relationships and workplace activities.

Understanding how employment legislation affects the human resource process is critical for all managers and supervisors within the organization. The following sections provide an introduction to and a summary of the major laws of the Department of Labor

## Fair Labor Standards Act

Commonly referred to wage and hour law, the 1938 **Fair Labor Standards Act** (FSLA) establishes minimum wage, standards for wages and overtime pay, child labor standards, and record-keeping requirements. This federal statue governs full-time and part-time employees. Federal minimum wage may differ than state minimum wage laws. The Fair Labor Standards Acts sets overtime pay (all hours worked over a 40-hour workweek) at least 1 ½ times an employee's regular rate of pay for any non-exempt employee. However, there are exceptions to the minimum wage and overtime pay. For example, minimum wage variations may apply to student workers, apprentices, or workers with disabilities. And, overtime exceptions may apply to employees working outside sales or in professional salaried positions, such as administration.

## Equal Pay Act

The 1963 **Equal Pay Act**, an amendment to the FLSA, prohibits wage and benefit discrimination between women and men. Within the workplace, when men and women must received equal pay for equal work. Equal work does not mean identical jobs but rather the meaning is based upon substantially equal jobs. In other words, it is job content and not job titles that determines if jobs are substantially equal. The Equal Pay Act considers skills, effort, responsibility, and working conditions with an establishment—a physical place of business rather than the entire business. However, pay differentials are permitted when not based on gender. For example, pay differential may exist based on seniority or merit, such as, quantity and quality of production. Pay differentials may also exist due to education, experience, or training.

## Civil Rights Act

**Title VII of the Civil Rights Act** of 1964 outlaws discrimination based on race, color, religion, sex, or national origin in schools, the workplace, and public facilities. Signed into law by President Lyndon B. Johnson on July 2, 1964, President John F. Kennedy called for the bill in his 1963 civil right speech. In the workplace, Title VII prohibits discrimination in hiring, employment, and termination or layoff. Considered landmark legislation, Title VII applies to businesses with 15 or more employees and encompasses all terms of employment, such as conditions and benefits. For example, it is unlawful to make assumptions about skills or abilities based on stereotypes or treat people in similar jobs differently. Additionally, it is unlawful to retaliate against an individual who files a complaint. Remedies include reinstatement, back pay, attorney fees, and the possibility of damages for emotional pain and suffering. The Civil Rights Act of 1991 amended the procedures, such as, the right to trail by jury for discrimination claims and the possibility of emotional distress damages. The Equal Employment Opportunity Title VII has also been supplemented with legislation outlawing discrimination based on pregnancy, age, or disability. The Pregnancy Discrimination Act of 1978, prohibits discrimination against the condition of pregnancy, related medial conditions, or the intent to become pregnant. It is against the law, to not hire, fire or otherwise discriminate against expectant mothers or the likelihood of becoming pregnant. The Pregnancy Discrimination Act also addressed the docking of pay due to pregnancy and termination after maternity leave.

## Age Discrimination

The **Age Discrimination Act** of 1967, also an amendment to the FLSA, prohibits employment discrimination against individuals aged 40 years or older. Applicable to businesses with over 20 employees, the Age Discrimination Act (ADEA) prohibits age discrimination. For example, individuals cannot be discriminated against in hiring, promotion, pay, or termination based on age. Additionally, older workers cannot be denied health benefits or training opportunities based on their age. Since 1986, the Age Discrimination Act prohibited the practice of mandatory retirement for tenured employees. The Act provides limited exceptions for executives in policy-making positions. Remedies may include reinstatement, back pay, or damages.

## Americans with Disabilities Act

The**Americans with Disabilities Act** of 1990 is a wide-ranging civil right law that outlaws discrimination based on physical or mental disability. The American with Disabilities Act, which applies to any employer engaged in interstate commerce or having 15 or more employees, states that a 'covered entity shall not discriminate against a qualified individual with a disability.' Discrimination for disability may occur by an employer limiting or classifying a job or applicant in an adverse fashion, denying opportunity for employment or promotion to qualified applicants, or not making reasonable accommodations for a disabled employee. The determination of disability for a particular condition is considered on a case-by-case basis. However, the Americans with Disabilities Act (ADA) excludes certain conditions, such as, substance abuse.

## Sexual Harassment

Title VII of the Civil Rights Act of 1964 also prohibits sexual harassment as a form of sex discrimination. The law forbids the harassment of an employee based on their sex. The harasser or the victim may be either male or female and the victim does not need to be of the opposite sex. The harasser can be a supervisor, co-worker, or a non-employee. Additionally, the victim does not need to be the person harassed but instead can be anyone who found the conduct offensive. Moreover, harassment does not need to be of a sexual nature. However, harassment can include sexual harassment, such as, verbal or physical conduct of a sexual nature or unwelcome sexual advances. Unwelcome verbal or physical conduct constitutes sexual harassment when the conduct affects an individual's work performance or employment or creates a hostile, intimidating, or offensive work environment.

## Bona fide Occupational Qualifications

In general, the intent of this body of law is to make the above factors irrelevant in hiring, employment, and termination decisions. Still evolving as new court cases produce court decisions, the intent is to prohibit employers from discriminating in workplace decisions on the basis of gender, age, religion, color, national origin, race, or disability. In other words, hiring, employment, and termination decisions should be based on factors that are job related, reasonably necessary, or reasonably necessary to business operations. The only time an organization can use a protected category, such as gender or religion, to make employment and workplace decisions is when there is a bona fide occupational qualification.

Title VII of the 1964 Civil Rights Act states, it is not an unlawful act to hire and employ someone on the basis of gender, religion, or national origin when there is a **bona fide occupational qualification (BFOQ)** that is "reasonably necessary to the normal operation of that particular business or enterprise." For example, a Catholic church recruiting a new pastor can reasonably specify that being a Catholic is a bona fide occupational qualification. Still, it would not be acceptable for the church could specify race of national origin as a bona fide occupational qualification.

## Equal Employment Opportunity Commission

A federal agency, the Equal Employment Opportunity Commission (EEOC) administers all of the above laws. Responsible for enforcing federal employment laws, the **Equal Employment Opportunity Commission** has the authority to investigate charges of discrimination against employers with at least 15 employees (20 employees in cases of age discrimination), labor unions, and employment agencies. The scope and role of the Equal Employment Opportunity Commission also includes the authority to file lawsuits to protect individual's rights and the public interest. However, not all cases of discrimination result in the filing of EEOC lawsuits. Lastly, in addition to the above federal laws, there are two additional important sets of federal laws—National Labor Relations Act administered by the National Labor Relations Board and the Occupational Safety and Health Act administered by the Occupational Safety and Health Administration.

## National Labor Relations Act

The first is the set of labor laws enacted to protect employees right to unionize and the second are laws and regulations governing safety standards in the workplace. Congress enacted the **National Labor Relations Act** (NLRA) to protect the privilege and right of employees to organize and bargain collectively. In addition to guaranteeing employees the right to form and join unions, these labor laws regulate interactions between management and the labor unions representing employees. The National Labor Relations Act prohibits labor and management practices that can cause harm to the general welfare of works and the US economy. A federal agency, the **National Labor Relations Board** acts to prevent and remedy unfair labor practices committed by either private sector employers or unions. For more information about NLRA, see **www.nlrb.gov**.

## Occupational Safety and Health Act

| Human Resource Legislation | |
|---|---|
| **Legislation:** | **For More Information:** |
| Fair Labor Standards Act | www.dol.gov/whd/flsa/ |
| Equal Pay Act | www.eeoc.gov/laws/statutes/epa.cfm |
| Civil Rights Act | www.eeoc.gov/laws/statutes/titlevii.cfm |
| Age Discrimination | www.eeoc.gov/laws/types/age.cfm |
| Americans with Disabilities Act | www.ada.gov |
| Sexual Harassment | www.eeoc.gov/laws/types/sexual_harassment.cfm |
| Equal Employment Opportunity Commission | www.eeoc.gov |
| National Labor Relations Act | www.nlrb.gov |
| Occupational Safety and Health Act | www.osha.gov |

Figure 10.1: Helpful Legislation Information

The **Occupational Safety and Health Act** (OSHA) requires that employers provide employees with a safe and healthful work environment. Specifically, the Occupational Safety and Health Act requires employers to protect employees from health and safety hazards on the job by providing a workplace that is "free from recognized hazards that are causing or are likely to cause death or serious physical harm." The **Occupational Safety and Health Administration**, a federal agency, is charged with setting and enforcing standards, providing training and outreach, and conducting workplace inspections. OSHA inspections are conducted without advance notice and may occur on-site or via phone. Inspection priorities include imminent danger, targeted inspections of high injury or high illness rate, chronic violators and cases involving worker complaints. Upon inspection, Employers not meeting OSHA standards may be fined. For more information about OSHA, see **www.osha.gov**.

It is important to understand that the laws covered in the first section of this chapter apply to the entire human resource management process. Obviously, these laws apply to hiring decisions but they apply to all workplace activities, such as, training, performance appraisals, promotion, compensation, and termination decisions.

# Recruitment

**Recruitment,** the first stage of the human resource management process, refers to the overall process of attracting, selecting, and interviewing suitable candidates. Quite obviously, the recruitment stage is when the employer-employee relationship is first established. During this stage, introductions are presented and first impressions are made. The recruiting process includes to steps:

1. The first step in the recruitment process involves finding qualified applicants.
2. Determining which candidates to hire is the second step in the recruitment process.

Developing a pool of qualified applicants begins with advertising the job opening. Depending upon the organization's philosophy and need, jobs can be advertised to employees working in the company or widely distributed outside of the company, or both. Regardless of corporate philosophy, effective recruitment results in the hiring of skilled and experienced employees who are a good fit with the organization's culture.

**Internal recruitment** refers to the process of developing a pool of qualified applicants and selecting a candidate from the existing workforce. Selecting and hiring an employee who already works in the company is advantageous to the organization since they are already familiar with the employee and their job performance. Also called "promotion from within," internal recruiting has numerous benefits for the organization and the employee. First, internal recruiting reduces startup and training time, and as a result saves the organization considerable time and costs. Second, since the employee is familiar with the organization's culture they are more likely to succeed in their new job. Third, recruiting from the existing workforce improves employee satisfaction, morale, and commitment. Many organizations committed to internal recruiting utilize advertise jobs to existing employees. Created by the organization, a **job posting** is an advertisement listing the job description and specification of the job that alerts employees to available vacancies.

| Promoting from Within | Hiring Externally |
|---|---|
| **Potential Advantages** | **Potential Advantage** |
| • Easily accessible applicants <br> • Quicker and less costly <br> • Employee is familiar with company <br> • Demonstrates to employees the organization values career development <br> • Lowers costs for some jobs <br> • Improve employee morale rather than upset it by making major changes | • More applicants as the information is reaching bigger talent pools <br> • Provides new perspectives, insights, and ideas from other industries and backgrounds <br> • Initiates a turnaround <br> • Reduce need for training if employee has prior experience in field <br> • Avoid internal politics <br> • Increases diversity |
| **Potential Disadvantages** | **Potential Disadvantages** |
| • Narrow perspective and ideas <br> • May not turn company around <br> • Job duties will require training and learning curve <br> • Occurrence of internal politics <br> • Difficult with rapid growth <br> • Ripple effect <br> • Fewer applicants as the talent pool is smaller | • Less information on applicants <br> • Time consuming <br> • More costly <br> • New hire requires more time to adjust to the organizational culture and systems <br> • May require higher pay for new hire <br> • Current organization members may resist new ideas from outsider |

Figure 10.2: Recruitment Advantages and Disadvantages

**External recruiting** refers to the process of developing a pool of qualified applicants and selecting a candidate from outside the company.

Commonly used external recruitment methods include advertising in newspapers, magazines, job search website, and job fairs. Companies also use referrals from current employees to increase the applicant pool. Other firms will use employment service agencies, such as professional search firms, to find, screen, and deliver qualified candidates. The basic advantage of external recruiting is the inflow of new ideas. However, corporate culture quickly absorbs new hires and the possibility of new innovative ideas and methodologies is usually not realized. Unlike utilizing your existing workforce to recruit and promote, external recruitment does allow the organization to change the company's diversity mix.

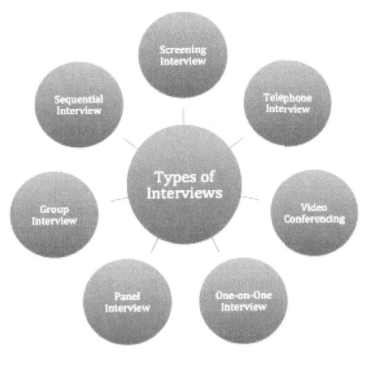

Figure 10.3: Types of Interviews

# Types of Interviews

Managers must make decisions on the type and format of interview process prior to opening the selection process to candidates. An **interview** is a formal conversation in which one or more company representatives evaluate the qualifications of a candidate. Either a hiring manager or a panel of company representatives ask job candidates job-related questions with the intent of determining the candidate's suitability for a position. Organizations use several types of interviews (Figure10.3) to assess qualifications and determine whether the applicant is suitable for employment:

1. Screening interviews are used to ensure that applicants meet the minimum requirements. Generally, in large companies when there are large applicant pools human resource department personnel will pre-screen applicants to ensure they meet the minimum requirements of the position.
2. Telephone interviews are also used to narrow the applicant pool. Popular due to the reduction in expense, telephone interviews are conducted to determine the suitability of the applicant.
3. Video Conferencing interviews are conducted utilizing technology. This type of interview is common when the candidate is not local. When geographic distance prevents a convenient or cost effective interview, many organizations conduct an interview via videoconference.
4. One-on-One interviews are the most common type of interview format. Often the last step in the hiring process, a one-on-one interview is traditionally conducted in person by a direct supervisor.

5. Panel interviews, conducted by two or more company representatives, are designed to reduce bias. Popular due to efficiency, the company will put together a selection committee. A designated person may ask questions or panel members may take turns asking questions.

6. Sequential/Serial interviews, conducted by two or more company representatives, require the candidate to meet with several people throughout the day. Interviews usually occur back-to-back and either candidates or company representatives move from one interview location to another. Once the rounds of interviews are completed, company representatives meet.

## Interview Formats

Three basic kinds of employment interviews provide candidates the opportunity to present themselves and the employer the opportunity to gain additional information about the candidate: unstructured, structured, and semi-structured.

Unstructured interviews may seem like a casual conversation. In **unstructured interviews**, questions are based on the candidate's application and resume. Without prearranged questions, interviewers are free to ask applicants a variety of questions. Unstructured interviews allow the interviewer to develop questions during the interview. The advantage of a natural flow and conversation style of the unstructured interview allows the interviewer to build rapport with the candidate and, as a result, the opportunity to discover important information which may not have seemed relevant before the interview. The major disadvantage of unstructured interviews is the lack of comparison data. Because there is not a consistent set of questions, it is difficult to draw patterns or comparisons between different candidates' responses.

The opposite of the unstructured interview format, **structured interviews** are highly organized with prearranged and standardized questions. Since the goal of structured interviews is to ensure that all candidates are presented with exactly the same questions in the same order, questions are prepared ahead of time. Generally, questions are concentrated on essential job duties and the interviewer utilizes a detailed, predetermined rating scale to score the candidates. The first major advantage of structured interviews is that data can be aggregated and comparisons can be made between candidates- even if the interviews occurred at different times. A second major advantage of this approach is a reduction in interviewer bias, as a result objective decisions are more likely to made ensuring the company gets the best candidate. The ability for organizations to ensure that interviewers ask only job-related questions of candidates, is a third major advantages of structured interviews The disadvantage of structured interviews is that the formality does not allow for a conversational style and discovery of additional, follow-up information. In order to counter this disadvantage, many organizations allow for follow-up questions by the interviewers.

The third approach, **semi-structured interviews** are a hybrid format between structured and unstructured interview formats. Semi-structured interviews are mostly comprised of structured questions, but some time is set aside for unstructured questions. The can probe for additional information and ask clarifying questions when information is ambiguous or mission. This allows for a little more of a 'laid-back' style as a result the interview is generally a little formal and more relaxed than a structured interview. Typically, there is an introductory period of establishing rapport and a closing stage when information about the company is shared and the interviewee can ask questions.

# Interview Questions

In addition to deciding which interview format will be used in the selection process, managers must determine what types of questions will be asked in the interview. Generally, interviews start with one or more background question about the candidate's employment history and education. Typically, the

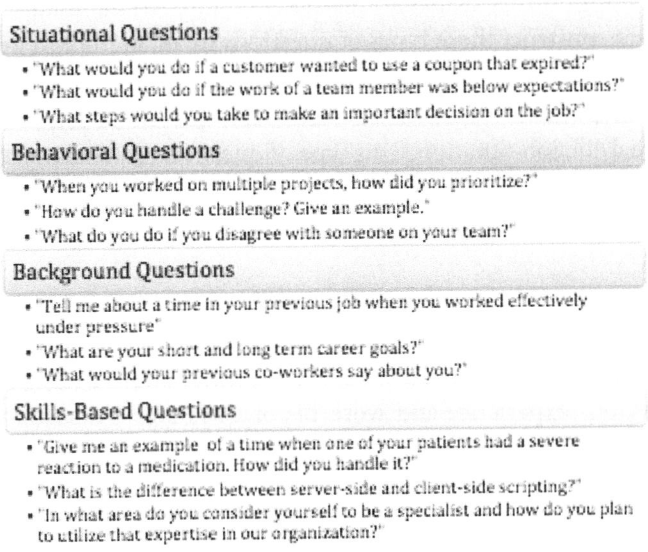

### Situational Questions

- "What would you do if a customer wanted to use a coupon that expired?"
- "What would you do if the work of a team member was below expectations?"
- "What steps would you take to make an important decision on the job?"

### Behavioral Questions

- "When you worked on multiple projects, how did you prioritize?"
- "How do you handle a challenge? Give an example."
- "What do you do if you disagree with someone on your team?"

### Background Questions

- "Tell me about a time in your previous job when you worked effectively under pressure"
- "What are your short and long term career goals?"
- "What would your previous co-workers say about you?"

### Skills-Based Questions

- "Give me an example of a time when one of your patients had a severe reaction to a medication. How did you handle it?"
- "What is the difference between server-side and client-side scripting?"
- "In what area do you consider yourself to be a specialist and how do you plan to utilize that expertise in our organization?"

Figure 10.4: Example Interview Questions

remaining questions are about the candidate's ability to work on a team, leadership skills, and job knowledge. Four kinds of questions are typically asked in structured interviews:

**Background questions** are straightforward questions that require applicants to speak about their work education, experience, and qualifications. For example, a background question may require the candidate to respond to specific job requirements, such as, any certification required for the position. Generally, background questions are the first questions presented to the applicant.

**Skill-based questions** ask applicants to speak about job knowledge. Common in technical, industrial, and manufacturing job positions, skill-based questions require the candidate to demonstrate their job knowledge. Interviewers construct these types of questions in an attempt to determine if the candidate has the practical skills and 'know how' to perform the job.

Also referred to as hypothetical questions, **situational questions** ask applicants how they would respond or react to a real-life job situation. This type of question establishes if the candidate has a good understanding of the job requirements. Situational questions are generally comprised of common job scenarios. Simply, this type of question requires the candidate to speak about how they would handle a particular issue.

Designed to elicit information about past performance, **behavioral questions** ask applicants to speak about previous job experiences. In an effort to determine the candidate's personality in resolving interpersonal interactions or work situations, behavioral questions are designed to compel candidates to reach into their previous experience and work history. Managers develop these types of questions around the skills and abilities considered necessary for the position.

# Performance Appraisals

The term **performance appraisal** refers to the systematic and periodic process by which a supervisor or manager examines and assesses how well an employee is performing their assigned duties and responsibilities and uses the results to provide feedback to the employee. Periodic performance appraisals help supervisors and managers gain an understanding employee's abilities and provide the organization and the employee with a formal feedback mechanism on job performance.

Also referred to as employee reviews, performance appraisals begin with the supervisor conducting an examination and evaluation of the employee's work performance—how well the employee is doing their job. During regularly scheduled intervals, the supervisor analyses and compares the employee's performance to set company standards, guidelines, and goals. After the supervisor completes the examination and evaluation, a meeting is set with the employee to discuss the findings and, if necessary, identify areas for future improvement.

Numerous methods and metrics exist designed to measure the quality and quantity of an employee's contribution. Although areas of evaluation vary from one organization to another depending on strategic plans, assessment categories are determined and set based on the particular needs of the department or division and the job function. Common evaluation categories can include: quality, dependability, collaboration, decision-making, and initiative or leadership.

When preparing and conducting performance appraisals, managers focus their attention in two broad categories—a past oriented review and future oriented focus. In addition to being *past focused* (an evaluation of the employee's performance during a set interval of time), performance appraisals should be *future focused* (discovering the reasons for poor performance and developing strategies to help the employee perform better in the future). A past oriented focus consists of assessing the employee's job performance in several categories, such as, dependability, attitude, productivity, and initiative. Typically, companies use checklists or rating scales, such as, a Likert scale with 1 representing poor performance and 5 representing exceptional performance to rate performance. Future oriented methods include setting performance standards by establishing goals and expectations for the employee in the upcoming quarter or year. In addition to evaluating the employee's contribution, the performance appraisal can be a powerful developmental tool. The type of focus depends on the industry and organization; however, most companies use a combination of past and future oriented methods.

Obviously, a central reason for reviewing job progress is to improve and enhance future performance. But, there are many fundamental reasons that organizations utilize systematic and periodic performance appraisals to assess an individual's job performance using pre-established criteria and organizational objectives. There are four broad goals of using performance appraisals to evaluate job progress:

1. Developmental Uses.
2. Administrative Decisions and Uses.
3. Organizational Maintenance.
4. Documentation.

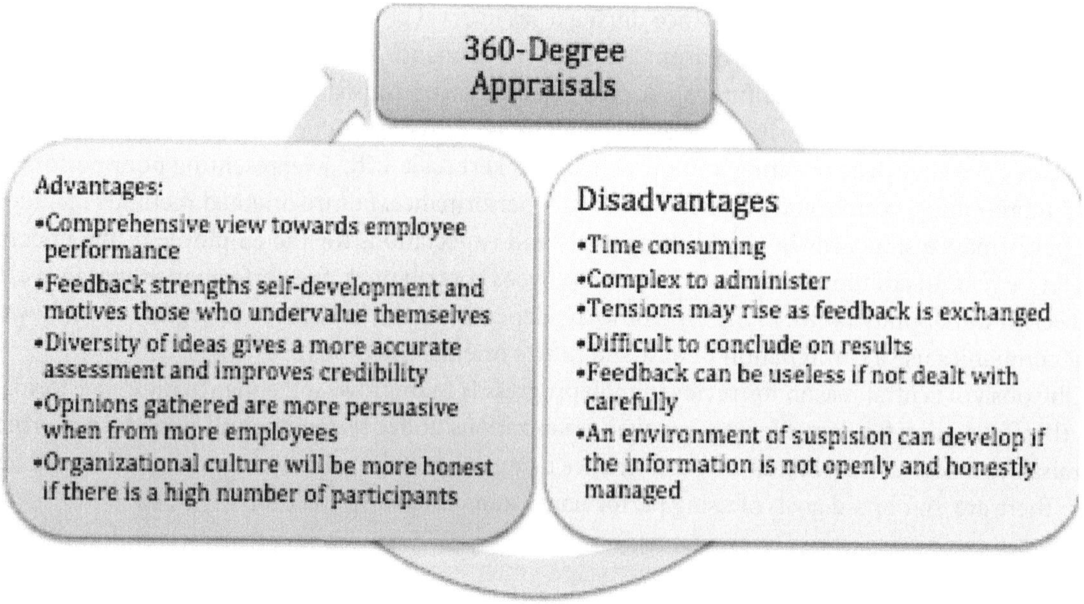

Figure 10.5: 360-Degree Appraisals Advantages and Disadvantages

# 360-Degree Feedback

Since performance appraisals help provide the manager and employee with a better understanding of the employee's performance, organizations routinely strive to develop accurate and effective job performance metrics and measures. In an effort to gather objective data, many organizations gather feedback on an employee's performance from multiple perspectives by utilizing 360- degree feedback systems. The term **360-degree feedback** refers to a systematic process of gathering information on the employee's performance from the people who work with them. Two categories of individuals participate in rate an employee—those in the vertical chain of command, such as direct reports and supervisors, and those in working relationships with the employee, such as peers and colleagues. Data is obtained and combined by reviewer category to ensure reviewers remain anonymous and complied into a feedback report for delivery to the supervisor and employee. The goal is to base performance on the input of many different people in an effort to provide a more complete and balanced assessment. Obviously, the major benefit of 360-degree feedback is that data comes from multiple sources instead of the traditional approach of one person—the boss.

### Poor Employee Performance

Performance problems, such as absenteeism or inability to perform the job, can stem from a variety of individual reasons. In most companies, when performance problems lead to employee termination the supervisor or manager has tried to find solutions to help the employee improve. Common in most organizations, prior to termination, supervisors or managers progress with the employee through some type of escalating discipline.

## Progressive Discipline Plans

Escalating discipline actions, commonly referred to as **progressive discipline plans**, is a process of formal efforts by the supervisor to provide feedback to the employee. Through the use of verbal and escalating written warnings, the supervisor is able to explain and document the performance problem. The key goal of a progressive discipline plan is to assist the employee in understanding why their performance problem does not meet expectations. However, in cases, where progressive discipline plans fail and the employee does improve his or her performance then the supervisor has substantial documentation for termination. Basically, there are four broad steps in progressive discipline plans:

1. Verbal warning.
2. First written warning.
3. Second written warning.
4. Termination.

Issued by the supervisor, a **verbal warning** is defined as an oral reprimands issued to the employee for poor performance. Generally, the supervisor will counsel the employee about his or her poor performance and make certain that the employee understands the job requirements and company expectations. During this step, the supervisor should provide clear feedback about the employee's performance and ascertain if there are any issues that contribute to the poor performance, such as technology problems.

The supervisor also issues written warnings, however, unlike verbal warnings, they are generally coordinated through the department of human resources. A **written warning** is defined as a written documentation of the verbal warning. Written warnings document all of the information covered previously in the verbal warning and any additional occurrences. Supervisors must be proficient at clearly and objectively documenting the poor performance and the expectations. Commonly, the employee being coached and counseled is asked to sign written warnings. Written warnings are part of an employee's file and generally housed both in the department by the supervisor and in the department of human resources. The length of time between written warnings varies from company to company and depends upon the impact and impact of the employee's performance deficiency. Additionally, companies may choose to bypass the verbal warning and proceed immediately with a written warning. Also, companies may issue one warning instead of proceeding with a progressive discipline plan. For example, a derogatory outburst at the workplace by an employee may cause an employer to issue only one written warning. Some behaviors, such as violence, will cause a company to immediate fire the employee. Generally, terminating the employee is not the first option. Most companies provide employees a chance to change their behavior.

In addition to supervisors and managers partnering with the department of human resources, most organizations provide basic human resource training to supervisors and managers. During training, supervisors will learn about when and how to discipline employees and the legalities of terminating employees, such as wrongful discharge. **Wrongful discharge**, also referred to as wrongful termination, involves an employee's claim that his or her firing breached their employment contract or public law. Most supervisory human resources training sessions revolve around helping the employee improve their performance through coaching and feedback but also include making certain that the company is above reproach in the case of employee termination.

# Compensation

**Compensation** is defined as the financial and nonfinancial exchange that occurs between organizations and employees in exchange for the employee's work. When formulating pay, most organizations take into account and consider two basic categories of equity–external and internal. Both internal and external equity are important in ensuring that individuals performing the jobs are compensated fairly.

**External equity** is defined as the comparison of wages paid to similar and comparable employees within parallel marketplaces. For example, comparable employees would include those in the same grade or with the same level of responsibility working at different companies but in the same industry and geographic location. External pay equity includes factors, such as employer industry and market focus. Turbulent and rapidly changing industries, such as technology, often pay better than industries with slower or unprofitable markets.

**Job evaluation** refers to the process of setting the worth of each job by evaluating the market value of the knowledge, abilities, and skills required to perform the job in a proficient manner. Commonly, after conducting a job evaluation, most companies default to paying current market wages. Also referred to paying the going rate, current market wages are determined by looking at typical wages by occupation. For example, companies frequently access and use research data, such as the **Occupational Employment Statistics**—a federal and state survey program containing information from the Department of Labor, the Bureau of Labor Statistics, and state workforce agencies.

Closely related to external equity, **internal equity** is defined as the comparison of wages paid to similar and comparable employees within the organization. For example, comparable employees would include those in the same grade or with the same level of responsibility within the company. Internal pay equity also includes additional factors, such as job experience and job performance.

Similar to pay grades used by the government, **salary ranges** help businesses establish a fixed framework of pay based on the level of education, knowledge, skill, and experience needed for each type of job. Salary ranges, also determined by accessing and using market research data, set minimum pay rate, maximum pay rate, and mid-range point for each particular job or function in the company. Quite often, similar jobs or functions determined to have the same worth are grouped. Pay ranges help to classify jobs and demonstrate the interrelations of the jobs in the organization. In other words, pay ranges establish the relationship of one job to another job. Many companies hire at or below the mid-range point to allow for pay increases while still keeping the employee in the pay range.

Since compensation strategies affect human resources practices, most companies spend a considerable amount of time designing pay structures and determining salaries. In order to ensure that salary and pay ranges are comparable and fair, organizations use job evaluations and salary ranges the foundation of their pay structures.

In addition to external and internal equity, companies must consider and determine organization-wide pay philosophies. An **organizational compensation philosophy**, also referred to as pay philosophy, is a financial representation of the company's commitment to how it values its workforce. Organizational compensation philosophies help companies explain the 'why' of employee pay. In an effort to be transparent, it is common for large organizations to develop a formal statement on the company's position regarding employee compensation. Additionally, it is important for organizations to review their pay philosophies periodically and make modifications based on current market and business factors. On a broad scale, three types of organizational compensation decisions form the platform of a company's compensation philosophy—pay-structure, pay-level, and pay-variability decisions.

## Organizational Compensation Decisions

**Pay-structure decisions** encompass the organization's judgment and choices about internal pay distributions—the extent to employees receive varying levels of pay. *Hierarchical pay structures* are designed with large pay differences from one level to another. Generally, the highest pay levels are reserved for top-level management. By contrast, *compressed pay structures* are designed with smaller pay differences and contain fewer pay levels. Generally, in compressed pay structures the pay between different levels is not as uneven. There are examples of successful organizations with both types of pay structures. In general, hierarchical pay structure fuel individual motivation and are best suited for independent type of work. Whereas, compressed pay structures are best suited for inter-dependent work environments.

**Pay-level decisions** encompass the organization's judgments and choices about whether to pay employees at levels below, above, or at current market wages. Organizations looking to attract and keep high performing employees are more likely to pay above-average wages. Additionally, above-average wages attract larger and more qualified candidates. Conversely, organizations offering below-market wages tend to experience low employee moral and widespread job dissatisfaction. In addition, below-market wages causing employee dissatisfaction can lead to absenteeism, higher worker compensation claims, and increased turnover.

**Pay-variability decisions** encompass the organization's judgments and choices about the extent to vary employee's pay with individual and organizational performance. Basic individual pay-variability decisions include rate of pay: hourly, salary, piecework, or commission. All of these terms refer to how an employee gets paid. An *hourly* rate employee is paid a set amount by the hour. A *salaried* employee is paid a set amount annually. This set amount is divided between pay periods. The distinction between hourly and salary depend upon the type of work performed and the employee's status as exempt or non-exempt from overtime. An employee paid *piecework* is compensated a set rate for item produced. And, lastly, an employee paid *commission* is compensated a set rate per sale or lead. Both piecework and commission based pay types are based on the employee's performance.

Organizational pay-variability decisions, designed to improve teamwork and collaboration, include profit sharing, gain-sharing plans, and employee stock ownership plans. Based on predetermined economic-based profitability decisions, **profit sharing** refers to the payment of a portion of the organization's profits to employees above their regular salaries and bonuses. Obviously, the more profit the company produces, the more profit is shared either directly or indirectly. Direct forms of profit sharing are paid to employees through a profit-sharing check. Similarly, **gain-sharing plans**, compensate employees by distributing cost savings to employees, usually in the form of a bonus check. More commonly, profit sharing plans provide indirect payments, such as company shares. Different from stock options,

**employee stock ownership plans** compensate employees by assigning and distributing shares of company stock based upon the company's profitability.

## Employment Benefits

**Employment benefits,** commonly referred to as employee benefits, include compensation paid to employees other than direct wages. First, there are three employee benefits mandated by law: social security, worker's compensation, and unemployment insurance. However, in addition to these benefits, it is common for companies to offer customary benefits. **Customary employment benefits** include paid holiday, paid vacations, sick leave, health insurance, life insurance, dental care, eye care, retirement plans and pensions, educational assistance, and discounts on company products and services.

Often, companies wanting to have a high performing workforce will offer cafeteria style benefits plans—giving employees the opportunity to choose the benefits which best suit their needs—and value-added employment benefits. **Value-added employment benefits**, designed to attract and retain high performers, include all of the customary employment benefits and also additional benefits, such as: day-care facilities, paid personal days, legal assistance, physical fitness facilities or gym memberships, alternative and flexible work schedules, and allowances for clothing, housing, meals, and entertainment.

Although employment benefits are unlikely to improve employee motivation or performance, high performing companies understand that they do affect job satisfaction. Additionally, value-added employment benefits can influence an employee's decisions about staying or leaving the organization and can influence the company's attractiveness level to job applicants.

## Employee Separations

**Employee separation**, a broad term, is defined as the parting of an employee from the organization for any reason. A critical human resource function, employee separations signal a break in the employer—employee relationship. There are four broad categories of employee separation:

1. Voluntary
2. Involuntary
3. Temporary
4. Permanent

Terminations are classified as voluntary or involuntary depending on the circumstances. **Voluntary separations** occur when an employee resigns from the company. Although employees resign for a variety of reasons, such as family demands, retirement, or a new job, it is the choice of the employee to leave the company. On the other hand, **involuntary separations** occur when the company decides to end the employer-employee relationship. Although involuntary separations occur for a variety of reasons, such as economic downturns or poor performance, it is the employer's choice to terminate the employee.

Involuntary employee separations, often referred to as 'terminations,' are classified as temporary or permanent. **Temporary terminations** can be for a specified or unspecified length of time. A **layoff** is a temporary termination due to a lack of work. Although layoffs may become permanent, it is not the initial intent. Often, layoffs occur due to seasonal demands, such as after the Christmas shopping season, or temporary demand common in certain industries, such as the decline in construction during inclement weather. Simply, a layoff occurs when an organization eliminates a job regardless of the employee's performance. However, the laid-off employee does not have a guarantee of being re-hired.

On the other hand, **permanent terminations** are meant to be lasting and signal an end to the employer—employee relationship. Generally, permanent terminations occur due to a company restructure or poor employee performance. Company restructures, sometimes referred to as "right sizing," involve a reduction in workforce due to the elimination of jobs. The planned elimination of jobs, downsizing and outsourcing are the two types of permanent terminations attributed to organizational restructures.

## Downsizing and Outsourcing

**Downsizing** involves releasing employees because the organization no longer requires their job. Simply, a restructure or reorganization of the company has eliminated their job. For example, technology or improved work processes can cause the elimination of company jobs. Other times, positions are eliminated due to organizational realignments or redundancies in work processes.

**Outsourcing** is also a type of company restructure that involves the elimination of jobs. Also, referred to as off-shoring, outsourcing involves the company transferring the work to another organization. Although work can be transferred domestically or overseas, generally work is transferred over-seas to reduce employee labor costs. Common work functions off-shored include call centers, such as customer service, information technology helpdesks, and assembly operations.

Although organizations commonly outsource jobs an interesting and recent trend involves organizations re-shoring divisions, departments, and work functions. **Re-shoring** occurs when an organization brings the outsourced work back in-house. As organizations began to feel to effects of outsourcing, for example poor customer service due to tight scripts and language barriers, companies suffered customer dissatisfaction and as a result experienced a decline in their customer base. Simply, when a company decides to re-shore previously outsourced work it can be due to a variety of reasons, such as, quality control or customer retention.

## Employee Turnover

**Employee turnover** is defined as the rate at which companies lose employees. Basically, employee turnover happens when employees either voluntarily or involuntarily leave a company. Measured by companies and industries, employee turnover is an important metric since it is costly for companies to replace employees. High employee turnover is concerning to most companies because of the costs associated with recruiting, hiring, and training new employees. However not all types of employee turnover are bad for organizations, so high performing organizations track employee turnover through the lens of two critical elements of is it good or bad for the organization.

**Functional turnover** is defined as the loss of poor-performing employees. Functional turnover occurs when underperforming employees voluntarily or involuntarily leave the company. Consequently, the organizations is gaining the opportunity to replace an under performing or poor performing employee with a better, more productive worker. In these instances, the company has the opportunity increase efficiency and effectiveness and, as a result, to improve their bottom line. For example, the company may replace a low performing salesperson with a higher performing salesperson or reduce costly errors by hiring a more effective machinist.

**Dysfunctional turnover**, the exact opposite of functional turnover, is defined as the loss of high-performing employees. Costly to organizations, dysfunctional turnover occurs when high-performing employees voluntarily leave the organization. Since high performing employees are rarely terminated, they usually leave the organization to seek different job opportunities. Although high performers quit their jobs for external opportunities due to various reasons, the most common is low potential to advance.

A major concern to competitive and productive organizations is dysfunctional employee turnover. If the organization is loosing high performers, then managers should examine the reasons and take steps to reduce the loss of their most productive employees. Generally, human resource managers will conduct a four-prong evaluation system to identify the causes of dysfunctional turnover.

1. Examine pay structures (is there a need to raise salary levels?).
2. Evaluate benefits plans (can enhancements be made to benefits plans?).
3. Review job design (is there an opportunity to improve working conditions and increase incentives through job design?).
4. Explore advancement opportunities (are there opportunities for internal advancement?).

An abundant amount of research has demonstrated that tying performance to pay is the best way to influence functional and dysfunctional turnover. Poor performing employees are more likely to *leave* when pay is tied to performance. Conversely, poor performing employees are more like to *stay* if pay is tied to other factors, such as seniority or cost of living increases. On the other hand, research has demonstrated that high performing employees are the exact opposite. High performing employees are more likely to *leave* if pay is not tied to performance. And, high performing employees are more likely to *stay* if pay is tied to performance.

Additionally, dysfunctional turnover is major concern to organizations because of the threat of culture of mediocrity. A **culture of mediocrity** is created when dysfunctional turnover is high and functional turnover is low. Organizations are keenly aware of the need to remain competitive and productive in today's business environment. Organizations unable to do are in danger of extinction.

## Summary of Chapter

- We examined how different employment laws affect human resource practice in the workplace.
- This chapter looked at the laws regarding harassment and sexual harassment in the workplace.
- We explored the different philosophies in recruiting and how companies use internal and external recruiting to find qualified job applicants.
- We explored the advantages and disadvantages of the three different approaches to interviews.
- This chapter also looked at the different types of questions managers use to determine a candidates ability to succeed at the job.
- This chapter discussed how managers use performance appraisal to give meaningful performance feedback. And, the common steps in progressive discipline plans.

- This chapter explained how companies use internal and external recruiting to find qualified job applicants.
- We discovered that organizational compensation philosophies are comprised of three types of pay decisions and that there are two important equities that companies need to consider when setting pay.
- We read about the three basic kinds of compensation decisions: pay level, pay variability, and pay structure.
- We read about the basic compensation strategies and explored how they affect human resource practices and learned about the compensation decisions that managers must make in today's marketplace.
- This chapter covered the role that employment benefits play in compensating employees in the workplace.
- We discussed employment benefits and the importance of value-added employment benefits to high-performing organizations.
- We learned about the four different kinds of employee separation: temporary, permanent, voluntary, and involuntary.
- We discussed the differences between downsizing and outsourcing, including the recent trend of re-shoring.
- This chapter also covered employee termination and the importance of tracking and managing functional and dysfunctional turnover.

## Discussion Questions

1. List how different employment laws affect human resource practices in the workplace.
2. Explain the law regarding harassment and sexual harassment in the workplace.
3. Explain how companies use recruiting to find qualified job applicants.
4. Provide an example of each of the four kinds of interview questions.
5. Discuss how managers use performance appraisal to give meaningful performance feedback.
6. Discuss the key steps a manager must follow in a progressive discipline situation.
7. Identify the basic pay decisions that comprise organizational compensation philosophies.
8. Explain why internal and external equity is important when establishing compensation strategies and explain how they affect human resource practice.
9. Describe the significance of considering pay equity and explain the different considerations in establishing internal and external pay equity.
10. List the types of compensation decisions managers must make in determine an employee's pay.
11. Discuss the financial and nonfinancial compensation that occurs between organizations and their employees in exchange for their work.
12. How can value-added employment benefit plans improve job satisfaction and increase the chance that employees will stay with companies? How can value-added employment benefits plans make organizations more attractive to job applicants?
13. Explain the differences between downsizing and outsourcing.
14. What are some factors that influenced the re-shoring trend?

15. How can companies influence functional and dysfunctional turnover?

# References

ADA. (n.d.). *Amendments Act of 2008 (AA) explained.* Retrieved July 25, 2014, from http://www.blr.com/hrtips/ada

Americans with Disabilities Act of 1990 - ADA - 42 U.S. Code Chapter 126. (2006, January 1). *Making the Law Easy to Understand.* Retrieved July 25, 2014, from http://finduslaw.com/americans-disabilities-act-1990-ada-42-us-code-chapter-126

Civil Rights Act of 1964 - CRA - Title VII - Equal Employment Opportunities - 42 US Code Chapter 21. (n.d.). *Making the Law Easy to Understand.* Retrieved July 25, 2014, from http://finduslaw.com/civil-rights-act-1964-cra-title-vii-equal-employment-opportunities-42-us-code-chapter-21

Disabilities (ADA) News. (n.d.). *Disabilities (ADA) News.* Retrieved July 25, 2014, from http://hr.blr.com/HR-news/Discrimination/Disabilities-ADA

Facts About Equal Pay and Compensation Discrimination. (n.d.). *Facts About Equal Pay and Compensation Discrimination.* Retrieved July 25, 2014, from http://www.eeoc.gov/eeoc/publications/fs-epa.cfm

Help Navigating DOL Laws and Regulations. (n.d.). *Compliance Assistance News Room.* Retrieved July 25, 2014, from http://www.dol.gov/compliance/

H.R. 7152. PASSAGE.—House Vote #128—Feb 10, 1964. (n.d.). *GovTrack.us.* Retrieved July 25, 2014, from https://www.govtrack.us/congress/votes/88-1964/h128

HR. 7152. PASSAGE.—Senate Vote #409—Jun 19, 1964. (n.d.). *GovTrack.us.* Retrieved July 25, 2014, from https://www.govtrack.us/congress/votes/88-1964/s409

H.R. 7152. CIVIL RIGHTS ACT OF 1964. ADOPTION OF A …—House Vote #182—Jul 02, 1964. (n.d.). *GovTrack.us.* Retrieved July 25, 2014, from https://www.govtrack.us/congress/votes/88-1964/h182

Laws & Guidance. (n.d.). *Laws & Guidance.* Retrieved July 25, 2014, from http://www.eeoc.gov/policy/adea.html

Milestones: 1972. (n.d.). *Milestones in the History of the U.S. Equal Employment Opportunity Commission: 1972.* Retrieved July 25, 2014, from http://www.eeoc.gov/eeoc/history/35th/milestones/1972.html

National Research Council. *Pay for Performance: Evaluating Performance Appraisal and Merit Pay.* Washington, DC: The National Academies Press, 1991.

S. 1745 (102nd): Civil Rights Act of 1991 (On Passage …—Senate Vote #238—Oct 30, 1991. (n.d.). *GovTrack.us.* Retrieved July 25, 2014, from https://www.govtrack.us/congress/votes/102-1991/s238

S. 1745 (102nd): Civil Rights Act of 1991 (On Passage …—House Vote #386—Nov 07, 1991. (n.d.). *GovTrack.us.* Retrieved July 25, 2014, from https://www.govtrack.us/congress/votes/102-1991/h386

Summary of the Major Laws of the Department of Labor. (n.d.). *U.S. Department of Labor.* Retrieved July 25, 2014, from http://www.dol.gov/opa/aboutdol/lawsprog.htm

42 U.S. Code § 12101—Findings and purpose. (n.d.). *LII/Legal Information Institute.* Retrieved July 25, 2014, from http://www.law.cornell.edu/uscode/text/42/12101

42 U.S. Code § 12111—Definitions. (n.d.). *LII/Legal Information Institute.* Retrieved July 25, 2014, from http://www.law.cornell.edu/uscode/text/42/12111

42 U.S. Code § 12112—Discrimination. (2012, January 3). *LII/Legal Information Institute.* Retrieved July 25, 2014, from http://www.law.cornell.edu/uscode/text/42/12112

P. S. Greenlaw & J. P Kohl, "Employer 'Business' and 'Job' Defenses in Civil Rights Actions," *Public Personnel Management* 23, no. 4 (1994): 573.

Greenlaw & Kohl, "Employer 'Business' and 'Job' Defenses in Civil Rights Actions."

W. Peirce, C. A. Smolinski, & B. Rosen, "Why Sexual Harassment Complaints Fall on Deaf Ears," *Academy of Management Executive* 12, no. 3 (1998): 41–54.

"Facts about Sexual harassment," U.S. Equal Employment Opportunity Commission. |Online| available at http://www.eeoc.gov/facts/fs-sex.html, 23 May 1999.

Peirce, Smolinski, & Rosen, "Why Sexual Harassment Complaints Fall on Deaf Ears."

R. D. Gatewood & H. S. Field, *Human Resource Selection* (Fort Worth, TX: Dryden Press, 1998).

J. A. Breaugh, *Recruitment: Science and Practice* (Boston: PWS-Kent, 1992).

J. Breaugh & M. Starke, "Research on Employee Recruitment: So Many Studies, So Man Remaining Questions" *Journal of Management* 26 (2000): 405–434.

J. Hunter, "Cognitive Ability, Cognitive Aptitudes, Job Knowledge, and Job Performance," *Journal of Vocational Behavior* 29 (1986): 340–362.

J. R. Glennon, L. E. Albright, & W. A. Owens, *A Catalog of Life History Items* (Greensboro, NC: The Richardson Foundation, 1966).

Gatewood & Field, *Human Resources Selection.*

J. M. Digman, "Personality Structure: Emergence of the Five-Factor Model," *Annual Review of Psychology* 41 (1990): 417–440; M. R. Barrick & M. K. Mount, "The Big Five Personlity Dimensions and Job Performance: A Meta-Analysis," *Personnel Psychology* 44 (1991): 1–26.

J. Cortina, N. Goldstein, S. Payne, K. Davison, & S. Gilliland, "The Incremental Validity of Interview Scores Over and Above Cognitive Ability and Conscientiousness Scores," *Personnel Psychology* 53, issue 2 (2000): 325–351; F. L. Schmidt & J. E. Hunter, "The Validity and Utility of Selection Methods in Personnel Psychology: Practical and Theoretical Implications of 85 Years of Research Findings," *Psychology Bulletin* 124, no. 2 (1998): 262–274.

M. A. Campion, D. K. Palmer, & J. E. Campion, "A Review of Structure in the Selection Interview," *Personnel Psychology* 50, no. 3 (1997): 655–702.

T. Judge, "The Employment Interview: A Review of Recent Research and Recommendations for Future Research," *Human Resource Management Review* 10, issue 4 (2000): 383–406.

D. L. Kirkpatrick, "Four Steps to Measuring Training Effectiveness," *Personnel Administrator* 28 (1983): 19–25.

J. Yankovic, "Are the Reviews In?" *Pittsburgh Business Times* 16 (28 October 1996): 7.

D. J. Woehr & A. I. Huffcutt, "Rater Training for Performance Appraisal: A Quantitative Review," *Journal of Occupational and Organizational Psychology* 67, no. 3 (1994): 189–205.

D. A. Waldman, L. E. Atwater, & D. Antonioni, "Has 360 Feedback gone Amok?" *Academy of Management Executive* 12, no. 2 (1998): 86–94.

H. H. Meyer, "A Solution to the Performance Appraisal Feedback Enigma," *Academy of Management Executive* 5, no. 1 (1991): 68–76.

G.C. Thornton, "Psychometric Properties of Self-Appraisals of Job Performance," *Personnel Psychology* 33 (1980): 263–271.

Meyer, "A Solution to the Performance Appraisal Feedback Enigma."

G. T. Milkovich & J. M. Newman, *Compensation*, 4th ed. (Homewood, IL: Irwin, 1993).

M. L. Williams & G. F. Dreher, "Compensation System Attributes and Applicant Pool Characteristics," *Academy of Management Journal* 35, no. 3 (1992): 571–595.

M. Bloom, "The Performance Effects of Pay Dispersion on Individuals and Organizations," *Academy of Management Journal* 42, no. 1 (1999): 25–40.

L. Lavelle, F. Jespersen, S. Ante, & J. Kerstetter, "Executive Pay: The Days of Fantasyland CEO Pay Package Appear to Bo in the Past, A 33% Decline in Compensation Has Returned America' Bosses to the Year 1996," *Business Week*, 21 April 2003, 86.

W. Grosman & R. E. Hoskisson, "CEO Pay at the Crossroads of Wall Street and Main: Toward the Strategic Design of Executive Compensation," *Academy of Management Executive* 12, no. 1 (1998): 43–57.

J. S. Rosenbloom, "The Environment of Employee Benefit Plans," in *The Handbook of Employee Benefits*, ed. J. S. Rosenbloom (Chicago: Irwin, 1996), 3–13.

"Employer Costs for Employee Compensation Summary," Bureau of Labor Statistics, [Online] available at http://www.bls.gov/news.release/ccc.nr0.htm, 1 June 2003.

A. E. Barber, R. B. Dunham, & R. A. Formisano, "The Impact of Flexible Benefits on Employee Satisfaction: A Field Study," *Personnel Psychology* 45 (1992): 55–75; B. Heshizer, "The Impact of Flexible Benefits on Job Satisfaction and Turnover Intentions," *Benefits Quarterly* 4 (1994): 84–90; D. M. Cable & T. A. Judge, "Pay Preferences and Job Search Decisions: A Person-Organizations Fit Perspective," *Personnel Psychology* 47 (1994): 317–348.

B. T. Beam & J. J. McFadden, *Employee Benefits* (Chicao: Dearborn Financial Publishing, 1996).

M. Bordwin, "Employment Law: Beware of Time Bombs and Shark-Infested Waters," *HR Focus*, April 1995, 19.

T. Bland, "Fire at Will, Repent at Leisure," *Security Management* 44 (May 2000), 64.

J. R. Morris, W. F. Cascio, & C. E. Young, "Downsizing After All These Years; Questions and Answers about Who Did It, How Many Did It, and Who Benefited from It," *Organizational Dynamics* 27, no. 3 (1998): 83–95.

K. E. Mishra, G. M. Sprietzer, & A. L. Mishra, "Preserving Employee Morale during Downsizing," *Sloan Management Review* 39, no. 2 (1998): 83–95.

J. Ackerman, "Helping Layoff Survivors Cope: Companies Strive to Keep Morale High," *Boston Globe*, 30 December 2001, H1.

D. R. Dalton, W. D. Todor, & D. M. Krackhardt, "Turnover Overstated: The Functional Taxonomy," *Academy of Management Review* 7 (1982): 117–123.

J. R. Hollenbeck & C. R. Williams, "Turnover Functionality versus Turnover Frequency: A Note on Work Attitudes and Organizational Effectiveness," *Journal of Applied Psychology* 71 (1986): 606–611.

C. R. Williams, "Reward Contingency. Unemployment , and Functional Turnover," *Human Resource Management Review* 9 (1999): 549–576.

# CHAPTER 11

## Motivation

---

*"The will to win, the desire to succeed, the urge to reach your full potential … these are the keys that will unlock the door to personal excellence.*
— Confucius

*"Our greatest weakness lies in giving up. The most certain way to succeed is always to try just one more time."*
— Thomas A. Edison

*"I've missed more than 9000 shots in my career. I've lost almost 300 games. 26 times I've been trusted to take the game winning shot and missed. I've failed over and over and over again in my life. And that is why I succeed."*
— Michael Jordan

*"If you can dream it, you can achieve it."*
— Zig Ziglar

---

### Chapter Learning Objectives:

After reading this chapter you should be able to:

- Discuss the importance of motivation in organizations.
- Identify the different motivational theories and approaches.
- Understand the methods for enhancing motivation in organizations.
- Understand why motivation is critically important to organizations.
- Learn the differences between intrinsic and extrinsic motivation.
- Understand why expectancy, valence, and instrumentality are important to work motivation.
- Learn why equity and inequity is important in motivation.
- Learn why organizational justice is so important and how to promote it.

# Motivation

Motivation focuses on the internal and external factors that stimulate desire and energy in people to be continually interested and committed to a job, a role, or to make an effort to attain a goal. Motivation results from the interaction of both conscious and unconscious factors such as the intensity of desire or need, the incentive or reward value of the goal and the expectations of the individual and of his or her peers. From the manager's viewpoint, the objective is to motivate people to behave in ways that are in the organization's best interest. This chapter provides an overview of the need-based, cognitive and behavioral theories of motivation, as well as a framework for enhancing motivation in organizations.

## Need-based Theories of Motivation

Need-based perspectives represent the starting point for most contemporary thought on motivation. The basic premise of need-based theories and models is that humans are motivated primarily by deficiencies in one or more important needs or need categories. Need theorists have attempted to identify and categorize the needs that are most important to people.

### Maslow's Hierarchy of Needs

The hierarchy of needs, developed by psychologist Abraham Maslow in the 1940s, is the best-known need theory. Influenced by the human relations school, Maslow argued that human beings are "wanting" animals: They have innate desires to satisfy a given set of needs. Furthermore, Maslow believed that these needs are arranged in a hierarchy of importance, with the most basic needs at the foundation of the hierarchy. Figure 11.1

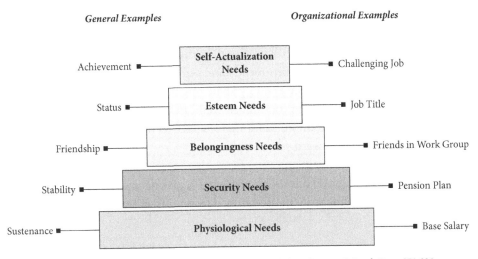

Adapted from Abraham H. Maslow, "A Theory of Human Motivation," *Psychological Review,* 1943, vol. 50, pp. 374–396.

Figure 11.1: Maslow's Hierarchy of Needs

shows Maslow's hierarchy of needs. The three sets of needs at the bottom of the hierarchy are called deficiency needs, because they must be satisfied for the individual to be fundamentally comfortable. The top two sets of needs are termed growth needs because they focus on personal growth and development.

The most basic needs in the hierarchy are **Physiological** needs. They include the needs for food, sex, and air. Next in the hierarchy are **Security** needs: things that offer safety and security, such as adequate housing and clothing and freedom from worry and anxiety. The third level in the hierarchy, **Belongingness** needs, are primarily social. Examples include the need for love and affection and the need to be accepted by peers. The fourth level, **Esteem** needs, actually encompasses two slightly different kinds of needs: the need for a positive self- image and self- respect and the need to be respected by others. At the top of the hierarchy are **Self-Actualization** needs. These involve a person's realizing his or her full potential and becoming all that he or she can be. Maslow believed that each need level must be satisfied before the level above it can become important. Thus, once physiological needs have been satisfied, their importance diminishes, and security needs emerge as the primary sources of motivation. This escalation up the hierarchy continues until the self- actualization needs become the primary motivators.

In most businesses, physiological needs are probably the easiest to evaluate and to meet. Adequate wages, toilet facilities, ventilation, and comfortable temperatures and working conditions are measures taken to satisfy this most basic level of needs. Security needs in organizations can be satisfied by such things as job continuity, a grievance system and an adequate insurance and retirement system. Most employees' belongingness needs are satisfied by family ties and group relationships both inside and outside the organization. In the workplace, people usually develop friendships that provide a basis for social interaction and can play a major role in satisfying social needs. Managers can help satisfy these needs by fostering a sense of group identity and interaction among employees. At the same time, managers can be sensitive to the probable effects on employees of family problems or lack of acceptance by coworkers. Esteem needs in the workplace are met at least partially by job titles, choice offices, merit pay increases, awards, and other forms of recognition. Of course, to be sources of long-term motivation, tangible rewards such as these must be distributed equitably and be based on performance. Self-actualization needs are perhaps the hardest to understand and the most difficult to satisfy. For example, it is difficult to assess how many people completely meet their full potential. In most cases, people who are doing well on Maslow's hierarchy will have satisfied their esteem needs and will be moving toward self-actualization. Working toward self- actualization, rather than actually achieving it, may be the ultimate motivation for most people. In recent years there has been a pronounced trend toward people leaving well- paying but less fulfilling jobs to take lower-paying but more fulfilling jobs such as nursing and teaching. This might indicate that they are actively working toward self-actualization.

Maslow's needs hierarchy makes a certain amount of intuitive sense. And because it was the first motivation theory to become popular, it is also one of the best known among practicing managers. However, the theory's primary contribution seems to lie in providing a general framework for categorizing needs.

## Herzberg's Dual Structure Theory

Frederick Herzberg and his associates developed the dual-structure or two factor theory in the late 1950s and early 1960s. Herzberg began by interviewing approximately two hundred accountants and

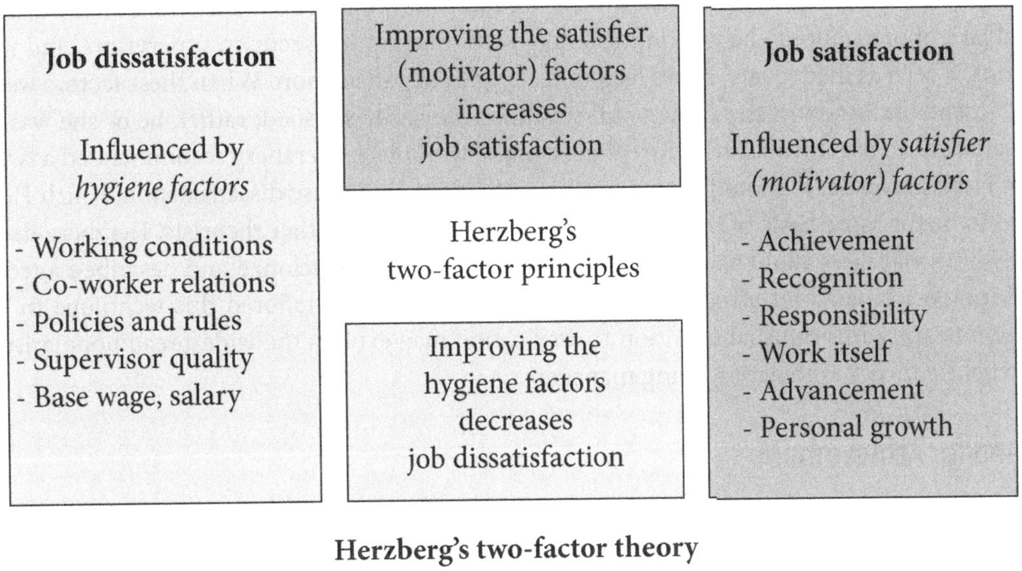

| Job dissatisfaction | Improving the satisfier (motivator) factors increases job satisfaction | Job satisfaction |
|---|---|---|
| Influenced by *hygiene factors*<br><br>- Working conditions<br>- Co-worker relations<br>- Policies and rules<br>- Supervisor quality<br>- Base wage, salary | Herzberg's two-factor principles<br><br>Improving the hygiene factors decreases job dissatisfaction | Influenced by *satisfier (motivator) factors*<br><br>- Achievement<br>- Recognition<br>- Responsibility<br>- Work itself<br>- Advancement<br>- Personal growth |

**Herzberg's two-factor theory**

Adapted from: John Schermerhorn, Principles of Management,12th Edition, Wiley (2013).

Figure 11.2: Herzberg's Dual Structure Theory

engineers in Pittsburgh. He asked them to recall times when they felt especially satisfied and motivated by their jobs and times when they felt particularly dissatisfied and unmotivated. He then asked them to describe what caused the good and bad feelings. To his surprise, Herzberg found that entirely different sets of factors were associated with the two kinds of feelings about work. For example, a person who indicated "low pay" as a source of dissatisfaction would not necessarily identify " high pay" as a source of satisfaction and motivation. Instead, people associated entirely different causes, such as recognition or achievement, with satisfaction and motivation. The findings led Herzberg to conclude that the prevailing thinking about satisfaction and motivation was incorrect. Herzberg reasoned, one set of factors should therefore influence movement back and forth along the continuum. But because his research had identified differential influences from two different sets of factors, Herzberg argued that two different dimensions must be involved. Thus, he saw motivation as a dual-structured phenomenon.

In the dual-structure concept, there is one dimension ranging from satisfaction to no satisfaction and another ranging from dissatisfaction to no dissatisfaction. The two dimensions must presumably be associated with the two sets of factors identified in the initial interviews. Thus, this theory proposed, employees might be either satisfied or not satisfied and, at the same time, dissatisfied or not dissatisfied. **Motivation Factors** such as achievement and recognition were often cited by people as primary causes of satisfaction and motivation. When present in a job, these factors apparently could cause satisfaction and motivation; when they were absent, the result was feelings of no satisfaction rather than dissatisfaction.

The other set of factors, **Hygiene Factors**, came out in response to the questions about dissatisfaction and lack of motivation. The respondents suggested that pay, job security, supervisors, and working conditions, if seen as inadequate, could lead to feelings of dissatisfaction. When these factors were considered acceptable, however, the person still was not necessarily satisfied; rather, he or she was simply not dissatisfied. To use the dual-structure theory in the workplace, Herzberg recommended a two-stage process. First, the manager should try to eliminate situations that cause dissatisfaction, which Herzberg assumed to be the more basic of the two dimensions. Unlike many other theorists, Herzberg described explicitly how managers could apply his theory. In particular, he developed and described a technique called " job enrichment" for structuring employee tasks. Herzberg tailored this technique to his key motivation factors. This unusual attention to application may explain the widespread popularity of the dual- structure theory among practicing managers.

## The Need for Achievement

The need for achievement is most frequently associated with the work of David McClelland. This need arises from an individual's desire to accomplish a goal or task more effectively than in the past. Individuals who have a high need for achievement tend to set moderately difficult goals and to make moderately risky decisions. High-need achievers also want immediate, specific feedback on their performance. They want to know how well they did something as quickly after finishing it as possible. For this reason, high- need achievers frequently take jobs in sales, where they get almost immediate feedback from customers, and avoid jobs in areas such as research and development, where tangible progress is slower and feedback comes at longer intervals. Preoccupation with work is another characteristic of high-need achievers. They think about it on their way to the workplace, during lunch, and at home. They find it difficult to put their work aside, and they become frustrated when they must stop working on a partly completed project. Finally, high-need achievers tend to assume personal responsibility for getting things done. They often volunteer for extra duties and find it difficult to delegate part of a job to someone else. Accordingly, they derive a feeling of accomplishment when they have done more work than their peers without the assistance of others.

Although high-need achievers tend to be successful, they often do not achieve top management posts. The most common explanation is that although high need for achievement helps these people advance quickly through the ranks, the traits associated with the need often conflict with the requirements of high-level management positions. Because of the amount of work they are expected to do, top executives must be able to delegate tasks to others. In addition, they seldom receive immediate feed-back, and they often must make decisions that are either more or less risky than those with which a high- need achiever would be comfortable. High-need achievers tend to do well as individual entrepreneurs with little or no group reinforcement. Steve Jobs, the cofounder of Apple Computer, and Bill Gates, the cofounder of Microsoft, are both recognized as being high-need achievers. Their need for achievement was the desire to accomplish a task or goal more effectively than it was done in the past.

## The Need for Affiliation

Individuals also experience the need for affiliation or the need for human companionship. Researchers recognize several ways that people with a high need for affiliation differ from those with a lower need.

Individuals with a high need tend to want reassurance and approval from others and usually are genuinely concerned about others' feelings. They are likely to act and think as they believe others want them to, especially those with whom they strongly identify and desire friendship. As we might expect, people with a strong need for affiliation most often work in jobs with a lot of interpersonal contact, such as sales and teaching positions. A recent Gallup survey suggests that people who have at least one good friend at work are much more likely to be highly engaged with their work and to indicate higher levels of job satisfaction.

## The Need for Power

Another individual need is the need for power or the desire to control one's environment, including financial, material, informational, and human resources. People vary greatly along this dimension. Some individuals spend much time and energy seeking power; others avoid power if at all possible. People with a high need for power can be successful managers if three conditions are met. First, they must seek power for the betterment of the organization rather than for their own interests. Second, they must have a fairly low need for affiliation because fulfilling a personal need for power may well alienate others in the workplace. Third, they need plenty of self- control to curb their desire for power when it threatens to interfere with effective organizational or interpersonal relationships.

# Cognitive Theories of Motivation

## Equity Theory

The equity theory of motivation is based on the relatively simple premise that people in organizations want to be treated fairly. The theory defines equity as the belief that we are being treated fairly in relation to others and inequity as the belief that we are being treated unfairly compared with others. Equity theory is just one of several theoretical formulations derived from social comparison processes. Social comparisons involve evaluating our own situation in terms of others' situations.

People in organizations form perceptions of the equity of their treatment through a four-step process. First, they evaluate how they are being treated by the firm. Second, they form a perception of how a "comparison-other" is being treated. The **Comparison-Other** might be a person in the same work group, someone in another part of the organization, or even a composite of several people scattered throughout the organization. Third, they compare their own circumstances with those of the comparison-other and then use this comparison as the basis for forming an impression of either equity or inequity. Fourth, depending on the strength of this feeling, the person may choose to pursue one or more of the alternatives discussed in the next section. Equity theory describes the equity comparison process in terms of an input-to-outcome ratio. **Inputs** are an individual's contributions to the organization, such factors as education, experience, effort, and loyalty. **Outcomes** are what the person receives in return, such as pay, recognition, social relationships, intrinsic rewards, and similar things. In effect, then, this part of the equity process is essentially a personal assessment of one's psychological contract. If the two sides of this psychological equation are comparable, the person experiences a feeling of equity; if the two sides do not balance, a feeling of inequity results.

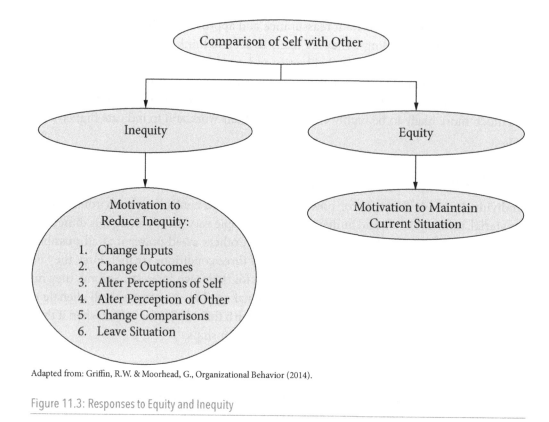

Adapted from: Griffin, R.W. & Moorhead, G., Organizational Behavior (2014).

Figure 11.3: Responses to Equity and Inequity

Figure 11.3 summarizes the results of an equity comparison. If a person feels equitably treated, she is generally motivated to maintain the status quo. For example, she will continue to provide the same level of input to the organization as long as her outcomes do not change and the ratio of inputs and outcomes of the comparison-other do not change. But a person who is experiencing inequity is motivated to reduce it. Moreover, the greater the inequity, the stronger the level of motivation.

People may use one of six common methods to reduce inequity. First, we may change our own inputs. Thus, we may put more or less effort into the job, depending on which way the inequity lies, as a way to alter our ratio. If we believe we are being underpaid, for example, we may decide not to work as hard. Second, we may change our own outcomes. We might, for example, demand a pay raise, seek additional avenues for growth and development, or even resort to stealing as a way to " get more" from the organization. Or we might alter our perceptions of the value of our current outcomes, perhaps by deciding that our present level of job security is greater and more valuable than we originally thought. A third, more complex response is to alter our perceptions of ourselves and our behavior. After perceiving an inequity, for example, we may change our original self- assessment and decide that we are really contributing less but receiving more than we originally believed. For example, we might decide that we are not really working as many hours as we had first thought, admitting, perhaps, that some of our time spent in the office is really just socializing and not actually contributing to the organization. Fourth, we may alter our perception of the comparison-other's inputs or outcomes. After all, much of our assessment of other people is based on perceptions, and perceptions can be changed. For example, if we feel under rewarded, we may decide that our comparison-other is working more hours than we originally believed, say by coming in on weekends and taking work home at night. Fifth, we may change the object of comparison. We may conclude, for instance, that the current comparison-other is the boss's personal favorite, is unusually lucky, or has special skills and abilities. A different person would thus provide a more valid basis for comparison. Indeed, we might change comparison-others fairly often. Finally, as a last resort, we may simply leave the situation. That is, we might decide that the only way to feel better about things is to be in a different situation altogether. Transferring to another department or seeking a new job may be the only way to reduce the inequity.

## Expectancy theory

Victor Vroom is generally credited with first applying the theory to motivation in the workplace. The theory attempts to determine how individuals choose among alternative behaviors. The basic premise of expectancy theory is that motivation depends on how much we want something and how likely we think we are to get it.

Figure 11.4 summarizes the basic expectancy model. The model's general components are effort, performance, and outcomes. Expectancy theory emphasizes the linkages among these elements, which are described in terms of expectancies and valences. **Effort-to-Performance Expectancy** is a person's perception of the probability that effort will lead to successful performance. If we believe our effort will lead to higher performance, this expectancy is very strong, perhaps approaching a probability of 1.0, where 1.0 equals absolute certainty that the outcome will occur. If we believe our performance will be the same no matter how much effort we make, our expectancy is very low, perhaps as low as 0, meaning that there is no probability that the outcome will occur. A person who thinks there is a moderate relationship between effort and subsequent performance, the normal circumstance, has an expectancy somewhere between 1.0 and 0. **Performance-to-Outcome Expectancy** is a person's perception of the probability that performance will lead to certain other outcomes. If a person thinks a high performer is certain to get a pay raise, this expectancy is close to 1.0. At the other extreme, a person who believes raises are entirely independent of performance has an expectancy close to 0. Finally, if a person thinks performance has

Adapted from: Griffin, R.W. & Moorhead, G., Organizational Behavior (2014).

Figure 11.4: Vroom's Expectancy Theory

some bearing on the prospects for a pay raise, his or her expectancy is somewhere between 1.0 and 0. In a work setting, several performance-to-outcome expectancies are relevant because, as Figure 11.4 shows, several outcomes might logically result from performance. Each outcome, then, has its own expectancy. For example, New England Patriot's quarterback, Tom Brady, may believe that if he plays aggressively all the time, he has a great chance of leading his team to the playoffs. Playing aggressively may win him individual honors like the Most Valuable Player award, but he may also experience more physical trauma and throw more interceptions.

An **Outcome** is anything that might potentially result from performance. High-level performance conceivably might produce such out-comes as a pay raise, a promotion, recognition from the boss, fatigue, stress, or less time to rest, among others. The **Valence** of an outcome is the relative attractiveness or unattractiveness, the value of that outcome to the person. Pay raises, promotions, and recognition might all have positive valences whereas fatigue, stress, and less time to rest might all have negative valences. The strength of outcome valences varies from person to person. Work-related stress may be a significant negative factor for one person but only a slight annoyance to another. Similarly, a pay increase may have a strong positive valence for someone desperately in need of money, a slight positive valence for someone interested mostly in getting a promotion, or for someone in an unfavorable tax position, even a negative valence!

The basic expectancy framework suggests that three conditions must be met before motivated behavior occurs. First, the effort-to-performance expectancy must be well above zero. That is, the worker must reasonably expect that exerting effort will produce high levels of performance. Second, the performance-to-outcome expectancies must be well above zero. Thus, the person must believe that performance will realistically result in valued outcomes. Third, the sum of all the valences for the potential outcomes relevant to the person must be positive. One or more valences may be negative as long as the positives outweigh the negatives. For example, stress and fatigue may have moderately negative valences, but if pay, promotion, and recognition have very high positive valences, the overall valence of the set of outcomes associated with performance will still be positive. Conceptually, the valences of all relevant outcomes and the corresponding pattern of expectancies are assumed to interact in an almost mathematical fashion to determine a person's level of motivation. Most people do assess likelihoods of and preferences for various consequences of behavior, but they seldom approach them in such a calculating manner.

## Learning Theory

Learning is another important component in employee motivation. In any organization, employees quickly learn which behaviors are rewarded and which are ignored or punished. Thus, learning plays a critical role in maintaining motivated behavior. Learning is a relatively permanent change in behavior or behavioral potential that results from direct or indirect experience.

**Classical Conditioning**, developed by Ivan Pavlov, is a simple form of learning in which a conditioned response is linked with an unconditioned stimulus. In organizations, however, only simple behaviors and responses can be learned in this manner. For example, suppose an employee receives very bad news one day from his boss. It's possible that the employee could come to associate, say, the color of the boss's suit that day with bad news. Thus, the next time the boss wears that same suit to the office, the employee may experience dread and foreboding. But this form of learning is obviously simplistic and not directly relevant to motivation. Learning theorists soon recognized that although classical conditioning offered some interesting insights into the learning process, it was inadequate as an explanation of human learning. Because of the shortcomings of classical conditioning, theorists eventually moved on to other approaches that seemed more useful in explaining the processes associated with complex learning.

Although it is not tied to a single theory or model, contemporary learning theory generally views learning as a cognitive process; that is, it assumes that people are conscious, active participants in how they learn. First, the cognitive view suggests that people draw on their experiences and use past learning as a basis for their present behavior. These experiences represent knowledge, or cognitions. For example, an employee faced with a choice of job assignments will use previous experiences in deciding which one to accept. Second, people make choices about their behavior. The employee recognizes that she has two alternatives and chooses one. Third, people recognize the consequences of their choices. Thus, when the employee finds the job assignment rewarding and fulfilling, she will recognize that the choice was a good one and will understand why. Finally, people evaluate those consequences and add them to prior learning, which affects future choices. Faced with the same job choices next year, the employee will probably be motivated to choose the same one. As implied earlier, several perspectives on learning take a cognitive view. Perhaps foremost among them is reinforcement theory. Although reinforcement theory per se is not really new, it has only been applied to organizational settings in the last few years.

**Learning Reinforcement Theory** or "operant conditioning" is generally associated with the work of B. F. Skinner. In its simplest form, reinforcement theory suggests that behavior is a function of its consequences. Behavior that results in pleasant consequences is more likely to be repeated and behavior that results in unpleasant consequences is less likely to be repeated. Reinforcement theory also suggests that in any given situation, people explore a variety of possible behaviors. Future behavioral choices are affected by the consequences of earlier behaviors. Cognitions, as already noted, also play an important role. Therefore, rather than assuming the mechanical stimulus-response linkage suggested by the traditional classical view of learning, contemporary theorists believe that people consciously explore different behaviors and systematically choose those that result in the most desirable outcomes. The consequences of behavior are called reinforcement. Managers can use various kinds of reinforcement to affect employee behavior. There are four basic forms of reinforcement: positive reinforcement, avoidance, extinction, and punishment.

| | |
|---|---|
| **Positive reinforcement** | After a person exhibits positive behavior, they are given a reward or desirable outcome. |
| **Negative reinforcement (avoidance)** | After exhibiting positive behavior, the person will avoid or escape unpleasant circumstances. |
| **Extinction** | A person will cease to exhibit a specific behavior because rewards or desirable consequences aren't given. |
| **Punishment** | A person will cease to exhibit a specific behavior because rewards or desirable consequences aren't given. |

Adapted from: Griffin, R.W. & Moorhead, G., Organizational Behavior (2014).

Figure 11.5: Forms of Reinforcement

**Positive Reinforcement** is a reward or other desirable consequence that follows behavior. Providing positive reinforcement after a particular behavior motivates employees to maintain or increase the frequency of that behavior. A compliment from the boss after an employee has completed a difficult job and a salary increase following a worker's period of high performance are examples of positive reinforcement. Avoidance, also known as **Negative Reinforcement**, is another means of increasing the frequency of desirable behavior. Rather than receiving a reward following a desirable behavior, the person is given the opportunity to avoid an unpleasant consequence. For example, suppose that a boss habitually criticizes employees who dress casually. To avoid criticism, an employee may routinely dress to suit the supervisor's tastes. The employee is thus motivated to engage in desirable behavior to avoid an unpleasant, or aversive, consequence. **Extinction** decreases the frequency of behavior, especially behavior that was previously rewarded. If rewards are withdrawn for behaviors that were previously reinforced, the behaviors will probably become less frequent and eventually die out. For example, a manager with a small staff may encourage frequent visits from subordinates as a way of keeping in touch with what is going on. Positive reinforcement might include cordial conversation, attention to subordinates' concerns, and encouragement to come in again soon. As the staff grows, however, the manager may find that such unstructured conversations make it difficult to get her own job done. She then might begin to brush off casual conversation and reward only to the point business conversations. Withdrawing the rewards for casual chatting will probably extinguish that behavior. We should also note that if managers, inadvertently or otherwise, stop rewarding valuable behaviors such as good performance, those behaviors also may become extinct. Punishment, like extinction, also tends to decrease the frequency of undesirable behaviors. **Punishment** is an unpleasant, or aversive, consequence of a behavior. Examples of punishment are verbal or written reprimands, pay cuts, loss of privileges, layoffs, and termination. Many experts question the value of punishment and believe that managers use it too often and use it inappropriately. In some situations, however, punishment may be an appropriate tool for altering behavior. Many instances of life's unpleasantness teach us what to do by means of punishment. Furthermore, certain types of undesirable behavior may have far reaching negative effects if they go unpunished. For instance, an employee who sexually harasses a coworker, a clerk who steals money from the petty cash account, and an executive who engages in illegal stock transactions all deserve punishment.

# Behavioral Theories of Motivation

## Goal Setting Theory

Goal setting is a very useful method of enhancing employee performance. From a motivational perspective, a goal is a meaningful objective. Goals are used for two purposes in most organizations. First, they provide a useful framework for managing motivation. Managers and employees can set goals for themselves and then work toward them. Thus, if the organization's overall goal is to increase sales by 10 percent, a manager can use individual goals to help attain that organizational goal. Second, goals are an effective control device. Comparing people's short-term performances with their goals can be an effective way to monitor the organization's longer-term performance.

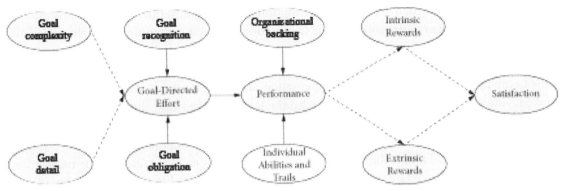

Adapted from: Griffin, R.W. & Moorhead, G., Organizational Behavior (2014).

Figure 11.6: Goal Setting Theory

A person who achieves a goal will be proud of having done so whereas a person who fails to achieve a goal will feel personal disappointment, and perhaps even shame. People's degree of pride or disappointment is affected by their self-efficacy, the extent to which they feel that they can still meet their goals even if they failed to do so in the past. The research of Edwin Locke and his associates most clearly established the utility of goal-setting theory in a motivational context. Locke's goal-setting theory of motivation assumes that behavior is a result of conscious goals and intentions. Therefore, by setting goals for people in the organization, a manager should be able to influence their behavior. Given this premise, the challenge is to develop a thorough understanding of the processes by which people set their goals and then work to reach them. **Goal Difficulty** is the extent to which a goal is challenging and requires effort. If people work to achieve goals, it is reasonable to assume that they will work harder to achieve more difficult goals. But a goal must not be so difficult that it is unattainable. Reinforcement also fosters motivation toward difficult goals. A person who is rewarded for achieving a difficult goal will be more inclined to strive toward the next difficult goal than will someone who received no reward for reaching the first goal. **Goal Specificity** is the clarity and precision of the goal. A goal of " increasing productivity" is not very specific, whereas a goal of " increasing productivity by 3 percent in the next six months" is quite specific. Some goals, such as those involving costs, output, profitability, and growth, can easily be stated in clear and precise terms. Other goals, such as improving employee job satisfaction and morale, company image and reputation, ethical behavior, and social responsibility, are much harder to state in specific terms. Like difficulty, goal specificity has been shown to be consistently related to performance.

## Organizational Reward Systems

As noted earlier, one of the primary purposes of performance management is to provide a basis for rewarding employees. We now turn our attention to rewards and their impact on employee motivation and performance. The **Reward System** consists of all organizational components, including people, processes, rules and procedures, and decision-making activities involved in allocating compensation and benefits to employees in exchange for their contributions to the organization. **Rewards** constitute many of the inducements that organizations provide to employees as their part of the psychological contract. Rewards also satisfy some of the needs employees attempt to meet through their choice of work-related behaviors. The purpose of the reward system in most organizations is to attract, retain, and motivate qualified employees. The organization's compensation structure must be equitable and consistent to ensure equality of treatment and compliance with the law. Compensation should also be a fair reward for the individual's contributions to the organization, although in most cases these contributions are difficult, if not impossible, to measure objectively. Given this limitation, managers should be as fair and as equitable as possible. Finally, the system must be competitive in the external labor market for the organization to attract and retain competent workers in appropriate fields. Beyond these broad considerations, an organization must develop its philosophy of compensation based on its own conditions and needs, and this philosophy must be defined and built into the actual reward system. The organization needs to decide what types of behaviors or performance it wants to encourage with a reward system because what is rewarded tends to recur. Possible behaviors include performance, longevity, attendance, loyalty, contributions to the " bottom line," responsibility, and conformity. Performance measurement, as described earlier, assesses these behaviors, but the choice of which behaviors to reward is a function of the compensation system.

It is also important for the organization to recognize that organizational rewards have many meanings for employees. **Intrinsic** and **Extrinsic** rewards carry both surface and symbolic value. The surface value of a reward to an employee is its objective meaning or worth. A salary increase of 5 percent, for example, means that an individual has 5 percent more spending power than before whereas a promotion, on the surface, means new duties and responsibilities. But managers must recognize that rewards also carry symbolic value. If a person gets a 3 percent salary increase when everyone else gets 5 percent, one plausible meaning is that the organization values other employees more. But if the same person gets 3 percent and all others get only 1 percent, the meaning may be just the opposite, the individual is seen as the most valuable employee. Thus, rewards convey to people not only how much they are valued by the organization but also their importance relative to others. Managers need to tune in to the many meanings rewards can convey, not only to the surface messages but to the symbolic messages as well.

Most organizations use several different types of rewards. The most common are base pay, incentive systems, benefits, perquisites, and awards. These rewards are combined to create an individual's compensation package. **Base Pay** is for most people, the most important reward for work is the pay they receive. Obviously, money is important because of the things it can buy, but as we just noted, it can also symbolize an employee's worth. Pay is very important to an organization for a variety of reasons. For one thing, an effectively planned and managed pay system can improve motivation and performance. For another, employee compensation is a major cost of doing business, much as 50 to 60 percent in many organizations, so a poorly designed system can be an expensive proposition. Finally, since pay is considered a major source of employee dissatisfaction, a poorly designed system can result in problems in other areas such as turnover and low morale.

**Incentive Systems** are plans in which employees can earn additional compensation in return for certain types of performance. Examples of incentive programs include the following: 1) **Piecework** programs, which tie a worker's earnings to the number of units produced; 2) **Gain-sharing** programs, which grant additional earnings to employees or work groups for cost- reduction ideas; 3) **Bonus** systems, which provide managers with lump-sum payments from a special fund based on the financial performance of the organization or a unit; 4) **Long-term compensation**, which gives managers additional income based on stock price performance, earnings per share, or return on equity; 5) **Merit pay** plans, which base pay raises on the employee's performance; 6) **Profit- sharing** plans, which distribute a portion of the firm's profits to all employees at a predetermined rate; 7) **Employee stock option** plans, which set aside stock in the company for employees to purchase at a reduced rate. Plans oriented mainly toward individual employees may cause increased competition for the rewards and some possibly disruptive behaviors, such as sabotaging a coworker's performance, sacrificing quality for quantity, or fighting over customers. A group incentive plan, on the other hand, requires that employees trust one another and work together. Of course, all incentive systems have advantages and disadvantages. Long-term compensation for executives is particularly controversial because of the large sums of money involved and the basis for the payments. Indeed, executive compensation is one of the more controversial subjects that U. S. businesses have had to face in recent years. When a firm is growing rapidly, and its profits are also growing rapidly, relatively few objections can be raised to paying the CEO well. However, objections arise when an organization is laying off workers, its financial performance is perhaps less than might be expected, and the CEO is still earning a huge amount of money.

Another major component of the compensation package is **Indirect Compensation**, also commonly referred to as the employee benefits plan. Typical benefits provided by businesses include the following: 1) **Payment for time not worked**, both on and off the job. On-the-job free time includes lunch, rest, coffee breaks, and wash-up or get-ready time. Off- the- job time not worked includes vacation, sick leave, holidays, and personal days. 2) **Social Security** contributions. The employer contributes half the money paid into the system established under the Federal Insurance Contributions Act (FICA). The employee pays the other half. 3) **Unemployment** compensation. People who have lost their jobs or are temporarily laid off get a percentage of their wages from an insurance- like program. 4) **Disability and workers' compensation** benefits. Employers contribute funds to help workers who cannot work due to occupational injury or ailment. 5) **Life and health insurance** programs. Most organizations offer insurance at a cost far below what individuals would pay to buy insurance on their own. 6) **Pension or retirement** plans. Most organizations offer plans to provide supplementary income to employees after they retire. A company's Social Security, unemployment, and workers' compensation contributions are set by law. But deciding how much to contribute for other kinds of benefits is up to each company. Some organizations contribute more to the cost of these benefits than others. Some companies pay the entire cost; others pay a percentage of the cost of certain benefits, such as health insurance, and bear the entire cost of other benefits. In many organizations today, benefits now account for 30 to 40 percent of the payroll.

**Perquisites** are special privileges awarded to selected members of an organization, usually top managers. For years, the top executives of many businesses were allowed privileges such as unlimited use of the company jet, motor home, vacation home, and executive dining room. In Japan, a popular perquisite is a paid membership in an exclusive golf club; a common perquisite in England is first- class travel. More than anything else, though, perquisites seem to add to the status of their recipients and thus may increase job satisfaction and reduce turnover.

**Award Programs** can be an effective means of motivation. At many companies, employees receive awards for every-thing from seniority to perfect attendance, from zero defects to cost reduction suggestions. Award programs can be costly in the time required to run them and in money if cash awards are given. But award systems can improve performance under the right conditions.

# Enhancing Performance in Organizations

| 8 Ways Leaders Can Motivate Employees Beyond Money |
| --- |
| Energize your team. |
| There's more to life than work. |
| Put your people first |
| Act with integrity. |
| Be a great communicator. |
| Be a great listener |
| Be a problem solver |
| Lead through experience and competence, not through title or position. |

Adapted from: Martin Zwilling, Forbes Magazine (2012).

Managers can use a variety of methods to enhance performance in organizations. The need and process based perspectives on motivation explain some of the factors involved in increasing the potential for motivated behavior directed at enhanced performance. Managers can then use such means as goal setting, job design, flexible work arrangements, performance management, rewards, and organizational behavior motivation to help translate this potential into actual enhanced performance.

## Motivation and Work Design

Work design is an important method managers can use to enhance employee performance. When work design is addressed at the individual level, it is most commonly referred to as **Job Design**; it can be defined as how organizations define and structure jobs. As we will see, properly designed jobs can have a positive impact on the motivation, performance, and job satisfaction of those who perform them. On the other hand, poorly designed jobs can impair motivation, performance, and job satisfaction. The first widespread model of how individual work should be designed was **Job Specialization**. For example, a worker who applies safety decals to a piece of equipment as that equipment moves down an assembly line is performing a specialized job. On the surface, job specialization appears to be a rational and efficient way to structure jobs. The jobs in many factories, for instance, are highly specialized and are often designed to maximize productivity. In practice, however, performing those jobs can cause problems, foremost among them the extreme monotony of highly specialized tasks. Managers began to recognize that although job specialization might lead to efficiency, if carried too far, it would have a number of negative consequences.

Job rotation and job enlargement seemed promising but eventually disappointed man-agers seeking to counter the ill effects of extreme specialization. They failed partly because they were intuitive, narrow approaches rather than fully developed, theory-driven methods. Consequently, a new, more complex approach to task design, job enrichment, was developed. **Job enrichment** is based on the dual-structure theory of motivation. That theory contends that employees can be motivated by positive job-related experiences such as feelings of achievement, responsibility, and recognition. To achieve these, job enrichment relies on vertical job loading, not only adding more tasks to a job, as in horizontal loading, but also giving the employee more control over those tasks.

Employee involvement in their work can also play an important role in motivation. Involvement is most often enhanced through what are called **participative management** and empowerment. In most cases managers who use these techniques are attempting to enhance employee motivation. In a sense, participation and empowerment are extensions of job design because each fundamentally alters how employees in an organization perform their jobs. Participation occurs when employees have a voice in decisions about their own work. **Empowerment** is the process of enabling workers to set their own work goals, make decisions, and solve problems within their spheres of responsibility and authority. Thus, empowerment is a somewhat broader concept that promotes participation in a wide variety of areas, including but not limited to work itself, work context, and work environment.

Beyond the actual redesigning of jobs and the use of employee involvement, many organizations today are experimenting with a variety of **flexible work arrangements**. These arrangements are gen-erally intended to enhance employee motivation and performance by giving workers more flexibility about how and when they work. Among the more popular flexible work arrangements are variable work schedules, flexible work schedules, extended work schedules, job sharing, and telecommuting.

| Top 10 Ways to Destroy Motivation at Work |
| --- |
| Treat employees like children. |
| Make rules for the many because of the behavior of a few. |
| Focus on mistakes and errors no matter how trivial they are in comparison with successes. |
| Apply policies unfairly and inequitably. |
| Stomp on employee initiative and ideas. |
| Tell employees that they're empowered but then review and retain veto power over the smallest decisions. |
| Hold meetings, coaching sessions, and performance reviews in which the manager does the majority of the talking. |
| Violate employee confidentiality by sharing information inappropriately. |
| Measure aspects of work for employee review that the employee can't control. |
| Set unattainable goals and penalize employees for not meeting them. |

Adapted from: Susan M. Heathfield, About.com, Human Resources (2014).

# Summary of Chapter

Motivation starts with a need. People search for ways to satisfy their needs and then behave accordingly. According to Abraham Maslow, human needs are arranged in a hierarchy of importance, from physiological to security to belongingness to esteem and, finally, to self-actualization. In Herzberg's dual-structure theory, satisfaction and dissatisfaction are two distinct dimensions instead of opposite ends of the same dimension. Motivation factors are presumed to affect satisfaction and hygiene factors are presumed to affect dissatisfaction. Other important individual needs include the needs for achievement, affiliation, and power.

The equity theory of motivation assumes that people want to be treated fairly. It hypothesizes that people compare their own input-to-outcome ratio in the organization with the ratio of a comparison-other. If they feel their treatment has been inequitable, they take steps to reduce the inequity. Expectancy theory, follows from the assumption that people are motivated to work toward a goal if they want it and think that they have a reasonable chance of achieving it. Learning also plays a role in employee motivation. Various kinds of reinforcement provided according to different schedules can increase or decrease motivated behavior. Organizations can use learning and reinforcement principles to enhance employee motivation and performance by effective measurement of performance and the provision of rewards to employees after they perform at a high level.

The goal-setting theory of motivation suggests that appropriate goal difficulty, specificity, acceptance, and commitment will result in higher levels of motivated performance. Rewards for achieving goals in the form of money, indirect compensation or benefits, perquisites, awards, and incentives can be effective motivators. Factors such as motivational impact, cost, and fit with the organizational system must be considered when designing or analyzing a reward system. The effective management of a reward system requires that performance be linked with rewards.

Managers seek to enhance employee performance by capitalizing on the potential for motivated behavior to improve performance. Methods often used to translate motivation into performance include work design, job enrichment, participation and empowerment, alternative work arrangements, performance management, goal setting, and rewards. Employee involvement using participative management and empowerment can help improve employee motivation in many business settings. Flexible work arrangements are commonly used today to enhance motivated job performance. Among the more popular alternative arrangements are compressed workweeks, flexible work schedules, extended work schedules, job sharing, and telecommuting.

Work motivation explains why employees behave as they do. We looked at four theories on work motivation—need theory, expectancy theory, equity theory, and the organizational justice theory and learned that each theory answers different questions on how to motivate workers. In this chapter we also covered:

- Motivation is different than performance and that other factors beside motivation influence performance.
- Intrinsically motivated behavior is behavior that is performed for its own sake whereas extrinsically motivated behavior is behavior that is performed to acquire material or social rewards or to avoid punishment.

- The Needs Theory of motivation examines those needs that workers are motivated to satisfy on the job.
- Expectancy Theory looks at how workers decide what behaviors to engage in on the job and how much effort to expend. Three components of the Expectancy Theory are valence (how desirable an outcome is to a worker), instrumentality (the perception about the extent of performance will lead to the achievement of a particular outcome), and expectancy (the perception about the extent to which effort will result in a certain level of performance). All three components combine to determine worker motivation.
- Equity Theory compares workers own outcome/input ratio to the outcome/input ratio of a referent. When unequal ratios exist, tension is created. When ratios are equal, workers are motivated to maintain their current level of outcome to input or raise their inputs to increase their outcome.
- There our four forms of Organizational Justice - distributive, procedural, interpersonal, and informational. Perceptions of organizational justice can have significant impact on employee motivation, attitudes, and behavior.

# References

Griffin, R.W. & Moorhead, G (2008). Organizational Behavior, 10th edition, South-Western Cengage.

Griffin, R.W. & Moorhead, G (2010). Organizational Behavior, 11th edition, South-Western Cengage.

Griffin, R.W. & Moorhead, G (2012). Organizational Behavior, 11th edition, South-Western Cengage.

Griffin, R.W. & Moorhead, G (2014). Organizational Behavior, 11th edition, South-Western Cengage.

Heathfield, S.M. (2014). Top Ten Ways to Destroy Motivation at Work, About.com, Human Resources.

Maslow, A.H. (1943). A Theory of Human Motivation, *Psychological Review*, vol. 50, pp. 374–396.

Schermerhorn, J. (2013). Principles of Management, 12th Edition, Wiley.

Zwilling, M. (2012). Eight Ways Leaders Can Motivate Employees Beyond Money, Forbes Magazine.

# PART 4

# Leading

# CHAPTER 12

## Leadership

---

*"Leadership is the capacity to translate vision into reality."*

– Warren Bennis

*"A leader is best when people barely know he exists, when his work is done, his aim fulfilled, they will say: we did it ourselves."*

– Lao Tzu

*"Leaders become great, not because of their power, but because of their ability to empower others."*

– John Maxwell

*"Outstanding leaders go out of their way to boost the self-esteem of their personnel. If people believe in themselves, it's amazing what they can accomplish."*

– Sam Walton

---

### Chapter Learning Objectives:

After reading this chapter you should be able to:

- Discuss the importance of leadership in organizations.
- Understand the differences between leadership and management.
- Identify the different leadership theories and approaches.
- Explain the strengths and limitations of each leadership theory and approach.

# Leadership

**Leadership** is a process whereby an individual influences a group of individuals to achieve a common goal (Northouse). The focus of leadership research can include group processes, a personality perspective, an act or behavior, the power relationship between leaders and followers and an instrument of goal achievement. Leadership involves influence, occurs within a group context and involves goal attainment.

# Leadership and Management

Although there are similarities, leadership is different from management. Leadership is largely motivational in nature whereas management focuses on maintaining performance. Kotter notes that managers produce order and consistency while leaders produce change and movement (Figure 12.1). However, while the activities of management and leadership may be played out differently, both are essential for an organization to prosper is can be seen in Figure 12.2.

| LEADERSHIP<br>Produces Change & Movement | MANAGEMENT<br>Produces Order & Consistency |
|---|---|
| **Establishing Direction**<br>- Create a vision<br>- Clarify big picture<br>- Set strategies | **Planning and Budgeting**<br>- Establish agendas<br>- Set timetables<br>- Allocate resources |
| **Aligning people**<br>- Communicate goals<br>- Seek commitment<br>- Build teams and coalitions | **Organizing and Staffing**<br>- Provide structure<br>- Make job placements<br>- Establish rules and procedures |
| **Motivating and Inspiring**<br>- Inspire and energize<br>- Empower subordinates<br>- Satisfy unmet needs | **Controlling and Problem Solving**<br>- Develop incentives<br>- Generate creative solutions<br>- Take corrective action |

Adapted from *Leadership: Theory and Practice, Fourth Edition*, Peter Northouse, 2006.

Figure 12.1: Management versus Leadership

Figure 12.2: Leadership compliments Management

# Leadership Theories and Approaches

## The Trait Approach

This approach focuses exclusively on leader and the traits that leaders exhibit (see the chart below). Organizations can use personality assessments to find the "right" people with the assumption that certain leader traits will increase organizational effectiveness. Position descriptions specify certain characteristics or traits for specific positions and personality assessment measures, such as the Leadership Trait Questionnaire and the Myers Briggs Personality Inventory are used to establish the right fit.

The strengths of such an approach is that it is intuitively appealing given the perception that leaders are different in that they possess special traits. People want to view their leaders as being gifted or possessing special characteristics. This approach also has a degree of credibility due to a century of research support and it highlights the leadership component in the leadership process. It provides a deeper level understanding of how leader/personality is related to the leadership process, as well as providing benchmarks for what to look for in a leader.

The limitations of such an approach is that it fails to establish a definitive list of leadership traits and thus endless lists have emerged. It also doesn't take into account situational effects, as leaders in one situation may not be leaders in another situation. The list of most important leadership traits is highly subjective as is the experience and observations that serve as basis for the identified leadership traits. And lastly, because it is assumed that effective leadership traits are inherent to an individual, versus acquired, it is not useful for training and development.

## The Skills Approach

The focus of the skills approach (Figure 12.3) is primarily descriptive in that it describes leadership from skills perspective and provides a structure for understanding the nature of effective leadership. Katz suggests that the importance of particular leadership skills varies depending where leaders reside in the management hierarchy. Mumford et al. suggest that leadership outcomes are direct result of a leader's skilled competency in problem solving, social judgment and knowledge.

One of the strengths of this approach is that it is the first approach to conceptualize and create a structure of the process of leadership around skills and by doing so, makes leadership available to everyone. It also provides an expansive view of leadership that incorporates a wide variety of components (i.e., problem-solving skills, social judgment skills) and provides a structure consistent with leadership education programs.

However, one shortcoming of this approach is that the breadth of the skills approach appears to extend beyond the boundaries of leadership, making it more general, less precise. It is also weak in predictive value in that it does not explain how skills lead to effective leadership performance.

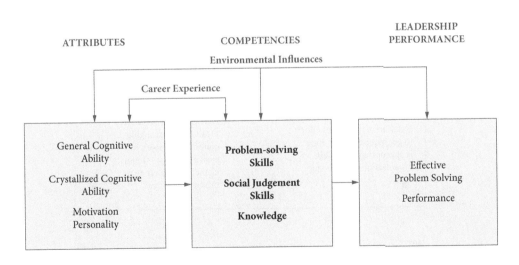

From *Leadership: Theory and Practice, Fifth Edition*, Peter Northouse, 2010.

Figure 12.3: Skills Approach Model

# The Style Approach

The focus of the style approach is a framework for assessing leadership in a broad way, as behavior with a task and relationship dimension. It offers a means of assessing in a general way the behaviors of leaders. The style approach marked a major shift in leadership research from exclusively trait focused to include behaviors and actions of leaders. At the conceptual level, a leader's style is composed of two major types of behaviors: task and relationship.

One of the strengths of this approach is the broad range of studies on leadership style that validates and gives credibility to the basic tenets of the approach. Also, the style approach is heuristic and leaders can learn a lot about themselves and how they come across to others by trying to see their behaviors in light of the task and relationship dimensions.

However, research has not adequately demonstrated how leaders' styles are associated with performance outcomes. Also, there is no universal style of leadership that could be effective in every situation. It also implies that the most effective leadership style is a high task and a high relationship combination (9,9 see Figure 12.4) and research to support this finding is limited.

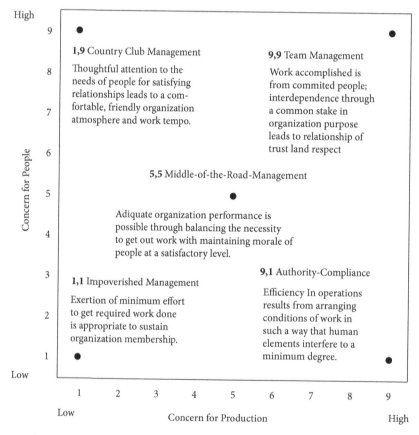

Adapted from Robert R. Blake and Anne Adams McCanse. *Leadership Dilemmas-Grid Solutions* (Houston, TX: Gulf. 1991), 29, formerly the Management Grid figure by Robert R. Blake and Jane S. Mouton.

Figure 12.4: The Leadership Style Grid

## The Situational Approach

The focus of this approach is centered on the idea that subordinates vacillate along the developmental continuum of competence and commitment, therefore leader effectiveness depends upon assessing subordinate's developmental position and adapting his/her leadership style to match the subordinate developmental level. The situational approach requires leaders to demonstrate a strong degree of flexibility (Figure 12.5).

On of the strengths of this approach is that it is perceived as providing a credible model for training employees to become effective leaders. It is a straightforward approach that is easily understood and applied in a variety of settings. It also clearly outlines what you should and should not do in various settings. Situational leadership stresses that effective leaders are those who can change their style based on task requirements and subordinate needs and the premise that leaders need to treat each subordinate according to his/her unique needs.

However, the lack of an empirical foundation raises theoretical considerations regarding the validity of the approach. Additional research is required to determine how commitment and competence are conceptualized for each developmental level as the conceptualization of commitment itself is very unclear. Also, studies fail to support basic prescriptions of situational leadership model. It does not account for how particular demographics influence the leader-subordinate prescriptions of the model and fails to adequately address the issue of one-to-one versus group leadership in an organizational setting.

| HIGH DIRECTIVE BEHAVIOR | | | LOW DIRECTIVE BEHAVIOR |
|---|---|---|---|
| **Directive Behavior** | | | |
| DIRECTING | COACHING | SUPPORTING | DELEGATING |
| S1- Defining Planning/ Prioritizing, Orienting, Teaching/showing and telling how, Checking/ monitoring, Giving feedback | S2-Exploring/asking, Explaining/clarifying, Redirecting, Sharing feedback, Encouraging, Praising | S3-Asking/listening, Reassuring, Facilitating self-reliant problem solving, Collaborating, Encouraging feedback, Appreciating | S4 - Allowing/trusting, Confirming, Empowering, Affirming, Acknowledging, Challenging |
| Characteristics: | Characteristics: | Characteristics: | Characteristics: |
| High Directive and Low Supportive Behavior | High Directive and High Supportive Behavior | Low Directive and High Supportive Behavior | Low Directive and Low Supportive Behavior |
| **Development of Individual** | | | |
| D1 | D2 | D3 | D4 |
| Low Competence | Low to some Competence | Moderate to High Competence | High Competence |
| High Commitment | Low Commitment | Variable Commitment | High Commitment |

**DEVELOPING**  **DEVELOPED**

Adapted from *Leadership and the One Minute Manager: Increasing Effectiveness Through Situational Leadership,* Kenneth Blanchard, 1985.

Figure 12.5: Situational Leadership

## The Path-Goal Theory

The path-goal theory maintains that it is the leader's job is to help subordinates reach their goals by directing, guiding and coaching them along the way. Leaders must evaluate task and subordinate characteristics and adapt leadership their style to fit those characteristics. The theory suggests which style is most appropriate for specific characteristics and leaders should choose a leadership style that best fits the needs of subordinates and their work. Path-goal theory provides a set of assumptions about how different leadership styles will interact with subordinate characteristics and the work situation to affect employee motivation. Path-goal theory is complex but also pragmatic in its approach.

One of the strengths of this theory is that it is a useful theoretical framework for understanding how various leadership behaviors affect the satisfaction of subordinates and their work performance. It also attempts to integrate the motivation principles of expectancy theory into a theory of leadership. Path-goal theory provides a practical model that underscores and highlights the important ways leaders help subordinates.

However, interpreting the meaning of the theory can be confusing because it is so complex and incorporates so many different aspects of leadership; consequently, it is difficult to implement. Furthermore, empirical research studies have demonstrated only partial support for path-goal theory because it fails to adequately explain the relationship between leadership behavior and worker motivation. Lastly, the path-goal theory approach treats leadership as a one-way event in which the leader affects the subordinate.

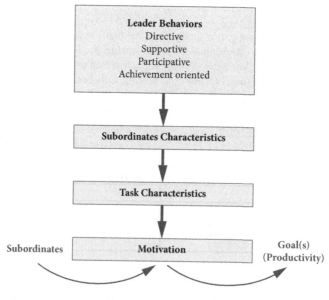

From *Leadership: Theory and Practice, Fifth Edition,* Peter Northouse, 2010.

Figure 12.6: Path-Goal Theory Matrix

## The LMX Theory

The Leader-Member Exchange theory, or LMX, works in two ways: it describes leadership and it prescribes leadership. The central concept is the dyadic relationship between leaders and their subordinates. It suggests that it is important to recognize the existence of in-groups and out-groups within an organization. There are significant differences in how goals are accomplished using in-groups versus out-groups and relevant differences in in-group versus out-group behaviors. The theory is best understood within the Leadership Making Model (Figure 12.7). In this model, leaders should forms special relationships with all subordinates, offer each subordinate an opportunity for new roles/responsibilities and should nurture high-quality exchanges with all subordinates. Rather than concentrating on differences, leaders focus on ways to build trust and respect with all subordinates resulting in the entire work group becoming an in-group.

The strength of LMX theory is that it validates our experience of how people within organizations relate to each other and the leader. It also is the only leadership approach that makes the dyadic relationship the centerpiece of the leadership process. LMX theory directs our attention to the importance of communication in leadership and has a solid research foundation on how the practice of LMX theory is related to positive organizational outcomes.

However, critics of this approach argue that it inadvertently supports the development of privileged groups in the workplace and appears unfair and discriminatory. Also the basic theoretical ideas of LMX are not fully developed and not enough is known about creating high-quality leader-member exchanges, nor the means to achieve building trust, respect, and obligation. Also, because of various scales and levels of analysis, the precise measurement of leader-member exchanges is questionable.

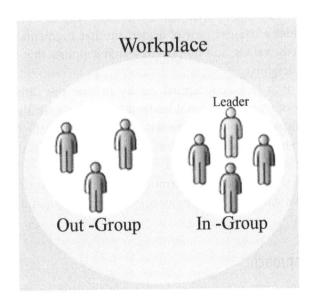

Figure 12.7: LMX Leadership Making Model

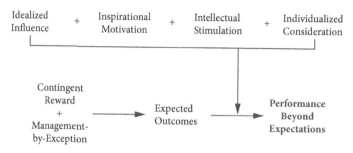

Adapted from *Leadership: Theory and Practice, Fifth Edition,* Peter Northouse, 2010.

Figure 12.8: The Effect of Transformational Leadership

## The Transformational Leadership Approach

Transformational leaders empower and nurture followers, stimulate change by becoming strong role models for followers, commonly create a vision, require leaders to become social architects, build trust and foster collaboration. This theory describes how leaders can initiate, develop, and carry out significant changes in organizations.

Transformational leadership has been widely researched, including a large body of qualitative research centering on prominent leaders and CEOs in major firms. People are attracted to transformational leadership because it makes sense to them and treats leadership as a process occurring between followers and leaders. It provides a broader view of leadership that augments other leadership models and emphasizes followers' needs, values, and morals. Research supports that transformational leadership is an effective form of leadership.

However, critics argue that it lacks conceptual clarity in that the dimensions are not clearly delimited and the parameters of transformational leadership overlap with similar conceptualizations of leadership, as some transformational factors are not unique solely to the transformational model. Also, transformational leadership treats leadership more as a personality trait or predisposition than a behavior that can be taught. Some say it is elitist and antidemocratic, suffers from heroic leadership bias and has the potential for abuse. Furthermore, research on transformational leadership is based primarily on qualitative data and the measurement of transformational leadership has been questioned.

## The Servant Leadership Approach

Servant leadership is different from many other leadership theories in that it is concerned with putting followers first and the outcomes that are likely to emerge. It works best when leaders are altruistic and have a strong motivation to help others and it is important for followers to be receptive

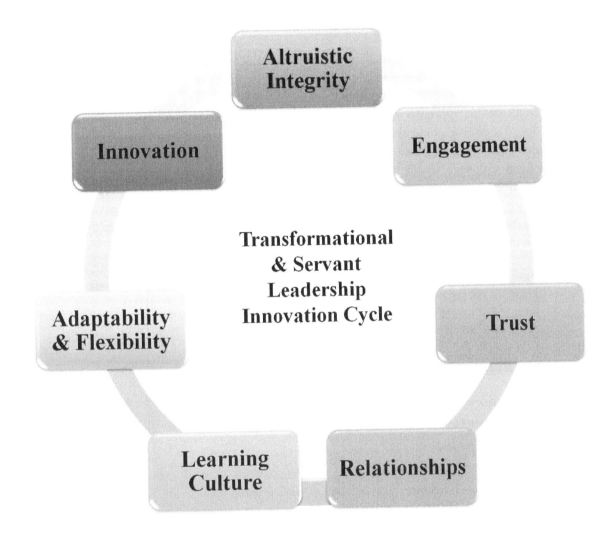

Figure 12.9: The Servant Leadership Approach

to this style of leadership. In the proper context, servant leadership can result in community and societal change.

The strength of this approach is that it makes altruism the central component of the leadership process. It also provides a counterintuitive approach to the use of influence in that leaders should share control. However, it may not be effective when subordinates are not open to being guided, supported, and empowered.

However, one shortcoming of this approach is that researchers are unable to reach a consensus on a common definition or theoretical framework for servant leadership. Also, the prescriptive overtone which suggests that good leaders "put others first" conflicts with other principles of leadership such as directing, concern for production, etc. It can also sound moralistic, which may deter some researchers.

## The Team Leadership Approach

This model provides a cognitive map to identify group/team needs and offers suggestions on appropriate corrective actions. It assists leader in making sense of the complexity of groups and provides suggested actions to improve group effectiveness.

The strength of this approach is that it provides answers to what constitutes excellent teams. It also provides a cognitive guide that assists leaders in designing and maintaining effective teams and recognizes the changing role of leaders and followers in organizations However, the complete model has not been totally supported or tested and may not be practical as the model is complex and doesn't provide easy answers for difficult leader decisions. It also fails to provide much guidance for handling everyday interactions and complications of team management. Furthermore, the model lacks the focus required on how to teach and provide skill development in areas of diagnosis and action taking.

| CHARACTERISTICS of Team Excellence (Larson & LaFasto, 1989) | CONDITIONS of Group Effectiveness (Hackman & Walton, 1986) |
|---|---|
| Clear, elevating goal | Clear, engaging direction |
| Results-driven structure | Enabling structure |
| Competent team members | |
| Unified commitment | |
| Collaborative climate | |
| Standards of excellence | Enabling context |
| External support | Adequate material resources |
| Principled leadership | Expert coaching |

From *Leadership: Theory and Practice, Fifth Edition,* Peter Northouse, 2010.

Figure 12.10: Factors for Group or Team Effectiveness

## The Psychodynamic Approach

The primary consideration of this approach is to raise awareness of leaders and followers to their own personality types and the implications of these types on their work and relationships. Various personal assessments are used to determine Psychological types (Myers Briggs Typology Inventory or similar method or questionnaires).

One of the strengths of this approach is that it results in an analysis of the relationship between a leader and a follower. It also emphasizes the leader's need for insight and discourages manipulative techniques in leadership.

However, critics argue that it is based upon the psychology of the abnormal rather than the normal and the MBTI may have reliability or validity problems. It also focuses primarily on personalities of leader and followers that dictate nature of relationship between them. It rejects the notion that emotional reactions occur toward leaders, followers and coworkers, and that those reactions arise from predispositions in individuals. Lastly, it does not lend itself to traditional training paradigm.

## The Ethical Leadership Approach

This approach is concerned with the kinds of values and morals an individual or society ascribes as desirable or appropriate and focuses on the virtuousness of individuals and their motives. Ethical leaders treat other people's values and decisions with respect, allow others to be themselves with creative wants and desires and approach others with a sense of unconditional worth and value individual differences, Figure 12.12 is a list of the top 10 world's greatest ehtical leaders.

This approach provides a body of timely research on ethical issues and provides direction on how to think about ethical leadership and how to practice it. It also suggests that leadership is not an amoral phenomenon and that ethics should be considered as integral to the broader domain of leadership. Furthermore, it highlights principles and virtues that are important in ethical leadership development.

However, it lacks a strong body of traditional research findings to substantiate the theoretical foundation. It also relies heavily on writings of just a few individuals that are primarily descriptive and anecdotal in nature, and are strongly influenced by personal opinion and a particular worldview.

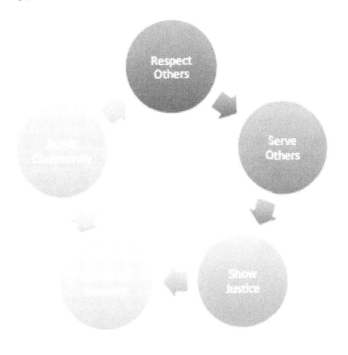

Figure 12.11: Principles of Ethical Leadership

**The World's 50 GREATEST LEADERS**

| 1. Pope Francis | Pontiff | Catholic Church |
|---|---|---|
| 2. Angela Merkel | Chancellor | Germany |
| 3. Alan Mulally | CEO | Ford Motor Company |
| 4. Warren Buffett | CEO | Berkshire Hathaway |
| 5. Former President Bill Clinton | Founder | The Clinton Foundation |
| 6. Aung San Suu Kyi | Chair | National League for Democracy |
| 7. General Joe Dunford | Commander | U.S. Forces Afghanistan |
| 8. Bono | Lead Singer | U2 |
| 9. Dalai Lama | Tibetan Spiritual Leader | India |
| 10. Jeff Bezos | CEO | Amazon.com |

*Adapted from: fortune.com/2014/03/20/ fortune-ranks-the-worlds-50-greatest-leaders/*

Figure 12.12: Top 10 of the Fortune World's 50 Greatest Leaders

# Summary of Chapter

There are a variety of approaches to leadership and no one theory or model can describe all of the elements essential to effective leadership behavior. Each approach has its strengths and limitations and some theories have stronger research to support their assumptions than others. Leadership is a multifaceted concept and leadership theory continues to evolve as new understandings of the phenomena are discovered. It is important for leaders to assess themselves, their followers and the dynamics of each situation to have a better understanding of what is best to achieve organizational purposes. As the complexity of the world and work environments increase, the need for effective leadership grows exponentially.

# References

*Leadership: Theory and Practice, Fourth Edition,* Peter Northouse, Sage Publications, Thousand Oaks, CA., 2006.
*Leadership: Theory and Practice, Fifth Edition,* Peter Northouse, Sage Publications, Thousand Oaks, CA., 2010.
*Leadership: Theory and Practice, Sixth Edition,* Peter Northouse, Sage Publications, Thousand Oaks, CA., 2013.

# CHAPTER 13

## Managing Communication

*"Communication–the human connection–is the key
to personal and career success."*

– Paul J. Meyer

### Chapter Learning Objectives:

After reading this chapter you should have a good understanding of:

- The communication process and the role that perception plays in communication.
- The different strategies that help supervisors manage effective one-on-one communication.
- The types of communication channels that managers can utilize to ensure effective organization-wide communication.
- The importance of non-verbal communications and the affect of non-verbal communication on perception.

- The different methods of improving transmission by getting the message our and into the organization.
- The importance of improving the reception among the intended audience.
- The effects of perception on the communication process and how to improve reception.
- The basic skills of feedback and the steps necessary to communicate feedback to employees.

Coupled with globalization, the information age is driving the need for organizations to communicate effectively. As businesses seek to compete in a global marketplace, the need to manage, access, and distribute information has become critical. Organizations recognizing the need to create and develop communication environments are struggling to create communication systems that have the ability to integrate decentralized workforces and enhance customer experiences.

Obviously, better and faster business communication is a key component of the framework to meet the increasing and ever changing demands of the marketplace. Indeed, to a large extent, the success of today's organization depends on the effectiveness and efficiency of its communication. So it isn't surprising that several significant business trends involve business communications.

First, businesses are intentionally concentrating their efforts on creating and delivering content communications and environments that will facilitate and support a connected workforce. Employees will be able to access shared resources and have information at their fingertips. For example, employees will be able to and access company policies and procedures instantly.

Second, organizations are deliberately shedding the concept and strategy of outsourcing. As companies recognize the deficiencies of outsourcing, it is quickly being replaced by embracing geographically remote employees. The idea of allowing a outsourced customer service center to determine your customer satisfaction rate, is being replaced as organizations are finding the benefits of integrating and empowering remote staff.

As organizations compete for market share in today's competitive environments, effective communication is a critical and necessary skill for leaders, managers and workers. If this weren't reason enough to learn how to communicate effectively, consider that many college professors believe effective oral communication, such as listening and following instructions is one of the most important skill sets for college graduates. According to research conducted by the National Association of Colleges and Employers (NACE) the most important proficiency a college graduate can possess is effective communication skills. Recently, NACE, a leading source of information about the employment of college graduate, conducted a poll and found that 79% of those polled reported that most college students did not have effective communication skills. Interestingly, along with effective communication, NACE found that soft skills were important to adapt to different workplace environments. Additionally, NACE found that the following skills—strong work ethic, teamwork skills, analytical skills and initiative—rounded out the top five.

## The Communication Process

Derived from the Latin word 'communicare', **communication** is the process of sharing information between people—transmitting information from one person to another. **Business communication**, a key function of management, involves transmitting information about and within the organization. Generally, the level of formality distinguishes business communication. In business, communication tends to be more formal than that associated with personal communication.

Business communications are utilized within for-profit companies, non-profit organizations, and governmental agencies. **External communication** involves information shared and transmitted to all stakeholders, such as, customers and vendors. It involves employees communicating with anyone outside the organization. **Internal communication** involves information shared and transmitted within the confines of the organization. It involves employees within the organization communicating with each other.

Most companies utilize a variety of transmission channels, such as, email and web conference, in the communication process. Despite the environment, basically, there are five major components in the communication process, the:

1. Sender (message to convey, transmitting the message, encoding the message)
2. Message (the subject matter, opinion, fact, idea, information)
3. Communication channel (media through which message is delivered, links sender and receiver)
4. Receiver (receives messages, decodes message, and interprets message, provides feedback)
5. Feedback (a signal from the receiver to the sender)
6. Noise (interferes with the communication process)

The **sender**, who begins the communication process, composes a message he or she wants to convey to another person. In essence, the message is what the sender wants someone else to know. The next step is encoding the message. **Encoding** means selecting a form for the message, such as, written or verbal, that can be recognized and acknowledged by the receiver. The sender transmits the message using a communication channel. Selected by the sender, the **communication channel** is the media through which the message is transmitted. The communication channel links the message to the sender and receiver. Some communication channels allow for immediate feedback. For example, using the phone or face-to-face as the communication channel allows the sender to receive immediate feedback. While other communication channels, do not allow the sender to receive immediate feedback. For example, using text or email as the communication channel does not allow the sender to receive immediate feedback, as he or she must wait for the receiver to respond.

Once the message is received, the **receiver** decodes and interprets the message. **Decoding** is the process by which the receiver interprets the communication. For example, the receiver will translate the message using their knowledge, background and experience. At times, the message, as understood by the receiver,

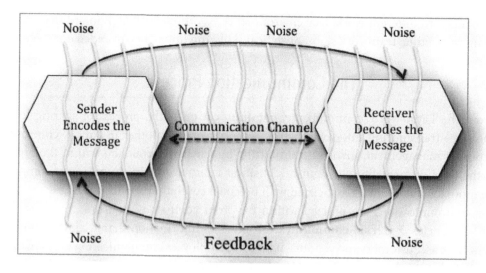

Figure 13.1: The Communication Process

isn't the message the sender intended. Because of perceptual filters, receivers may translate a vastly different meaning to a message than that which the sender intended. The third step of the communication exchange process takes place when the receiver supplies the sender with feedback. **Feedback,** a return message from the receiver to the sender, indicates the receiver's translation and understanding of the message. Feedback, the final link in the communication process chain, is extremely helpful as it makes senders aware of possible miscommunications. Once the sender is aware of a miscommunication he or she is able to offer continued communications, such as clarifications, until the receiver understands the message as intended.

Feedback may take the form of a non-verbal, written, or oral response from the receiver to the sender. A **feedback signal** is the interpretation of the message by the receiver. Often, this signal is influenced by such factors as the receivers experience, background, or emotional state. **Non-verbal communication**, which includes gestures and facial expressions, is any communication that does not involve words. In other words, it is expressed. Non-verbal communication is the transmission of messages by a medium other than writing or speech. However, non-verbal communication does include aspects of speech itself, such as, accent, pitch, and tone. Certainly, the importance of non-verbal communication is well documented. Research suggests that 45-93 percent of an oral communication is influenced by non-verbal feedback. Obviously, non-verbal feedback can demonstrate to the sender that the receiver accepts or discounts the message. Additionally, non-verbal communication can contradict the verbal communication message spoken by the sender. Two types of non-verbal communications include:

1. Kinesics
2. Paralanguage

From the Greek word *kinesis*, meaning "movement," **kinesics** involves facial and body movements. For example, these movements may include facial expressions, eye contact, and hand gestures, such as, tapping fingers or jiggling coins. Kinesics can be used to signal approval or disapproval of a message. For example, a smile or a nod can demonstrates the receiver's approval. Conversely, a finger to the lips may indicate that the receiver doesn't want to hear the message. **Paralanguage** involves vocal characterizers and qualifiers. For example, vocal characterizers include laughing, yelling, crying. While, vocal qualifiers include volume, pitch, and tempo. Often, speaking patterns, such as silence, hesitation, or yelling, are utilized to send a signal. Pitch and tone can cause a sentence to become a command. Non-verbal communication, a critical link in the feedback process of oral communications, has multiple functions. It can be used to repeat the message, augment, accent, or regulate the message. Regardless of the intended function, non-verbal communication is very helpful and informative.

Unfortunately, feedback doesn't always occur. Due to the ease and commonplace of communication, senders and receivers often assume that they share a common understanding of the message. And, therefore, do not use feedback to improve their understanding. If the receiver is rash or emotionally based, then message can seem personal to the receiver. Not utilizing feedback in the communication process is a serious mistake. In addition to the background and experiences of the receiver, messages are transmitted with and against a backdrop of noise. **Noise,** anything interfering with the transmission of the intended message, prevents the message from being interpreted by the receiver as intended by the sender. Noise may occur in any of the following five situations:

1. Sender is not sure what message to communicate.
2. Message is not clearly encoded.
3. Wrong communication channel is chosen.
4. Message is not decoded or received properly.
5. Receiver doesn't have the knowledge, experience, or time to understand the message.

As we are learning, the communication process can be complicated. If leaders and managers assume that communication is easy, the receiver may not translate and interpret the message as intended by the sender.

Step 1: State the purpose
- "I want to talk to you about…"
- "I have a concern about…"

Step 2: Specifically describe your observations
- "This morning, when you were talking with Bob, I noticed you were raising your voice…"

Step 3: Describe your reactions
- "I felt uncomfortable as Bob was getting very embarrassed and that type of behavior is not acceptable in this department"

Step 4: Give the other person the opportunity to respond
- "What are your thoughts?"
- "How did you view this situation?"

Step 5: Offer specific suggestions
- "Joe, I understand it can be frustrating working with customers at times, but I like to write myself encouraging notes to remind myself to maintain my patience and remain calm"

Step 6: Summarize and express support
- "In those hard situations, I expect you to come to me if there is a problem or find ways to calm yourself down to ensure the customers know that we value them."

Figure 13.2: Steps to Giving Feedback

# Formal Communication Channels

The **formal communication channel** is the system of official organizational channels that carry approved information and messages. For example, the formal communication channel may carry organizational edicts such as, policies and procedures, and transmitted via formal communication systems, such as, company emails, and website. Basically, three formal communication channels exit: downward communication, upward communication, and horizontal communication.

    **Downward communication** includes the communication that flows from upper to lower levels in an organization. Generally, downward communication contains the issuing of orders down the organizational hierarchy. For example, downward communication is utilized to give employees job-related information.

    **Upward communication** includes the communication that flows from lower levels to upper levels in an organization. Generally, upward communication contains feedback about operations and situations. For example, upward communications help higher-level managers understand organizational performance problems and workplace situations.

    **Horizontal communication** flows among employees at the same organizational level. For example, horizontal communication occurs when two supervisors coordinate the schedule of shared employees. Generally, horizontal communication facilitates coordination and cooperation between different personnel in the same company by allowing coworkers to share important information. Horizontal communication can also help coworkers discuss situations and resolve problems without involving upper levels of management.

# Informal Communication Channels

Conversely, the informal communication channel generally arises from a lack of complete or truthful messages from the formal communication channel. Organizations that have robust grapevines often have formal communications that are encrypted. **Encryption** refers to the sending of messages that are not readily understood.

The **informal communication channel**, sometimes called the "**grapevine**," includes transmissions of employee-to-employee messages that occur outside of formal communication channels. The grapevine, arising out of curiosity, is the workers need to know what is going on and how it might affect them or their coworkers. When formal communication channels do not supply sufficient or complete information, employees create the information. The grapevine is an attempt by workers to understand a situation. Workers create a network design to supply information about the current situation.

Grapevines arise out of informal communication networks, it is about who knows whom in the organization. Interestingly, research has proven that grapevines contain highly accurate information. First, because grapevines help supply missing information that is not available through formal channels, information spreads rapidly. Second, because grapevine information is typically carried through face-to-face channels, senders can get feedback to make sure they understand the message thus reducing misunderstanding. Third, because most of the information in an organization moves through the grapevine, workers usually verify the accuracy of information. This is accomplished by verifying the interpretation of the message with others.

All communication, both formal and informal, impacts the organization. When managers withhold information or send encrypted messages, it is generally a bad communication practice. The absence of information or encrypted information from upper-level management, fuels the grapevine. A better management strategy is to inform employees honestly and, when possible, completely.

## Communication Mediums

All communication involves the transfer of a message (information, ideas, commands, etc) from one person to another. Basically, in business, there are two types of communication media –oral and written. **Oral communication**, which includes face-to-face and telephone calls, is defined as transmitting verbal messages. A rich communication media, oral communication is a dynamic transfer of information because it allows for feedback and non-verbal communication, such as facial expressions and body language. The sender is able to engage the audience by using simple and complex forms of non-verbal communication. Likewise, the receiver is able to collect and assess non-verbal communication. **Written communication**, which includes letters and emails, is defined as transmitting messages in print form. Although oral communications comprise the bulk of our daily communications, published messages, email in particular, is changing the way employees in the workplace communicate. Written forms of communication allow the pace to be controlled by the sender and receiver.

While oral communications are capable of a higher level of immediacy, they commonly suffer from a lower level of retention. Conversely, written communication has the advantage of being more precise because written words can be carefully chosen. However, written communication is not well suited for emotional or ambiguous messages.

# Managing Communication in the Workplace

Business communications, the lifeblood of productive organizations, are designed to promote and affect change and drive action. Without effective business communications, both the internal and external structure of an organization can face challenges. Ineffective communications can lead to misunderstandings and give rise to problems. On the other hand, effective communications foster understanding and boost the bottom line of a business. Since communication is the foundation of workplace interactions, it is critical for managers and employees to master good communication skills.

For managers and supervisors operating at all levels of the organization, the ability to communicate effectively is an essential skill. Businesses rely on their managers to interact effectively with employees, co-workers, and supervisors. In the workplace, managers utilize both one-on-one and organizational-wide communications to exchange information.

## One-On-One Communication

Managers spend a significant portion of their workday interacting with others and communicating one-on-one. Many of these interactions are pleasant or routine. However, some interactions, such as giving feedback can be difficult as they may involve unpleasant messages and emotionally charged conversations. Yet, giving feedback is the only way to make certain the behavior is likely to change. Managers and supervisors can use feedback to help employees focus on important issues. In the workplace, feedback should be delivered to help workers do the right things, do things the right way, and perform at higher levels. Indeed, managers may find that their most productive employees are likely to be motivated by well-delivered feedback.

Although performance appraisals are scheduled on a regular basis in most organizations, feedback does not need to be limited to a scheduled date and time, it can occur when most appropriate. Moreover, certain feedback can be informal, such as, positive feedback, or formal, such as a performance appraisal. Regardless of the time or formality, feedback must be effective in order to improve job performance, reduce confusion regarding expectations and current performance, promote professional and personal growth in employees, and maintain or improve workplace morale.

In order for managers and supervisors to be effective, they must be skilled at giving praise feedback and criticism feedback. Being an effective manager is not always easy, but there are some basic principals about delivering effective feedback:

1. Feedback should be delivered in the right setting. As a rule, it is acceptable to deliver positive feedback in public. However, this rule is general and can be tricky. It is best to consider the employee's personality and preference. On the other hand, constructive feedback should be delivered privately.
2. Feedback should be specific. Specific feedback focuses on incidents that are within the worker's control. It is important for the manager to supply specific information, such as, when and where it happened and what the results were. For example, if a manager witnesses an employee arriving late to work it is not helpful to tell the employee, "You are always late." It would be better to say, "In the last two weeks, you have been more than 15 minutes late four times." Remember to focus on observations and facts rather than inferences.

3. Feedback should be timely. As a rule, feedback should occur promptly following the observation or incident. Feedback is more effective when both the manager and the employee can recall the incident. When the feedback occurs closing following the observation, the incident is vivid and can be discussed in detail. Delayed feedback, for example attempting to discuss an incident that happened three months ago, is often problematic due to lack of recall and memory. Additionally, performance deficiencies should be addressed at the earliest possible opportunity. This will prevent the employee from forming poor habits.

4. Feedback should be task oriented versus employee oriented. Task oriented feedback focuses on the problem or the deficient performance rather that the personality of the employee. Feedback should be based on what an employee does or did rather than personality traits or generalizations. In order to be effective, is important for managers to be nonjudgmental while providing feedback. For example, it is not helpful for a manager to say, "You always talk too much." It is better to say, "I noticed that you talked during much of the department meeting. This prevented me from covering the agenda."

5. Feedback should be balanced. There are two important focuses when balancing feedback. First, employees should be provided with a balance of praise and criticism feedback. Second, employees should be provided with frequent feedback but not overloaded with feedback. If an employee is overloaded with feedback, he or she can be confused about what needs to be improved.

In addition to understanding the basic skills needed to deliver feedback, it is important for managers and supervisors need to recognize that feedback can be positive, constructive, or destructive. Positive feedback, acknowledging good performance, and constructive feedback, addressing areas in need of improvement should occur in the workplace. Conversely, managers should make every effort to avoid delivering destructive feedback.

**Positive feedback** is used to reinforce desired behavior. Positive feedback includes information or input to a staff member about a job well done. Perhaps, the news could stem from a customer comment. Or, perhaps, the manager may observe a staff member providing great customer service. Research suggests that positive feedback should outnumber constructive feedback. Consider the following steps when giving positive feedback as well as reinforcing great performance:

| | |
|---|---|
| 1. | **Describe the positive behavior.** Be specific in providing details. |
| 2. | **Explain why the behavior was positive.** It is helpful to describe how the positive behavior impacted the organization, department or customer. |
| 3. | **Thank the employee.** Acknowledge the employee's contribution with a verbal 'thank you.' If necessary, help the employee accept credit. |

Generally, **constructive feedback** addresses areas of improvement with the intention to be helpful or corrective. At times, constructive feedback is encouraging. Generally, based on observation, constructive feedback is information-specific or issue-focused and aimed at correcting performance deficiencies, providing additional information or resources to correct the deficiency, and motivating employees. Consider the following steps when giving constructive feedback:

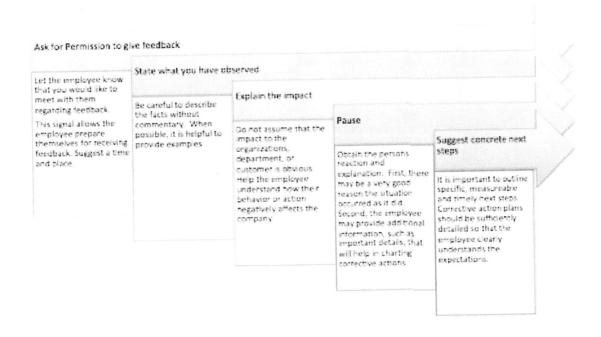

Ask for Permission to give feedback

Let the employee know that you would like to meet with them regarding feedback.

This signal allows the employee prepare themselves for receiving feedback. Suggest a time and place.

State what you have observed

Be careful to describe the facts without commentary. When possible, it is helpful to provide examples

Explain the impact

Do not assume that the impact to the organizations, department, or customer is obvious. Help the employee understand how their behavior or action negatively affects the company

Pause

Obtain the persons reaction and explanation. First, there may be a very good reason the situation occurred as it did. Second, the employee may provide additional information, such as important details, that will help in charting corrective actions

Suggest concrete next steps

It is important to outline specific, measurable and timely next steps. Corrective action plans should be sufficiently detailed so that the employee clearly understands the expectations.

Figure 13.3: Steps to Give Constructive Feedback

In order for feedback to be constructive instead of destructive, it should be focused on specific behaviors and be problem/solution orientated. **Destructive feedback**, which tends to occur in the form of generalized or subjective comments, is critical and disapproving without any intention of being helpful. Although destructive feedback often occurs when poor performance is witnessed or when there is a lack of agreed upon performance standards, it is delivered in a way that negatively impacts the employee. In the worse of scenarios, destructive feedback is a personal criticism that does not improve performance. Often, destructive feedback produces a negative or defensive reaction from the recipient. At times, employees respond to destructive feedback with verbal or physical aggression. In order to reduce the chances of delivering destructive feedback, managers should be cautious in entering conversations with subordinates when frustrated.

Providing one-on-one feedback is one of the most powerful tools managers have to develop their staff.

And, since giving regular and frequent feedback is part of a manager's job, it is important to be aware of the most common mistakes new managers make when learning to give feedback. Many new managers and supervisors make one of the two most common mistakes when delivering feedback.

Figure 13.4: Common Mistakes in Delivering Destructive Feedback

## Improving Reception by Listening

Effective listening skills are an essential part of communication. Not just hearing, but listening is important for managerial success at all levels of the organization. Although hearing and listening are used interchangeably, they mean two very different things. **Hearing**, involuntary and uncontrollable, involves receiving and perceiving sounds. On the other hand, **listening** requires attention, as it is a conscious effort to hear and understand. Typically, active and empathic listening are the two most important listening skills that managers must develop in order to possess competent listening skills.

Active listening involves assuming half they responsibility for successful communication. **Active listening** is the process of participating in giving the speaker nonjudgmental feedback that demonstrates you accurately heard the sender. Simply active listening involves listening to the sender and making verifying understanding prior to providing feedback. Active listeners practice listening carefully to what the speaker has to say and seek to understand the message. Generally, active listeners put the speaker at ease by maintaining interest and eye contact. In addition, they show the sender that they are attentively listening by nodding and making engaging in short statements to gain more information or seek clarification. Three key elements can help managers and supervisors become better active listeners.

1. Clarifying
2. Paraphrasing
3. Summarizing

**Clarifying,** asking the sender to explain or provide more details, helps the receiver understand confusing or ambiguous statements. Similarly, **paraphrasing**, restating what was said to you in your own words, is helps the receiver understand and provides the opportunity for the sender to further expand upon the message. **Summarizing** involves providing a review of the sender's main points or emotions. Since each of these key elements help the receiver understand and acknowledge the message, the receiver should refrain from interrupting. Instead, the receiver can use the natural breaks in the speaker's delivery as a time to clarifying, paraphrase or summarize.

Active listeners make a conscious effort to hear the words, but, more importantly, they try to understand the complete message. Active listening is achieved by attentively listening without distraction and without forming counter arguments. It is important to withhold evaluation, counter arguments, or criticism until after the message is accurately and completely received. Until then, the manager should respond appropriately with respect and with the intent to understand in order to receive the complete message accurately.

**Empathetic listening** is defined as the ability to understand another person's feelings, concerns, or emotional state. This means understanding the sender's personal perspective—how they feel. Empathic listening is a built upon active listening. First the sender must understand the message. However, more advance than active listening, empathic listening requires the receiver to recognize and understand the feelings, perceptions, and motives of the sender. Simply, empathic listening is the receiver's ability and willingness to appreciate the situation without judgment. Unlike sympathy, listening empathically does not necessarily involve agreeing with the sender's perspective or being affected by the sender's perceptions, but instead the ability to see the world through the other person's eyes. Two key elements can help managers and supervisors become better empathic listeners.

1. Understanding feelings
2. Reflecting feelings

Effective empathetic listener depends on **understanding feelings**–the receiver's desire to understand and reflect the sender's feelings. It is critical to genuinely desire to understand the sender's perspectives and emotions. On the other hand, **reflecting feelings** involves indicating that you understand the sender's emotions. Unlike active listening, reflecting feelings is focused on the affective part of the message.

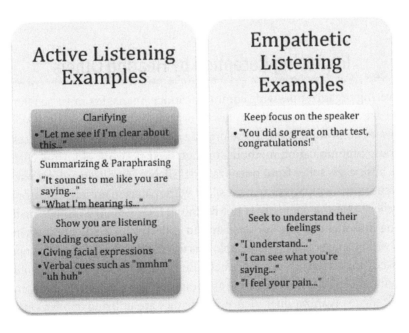

Figure 13.5: Listening Example Responses

# Organization-Wide Communication

While managing one-on-one communication is critical, managers must also be able to communicate effectively with audiences throughout the organization. Often, managers are called to converse with large and diverse audiences. Although the bulk of organization-wide communication occurs through email, new technology has enabled a wide variety of electronic mediums. Recently, organizations have begun utilizing online discussion forums, televised or videotaped speeches, and voice broadcasting to communicate with employees throughout the organization.

Discussion forums are another means of electronically promoting organization-wide communication. **Online discussion forums**, the in-house equivalent of an Internet forum, is an online discussion available to employees across the organization. Often found in Company Intranet sites, online discussion forums allow employees to ask questions, offer assistance, and share knowledge. Employees are able to share expertise and collaborate online without leaving their work location. This is especially convenient for larger organizations or organizations with multiple geographic locations.

Increasing in popularity televised or videotaped speeches are often used for smaller audiences or multiple-location audiences. **Televised/videotaped speeches**, generally made by top-level managers, can be simultaneously broadcast or videotaped for later distribution and viewing. Quite often, televised or videotaped speeches include either televised or electronic visuals. Although this type of communication can be costly, the organization is able to send a consistent message to everyone.

Similar to voice mail, **voice broadcasting** is a mass communication technique capable of broadcasting thousands of telephone messages at once. Voice broadcasting allows organizations to send voice messages to thousands of employees. Businesses are able to send a recorded message quickly and inexpensively to everyone in the company. The convenience of broadcast voice mail allows managers to deliver a consistent message to everyone in the organization.

# Improving Reception by Hearing Others

In addition to delivering organization-wide communications, managers must be attentive and receptive to what employees are feeling and thinking. Some organizations have become skilled at downward, horizontal, and upward communication. These organizations practice open and accessible communication, utilizing various communication methods through their network of formal channels.

However, some businesses suffer from organizational silence. A collective-level phenomenon, **organizational silence** occurs when employees remain silent with management regarding organizational issues. Once employees believe that the company is not listening, their opinions do not matter, or they will be punished for sharing information, they consciously and collectively decide not to share their knowledge, beliefs, or opinions with management. When employees withhold information about operational problems or organizational issues, the company does not benefit. Employees remain silent on problems and solutions. This, in turns, prevents effective decision-making and impedes organizational development and change. In order to prevent or reduce organizational silence, companies are utilizing anonymous company hotlines, survey feedback, and informal small and large group meetings. Designed to help the company improve reception, these communication channels help the organization hear what employees feel and think.

**Company hotlines** are generally toll free phone numbers that any employee can call anonymously and leave information. This information is generally for upper management but it is also information that the employee feels is sensitive in nature. Most companies hire outside firms to run their hotlines. Basically, the philosophy is to maintain complete anonymity of the caller. However, if an outside vendor reports to the Human Resources Manager, then there are other complications, such as conflict of interest if the company hotline call is regarding human resources.

**Survey feedback** is information collected by the company via a survey instrument. Surveys are generally sent to all involved employees, analyzed and the reviewed by committee. The committee members use the information to develop action plans for improvement. Many organizations make use of survey feedback by surveying their managers and employees several times a year. Such surveys may be categorized as 360 degree. This means that the organization is gathering data on an employee from horizontal, such as, peers and vendors, and vertical sources, such as bosses and subordinates.

# Perception and Communication Problems

Perception is defined as the process of experiencing the world around us. By creating awareness of objects and events in their world, individuals attend to, organize, interpret, and store information. The basic perception process occurs in four stages:

1. Stimulation (an action on various nerve agents).
2. Organization (arranging the information).
3. Interpretation-evaluation (ability to reveal meanings and relationships socially).
4. Storage-memory (ability to store and recall information).

Basically, as employees perform their work, they are exposed to a wide variety of stimuli, such as occurrences and communications and arrange the information in a meaningful way. Employees experience stimuli through their perceptual filters—based on past experiences and exposures. Through the lens of perceptual filters, employees interpret and assign meaning to the stimuli. In one-on-one and organization-wide communication, perception is a subjective, active and creative process. Perception, a cognitive progression of interpretations, begins with how the receiver perceives the sender's communication and interprets what they sensed. In other words, employees are likely to notice and pay attention to and different stimuli, such as workplace occurrences or communications. Moreover, different employees are likely to interpret the one communication message differently. So, different employees may end up with different interpretations and understandings.

## Perception Problems

Managers and supervisors must be aware that perception creates communication problems in the workplace. Often, employees exposed to the same organizational communication or information end up with dissimilar views, ideas and understandings. Two of the most common perception problems are:

1. Selective perception
2. Closure.

Selective perception is defined as the tendency to notice and accept stimuli consistent with our experiences, values, beliefs, and expectations while discounting or ignoring stimuli that is inconsistent. On the other hand, closure is defined as the tendency to 'fill in the gaps' when information is missing. Basically, employees may make assumptions about missing information. Most likely the assumptions will be based on interpretations of past experiences and exposures.

At work, it is important for managers and supervisors to share information clearly and accurately. Additionally, information should be shared in the most complete manner appropriate. Additionally, it is important for all levels of managers to be transparent in one-on-one and organization-wide communications. This will help management reduce perception problems and build trust, resulting in improved employee morale.

# Summary of Chapter

1. This chapter has focused on outlining the basic components of the communication process and the role that perception plays in communication.
2. We explored the different strategies that help managers and supervisors manage effective one-on-one communication with their subordinates.
3. We examined the types of communication channels that managers can utilize to ensure effective organization-wide communication.
4. This chapter discussed the importance of non-verbal communications and the affect of non-verbal communication on perception.
5. We read about the different methods of improving transmission by getting the message out and into the organization including the importance of improving the reception among the intended audience.
6. We learned about the basic types of feedback and the steps needed to effectively communicate feedback to employees. We also examined the basic skills necessary in delivering feedback.
7. We learned the importance of listening for managerial and business success and discussed key active listening criteria.

# Discussion Questions

1. Describe the basic elements of the communication process.
2. Explain the role that perception plays in communication and communication problems.
3. Describe the two basic types of communications found in organizations.
4. Explain the importance of non-verbal communication and how the different types affect the reception and interpretation of the intended message.
5. What types of strategies can supervisors utilize to manage effective one-on-one communication?
6. Identify the techniques needed to deliver effective positive and constructive feedback.
7. Describe how managers can manage effective organization-wide communication.
8. List examples of organizational communications that may fuel the grapevine.

# References

Berlo, D. K. (1960). *The process of communication: An introduction to theory and practice*. New York: Holt, Rinehart & Winston.

Job Outlook, National Association of Colleges and Employers. (2011). Retrieved November 27, 2011, from http://www.naceweb.org

NACE Poll: College students' communication skills. (2011). Retrieved November 28, 2011, from http://www.naceweb.org

Business Communication. (n.d.). Retrieved July 25, 2014, from http://www.newagepublishers.com/samplechapter/001680.pdf

Giving Constructive Feedback. (n.d.). . Retrieved July 25, 2014, from https://www.cabrillo.edu/services/jobs/pdfs/giving-feedback.pdf

How to Develop Skills in Empathy. (n.d.). *How to Develop Skills in Empathy*.

Non Verbal Communication. (n.d.). *Non Verbal Communication*. Retrieved July 25, 2014, from http://www.andrews.edu/~tidwell/bsad560/NonVerbal.html

Active Listening: Hear What People are Really Saying. (1996, January 1). *Active Listening*. Retrieved July 25, 2014, from http://www.mindtools.com/CommSkll/ActiveListening.htm

# PART 5

# Controlling

# CHAPTER 14

## An Introduction to Control

*"People in any organization are always attached to the obsolete—the things that should have worked but did not, the things that once were productive and no longer are."*

– Peter F. Drucker

### Chapter Learning Objectives:

After reading this chapter you should have a good understanding of:

- The different types of control found in organizations today.
- Regulatory processes and the importance of control to organizations.
- The basic role of control and three major steps in the control process.
- The key elements of internal and external control standards.
- Gap concepts involved in comparing actual performance to desired performance.

- How managers use contemporary management techniques to improve performance and increase productivity.
- Corrective action tools available to help managers repair deficiencies.
- Contemporary control approaches and how managers can achieve organizational goals utilizing the balanced scorecard methodology.

Control, a regulatory process, establishes the standards necessary to achieve organizational goals. In his 1916 classic, Administration Industrielle et Generale, **Henry Fayol** defined the function of control in terms of ensuring that all workplace activities occur within the parameters of the plan and accompanying principles. Control, used to compare actual performance against desired performance standards, includes the establishment of clear expectations and standards, identification methods to compare actual performance to desired performance, and strategies for taking corrective action if the actual performance does not meet desired performance. Simply, the purpose of control is to identify deviations and deficiencies in performance and take corrective action. Accordingly, the first section of this chapter will examine methods to establish control standards.

The middle section of this chapter will explore comparing standards and corrective actions. The previous phase of establishing standards laid the foundation for the second step in the control process—comparing actual performance against desired performance. This step is the active principle of the control process and managers utilize a variety of different methods to compare actual performance to desired performance. The last step in the control process, corrective action, is perhaps the most difficult for new managers. Yet, effective managers must be able to identify and carry out corrective actions when necessary to restore performance to standards.

Lastly, we will examine what to control and the trend towards the balanced scorecard. Managers in organization grapple with the delicate balance of control. Too much control weakens employee initiative and contribution and lowers workplace moral. On the other hand, quite often too little control does not produce alignment between organizational mission and vision and departmental processes and procedures.

## Organizational Control

The mission and vision of the business first determine the direction for organizational control. The drivers of organizational control are the goals and strategic plans of the company. Strategic plans are translated into departmental goals and objectives with specific performance measures. Control processes helps managers review and evaluate workplace activities and determine if those activities are on target to help the company meet its goals.

The organizational control framework keeps the business functions, processes, and tasks on track. Throughout the process managers monitor and evaluate their department's strategy, structure, and workplace activities to determine if they are working as intended. If performance deficiencies exist, then managers must decide how they can be corrected. And, if standards are met, then manager work on how to improve processes and procedures. Organizational control also focuses on challenges facing the company, anticipating future events, and working to take advantage of strategic opportunities.

## Types of Control

Management controls refer to the processes and systems managers utilize to foster, promote, and restrict the actions of groups and individuals in order to achieve departmental objectives and organizational goals. In the workplace, management control encompasses two broad and different categories of control—normative and regulative.

## Normative

**Normative control** refers to governing employee behavior through accepted patterns of behavior, including team norms and organizational culture. Normative controls represent shared forms of control since they govern workplace behavior through norms-accepted patterns of behavior and action. Typically, normative controls are implicit as they evolve from company-wide values and beliefs. In other words, normative controls are not written or codified. Rather they are implied and accepted guides for employee behavior and action.

Companies create normative controls in three ways. First, organizations create normative control through the hiring process. Typically, normatively controlled companies will screen and select applicants based on their attitudes and values. Second, organizations create normative control by sharing organizational stories, values, and beliefs in new employee orientation. Third, organizations create normative control through team norms and organizational culture. In normatively controlled companies, employees observe others in the workplace and learn what they should and should not do. Both team norms and organizational culture are covered in detail in previous chapters.

| Type of Regulative Control | Description | Possible Advantages | Possible Disadvantages |
|---|---|---|---|
| **Team Norms** | Informal and implicit team rules and responsibilities. | 1. Common goals lead to great employee involvement. 2. Collective power allows for group synergy. | 1. Self preservation may lead to group mobilization. 2. Teams are susceptible to groupthink. |
| **Organizational Culture** | Shared organizational beliefs, values, and traditions. | 1. Organizational commitment may lead to better employee loyalty. 2. Company may be able to build strong culture without being rule-bound. | 1. Overpowering cultures can be invasive to employees. 2. Disenfranchised employees may not find work meaningful or lose faith in the company. |

For example, Nordstrom sees customer service as a strategic competitive advantage. Nordstrom's website let's everyone know their one goal, "*Make customers feel good. We work hard every day with the goal of making customers feel good. The customer is tops in our book.*"

By uprooting the traditional structure and placing the customer at the top of the corporate pyramid, Nordstrom embeds customer service into the organizational culture instead of acting as if customer service is a separate function or department. To achieve a culture of customer service, Nordstrom ensures that policies and procedures support organizational culture and norms. Their efforts focus on creating alignment throughout the organization. As an example, for many years, Nordstrom had a one-paragraph employee handbook, "*We're glad to have you with our Company. Our number-one goal is to provide outstanding customer service. Set both your personal and professional goals high. We have great*

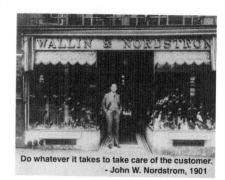

Do whatever it takes to take care of the customer.
- John W. Nordstrom, 1901

*confidence in your ability to achieve them. Nordstrom Rules: Rule #1: Use your good judgment in all situations. There will be no additional rules."*

# Regulative

The opposite of normative controls, **regulative controls** refer to the process of governing employee behavior by establishing bureaucratic controls, financial controls, and quality controls. Regulative controls are driven from the top-down and find their roots in long standing policies and procedures. Commonly referred to as standard operating procedures, these processes and procedures tend to be rigid and inflexible. Contemporary organizations are becoming more flexible, flattening their hierarchical structures, and empowering their employees to provide great customer service and improve the bottom line. Nonetheless, both large and small organizations rely heavily on regulative controls to ensure standards are met and company goals are achieved.

| Type of Regulative Control | Description | Possible Advantages | Possible Disadvantages |
|---|---|---|---|
| **Bureaucratic Control (stems from authority and chain of command)** | Generally codified in the form of standard operating policies and procedures. Formal and explicit. | 1. Standardization ensures that outcomes are predictable. 2. Allows for efficiency in routine problems and situations. 3. Lower training costs. | 1. Rules are difficult to dismantle. 2. Companies may become rigid, inflexible, and slow to respond to customers or market changes. 3. Tendency to be punishment focused. |
| **Financial Control** | Management and control of key financial targets. | 1. Proven methods to asses the strength of the company. 2. Investors and analysts can gain insight into the companies financial performance. For example, economic value added helps managers assess whether they are performing well enough to pay the cost of the capital needed to run the business. | 1. Financial measures are past oriented. 2. Linking rewards to key financial targets may lead to short-term decision-making. 3. Managers may be tempted to focus internally and miss external factors, such as, customer satisfaction. |
| **Quality Control** | Acceptable levels of variations in product or process. | 1. Products defects are uncovered and reported prior to distribution. 2. Increased likelihood of a quality product reduces risk of recalls, etc. | 1. Visual inspection relies on the competence and integrity of the employee. 2. Requires collection and sifting of data by knowledgeable personnel. |

Organizational control processes provide managers with the mechanisms to help regulate the quantity and quality of goods and services produced. Regulatory control systems allow managers to systematically assess the organization's efficiency and effectiveness in producing and distributing goods and services. Without a control process, managers would not have an orderly method to understand the performance of their department or division. Without a good understanding of performance, managers would have no idea how to improve workplace activities.

Throughout the control process, managers monitor and regulate the effectiveness and efficiency of their department, division, and work group. Managers play a significant role in the control process as it their responsibility to ensure that activities under their direction support the achievement organizational goals and objectives. Effective managers consistently monitor the performance of their department and find ways to improve performance.

## Bureaucratic Control

When managerial control is discussed at the workplace, managers and employees generally think of bureaucratic control. Similar to all regulatory control types, bureaucratic control is driven from the top levels of the organization and information generally flows from the top down. **Bureaucratic control** refers to the system of rules and standard operating procedures that regulate workplace activities and behaviors. Simply, bureaucratic control is the use of formalized policies and procedures to influence employee behavior. Policies are procedures are in written form, such as, an employee manual.

Generally, bureaucratic organizational structures have numerous layers of management and foster a company culture of rules and regulations with closely controlled operational processes, procedures, and tasks. Standardization ensures that workplace activities are accomplished in an effective and efficient manner. In an effort to improve productivity, bureaucratic organizations will often benchmark and adopt best practices. On the other hand, bureaucratic structures must be cautious not to discourage innovation and creativity. Bureaucratically controlled companies rigid in their policy-driven and decision-making may become resistant to change. If the organization becomes inflexible, then it may be slow to respond to customers or competitors or unable adapt to changing conditions in the marketplace or environment. Additionally, managers in bureaucratically controlled organizations must be cautious to balance punishment with reward. The lack of balance between reward and punishment will cause poor employee moral.

## The Control Process

Control processes center on ensuring that performance does not deviate from established standards. The **control process** consists of three essential steps—establishing performance standards, comparing actual performance against performance standards, and taking corrective action if necessary. Yet, the control process is not a one-time workplace management activity; instead it is a continuous, dynamic process that reoccurs over time. In order to set, maintain, and improve performance levels, managers repeat and refine the entire process daily, weekly, and monthly.

To varying degrees, managers at all levels in the organization engage in the managerial function of control. So, it is important for managers to differentiate between the managerial functions of control and behavioral control. The managerial function of control is primarily concerned with ensuring that work activities are contributing to and in alignment with organizational goals and departmental objectives.

Managers ensure that subordinates work performance meets pre-established standards. The control function does not suggest that managers attempt to control an employee's personality. Control is achieved when the employee's workplace behavior and actions conform to company standards, processes, and procedures. The overreaching aim of the managerial function of control is to ensure company objectives and goals are accomplished.

Control is achieved when behavior and work procedures conform to established standards and organizational or departmental goals are accomplished. By contrast, **control loss** occurs when workplace behavior and procedures do not conform to established standards. Typically, control loss prevents the accomplishment of goals. When control losses occur, managers need to analyze and identify what corrective actions can be taken to prevent these mistakes from occurring again in the future.

# Establishing Standards

The control process starts when managers begin the task of setting goals and establishing standards. **Standards** are defined as a basis of comparison for measuring the degree to which workplace performance is satisfactory or unsatisfactory. Designing and establishing effective standards begins with a plan. In order to accomplish this task, managers must understand the internal environment (who is doing what and how well) and be able to scan and understand the external environment (what are others doing and how well). This is generally accomplished by monitoring. In Chapter One, you learned about the different managerial roles as identified by **Henry Mintzberg**. A subcategory of the information managerial roles, **monitoring** is defined as actively seeking and obtaining a wide variety of information, both internal and external, to develop a thorough understanding of the organization and its environment.

## Internal Standards

**Internal standards** refer to the process of setting and monitoring systematic performance standards in an effort to ensure workplace tasks and activities are conducted in an effective and efficient manner. There are three common techniques and types of internal standards—standardization of work skills, standardization of outputs, and standardization of work processes.

1. **Standardization of work skills** involves hiring employees who possess the necessary skills, knowledge, and abilities to perform the tasks required by the job and make necessary decision regarding those tasks. For example, most firms consider engineers and doctors as self-controlling.
2. **Standardization of outputs** involves providing employees with precise product, quality, and performance specifications. The goal is to maintain control by gauging outputs against performance specifications.
3. **Standardization of work processes** involves reducing or eliminating an employee's discretion to deviate from the set standards by developing rules, regulations, and operating procedures. All

approaches to internal standards focus on developing systematic performance standards designed to monitor workplace tasks and activities.

## External Standards

**External standards** refer to the process of systematically scanning the environment and identifying best practices. The concept of **best practices** implies the organization or industry executes methods, processes, or techniques that accomplish desired outcomes in the most effective and efficient manner. Simply, best practices are methods and techniques that consistently demonstrate superior results. **Industry wide best practices** define guidelines (such as ethics) and methods (techniques and processes) that represent the most efficient or prudent course of action for a commercial or professional procedure or process. Generally, industry wide best practices are set and governed by an authority. Typically, organizations identify and use the best practices of other companies in benchmarking.

## Benchmarking

**Benchmarking** refers to the process of comparing a set of product or customer metrics, measurements, and performance from one company to those of another company. The goal of benchmarking is to set appropriate performance metrics and measurement for your organization based on the performance metrics of similar companies and similar processes. Also referred to as best practices, benchmarking is a strategic management process that allows organizations to evaluate critical aspects of their functions in relation to other organizations. Generally, managers select both peer and aspirant organizations as comparisons. A **peer** organization is defined as an organization in the same industry equal or similar in scope and size. An **aspirant** organization is defined as an organization in the same industry but in a better competitive position or larger in scope and size—a leader in the field. Identifying peer organizations,

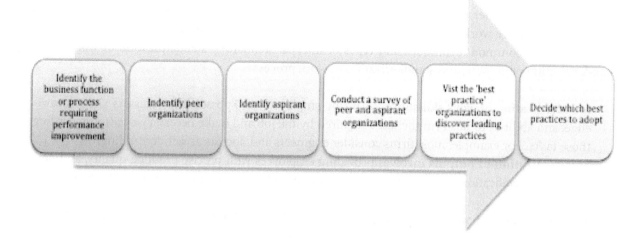

Figure 14.1: Process of Benchmarking

allows managers to plan improvements. Identifying aspirant organizations allows managers to develop future oriented strategies.

Utilizing benchmarking as a process improvement methodology has many advantages. First, benchmarking can be applied to any business function or process. Second, it has the flexibility to be low cost, low technology for small businesses or more robust with software for technical and product benchmarking. The most common costs are site visit costs (to visit peer or aspirant companies), time costs (researching, traveling), and technology and database costs (these costs have been reduced dramatically due to the internet). Third, benchmarking can be applied internally (comparing performance between departments, divisions, and teams within the organization) and externally (comparing to other companies in a specific industry or across industries).

The wide appeal of benchmarking has lead to the emergence of various benchmarking methodologies. Within these broad methodologies there are three specific types of benchmarking categories: process, performance, and strategic benchmarking. The typical benchmarking methodology contains six processes as seen below:

In all benchmarking methodologies, the goal is to learn how well the selected comparison organizations perform, and, more importantly, the business processes that enable those organizations to perform more effectively and efficiently. Simply put, it is looking at companies that perform the same business functions more successfully and finding out why.

## Setting Control Standards

Setting control standards requires formal target setting. **Standards of performance** are set as performance targets against which actual performance will be measured. Standards vary from company to

### Stretch Goals

Stretch goals have different roles than performance goals and targets. Coined by Jack Welch, many organizations utilize the concept of stretch goals to promote organizational effectiveness and achieve objectives. Stretch goals are defined as goals that are a little difficult. By definition, stretch goals are goals that you may not know how to immediately reach as they are sufficiently beyond current levels of achievement. Actually, managers and employees may lack a clear idea of how to reach reach them. According to Welch, there are two major purposes of stretch goals:

1. Improve organizational effectiveness.
2. Personal growth and professional development.

Today, organizations utilize stretch goals to force innovation and creativity. Faced with stretch goals, managers and their staff must utilize collaboration, cooperation, and innovation as they acknowledge that existing methods and systems are insufficient insufficient and explore new ideas and avenues.

company. However, common performance standards include quality, efficiency, innovation, safety, and responsiveness to customers.

After top executives set the organization's overall strategy and goals, performance goals are set for departments and divisions to help the organization achieve its goals. Department and division managers develop business unit performance standards and goals, while functional managers develop specific performance targets and standards for different functions under their responsibility.

Typically, organizations require that standards of performance be aligned to organizational goals and objectives since performance goals and target set at one level affect those at other levels. **Alignment of performance standards** refers to the harmony of goals at each level. Throughout the organization, performance standards should support and be congruent with the organizational strategy and goals. This requires the coordination and collaboration of managers at all levels in the organization.

Performance standards, also referred to as performance targets, should be measurable, clear and specific and set realistically achievable outcomes. Performance targets are derived from core business functions, processes, and tasks. They do not represent difficult outcomes, innovative projects, or long term goals. Simply, performance standards help employees understand what is expected of them.

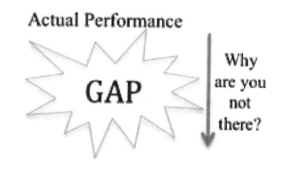

Figure 14.2: Desired Performance

## Comparing Standards

The previous phase of establishing standards laid the foundation for the second step in the control process-comparing actual performance against desired performance. This next step is the active principle of the control process. **Comparing standards** is defined as the process of identifying and analyzing performance deviations. Managers utilize different methods to compare actual performance to desired performance, such as, walking around the plant or obtaining computer generated company reports measuring results.

### Gap Analysis

A contemporary management technique, the gap analysis helps managers compare a departments' actual performance against established performance goals and standards. Simply, the term **gap analysis** refers to the comparison of actual performance against desired performance. Gap analysis methodology consists of identifying present levels of performance or competencies, measuring them against desired or established levels, and identifying the gap or distance between the two. Common gap analysis techniques consist of three steps:

1.  Current State. What is (identifying and listing current/actual performance levels)
2.  Future State. What should be (listing defined and established/desired standards)

## Gap Performance Analysis Example

| Key Outputs | Key Goals | Key Tasks | Performance Gaps | Root Cause |
|---|---|---|---|---|
| • 15 Orders To Be Shipped | • Ship 100% of orders within two days | • Package Product <br> • Prepare to Ship <br> • Send Shipment to Customer | • Product was not finished <br> • Shipment was late | • 5 wrong zip codes <br> • 7 incorrect postage codes <br> • 3 back orders |

Figure 14.3: Gap Performance Analysis Example

3.  Highlighting gaps (identifying the distance between what is and what should be).

Highlighting gaps includes identifying and recording all elements and component between the current state and the future state. Gap elements should be specific and descriptive, such as, 15 delays in orders shipped. Once gap elements are determined and defined, then managers begin the task of conducting a root cause analysis to determine the factors contributing to gap elements. **Root cause analysis** is a method of problem solving that identifies the preliminary cause of a discrepancy or deviation. Managers should list the contributing factors in relevant, objective, and specific terms. For example, the 15 delayed orders shipped could be attributable due to different factors, such as, 5 wrong zip codes, seven incorrect postage calculated, and three back orders. Each of these different factors may require different remedies, such as training. Additionally, each of these different factors could stem from different departments or positions. For example, the customer service department may take the zip code information with the order while the distribution center operates the postage meter.

The gap analysis is an effective tool in helping managers analyze and understand performance discrepancies. Additionally, the gap analysis is particularly helpful in new business setting, changes to production or operation functions, and in prioritizing and allocating resources.

## Corrective Action

The last step in the control process is perhaps the most difficult for new managers. After identification of performance deficiency and analysis of performance deviation, managers need to identify all possible remedies and chart a course of action. **Corrective action** refers to the process of identifying and implementing remedies to repair deficiencies. Remedies should directly address the factors responsible identified in the comparing standards stage.

Once the deviation from the established standards has been identified and analyzed, the manager develops and implements solutions to correct them. Solutions can take many forms, such as training employees, revising processes, and creating new procedures.

Corrective action should occur as close as possible in time to the employee's poor performance or mistake. Addressing issues in a timely manner allows managers to help employees make quick adjustments in their effort and direction. When possible, managers attempt to prevent deviations before they occur. Whether preventative or after the fact, corrective action means addressing and correcting problems when discovered. To minimize workplace deviations and ensure that corrective actions are effective, managers utilize three types of control methods.

# Feedback Mechanisms

There are three basic types of control feedback mechanisms: feedback control, concurrent control, and feed-forward control.

**Feedback control** refers to mechanisms that gather information about performance deficiencies *after* they occur. Feedback control focuses on outcomes and results. Although the manager is notified after the occurrence, this information is used to address, correct, or prevent future performance deficiencies. Research has clearly demonstrated that effective feedback improves organizational performance and employee performance. Effective feedback is beneficial in helping the employee correct the deficiency, prevent future occurrences, and improve performance.

**Concurrent control** refers to mechanisms that gather information about performance deficiencies *as* they occur. Concurrent control also focuses on outcomes and results but is an improvement over feedback due to immediate notification. Concurrent control attempts to eliminate or reduce the delay that occurs in feedback control. By eliminating or reducing the delay between performance and feedback about the deficiency, the occurrence is still vivid for the employee. The employee is more likely to recall specifics and can contribute to finding possible solutions.

**Feed-forward control** refers to mechanisms that gather information about performance deficiencies *before* they occur. Feed-forward control provides information to the manager about performance deficiencies by monitoring inputs, not outcomes or results. The primary advantage of feed-forward control is the proactive attempt to prevent or minimize performance deficiencies *before* they occur.

For example, Home Depot utilizes a variety of control mechanisms to ensure employees' performance is aligned with organizational values. One of Home Depot's eight core values is excellent customer service. Using feedback control, Home Depot tracks the customer service experience by printing a web survey link on each receipt. The survey begins by asking customers to enter information from their receipt and continues through a series of customer experiences questions. Associates who provide exceptional customer service are recognized and awarded a Home Depot Values badge that can be worn on their smocks.

The Home Depot Value of Excellent Customer Service: "Along with our quality products, service, price and selection, we must go the extra mile to give customers knowledgeable advice about merchandise and to help them use those products to their maximum benefit."

# Continuous Improvement

Since control is an on-going and dynamic process, corrective action is not a one-time achievement or result. Managers repeat the entire control process over time. However, most contemporary companies have adopted a culture of continuous improvement to help them identify opportunities for improvement and integrate those improvements into daily routines, tasks and processes. This type of commitment to continuous improvement is aimed at increasing effectiveness and efficiency, reducing waste, and cutting costs by find opportunities to improve workplace activities.

The **continuous improvement process** is defined as an on-going and dynamic effort to improve products, services, processes and tasks. Also known as continual improvement process, the goal is to improve organizational efficiency, effectiveness and flexibility by continually identifying opportunities for workplace improvement and making continuously working towards incremental improvement of goods, services, or processes. A pioneer in the field, W. Edward Deming considered continuous improvement as part of the management system. The basic cycle of continuous improvement processes contain four steps:

1. Identify opportunities for improvement in process or workflow (many times this begins with a gap analysis).
2. Plan how to improve the workplace process or procedure.
3. Execute the change (implement the selected plan).
4. Review how the change is working (monitor the effect of the implemented change).

Continuous improvement processes can be either formal or informal. Today, most companies utilize one or more types of continuous improvement processes as many organizations are working to constantly cut costs, reduce waste, and improve efficiency and effectiveness.

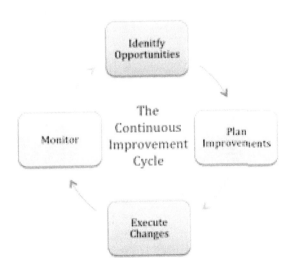

Figure 14.4: The Continuous Improvement Cycle

# What Should Organizations Control?

This chapter started by examining organizational control and need to align control to the organization's strategy, goals, and objectives. Obviously, deciding what the organization should control is very important as it has critical implications for most companies. Unfortunately, in many companies, financial measures are the only measures of performance. Historically, companies analyze financial control as achieved through cash flow, income statements, financial ratios and cost-cutting budgets. Forward thinking organizations have also added the measure of economic value added (EVA). Unlike traditional financial measures, economic value added allows managers to assess if their division or department is performing well enough to pay the cost of the capital needed to operate the business unit.

Today's competitive organizations support a more strategic and balanced approach to performance management. The balanced scorecard encourages managers to measure and control the organization's performance utilizing four perspectives: financial, customer, internal operation, and innovation and learning. Effective managers understand the push and pull of different stakeholders and, as a result, the need for a balanced approach to understanding and diagnosing performance.

## Balanced Scorecard

A strategic management tool, the term **balanced scorecard** refers to a performance metric tool and semi-standardized, structured report used to identify and improve internal functions and, as a result, external outcomes. Developed by **Robert Kaplan** and **David Norton** in 1992, the balanced scorecard

Figure 14.5

provides a methodology to align business activities to organizational strategy and monitor the performance of strategic goals. A typical balanced scorecard contains several characteristics:

1. It is a mix of financial and non-financial metrics and data.
2. The focus is on monitoring a limited number of mission important data items.
3. Selections of mission driven metrics and data items are driven from the strategic agenda of the organization.

Traditionally, companies use standard financial and accounting measures, such as return on investments, return on capitol, and return on assets, to measure performance. The financial and accounting perspectives are important and valuable but limited. A contemporary approach to measure performance, the balanced scorecard encourages managers to look beyond the traditional financial and accounting measures in an effort to provide a more comprehensive, holistic assessment of the organization's overall performance. As a methodology, the balanced scorecard breaks down broad organizational goals into vision and mission, strategies and objectives, tactical activities, and metrics. Utilizing four different perspectives to track company performance, the balanced scorecard methodology examines:

1. Financial performance (the most traditional performance indicator). How do our shareholders see us?
2. Customer analysis (customer satisfaction and retention). How do our customers see us?
3. Internal analysis (operations, production). Are we excelling at our core competencies and critical capacities?
4. Learning and Growth (effectiveness of management). Are we improving and creating value?

Due to the straightforward approach provided by balanced scorecard coupled with it's ability to link collected metrics to company goals, it is now utilized extensively by organizations around the world. The balanced scorecard gained in popularity due to the advantages it offers over traditional control processes (which solely provide financial measures). First, it compels managers at every organizational level to examine each of the four areas and set specific goals and measure performance in each category. This allows managers to measure what matters and make data driven decisions. Second, it ensures organizational alignment, which in-turn improves communication and builds collective and individual accountability. This allows managers to develop strategically focused plans and empower cross-functional teams to work towards aligning different functions and systems from a shared vision. Third, it enables the strategic setting of priorities and projects. This allows organizations to develop a prioritization framework.

# Summary of Chapter

1. This chapter has focused on the importance of organizational control and outlining the basic control process.
2. We explored the three major steps in the regulatory control process.
3. We learned about establishing standards and looked at the differences between internal and external control.
4. This chapter discussed the differences between normative and bureaucratic control.
5. We examined the contemporary trends of benchmarking and best practices. And, learned how managers can utilize these methods to increase effectiveness and efficiency.
6. This chapter discussed the importance of comparing standards and how managers can use a gap analysis to compare actual performance to desired or established performance.
7. We learned that corrective action, if needed, is necessary to repair performance deficiencies and examined the three basic methods of feedback control, concurrent control, and feed-forward control.
8. We looked three different types of control methods—feedback, concurrent, and feed-forward.
9. This chapter looked at the two basic kinds of control—normative and regulative—and how organizations use control to achieve company goals and objectives.
10. We studied the balanced scorecard—a strategic performance management tool developed by Robert Kaplan and David Norton.

# Discussion Questions

1. Explain the significance of control functions to organizations.
2. Describe the basic regulatory control process.
3. Explain why must the control process begin with the establishment of clear performance standards.
4. Outline the steps involved in comparing actual performance to desired performance.
5. Discuss the corrective action process and how it is used to repair performance deficiencies.
6. Identify the differences between feedback, concurrent, and feed-forward control methods.
7. Discuss how managers utilize the gap analysis to increase organizational performance. Why is it important to analyze performance discrepancies?
8. Why is benchmarking important to organizations? List the differences between peer and aspirant distinctions.
9. How can 'controlling' help a manager reach department goals and achieve more efficiency and effectiveness in departmental functions?
10. Explain the balanced scorecard approach to control and how manager utilize it to optimize and balanced control of performance.
11. How should managers obtain control? How do managers need to be careful when attempting to obtain control?
12. Is control necessary or possible in all situations?

# References

Anderson, P., and M. Pulich. "Managerial Competencies Necessary in Today's Dynamic Health Care Environment." Health Care Manager 21, no. 2 (2002): 1–11.

Baldrige Products and Services. (2010, March 25). *Baldrige Homepage*. Retrieved from http://www.nist.gov/baldrige/

Barnett, T. (n.d.). Reference for Business. *Management Functions*. Retrieved from http://www.referenceforbusiness.com/management/Log-Mar/Management-Functions.html#ixzz37qknucpJ

C. A. Reeves & D. A. Bednar, "Defining Quality: Alternatives and Implications," *Academy of Management Review* 19 (1994): 419–445.

C. B. Furlong, "12 Rules fo Customer Retention," *Bank Marketing* 5 (January 1993): 14.

C. C. Manz & H. P. Sims Jr., "Self-Management as a Substitute for Leadership: A Social Learning perspective." *Academy of Management Review* 5 (1980): 361–367.

C. Manz & H. Sims, "Leading Workers to Lead Themselves: The External Leadership of Self-Managed Work Teams." *Administrative Science Quarterly* 32 (1987): 106–128

Carroll, Stephen J., and Dennis J. Gillen. "Are the Classical Management Functions Useful in Describing Managerial Work?" Academy of Management Review 12, no. 1 (1980): 38–51.

Corrective and Preventive Action (CAPA). (2002). *Corrective and Preventive Action (CAPA)*. Retrieved from http://syque.com/improvement/corrective_preventive.htm

Definitions of General Management Terms. (2014). *Definitions of General Management Terms*. Retrieved from http://balancedscorecard.org/Resources/About-the-Balanced-Scorecard/Definitions

Droege, S. B. (n.d.). Management Control. *Management Control*. Retrieved from http://www.referenceforbusiness.com/management/Log-Mar/Management-Control.html

Fayol, Henri. General and Industrial Administration. London: Sir Issac Pitman & Sons, Ltd., 1949.

G. Colvin, "America's Best & Worst Wealth Creator: The Real Champions Aren't Always Who You Think. Here's an Eye-Opening Look at Which Companies Produce and Destroy the Most Money for Investors-Plus a New Tool for Spotting Future Winners," *Fortune*, 18 December 2000, 207.

H. Koontz & R. W. Bradspies, "Managing through Feedforward Control: A Furture-Directed View." *Business Horizons*, June 1972, 25–36.

Home Depot Values. (n.d.). *Home Depot*. Retrieved from https://corporate.homedepot.com/OurCompany/Values/Pages/default.aspx

J. R. Barker, "Tightening the Iron Cage: Concertive Control in Self-Managing Teams." *Administrative Science Quarterly* 38 (1993): 408–437.

J. Slocum & H. A. Sims, "Typology for Integrating Technology, Organization and Job Design." *Human Relations* 33 (1980): 193–212.

Koontz, Harold, and Cyril O'Donnell. Principles of Management: An Analysis of Managerial Functions. New York: McGraw-Hill Book Co., 1955.

Lamond, David. "A Matter of Style: Reconciling Henri and Henry." Management Decision 42, no. 2 (2004): 330–356.

Landauer, S., & Kerr, S. Using Stretch Goals to Promote Organizational Effectiveness and Personal Growth: General Electric and Goldman Sachs. *Academy of Management Executive, 18*, 134–138.

M. H. Stocks & A. Harrell, "The Impact of an Increase in Accounting Information Level on the Judgment Quality of Individuals and Groups," *Accounting, Organizations and society*, October-November 1995, 685–700.

M. Weber. *The Protestant Ethic and the Spirit of Capitalism* (New York: Scribner's. 1958)

Malcolm Baldrige National Quality Award (MBNQA). (2012). *ASQ*. Retrieved from http://asq.org/learn-about-quality/malcolm-baldrige-award/overview/overview.html

Martin, J. R. (n.d.). Summary of the Balanced Scorecard Concepts. *Balanced Scorecard Summary*. Retrieved from http://www.maaw.info/BalScoreSum.htm

Mintzberg, Henry. The Nature of Managerial Work. New York: Harper & Row, 1973.

Noone, L. (2008). How To Write Them & How To Make Them Work For You. Retrieved from http://staffperformancesecrets.com/wp-content/uploads/2010/05/PerformanceStandards6.pdf

Noone, L. (2010, April 13). Why Performance Standards Are Essential For Managing Employee Performance. *Why Performance Standards Are Essential For Managing Employee Performance*. Retrieved from http://staffperformancesecrets.com/2010/04/performance-standards–3/

Nordstrom Careers. (2013). *Careers*. Retrieved from http://about.nordstrom.com/careers/#/about-us/mainWhat is Continuous Improvement? (n.d.). *Continuous Improvement*. Retrieved from http://leankit.com/kanban/continuous-improvement/

R. Leifer & P. K. Mills, "An Information Processing Approach for Deciding upon Control Strategies and Reducing Control Loss in Emerging Organizations." *Journal of Management* 22 (1996): 113–137

R. S. Kaplan & D. P. Norton, "The Balanced Scorecard: Measures That Drive Performance." *Hard Business Review*, January-February 1992. 71–79

R. S. Kaplan & D. P. Norton, "Using the Balanced Scorecard as a Strategic Management System." *Harvard Business Review*, Janurary-February 1996, 75–85;

Robbins, Stephen P. and Mary Coulter. Management. Upper Saddle River, NJ: Prentice Hall, 1999.

S. G. Green & M. A. Welsh, "Cybernetics and Dependence: Reframing the Control Concept." *Academy of Management Review* 13 (1988): 287–30

The Benefits of Balancing Scorecard Strategic Planning and Management. (n.d.). Retrieved from https://www.balancedscorecard.org/Portals/0/PDF/BSC_Benefits_2pgs.pdf

# CHAPTER 15

## Managing Service and Manufacturing Operations

*"Operations Management keeps the lights on, Strategic Management provides the light at the end of the tunnel, and project management is the train engine that moves the organization forward."*

### Chapter Learning Objectives:

After reading this chapter you should have a good understanding of:

- The kinds of productivity and their importance in managing operations.
- The role quality plays in managing operations.
- The essentials of managing a service business.

- The different kinds of manufacturing operations.
- The types of inventory that is used in management.
- The different costs of maintaining an inventory.
- The various methods used to measure inventory.

# Productivity

In this chapter you will learn about *operations management*, the design and management of products, processes, services and supply chains. We will start with the basics of operations management: productivity and quality followed by managing operations and completing the chapter with inventory, examining the various types, measures, costs, and methods for managing inventory.

## Productions Systems

All organizations are production systems. *Production* is a method employed by organizations for making or providing essential goods and services for consumers. It is a process that puts *intangible inputs* like ideas, creativity, research, knowledge, wisdom, etc. in use or action. It is a way that transforms (convert) *tangible inputs* like raw materials, semi-finished goods and unassembled goods into *finished goods* or commodities.

*Productivity* is a measure of the efficiency of a person, machine, factory, system, etc., in transforming inputs into useful outputs. The fewer inputs it takes to create an output (or the greater number of output from one input), the higher the productivity. Productivity is a critical determinant of cost efficiency and is computed by dividing the average output per period by the total costs incurred or resources such as capitol, energy, material, or personnel consumed in that period. For example, let's say your car gets 40 miles (output) to the gallon (input), and your friend's car gets 25 miles (output) to the gallon (input), your car would be more productive than your friends.

## Why is Productivity important?

Productivity measures the efficiency of production. Higher productivity (doing more with less) results in lower costs for the company, lower prices for consumers, faster service, greater market share, and greater profits for the business. Increasing productivity can boost the level of competition in a market. When one firm is able to be more efficient with its resources, it encourages other companies to improve productivity as well in order to compete. For example, for every 1-second saved in the drive through lane at a fast food restaurant, sales are increased by 1 percent. Additionally, increasing the efficiency of drive through service by 10 percent adds approximately 10 percent to a fast-food restaurant's sales. With this data it is not surprising that companies try to reduce the average drive-through time. For example, Wendy's average drive-through time was 145.5 seconds; Taco Bell finished second with the average time of 146.7 second; and McDonald's has the longest average time of 184.2 seconds.

Productivity is the cornerstone of economic growth. We are richer than our grandparents and than the average person in the third world primarily because we are more productive. Productivity also affects our competitive position: the more productive we are the better we are able to compete on world markets. In short, productivity is the source of the high standard

$$\text{Productivity} = \frac{\text{Outputs}}{\text{Inputs}}$$

of living enjoyed by the developed economies relative to the third world or to the same economies fifty or one hundred years ago.

# Kinds of Productivity

One problem with trying to measure productivity is that a decision must be made in terms of identifying the inputs and outputs and how they will be measured. This is relatively easy when productivity of an individual is considered, but it becomes difficult when productivity involves a whole company or a nation.

*Partial productivity* is the simplest type of productivity measure; a single type of input is selected for the productivity ratio. The company or organization selects an input factor that it monitors in daily activity such as direct labor hours, *labor productivity,* is one factor that most companies' monitor because they pay their employees based on hours worked.

$$\text{Partial Productivity} = \frac{\text{Outputs}}{\text{Single Kind of Input}}$$

*Multifactor productivity* is an overall measure of productivity that assesses how efficiently a company uses all of the inputs (labor, capital, materials, and energy) necessary to make outputs. In illustrating the two productivity measurements: labor productivity can be represented as 1,000 cars/50 workers; and MFP can be represented as 1,000/(Labor + Capital + Materials + Energy). Thus, multifactor productivity is a more comprehensive measure of productivity than labor productivity or other single-factor productivity measures.

$$\text{Multifactor Productivity} = \frac{\text{Outputs}}{\text{Labor + Capital + Materials + Energy}}$$

As an example, the factors an airline may choose to determine its overall efficiency are the following:

- Labor: pilots, cabin attendants, maintenance mechanics, ticket sales people, etc.;
- Capital: airplanes, air terminals, etc.;
- Land: on which to build the air terminals, runways, and maintenance facilities; and
- Intermediate inputs: airplane fuel, etc.

Managers should use both partial and multifactor productivity measures as they provide a holistic view of the organizational performance. Multifactor productivity indicates a company's level of productivity relative to its competition. Partial productivity indicates the specific contribution that each factor makes to the overall productivity and provides managers the information necessary to determine what factors need to be adjusted or in what areas adjustments can make the greatest difference in increasing productivity.

# Quality

*Quality* in defined by people in many ways. Some think of quality as superiority or excellence of a product or service, others view it as a lack of manufacturing or service defects, still others think of quality as it relates to the product features or price.

A recent study was conducted asking managers to define quality, the results produced several different responses, including: perfection, consistency, eliminating waste, speed of delivery, compliance with policies and procedures, providing good usable products, doing it right the first time, pleasing the customer, total customer service, and satisfaction. Most managers agreed that the main reason to pursue quality is to satisfy the customer.

The American National Standards Institute (ANSI) and the American Society for Quality (ASQ) define quality as a product or service free of defects, such as the number of problems per 100 cars, or the characteristics of a product or service that satisfy customer needs. Today's cars are of higher quality than those made 20 years ago in both defects and characteristics. Not only do they have fewer problems per 100 cars, the also have a number of additional standard features such as; power brakes, power windows, power steering, stereo, navigation, CD/MP3, air bags, and cruise control to name but a few.

---

### Trouble in Toyland

The wake-up call for Mattel came just as it was preparing to announce that the company would recall 1.5 million Chinese-made toys that were tainted with lead paint.          "I've got bad news," interrupted David Lewis, senior vice president of Operations Asia for Mattel. He had just taken a call from the company's safety lab in Shenzhen, China, where toys made by outside companies are tested. "We've had another failure. It was one of the toys in the Pixar cars."

Mattel's difficulties stem from two sources: lead paint and small magnets. Lead, if ingested over time, can cause serious developmental and other health problems in young children.

On August 2, 2007, the company announced a recall of approximately 1.5 million Fisher-Price toys that contain lead paint including Ernie, Elmo, Dora the Explorer and Big Bird. On August 14, 2007, Mattel announced a second and much bigger lead paint recall involving 436,000 "Sarge" toy cars (253,000 in the U.S. and 183,000 outside the U.S.).

It also recalled approximately 18.2 million (9.5 million in the U.S.) Barbie, Polly Pocket, Doggie Day Care and Batman toys and accessories whose small, high-powered magnets can come loose and, if swallowed, bond together to cause intestinal perforation.

The magnets "measure 1/8 inch in diameter and are embedded in the hands and feet of some dolls, and in plastic clothing, hairpieces and other accessories to help the pieces attach to the doll or the doll's house and can cause serious injury or death to children who swallowed more than one magnet.

Consumers today are intelligent enough to recognize quality issues that firms face today, and the organization that doesn't heed its customers is in for a rude awakening, or, at worst, a quick demise.

## The Importance of Quality

Your customers expect you to deliver quality products. If you do not, they will quickly look to your competition. Quality is critical to *satisfying your customers* and retaining their loyalty so they continue to buy from you in the future. Quality products make an important contribution to long-term revenue and profitability and enable firm's to charge and maintain higher prices.

Quality influences the *company's reputation*. The growing importance of social media means that customers can easily share both favorable opinions and criticism a product quality on forums, product review sites and social networking sites, such as Facebook and Twitter. Just think of how quickly and how many friends and family members you can alert to a company with poor quality products.

A company with a strong reputation for quality can provide a competitive advantage in markets that are very competitive. Poor quality or a product failure that results in a product recall campaign can create negative publicity and damage your reputation.

Certain customers may require the accreditation to a recognized quality standard or compliance to legislation.

For example, public sector companies may insist that their suppliers achieve accreditation with quality standards. If you sell products in regulated markets, such as health care, food or electrical goods, you must be able to comply with health and safety standards designed to protect consumers. Accredited quality control systems play a crucial role in complying with those standards and can also help you win new customers or enter new markets by giving prospects independent confirmation of your company's ability to supply quality products.

Poor quality *increases costs*. If you do not have an effective quality control system in place, you may incur the cost of analyzing nonconforming goods or services to determine the root causes and retesting products after reworking them. In some cases, you may have to scrap defective products and incur additional production costs to replace them. If defective products reach customers, you will have to pay for returns and replacements and, in serious cases, you could incur legal costs for failure to comply with customer or industry standards.

The importance of quality cannot be underestimated, as statistics from various studies reveal:

- The average company never hears from more than 90 percent of its unhappy customers. For every complaint it receives, the company has at least 25 customers with problems, about one fourth of which are serious.
- Of the customers who make a complaint, more than 50 percent will do business again with the company if the complaint is resolved. If the customer feels that the complaint was resolved expeditiously, the number increases to nearly 95 percent.
- The average customer will tell fifteen or twenty others if they have a problem. Those whose complaints are satisfied satisfactorily will only tell five to seven others.
- It costs a company approximately six times more money to get a new customer than to keep a current customer.

# Products and Service Quality Dimensions

## Product Dimensions

Manager of products and service deal with different types of quality issues; the following section provides a brief overview of these dimensions. Although the details are unique to each, the customer-driven focus provides a unifying perspective.

Manufactured products have several quality dimensions including the following:

1. *Performance*—the product's primary operating characteristics.
2. *Features*—include the 'bells and whistles' of a product.
3. *Reliability*—the probability of a product's surviving over a specified period of time under stated conditions of use.
4. *Conformance*—the degree to which physical and performance characteristics of a product match pre-established standards.
5. *Durability*—the amount of use one gets from a product before it physically deteriorates or until replacement is preferable. As an example, when an LCD screen quits working it can't be repaired. Consequently, durability or the average time before failure is a key part of LCD quality.
6. *Serviceability*—refers to how easy or difficult it is to repair a product. The easier it is to maintain a working product or fix a broken product, the more serviceable that product is.
7. *Product failure*—means that the product can't be repaired. They can only be replaced.
8. *Aesthetics*—how a product looks, feels, sounds, tastes, or smells.
9. *Perceived quality*—subjective assessment resulting from image, advertising, or brand names.

Whereas high quality products are characterized by reliability, durability, and serviceability, service quality is quite different. There is no point in assessing the durability of a service because services don't last but are consumed the minute they are performed. As an example, once your pool service has cleaned your pool, the work is complete until the service is required next week to do it again. Rather that serviceability and durability, the quality of service interactions often depends on how the service provider interacts with the customer. Was the service provider friendly, rude, or helpful?

## Service Dimensions

*Service* can be defined as 'any primary or complementary activity that does not directly produce a physical product, it is the non-goods part of the transaction between the buyer and the seller.'

A service may be as simple as cleaning your pool or as complex as approving a home mortgage. Today services account for nearly 80 percent of the U.S. workforce and include hotels, health, legal, engineering, and other professional services, educational institutions, financial services, retailers, transportation, and public utilities.

Many of the key dimensions of product quality apply to services. For example, 'on time arrival', a dimension that measures service *performance;* frequent flyer awards and 'executive or business class' sections represent the *features* dimension. Although similar in many areas, service organizations have special dimensions that products cannot fill. The most important dimensions of service quality include the following:

1. *Reliability*—Are services delivered in the same fashion for every customer, and every time for the same customer? For example, when you take your clothes to the dry cleaner you don't want your buttons cracked or wrinkles down the front of your shirt. If your dry cleaner provides you with perfectly cleaned and pressed garments every time, they are providing reliable service.
2. *Responsiveness*—How much time must a customer wait? And, will a service be performed when promised?
3. *Completeness*—Are all the items in the order included?
4. *Assurance*—is the confidence that service providers are knowledgeable, courteous, and trustworthy. For example, Apple 'geniuses' are trained at Apple headquarters and can take care of everything from troubleshooting your problems to actual repairs. Geniuses are regularly tested on their knowledge and problem-solving skills to maintain their certification. Other Apple store employees are highly trained as well and are not allowed to help customers until they have spent two to four weeks shadowing experienced store employees.
5. *Courtesy*—Do frontline employees greet each customer cheerfully?
6. *Accessibility and convenience*—Is the service easy to obtain?
7. *Accuracy*—Is the service performed right the first time?

# The International Organization of Standardization

## ISO 9000/ISO 14000

As quality became a major focus for businesses throughout the world, many organizations developed standards and guidelines that were different and even conflicted from one country to another, within a country, or even within an industry.

In an effort to standardize quality requirements within a common market, the **International Organization for Standardization** was founded in 1946, composed of representatives from the national standards bodies of 91 nations. This body adopted a series of written quality standards in 1987, which were revised in 1994, and again in 2000. The most recent revision is called ISO 9000:2000 family of revisions.

ISO 9000, pronounced 'eye-so', is a series of standards that has been deemed to represent good quality management practices by international consensus, consisting of a set of standards and guidelines related to quality management systems. It is designed to help businesses ensure that they are meeting the needs of their customers and shareholders. The system is published by the International Organization of Standards (ISO), and deals with the fundamentals of quality management, developing and setting standards that facilitate the international exchange of goods and services for 162 countries. **ISO 9000** is a series of five international standards from ISO 9000 to ISO 9004, for achieving consistency in quality management and quality assurance in companies throughout the world.

**ISO 14000** is a series of international standards for managing, monitoring, and minimizing an organizations harmful effect on the environment. The actual environmental standards of ISO 14000 deal with how a company manages the environment inside its facilities and the immediate outside

environment. However, the standards also call for analysis of the entire life cycle of a product, from raw material to eventual disposal. These standards do not mandate a particular level of pollution or performance, but focus on awareness of the processes and procedures that can effect the environment.

Both the ISO 9000 and ISO 14000 are general and can be used for manufacturing any kind of product or delivering any kind of service. Ironically, ISO 9000 doesn't describe *how* to make a better-quality computer, car, or refrigerator. Instead, they describe how companies can extensively document (hence, standardize) the steps they take to create and improve the quality of their products.

ISO certification is intended to improve management performance at small companies. Becoming certified requires a two-phase audit performed by a third party accredited body, similar to what a certified public accountant verifies that a company's financial accounts are up-to-date and accurate. After initial certification, surveillance audits are performed annually to ensure a company's quality management system remains compliant, if it is not, its certification is suspended or cancelled.

## The Malcolm Baldrige National Quality Award

Named after the late Secretary of Commerce, Malcolm Baldrige, the U.S. Congress established in 1987 the ***Malcolm Baldrige National Quality Award*** to raise awareness of quality management and recognize U.S. companies that have implemented successful quality management systems. The President of the United States present up to three awards annually in six categories: manufacturing, service, small business, and education, healthcare and nonprofit.

The cost of applying for the Baldrige Award includes a $150 eligibility fee, an application fee of $7,500 for manufacturing firms and a $4,000 for small businesses and a site visitation fee of $20,000 to $40,000 for manufacturing firms and $15,000 to $20,000 for small businesses.

Although the fees seem extraordinary, firms receive a great deal of useful information about their businesses even if they don't win the award. Each company that applies receives an extensive report based on over 300 hours of assessment from at least eight business and quality experts.

An independent board of examiners judges organizations that apply for the Baldrige Award. Recipients are selected based on achievement and improvement in seven areas, 1,000 point scale, known as the **Baldrige Criteria for Performance Excellence:** (Figure 15.1).

1. **Leadership:** How upper management leads the organization, and how the organization leads within the community.
2. **Strategic planning:** How the organization establishes and plans to implement strategic directions.
3. **Customer and market focus:** How the organization builds and maintains strong, lasting relationships with customers.
4. **Measurement, analysis, and knowledge management:** How the organization uses data to support key processes and manage performance.
5. **Human resource focus:** How the organization empowers and involves its workforce.
6. **Process management:** How the organization designs, manages and improves key processes.

7. **Business/organizational performance results:** How the organization performs in terms of customer satisfaction, finances, human resources, supplier and partner performance, operations, governance and social responsibility, and how the organization compares to its competitors.

Companies that have been successful in winning the Baldrige Award have achieved superior financial performance. Since 1988, an investment in Baldrige Award winners would have outperformed the S&P's 500 stock index 80percent of the time.

### Total Quality Management (TQM)

**Criteria for the Baldrige National Quality Award**

| 2012 Categories/Items | Point Value |
|---|---|
| **1. Leadership** | **120** |
| Senior Leadership | 70 |
| Governance and Societal Responsibilities | 50 |
| **2. Strategic Planning** | **85** |
| Strategy Development | 40 |
| Strategy Implementation | 45 |
| **3. Customer Focus** | **85** |
| Voice of the Customer | 45 |
| Customer Engagement | 40 |
| **4. Measurement, Analysis, and Knowledge Management** | **90** |
| Measurement, Analysis, and Improvement of Organizational Performance | 45 |
| Management of Information, Knowledge, and Information Technology | 45 |
| **5. Workforce Focus** | **85** |
| Workforce Environment | 40 |
| Workforce Engagement | 45 |
| **6. Operations Focus** | **85** |
| Work Systems | 45 |
| Work Processes | 40 |
| **7. Results** | **450** |
| Product and Process Outcomes | 120 |
| Customer-Focused Outcomes | 90 |
| Workforce-Focused Outcomes | 80 |
| Leadership and Governance Outcomes | 80 |
| Financial and Market Outcomes | 80 |
| **TOTAL POINTS** | **1000** |

Figure 15.1: Baldrige Criteria for Performance Excellence

*Total Quality Management* (TQM) is a management approach to long–term success through customer satisfaction. TQM is not a specific tool or technique, it is a collaborative effort wherein all members of an organization participate in improving processes, products, services, and the culture in which they work. TQM is characterized by three principles: *customer focus and satisfaction, continuous improvement, and teamwork.*

- *Customer focus*—The customer ultimately determines the level of quality. No matter what an organization does to foster quality improvement, training employees, integrating quality into the design process, upgrading computers or software, or buying new measuring tools—the customer determines whether the efforts were worthwhile. The results of customer focus should be customer satisfaction, which occurs when the company's products or services meet or exceed customer's expectations.
- *Continuous Improvement*—A major focus of TQM is continual process improvement. **Continuous improvement** drives an organization to be both analytical and creative in finding ways to become more competitive and more effective at meeting stakeholder expectations. Continuous improvement usually results in a reduction of process **variation**, which is a deviation in the form, condition, or appearance of a product from the quality standard for that product. The less a product varies from the quality standard, or the more consistently a company's products meet a quality standard, the higher the quality.
- *Teamwork*—**Teamwork** is a collaboration of all employees participating in working toward common goals. Total employee commitment can only be obtained after fear has been driven from the workplace, when empowerment has occurred, and management has provided the proper environment. High-performance work systems integrate continuous improvement efforts with normal business operations. Self-managed work teams are one form of empowerment.

## Service Operations

Because services are different from goods, managing a service operation will be different from managing a manufacturing or production system. Let's begin this section by examining the differences between services and products using your computer for our scenario.

Imagine your trusty computer breaks down as you are writing your final project paper for this course. You have two choices. You can drive to Wal-Mart and purchase another computer for $700, or you can spend less (hopefully) to have it fixed at a computer repair shop. Either way, you will end up with the same thing, a working computer (a good), whereas the second option, dealing with the repair center, involves a service.

Services are different from produced goods in several ways.
- First, services are performed whereas goods are produced. Hence, since someone has to perform the service for you, services are more labor intensive than goods production.
- Second, goods are tangible whereas services are intangible, you can't touch the service that has been performed the same way that you can touch a product.

- Third, services are perishable and unstorable if you don't use them when they are available they are wasted. Whereas goods, such as printer paper, can be purchased and stored until you are ready to use it.

By their nature, service operations are often labor intensive and complex to manage. Repetition and consistency, typical hallmarks of excellence in service operations, can work against a company that is trying to achieve step-change improvements in processes and behaviors. Additionally, executives across many industries are finding it increasingly challenging to keep service costs in check (especially labor costs, the single largest cost component of any service operation) while maintaining service levels. Recent technological advances for example, self-service kiosks commonly found in airports, banks, and hotels have helped improve overall productivity, but technology is only one part of the solution.

Designing a tailored set of service models based on customer segments is a prerequisite for providing the desired services without overspending.

Whether the business is a retailer trying to optimize sales floor coverage, a hospital seeking to improve care delivery by better allocating nurses and beds, a hotel working to speed up check-in times, or a manufacturer delivering technical support in global markets, the leaders of the organization must rigorously and holistically manage the factors that affect service delivery and costs.

## Service-Providers Profit Chain

Any service business success is dependent on how well the employees deliver their service to customers. This however depends on how well management treats the service employees. This relationship is known as the *service-profit chain,* and is illustrated in Figure 15.2. The key element to the service-profit chain is the *internal service quality*, which is the quality of treatment that employees receive from management, payroll and benefits, and human resources (internal service provider). As Figure 15.2 shows, good internal service fosters employee satisfaction and service capability. *Employee satisfaction* occurs when companies treat their employees in a way that meets or exceeds the employee's expectation of internal service. The simple concept that the better employee's are treated the more likely they are to be satisfied, and satisfied employee's are more likely to provide high-quality, high-value service that satisfies customers.

Overall employee satisfaction is important because there is a positive relationship on service capability. *Service capability* is an employee's perception of his or her ability to serve customers well.

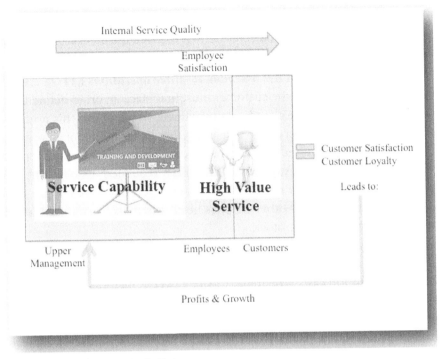

Figure 15.2: Service-Profit Chain

The final stage of the service-profit chain is the causal relationship that occurs when **high-value service** leads to **customer satisfaction,** which then leads to **customer loyalty,** which then creates **long-term profit and growth**.

Retaining customers is critical to a firm's long-term profit and growth as it costs as much as 10 times more to find a new customer then to keep an existing customer. In fact, keeping customers is so important that a firm could double their profits by simply keeping 5 percent more customers per year.

# Manufacturing Operations

Chevrolet makes cars and Apple makes computers. Shell Oil produces gasoline and diesel fuels, Glidden make paint. EAD (Airbus) makes aircraft, but Molson makes beer. Seagate makes hard drives, and General Electric makes appliances. The **manufacturing operations** of each of these companies all produce a physical product. However, as you can see, not all manufacturing operations are the same.

## Processing levels in Manufacturing Operations

Manufacturing operations can be classified based on the level of processing or assembly that occurs after the customer orders the product. The highest level of processing occurs in the **make-to-order operations (MTO)**. A make-to-order operation does not start processing or assembly until it receives a customer order.

One example of a make-to-order operation is comedian Jay Leno's customized motorcycle. The manufacturing company did not start assembling the motorcycle until it received the order from the customer. In fact, many of the specialized parts were not ordered until the manufacturing process had begun.

A moderate degree of processing occurs in the ***assemble-to-order operations (ATO)***. Assemble to order refers to a production method in which the customer must first place an order before the item is produced. The components of the products are already manufactured, which makes this process different from the *make-to-order* method, where everything is manufactured after receipt of an order.

Businesses often stock the inventory required to make the product, and as soon as an order is placed, they have everything they need to give the customer what has been requested. One benefit from this method makes it easier to customize orders for customers, because the products are not pre-made. For example, a jewelry maker can stock beads and other supplies needed to make customized jewelry, but still deliver unique jewelry using what he has in stock.

The lowest degree of processing occurs in the ***make-to-stock operations (MTS)***. The make-to-stock operations (also called build-to-stock) are a traditional production strategy used by businesses to match production with consumer demand forecasts. The make-to-stock (MTS) method forecasts demand to determine how much stock should be produced. If demand for the product can be accurately forecasted, the MTS strategy can be an efficient choice, if sales forecasts are incorrect, make-to-stock operations may end up building too many or too few products, or they make products with the wrong features or without the features that customers want. The relationship of each process discussed is illustrated in Figure 15.3.

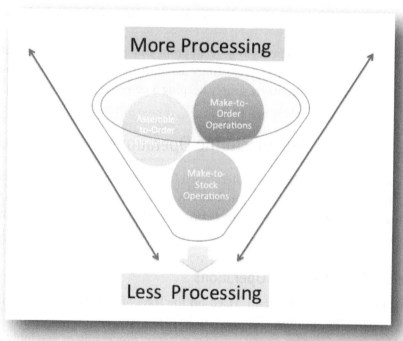

Figure 15.3: Processing in Manufacturing Operations

# Inventory

Day in and day out, the global flow of goods routinely adapts to all kinds of glitches and setbacks. For example, a supply breakdown of parts inventory in one factory in one country is quickly replaced by added shipments from suppliers elsewhere in the network. Sometimes, the problems span whole regions and require emergency action for days or weeks.

When the Eyjafyallayokull volcano erupted in Iceland in the spring of 2010, spewing ash across northern Europe and grounding air travel, inventory supply-chain were put to a test, juggling production and shipments worldwide to keep supplies flowing.

*Inventory* is the raw materials, work-in-process goods (WIP) and completely finished goods that are considered to be the portion of a business's assets that are ready or will be ready for sale.

Inventory represents one of the most important assets that most businesses possess, because the turnover of inventory represents one of the primary sources of revenue generation and subsequent earnings for the company's shareholders/owners.

## Kinds of Inventory

There are four kinds of inventory that manufacturers store: *raw materials, component parts, work-in-process,* and *finished goods.* The process of inventory for the manufacturing department begins when the purchasing department buys the required raw materials from the vendors.

*Raw materials inventory* are the basic inputs in the manufacturing process. They may include wood, metals, plastics and fabrics used in the production of goods. A manufacturer typically acquires raw materials from one or more producers or suppliers. Raw materials cost are recognized on a company's inventory at the point of acquisition and are considered a current asset the balance sheet. Over time, raw materials are pulled from inventory and used in the production of finished goods.

*Component parts inventory* are the basic parts used in manufacturing a product. These could include parts that have been fabricated, such as steel panels for the car body, or steel and iron that are melted and shaped into engine parts like pistons, crankshafts, and engine blocks. Some component parts may be purchased from the vendor rather than fabricated in-house.

Component parts then become partially assembled and become ***work-in-process inventory***. WIP inventory are materials that have entered the production process but is still not yet a finished product. Work in process (WIP) therefore refers to all materials and partly finished products that are at various stages of the production process. WIP excludes inventory of raw materials at the start of the production cycle and finished products inventory at the end of the production cycle, which is the finished goods inventory. ***Finished goods inventory*** are those goods that have completed the manufacturing process but have not yet been sold or distributed to the end user. This is the last step in the process after which the products are distributed to warehouses, distribution centers, wholesalers, and then to retailers for final sale to customer. This entire process is illustrated in Figure 15.4 below.

## Measuring Inventory

Have you ever worked in a retail store and been involved in taking the inventory? If so, most likely you were not too excited about the process of counting every item in the store and in the storeroom. Taking inventory is an extensive activity that is essential to the success of the company. This task has been made somewhat easier today with bar codes and scanners that can record and enter the data into the computers for tracking. Nonetheless, inventory levels vary from day to day and a count that was taken at the beginning of the month will likely be different from a count taken at the end of the month and a count taken on Friday will be different than a count taken on Monday.

Having too much or too little inventory can become very costly to a manufacturing operation. As such, managers need effective measures of inventory control to prevent inventory costs from becoming

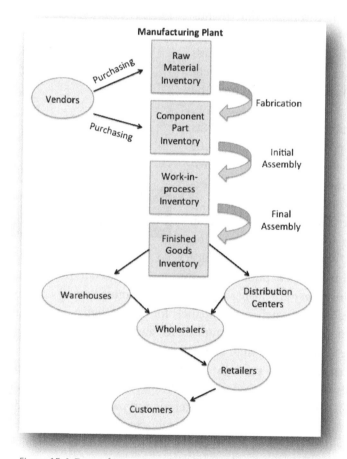

Figure 15.4: Types of Inventory in Manufacturing

too large. There are three basic inventory measurements that management use, they are: average *aggregate inventory, weeks of supply*, and *inventory turnover.*

***Average aggregate inventory*** is the median value of the overall inventory during a specified time period. The average aggregate inventory for a month can be determined by simply averaging the inventory counts at the end of each business day for that month. Determining the average aggregate inventory is one method that is used to determine firm performance. By compare the average aggregate inventory with the industry average aggregate inventory, a company can determine whether they are carrying too much or too little inventory.

The second common measurement of inventory is ***weeks of supply***. Weeks of supply tells the inventory manager how long the current on hand will last based on current sales demand. By keeping your eye on weeks of supply you can avoid inventory ***stock outs*** (running out of inventory) and lost sales. The basic calculation for weeks of supply is pretty simple: on hand inventory/average weekly units sold.

***Inventory turnover*** is the last common measurement of inventory manager's use. Inventory turnover is the number of times a company's inventory is sold and replaced over a given period. The days in the period can then be divided by the inventory turnover formula to calculate the days it takes to sell the inventory on hand or "inventory turnover days." For example, if a company keeps an average of 100 calculators in inventory each month, and they sold 1,000 calculators this year, the inventory turnover was 10 times this year. In general, the higher the number of inventory turnovers per year the better because that company can continue its daily operations with just a small amount of inventory on hand. For example, let's say we have two companies; Johnny's calculators and Haley's calculators, each company's have the identical inventory level of 10,000 calculators over the course of the year. If Johnny's company turns its inventory 2 times a year they will replenish the inventory every six-month and have an average inventory of 5000 calculators. By contrast, Haley's company turns their inventory 12 times per year and by doing so has an average inventory of 833 calculators. So, by turning its inventory more often, Haley's company has 83 percent less inventory on hand at any one time than the inventory carried by Johnny's company.

$$\text{Inventory Turnover} = \frac{\text{Sales}}{\text{Inventory}}$$

The average number of inventory turns varies from one industry to another with the automobile industry averaging 13 turns per year with the best in the industry turning its inventory 27.8 times per year. Dell computers has recorded an extraordinary inventory turnover of 500 times per year, this means that they measure their inventory not in days, but hours.

## The Cost of Maintaining Inventory

Carrying any inventory incurs costs. There are four kinds of costs that will be discussed in the following section: *ordering costs, setup costs, holding costs,* and *stock-out costs.* **Ordering costs** are those costs of ordering a new batch of inventory items and does not include the cost of the inventory itself. These include cost of placing a purchase order, entering data into the computer, costs of inspection of received inventory, documentation costs, getting and analyzing competitive bids, correcting mistakes, etc.

Ordering costs vary inversely with carrying costs. It means that the more orders a business places with its suppliers, the higher will be the ordering costs. However, more orders mean smaller average inventory levels and hence lower carrying costs.

**Setup costs** are the expenses associated each time a batch is produced. It consists of engineering cost of setting up, changing, or adjusting the production machines, *(downtime)* or the paperwork cost of processing the work order, and ordering cost to provide raw materials for the batch.

Setup cost may also include a new product or service line, or even initiating a new business of some type. The actual setup costs include any type of expense associated with the venture, ranging from research and development expenses all the way through to the creation of the production line. Businesses tend to look closely at the actual cost of setup involved with any project to ensure the venture has the potential to recover the costs and become profitable within a reasonable period of time.

**Holding costs** also referred to as 'carrying costs.' A holding cost is any expense that is incurred while maintaining an inventory of goods. The warehoused inventory may be raw materials awaiting use in production, or the inventory may be finished goods that are awaiting sale and shipment. There are several different types of holding costs that are likely to apply with the maintenance of any type of inventory.

Holding costs includes the cost of the storage facilities, wages and salaries paid to the employees working in the warehouse, insurance to protect the building and the inventory from damage and theft, utilities, inventory taxes, the cost of obsolescence, and the opportunity cost of spending money on inventory that could have been spent elsewhere in the company.

**Stock-out costs** are the cost associated with the lost opportunity caused by the exhaustion of the inventory. The exhaustion of inventory could be a result of various factors. The most notable amongst them is defective shelf replenishment practices. Stock-outs could prove very costly for a company, as it has been for Apple. Every year, Apple faces a delicate balancing act. It is critical for Apple to ensure that it has enough supplies of a new iPhone during the holiday season when demand is greatest. Shortages can often result in sales for its rivals, although too much inventory also is a concern. There are two basic kinds of stock-out costs. First, the company incurs the **transaction costs** of overtime work, shipping, etc. trying quickly to replace the out-of-stock items. The second cost is potentially more damaging, is the loss of customer goodwill, the inability of a company to deliver the product it promised. Stock-outs occur more often than you may think. For example, the average stock-out rate in the supermarket industry is 7.9 percent. Various retailers follow the concept of "**Safety Stock**" in order to avoid the situation of stock-outs by which they can increase their sales by 4 percent if they never run out of stock.

## Inventory Management

A business's inventory is one of its major assets and represents an investment that is tied up until the item is sold or used in the production of an item that is sold. Inventory also costs money to store, track and insure. Inventories that are mismanaged can create significant financial problems for a business, whether the mismanagement results in an inventory overage or an inventory shortage. **Inventory management** oversees and controls the ordering, storage, and use of components that a company will use in the production of its finished goods it will sell as well as the overseeing and controlling of quantities of finished products for sale.

Inventory management has two diametrically opposed goals: To *increase* inventory levels to a safe level avoiding stock-outs and to *minimize* the level of inventory the firm carries. The first is to avoid running out of stock and irritating and disappointing the customers. The second is to efficiently reduce inventory levels and costs as much as possible without harming the daily operations.

The following inventory management techniques are different ways of balancing the goals of inventory management: *economic order quantity* (EOQ), *just-in-time inventory* (JIT), and *materials requirement planning* (MRP).

**Economic order quantity (EOQ)** is an inventory-related equation that determines the optimum order quantity that a company should hold in its inventory given a set cost of production; demand rate (D), ordering costs (O), and holding costs (H). This is done to minimize variable inventory costs. The formula for EOQ is:

$$EOQ = \sqrt{\frac{2DO}{H}}$$

For example, if a manufacturing plant uses 80,000 gallons of paint a year (D), and the ordering costs (O) are $75 per order, and the holding costs (H) are $5 per gallon, the optimal order quantity is 1549.

Since the plant uses 80,000 gallons of paint per year, the approximate daily use is 219 gallons per day. Hence, the plant would order 1549 new gallons of paint approximately every 7.07 days.

As you can see the EOQ formulas focus on minimizing the holding and ordering costs, the JIT inventory management approach attempts to eliminate holding costs by reducing inventory levels to near zero.

**Just-in-time inventory systems (JIT)** are a management system in which materials or products are produced or acquired only as demand requires. Just-in-time inventory is intended to avoid situations in which inventory exceeds demand and places increased burden on your business to manage the extra inventory.

Manufacturers using JIT processes want to use materials for production at levels that meet distributor or retailer demand but not in excess. Retailers' only want to acquire and carry inventory that meets immediate customer demands, as excess inventory requires storage and management costs. There are two ways to promote JIT inventory systems: The first way is to promote tight coordination through close proximity. The second way is to promote tight coordination through close coordination with a shared information system that allows manufacturer and suppliers to know the quantity and kinds of parts inventory the other has in stock.

Close coordination can be achieved by the use of system known as *kanban*. Kanban is a Japanese word for 'card you can see' and is a simple visual signaling system to alert workers that it is time to reorder inventory. Toyota introduced and refined the use of kanban in a relay system to standardize the flow of parts in their production lines in the 1950s. Kanban was one of several tools Toyota developed to ensure that inventory was based on actual customer orders rather than managerial forecasts.

Companies need to control the types and quantities of materials they purchase, plan which products are to be produced and in what quantities and ensure that they are able to meet current and future customer demand, all at the lowest possible cost. Making a bad decision in any of these areas will make the company lose money. *Materials requirement planning (MRP)* is a computer-based production planning and inventory control system used to manage the manufacturing processes to aid in controlling costs. The three basic functions of the MRP system are; *inventory control, bill of material processing* and *master production scheduling.*

$$EOQ = \sqrt{\frac{2\,(80{,}000)(75)}{5}} = 1549 \text{ gallons}$$

$$\frac{80{,}000 \text{ gallons}}{365 \text{ days}} = 219 \text{ gallons/day}$$

$$\frac{1549 \text{ gallons}}{219 \text{ gallons per day}} = 7.07 \text{ days}$$

The *master production schedule* is a detailed schedule that indicates the quantity of each item to be produced, the planned delivery dates for those items, and the time by which each step of the production process must be completed in order to meet those delivery dates. The *bill of materials* identifies all the necessary parts and inventory, the quantity of inventory to be ordered, and the order in which the parts and inventory should be assembled. The kind, quantity, and location of inventory that is on hand or that has been ordered are found in the *inventory records*. When combined with the bill of materials, the resulting report indicates *what to buy, when to buy, and what it will cost to order.*

# Summary of Chapter

1. This chapter focused on managing service and manufacturing operations.
2. We discussed the kinds of productivity and their importance in managing operations.
3. We learned that at their core, companies are production systems that combine inputs (labor, capital, raw material) to produce outputs (such as finished goods).
4. In this chapter we learned that productivity is a measure of how many inputs it takes to produce or create an output, and that the greater the output for one input, or the fewer inputs it takes to create an output, the higher the productivity.
5. Partial productivity measures how much of a single kind of input (labor) is needed to produce an output whereas multifactor productivity is an overall measure of productivity that indicates how much labor, capital, materials, and energy are needed to produce an output.
6. We learned that quality might refer to a product or service free of deficiencies, or the characteristics of a product or service that satisfy customer needs.
7. Quality products usually possess three characteristics: reliability, serviceability, and durability.

8. We learned about ISO 9000, ISO 14000, the Baldrige Award, and TQM and how they can help a company improve its quality program.

9. We learned that services are different from goods and how the service-profit chain relates with success, employee satisfaction, and service capability, which lead to high-value service to customers.

10. This chapter discussed the four kinds of inventory, how to control inventory costs, and inventory management through economic order quantity (EOQ) formulas, just-in-time (JIT) inventory systems, and materials requirement planning (MRP).

# Discussion Questions

1. How do services differ from goods? Identify five ways.
2. Explain how just-in-time processes relate to the quality of an organization's outputs.
3. Identify the major concepts of TQM.
4. Identify the determinants of service quality. Describe two of them in a sentence or two each.
5. What is MRP? Identify four benefits from its use.
6. List the four types of inventory.
7. What are the main reasons that an organization has inventory?
8. List the typical cost components that constitute ordering costs in inventory systems.
9. What is a reorder point?
10. Haley has a part-time "cottage industry" producing seasonal plywood yard ornaments for resale at local craft fairs and bazaars. She currently works 8 hours per day to produce 16 ornaments.
    a. What is her productivity?
    b. She thinks that by redesigning the ornaments and switching from use of wood glue to a hot-glue gun she can increase her total production to 20 ornaments per day. What is her new productivity?
    c. What is her percentage increase in productivity?
11. The Fenton Box plant produces 500 cypress-packing boxes in two 10-hour shifts. What is the productivity of the plant?

# References

"Basic Concepts," American Society for Quality, accessed July 19, 2014, from www.asq.org/learn-about-quality/basic-concepts.html.

Briscoe, J., Fawcett, S., & Todd, R. (2005). "The Implementation and Impact on ISO 9000 among Small Manufacturing Enterprises," *Journal of Small Business Management* 43, 309.

Clark, K. (2005). 'An Eagle Eye for Inventory,' *Chain Store Age*, May Supplement, 8A.

Dean Jr. J.W., & Evans, J. (1994). *Total Quality Management, Organization, and Strategy*. St. Paul, MN: West.

Dean, Jr. J.W., & Bowen, D. E. (1994). 'Management Theory and Total Quality: Improving Research and Practice through Theory Development,' *Academy of Management Review,* 19: 392–418.

"FAQs—General Information on ISO," International Organization for Standardization, accessed July 20, 2014 from www.iso.org/iso/iso/support/faqs/faqs_general_information_on_iso.htm.

"Frequently Asked Questions about the Malcolm Baldrige National Quality Award," National Institute of Standards & Technology, accessed July 10, 2015, from www.nist.gov/public_affairs/factsheet/baldfaqs.htm.

Gruman, G. (2005). 'Supply on Demand: Manufacturers Need to Know What's Selling before They Can Produce and Deliver Their Wares in the Right Quantities,' *Info World,* April 18.

Hallowell, R., Schlesinger, L. A. & Zornitsky, J. (1996). 'Internal Service Quality, Customer and Job Satisfaction: Linkages and Implications for Management,' *Human Resource Planning,* 19: 20–31.

Heskett, J. L., Jones, T. O., Loverman, G. W., Sasser, Jr. W. E., & Schlesinger, L. A. (1994). 'Putting the Service-Profit Chain to Work. *Harvard Business Review.* March-April: 164–174.

"ISO 9000 Essentials" and "ISO 14000 Essentials," International Organization for Standardization, accessed July 20, 2014, from www.iso.org/iso/iso_catalogue/management_standards/iso_9000_iso_14000.htm.

Markland, R. E., Vickery, S. K., & Davis, R. A. "Managing Quality" in *Operations Management: Concepts in Manufacturing and Services.* Cincinnati, OH: South-Western, College Publishing. 1998.

Paravantis, J., Bouranta, N., & Chitiris, L. (2009). The Relationship between Internal and External Service Quality,' *International Journal of Contemporary Hospital Management,* (21): 275–293.

"2011-2012Criteria for Performance Excellence," Baldrige Performance Excellence Program, accessed July 19, 2014, from www.nist.gov/baldrige/publications/upload/2011_2012_Business_Nonprofit_Criteria.pdf.

# INDEX

# C

# CREDITS

CPSIA information can be obtained
at www.ICGtesting.com
Printed in the USA
FSOW03n2240220115
4751FS